deeper learning

Beyond 21st Century Skills

Solution Tree | Press

a division of
Solution Tree

555 North Morton Street
Bloomington, IN 47404
800.733.6786 (toll free) / 812.336.7700
FAX: 812.336.7790

email: info@solution-tree.com
solution-tree.com

Visit **go.solution-tree.com/21stcenturyskills** to access materials related to this book.

Printed in the United States of America

18   3 4 5

Library of Congress Cataloging-in-Publication Data

Deeper learning : beyond 21st century skills / James Bellanca, Editor ; contributors, Suzie Boss [and others].
      pages cm
 Includes bibliographical references and index.
  ISBN 978-1-936763-35-1 (perfect bound) 1. Learning ability.
2. Learning strategies. 3. Thought and thinking. 4. Teaching.
I. Bellanca, James A., 1937-
  LB1134.D38 2015
  370.15'23--dc23
                                        2014033229

Solution Tree
Jeffrey C. Jones, CEO
Edmund M. Ackerman, President

Solution Tree Press
President: Douglas M. Rife
Associate Acquisitions Editor: Kari Gillesse
Editorial Director: Lesley Bolton
Managing Production Editor: Caroline Weiss
Senior Production Editor: Edward M. Levy
Copy Editor: Rachel Rosolina
Proofreader: Ashante Thomas
Cover and Text Designer: Laura Kagemann

Dedication

To Reuven Feuerstein (1921–2014)

This year was saddened by the passing of Reuven Feuerstein, a great mind in the fields of education and psychology. Following in the footsteps of his teachers and mentors, Jean Piaget and André Rey, Reuven became one of the geniuses of developmental and cognitive psychology. In the mid-twentieth century, his theory of structural cognitive modifiability and his teaching method of mediated learning experience rocked the foundations of the education community. His work with children survivors of the Holocaust inspired these gallant propositions.

As the director of psychological services for the Youth Aliyah in Europe (immigration of young people), Reuven worked on improving the educational, psychological, and emotional needs of these young victims from their very traumatic experiences during the Nazi regime. He also began to question the then current beliefs regarding the stability of intelligence. He asked, "What if, instead of measuring a child's acquired knowledge and intellectual skills, the ability to learn was evaluated first? And what if their intelligence was not a fixed attribute? What if intelligence can be taught and was in fact the ability to learn?" (Feuerstein, Feuerstein, Falik, & Rand, 1979, 2003).

When he proclaimed to the public in the 1960s that intelligence was not fixed at birth, and that, indeed, the mind is flexible and modifiable throughout one's lifetime, people thought he was crazy; he was far ahead of his time in anticipating what we understand about the boundless possibilities of learning by all and our ability to change the structure of the brain. Twenty-first century neuroscientists are catching us up with precisely how that happens.

Over six decades, Reuven worked tirelessly to develop differentiated teaching methods and cognitive enrichment programs in order to create the structural change in thinking that produces metacognitive skills. He believed everyone can become a critical thinker, no matter their genetic makeup, economic status, or environmental or cultural differences. His seminal thoughts have not only changed the lives of millions around the globe but altered the belief systems we have had about educating children. Today, a growing number of educators around the globe are learning how to help every individual (educator, parent, and student). Reuven's methods and tools have had great influence, resting on his pioneering insistence that all of us can learn more, faster, and especially deeper for continuous growth in our thinking and learning abilities.

Until his last days, Reuven did his most beloved work, directly interacting with children and teaching adults how to do the same. Not only did he bring his great mind and vast array of skills to this work, he brought his generous heart. I and my family knew this not only professionally, but personally. Words will never be able to express the void that his passing has left.

In appreciation for what Reuven has brought to me, my family, and colleagues; to several of the contributing authors of this collection; to educators; and especially to the children who have benefited from his work, I dedicate to him this collection on deeper learning, a book that has grown from the seeds his thoughts planted in all of us.

—James A. Bellanca

Reference

Feuerstein, R., Feuerstein, S., Falik, L., & Rand, Y. (2003). *Dynamic assessments of cognitive modifiability. The learning essential assessment device.* Jerusalem, Israel: ICELP Press. (Original work published 1979)

Acknowledgments

A book this complex deserves many thanks.

First, thanks to the contributors. They each have busy schedules but have found time to keep the process going forward, promptly meeting big and little deadlines and presenting their best and deepest insight for our consideration. What each has written about the connection between 21st century skills and deeper learning and the importance of these skills, processes, and outcomes to the future of education in the United States has truly provided us with leading edge food for deeper thought.

Thanks to Douglas Rife, Solution Tree Press's president, for his support and encouragement in adding this book to the *Leading Edge* collection. This book allows us all to hear the voices of those who are most passionate about the most substantive reforms in our local, state, and national education endeavors.

Gratitude goes to the editorial staff at Solution Tree Press, but especially to Ed Levy, who did his usually precise and accurate job with polite but insightful author queries and helpful, prompt responses.

I thank Helen Soulé and Bernie Trilling, my colleagues in the Partnership for 21st Century Skills; Barbara Chow at the Hewlett Foundation; and Jay McTighe and Ken Kay at EdLeader21 for helping identify the issues, frame the essential questions, pick the authors, and set the tone of this book. Collaboration, communication, and critical and creative thinking in action!

I also want to celebrate the many teachers and school administrators with whom I and my colleagues at the Illinois Consortium have been toiling purposefully to integrate the 21st century skills and deeper learning outcomes into the most needy classrooms, often against giant obstacles held firmly in place by those who cling to the farm and factory ways of teaching and learning, ways that no longer work for these children who will be the leaders of tomorrow.

I especially want to celebrate the teachers and administrators at Reilly Elementary in Chicago. With almost no money, battered textbooks, too few technology tools, and a tsunami of mandates from the last century raining on them, these dedicated folks spent long and arduous hours and days, many outside the school week, taking multiple steps forward to transform instruction for their twelve hundred English language learners. Teachers and students alike learned from doing. Project-based learning became a reality in every classroom. Even though they lacked the resources of more favored schools, the Reilly family always and against great systemic odds, brought their hearts to make sure their students could become 21st century career and college ready. It is this faculty, and others like it, who happily, one small step at a time, are living the deeper learning paradigm.

☮ ☮ ☮ ☮

Rob Riordan, Stacey Caillier, and Ben Daley are indebted to Ron Berger of Expeditionary Learning for the idea of, and advice about, the "slice" as an introduction to project-based learning, in chapter 5.

Bernie Trilling extends special thanks to Peg Maddocks, executive director of NapaLearns, and Bob Pearlman, strategic consultant for 21st Century Schools and Districts and past director of strategic planning for the New Technology Foundation, for their help in developing the Napa Journey profile in chapter 7.

Charles Fadel wishes to thank all of the following for their insights, ideas, and contributions to chapter 8: John Abele, Laura Barragan-Montana, Peter Bishop, Dave Clune, Jillian Darwish, Keri Facer, Devin Fidler, Kurt Fisher, Elizabeth Hardwick, Irene Greif, Jennifer Groff, Ellen Hambrook, Christine Lee, Saeyun Lee, Beth Miller, Riel Miller, Rick Miller, Marco Morales, Melissa Panchuck, Robert Plotkin, Stephanie Rogen, Bernie Trilling, Erja Vitikka, Jim Wynn, and many others. All charts, graphs, and illustrations used in this chapter are the creation of the author unless otherwise noted.

Ken Kay and Valerie Greenhill would like to thank Martha Vockley for her support in the writing of their chapter.

Table of Contents

About the Editor ix

Preface *Barbara Chow* xi

Foreword Beyond the Rhetoric
James W. Pellegrino xv

Introduction Advancing a New Agenda
James A. Bellanca 1

Part I **How Does Deeper Learning Look and Sound?** 19

Chapter 1 Deeper Learning for Students Requires Deeper Learning for Educators
Richard DuFour and Rebecca DuFour 21

Chapter 2 Dispositions: Critical Pathways for Deeper Learning
Arthur L. Costa and Bena Kallick 55

Chapter 3 Paradigm Shift: Educating Creative and Entrepreneurial Students
Yong Zhao 83

Chapter 4 Powering Up Learning With PBL Plus Technology
Suzie Boss 111

Chapter 5 Developing Teachers for Deeper Learning
Rob Riordan, Stacey Caillier, and Ben Daley . . 137

Part II   **What Will Drive the Shift?** 157

Chapter 6   The Worst of Times, The Best of Times
Tony Wagner. 159

Chapter 7   Road Maps to Deeper Learning
Bernie Trilling. 177

Chapter 8   21st Century Curriculum: A Global Imperative
Charles Fadel 207

Chapter 9   Assessment Systems for Deeper Learning
Linda Darling-Hammond and David T. Conley. . 235

Part III   **What Lessons Will Work?**. 273

Chapter 10   Breakthrough Learning
Michael Fullan 275

Chapter 11   All or Nothing: A Deeper Learning Experience
Steven Zipkes. 287

Chapter 12   Ears to the Ground: School Leadership in the
New Millennium
Deborah Rosalia Esparza. 301

Chapter 13   The Pivotal Role of the District
Ken Kay and Valerie Greenhill 319

Chapter 14   Levers for Change: The Role of the States
Helen A. Soulé and Steven Paine 347

Glossary. 375

Index. 381

About the Editor

James A. Bellanca

James A. Bellanca began his career as a high school English teacher and went on to found two experimental alternative schools, a multicounty intermediate service agency, and Skylight Publishing and Professional Development. In his second career, he heads the Illinois Consortium's pro bono work with schools and districts making systemic changes to create a deeper learning agenda, advises the Partnership for 21st Century Skills as a senior fellow, edits the partnership's *Connecting the 21st Century Dots* blogazine, and continues his writing career with a focus on the how-to elements of 21st century skills and deeper learning.

James holds a master's degree in English from the University of Illinois at Urbana-Champaign.

To book James A. Bellanca for professional development, contact pd@solution-tree.com.

Preface

Barbara Chow

When the Organisation for Economic Co-operation and Development (OECD) released the 2012 results of the Programme for International Student Assessment (PISA), the findings of this assessment of fifteen-year-olds' critical-thinking skills kicked off a furious round of media coverage in the United States, including wild accusations, worries about our rankings, and criticisms of the worriers.

While the dust has not yet settled, the OECD report has reminded us of a few basic issues. Educational achievement in much of the world is improving, but in the United States, it remains stagnant. Our students' mathematics scores are below the international average—and their performance in reading and science is only average; in short, their abilities are simply not where they need to be in a globally competitive economy. Once the clear leaders, we are losing the race for excellence; we even have fewer and fewer top performers over time. The one place we excel is in our overconfidence: we believe we are doing well, but the facts do not support our complacency.

Our education system is at a critical crossroads. We can either carry on with what we have been doing—stand still as the world races ahead, endlessly debate the merits of every minor shift in the education reform discourse, and point fingers if we do not see immediate gains—or we can move forward.

This book is about moving forward. It is about grappling with the central educational challenge of our times—how to achieve excellence and how to do it equitably, rapidly, and at scale.

As you read this book, you'll see that an impressive set of experts believe that an excellent and equitable education system must deliver deeper learning outcomes for students. But you'll also see that those of us who support deeper learning do not have a singular point of view, or even exact agreement, about what the definition of *deeper learning* is. Some of us are big supporters of the new Common Core State Standards (CCSS); others are not, or feel that it is simply inadequate. Some of us think of deeper learning as a set of dispositions others would classify the same concepts differently. The Hewlett Foundation defines deeper learning as the ability to master rigorous academic content through the application of higher-order skills, including critical thinking and problem solving, communication, collaboration, learning to learn, and the development of an academic mindset (Hewlett Foundation, n.d.). But others would include a slightly different list and use slightly different terms.

This doesn't bother me, because reform is messy work, because we are diverse thinkers, and because our small differences are less important than our shared central beliefs. All of us in this movement believe that our students must be prepared for a radically different, exponentially changing world—a world with environmental and social problems of unimaginable horror and a punishing labor-force structure with little tolerance for mediocrity. As reformers, we are bound together by both fear of inaction and by hope that we can affix a new North Star for our education system—one in which all students graduate high school having earned their shot at the American dream.

I come to this work from the budget arena and proudly consider the Office of Management and Budget (OMB) my institutional home. For those of you who know the agency, the OMB mentality is not that of dreamers and hopeless optimists. Yet, even while taking a pragmatic, evidence-driven, hard-bitten approach to deeper learning, I see signs that make me hopeful. New small high schools dedicated to deeper learning principles have planted their flag in some of the highest poverty communities in the United States and are flourishing. Far-sighted school leaders have recognized that deeper learning requires a school culture that encourages autonomy, risk taking, and reflection, and have instituted these practices in hundreds of schools across the United States. Courageous district leaders are throwing off the shackles of a broken accountability system and forging a new compact with their community and their schools. New Common Core standards and assessments based on principles of coherence and focus have been adopted by forty-three states as of June 2014 and are moving us in the right direction (Common Core State Standards, 2014).

In 2015, OECD will retest students in the United States and around the world. Can we improve our educational standing? Prior PISA administrations have demonstrated that rapid improvement is possible if the right conditions are present. I hope you will take this book as a set of guideposts about what some of those conditions are.

References

Common Core State Standards. (2014). *Common Core standards adoption by state.* Accessed at www.ascd.org/common-core-state-standards/common-core -state-standards-adoption-map.aspx on July 31, 2014.

Hewlett Foundation. (n.d.). *What is deeper learning?* Accessed at www.hewlett.org /programs/education/deeper-learning/what-deeper-learning on July 31, 2014.

Foreword

Beyond the Rhetoric

James W. Pellegrino

The chapters in this volume are united by a common interest in changing the landscape of American education by promoting ideas that have come to be labeled as *deeper learning* and *21st century skills*. Much of what is discussed here is intended to illustrate what such terms might mean in the educational system, how they are connected, what it takes to create environments that promote their development and attainment, and some of the many systemic issues that need to be addressed for our educational system to properly prepare our youth for the world of today, in anticipation of the world of tomorrow. But what do these terms mean; why have they achieved such a degree of prominence in the thinking, writing, and actions of stakeholder groups; and what do we know from research that can help us think productively about their educational and social implications? To some extent, those were the questions posed to a National Research Council Committee in 2010 by various stakeholder groups. The response was a report titled *Education for Life and Work: Developing Transferable Knowledge and Skills in the 21st Century* (Pellegrino & Hilton, 2012). In what follows, I draw upon that work as a way of introducing some of the key ideas found in this volume.

The What: Issues of Construct Definition

As discussed in the 2012 National Research Council (NRC) report,

> Calls for such 21st century skills as innovation, creativity, and creative problem solving can also be seen as calls for deeper

learning—helping students develop transferable knowledge that can be applied to solve new problems or respond effectively to new situations. (Pellegrino & Hilton, 2012, p. 70)

Deeper learning can be understood as the process through which a person becomes capable of taking what was learned in one situation and applying it to new situations—in other words, learning for transfer. Through deeper learning, individuals acquire expertise in a discipline or subject area that goes beyond the rote memorization of facts or procedures; they understand when, how, and why to apply what they have learned. They recognize when a new problem or situation is related to what they have previously learned, and they can apply their knowledge and skills to solve them.

In contrast, research reviewed in Pellegrino and Hilton (2012) suggests that instead of being applicable to a range of contexts, these competencies are specific to—and intertwined with—knowledge of a particular discipline or subject area. For example, one does not just generically develop the capacity to solve problems. Rather, any competency in solving problems is situated in some domain such as chemistry, mathematics, cooking, or carpentry, and typically calls upon specialized knowledge and strategies specific to that domain of expertise. Many individuals and organizations have proposed lists of the competencies they believe to be important for the 21st century. The competencies vary widely, ranging from critical thinking and argumentation to flexibility and empathy, but the evidence reviewed in Pellegrino and Hilton (2012) suggests that it may be most productive to future work if they are conceptualized and organized into three broad domains:

1. The **cognitive** domain, which includes thinking, reasoning, and related skills

2. The **intrapersonal** domain, which involves self-management, including the ability to regulate one's behavior and emotions to reach goals

3. The **interpersonal** domain, which involves expressing information to others, as well as interpreting others' messages and responding appropriately

Although much research needs to be done to clarify the nature of these various constructs and determine how 21st century competencies are related to desired outcomes, there are some promising findings. Cognitive competencies, which have been the most extensively studied, show consistent, positive correlations of modest size with students' achieving higher levels of education, higher earnings, and better health. Among intrapersonal competencies, conscientiousness—which includes such characteristics as being organized, responsible, and hardworking—shows the strongest relationship with these same desirable outcomes. Conversely, antisocial behavior, which reflects deficits in both intrapersonal skills (such as self-regulation) and interpersonal skills (such as communication), is related to poorer outcomes (see the research studies reviewed in chapter 3 of Pellegrino & Hilton, 2012).

More research is needed to increase our understanding of relationships between particular competencies and desired outcomes, and we must especially look at whether the competencies are the cause of the outcomes or are simply correlated with them. This much is known, however: mastery of academic subject matter is not possible without deeper learning.

The Why: Some of the Relevant Rhetoric

It has always been widely recognized in the United States that public education has made a significant contribution to national prosperity, social cohesion, and the general welfare of citizens. Current economic, environmental, and social challenges point to the fact that

> education is even more critical today than it has been in the past. Today's children can meet future challenges if they have opportunities to prepare for their future roles as citizens, employees, managers, parents, volunteers, and entrepreneurs. To achieve their full potential as adults, young people will need to acquire the full range of skills and knowledge that facilitate mastery of English, mathematics, and other school subjects. They will need to learn in ways that support not only retention but also the use and application of skills and

knowledge—a process called "transfer" in cognitive psychology. (Pellegrino & Hilton, 2012, p. 15)

It is now well known that U.S. students' performance is not
impressive when compared to student performance in the other
industrialized nations making up the OECD. Part of the reason for
this is uneven learning and achievement among different groups.
Since the 1970s, disparities in the educational attainment of students
from high-income versus low-income families have grown enormously (Duncan & Murnane, 2011).

As a consequence, many have begun to call for new education policies that target the development of 21st century skills—a
broad array of transferable skills and knowledge. For example, the
Partnership for 21st Century Skills (P21), a nonprofit organization
that includes business, education, community, and governmental
groups, argues that student success in college and careers requires
four essential skills—the 4Cs: (1) critical thinking and problem
solving, (2) communication, (3) collaboration, and (4) creativity and
innovation (P21, 2010).

The partnership's report made a number of significant findings
as discussed in Pellegrino and Hilton (2012).

> Some state and local high-school reform efforts have begun
> to focus on a four-dimensional framework of college and
> career readiness that includes not only academic content but
> also cognitive strategies, academic behaviors, and contex-
> tual skills and awareness (Conley, 2011). At the international
> level, the U.S. secretary of education participates on the exec-
> utive board of the Assessment and Teaching of 21st Century
> Skills (ATC21S) project, along with the education ministers
> of five other nations and the vice presidents of Cisco, Intel,
> and Microsoft. This project aims to expand the teaching and
> learning of 21st century skills globally, especially by improv-
> ing assessment of these skills. In a separate effort, a large
> majority of sixteen OECD nations surveyed in 2009 reported
> that they are incorporating 21st century skills in their educa-
> tion policies, regulations, and guidelines (Ananiadou & Claro,
> 2009). Thus, it is clear that multiple stakeholder groups have

been energized and mobilized to consider the problem as well
as potential solutions. (p. 16)

Thus, as Pellegrino and Hilton (2012) note, there is considerable
interest in the idea of 21st century skills and many initiatives have
been undertaken to try to identify these skills or competencies. As
a consequence, various lists of terms have been developed by groups
in the United States and across the globe, in part to try to capture
the nature of these competencies and consider how they might be
developed both inside and outside the formal education process.
As noted earlier, one of the goals of the report *Education for Life
and Work: Developing Transferable Knowledge and Skills in the 21st
Century* (Pellegrino & Hilton, 2012) was to try to clarify the meaning
of terms like *deeper learning* and *21st century skills* and consider evidence in support of their relevance and contribution to attainment
of valued adult outcomes.

The Where: Deeper Learning and Disciplinary Standards

Deeper learning and the development of 21st century competencies do not happen separately from learning academic content.
Thus, it is important to consider the relationship among concepts
of deeper learning, 21st century competencies, and the disciplinary standards documents that have been introduced since 2010
(Achieve, 2013; National Governors Association Center for Best
Practices [NGA] & Council of Chief State School Officers [CCSSO],
2010a, 2010b). Given that these standards will likely shape curriculum and instruction for many years to come, Pellegrino and Hilton
(2012) consider how each of the different disciplinary standards
documents aligns with concepts of deeper learning and 21st century competencies. What follows is a glimpse of that alignment for
the area of mathematics learning.

Current U.S. teaching practices for mathematics often are at
odds with approaches that support deeper learning and transfer of
knowledge and skills. Studies of upper-elementary school and middle-grade classrooms reveal that students generally work alone on
low-level tasks that require memorizing and recalling facts and procedures—the hallmarks of rote learning. They do not engage in the

high-level cognitive processes, such as reasoning about ideas and solving complex problems. As Pellegrino and Hilton (2012) note,

> Although this pervasive approach to mathematics teaching has not been directly established as the cause of the generally low levels of achievement in mathematics by U.S. students, it is difficult to deny the plausibility of such a connection. In response, an array of reform initiatives has been aimed at changing how mathematics is taught and learned in American schools. (p. 113)

While reformers disagree over some things, they share the goal of giving students more opportunities to learn what is called *mathematics with understanding* and the related goal of promoting the teaching of mathematics *for* understanding. These goals reflect a focus on deeper learning in school mathematics. Studies since the 1950s have provided a solid body of evidence about the benefits of teaching mathematics in this way (see Silver & Mesa, 2011). Hallmarks of teaching mathematics for understanding include:

- The use of cognitively demanding mathematical tasks drawn from a broad array of content areas
- The use of teaching practices that support collaboration and discourse among students and that engage them in mathematical reasoning and explanation, real-world applications, and use of technology or physical models

The new Common Core standards identify several important learning goals: critical thinking, problem solving, constructing and evaluating evidence-based arguments, systems thinking, and complex communication. The new standards correspond most strongly with 21st century competencies in the cognitive domain, with the two most prominent areas of overlap in the themes of (1) argumentation and reasoning and (2) problem solving. The theme of argumentation and reasoning is explicitly stated in the second and third Standards for Mathematical Practice: "Reason abstractly and quantitatively" and "Construct viable arguments and critique the reasoning of others" (NGA & CCSSO, 2010b, p. 6). The CCSS also deal explicitly with problem solving; the first of the Standards for

Mathematical Practice is "Make sense of problems and persevere in solving them" (NGA & CCSSO, 2010b, p. 6).

Unlike competencies in the cognitive domain, those in the intrapersonal and interpersonal domains are not particularly prominent in the standards. However, the Standards for Mathematical Practice give some attention to the intrapersonal competencies of self-regulation, persistence, and the development of an identity as someone who can do mathematics.

While the CCSS for mathematics, the CCSS ELA, and the Next Generation Science Standards have a decided bias toward cognitive competencies, as one might expect given the disciplinary focus, they do not ignore—nor do they contradict—an emphasis on integration of the cognitive competencies with those in the interpersonal and the intrapersonal domains. In all three cases, the standards focus on key disciplinary ideas and practices that promote deeper learning and, in turn, support transfer.

The How: An Integrated System of Curriculum, Instruction, Assessment, and Teacher Development

As argued in the NRC report (Pellegrino & Hilton, 2012) and various chapters in this volume, helping students develop the full range of 21st century competencies will require numerous changes across the education system, including through curricula, assessments, and teacher education and professional development.

Curricula

Creating more specific instructional materials and strategies to help students develop transferable competencies requires additional research. Future curricula inspired by the concept of deeper learning should integrate learning across the cognitive, interpersonal, and intrapersonal domains in ways that are most appropriate for the targeted learning goals. Multiple stakeholder groups should actively support the development and use of curriculum and instructional programs that include research-based teaching methods to foster deeper learning, such as those Pellegrino and Hilton (2012) discuss.

Glimpses of such programs and their design principles are provided throughout this volume.

Assessments

The extent to which teachers will focus on helping students develop 21st century competencies will be strongly influenced by the degree to which these competencies are included in district, state, and national assessments. Recent policy developments offer an opportunity to address this challenge. With the support of the U.S. Department of Education, two large consortia of states, the Partnership for Assessment of Readiness for College and Careers (PARCC) and the Smarter Balanced Assessment Consortium (Smarter Balanced), are developing new assessments aligned with the Common Core State Standards. If these assessments—as well as those eventually developed based on new science standards—include facets of the 21st century competencies derived from the Common Core State Standards, it will create a powerful incentive for states, districts, schools, and teachers to emphasize these aspects of instruction. This volume considers the assessment landscape and how it must change to support an emphasis on deeper learning and the development of 21st century competencies.

Teacher Education and Professional Development

Current approaches to teacher development need to change substantially to support deeper learning and the development of transferable knowledge and skills. Researchers have identified many needed steps, including strengthening teachers' understanding of the subject matter they teach, their knowledge of how students learn, and their awareness of students' common misconceptions about the subject matter. Across the disciplines, teachers will need time to participate in the kinds of learning and teaching environments that promote deeper learning and transfer. "Experiencing instruction designed to support transfer will help them to design and implement such instruction in their own classrooms" (Pellegrino & Hilton, 2012, p. 188). As discussed in this volume, such environments are best structured as professional learning communities and require strong administrative support.

What's Next?

The chapters that follow, individually and collectively, provide various perspectives on one or more of these critical issues. Through a thoughtful analysis of those perspectives, we may better ascertain and agree about what we mean by *deeper learning* and *21st century competencies*, why they matter, and how best to create the contexts in which they can be developed so that our students may benefit.

References and Resources

Achieve. (2013). *Next generation science standards.* Accessed at www.nextgenscience .org/search-standards on April 1, 2014.

Ananiadou, K., & Claro, M. (2009). *21st century skills and competences for new millennium learners in OECD countries* (Working Paper No. 41). Paris: Organisation for Economic Co-operation and Development. Accessed at www.oecd-ilibrary.org/docserver /download/5ks5f2x078kl.pdf?expires=1396367109&id=id&accname=guest&checksum =5657B512D06C453C5A63141947A 9FCD7 on April 1, 2014.

Conley, D. (2011). *Crosswalk analysis of deeper learning skills to Common Core State Standards.* Unpublished manuscript.

Duncan, G. J., & Murnane, R. J. (Eds.). (2011). *Whither opportunity? Rising inequality, schools, and children's life chances.* New York: Sage Foundation.

National Governors Association Center for Best Practices & Council of Chief State School Officers. (2010a). *Common Core State Standards for English language arts and literacy in history/social studies, science, and technical subjects.* Washington, DC: Authors. Accessed at www.corestandards.org/assets/CCSSI_ELA percent20Standards.pdf on April 1, 2014.

National Governors Association Center for Best Practices & Council of Chief State School Officers. (2010b). *Common Core State Standards for mathematics.* Washington, DC: Authors. Accessed at www.corestandards.org/assets/CCSSI_Math percent20 Standards.pdf on April 1, 2014.

National Research Council. (n.d.). *Education for life and work: Guide for practitioners.* Accessed at www4.nationalacademies.org/xpedio/idcplg?IdcService =GET_FILE&dDocName= DBASSE_084153&RevisionSelectionMethod= Latest on May 13, 2014.

Organisation for Economic Co-operation and Development. (2010). *PISA 2009 results: What students know and can do—Student performance in reading, mathematics, and science, vol. I.* Paris: Author. Accessed at www.oecd.org/pisa/pisaproducts/48852548.pdf on April 1, 2014.

Partnership for 21st Century Skills. (2010). *21st century readiness for every student: A policymaker's guide.* Tucson, AZ: Author. Accessed at www.p21.org/storage /documents/policymakersguide_final.pdf on August 1, 2014.

Partnership for 21st Century Skills. (2011). *Overview of state leadership initiative.* Accessed at www.p21.org/index.php?option=com_content&task= view&id=505&Itemid=189 on April 1, 2014.

Pellegrino, J. W., & Hilton, M. L. (Eds.). (2012). *Education for life and work: Developing transferable knowledge and skills in the 21st century.* Washington, DC: National Academies Press.

Silver, E. A., & Mesa, V. (2011). Coordination characterizations of high-quality mathematics teaching: Probing the intersection. In Y. Li & G. Kaiser (Eds.), *Expertise in mathematics instruction: An international perspective* (pp. 63–84). New York: Springer.

Introduction

Advancing a New Agenda

James A. Bellanca

*The major aim of schooling is to enable students to
become the architects of their own education so that they
can invent themselves during the course of their lives.*

—Elliot W. Eisner

In 2010, with Ron Brandt—the longtime editor of the Association
for Supervision and Curriculum Development's prestigious professional journal, *Educational Leadership*—I edited this volume's
predecessor, *21st Century Skills: Rethinking How Students Learn*.
In that volume, leading voices from the U.S. education community
reported on emerging data about the need for the American school to
become more rigorous and to return to the inclusion of such valuable
skill sets as critical and creative thinking, problem solving, collaboration, and communication. Survey after survey claimed that these
skill sets, labeled 21st century skills, were becoming more and more
important as prerequisites for college coursework and later success
in the far-reaching global economy. Some of these voices claimed
that U.S. schools had become as obsolete as Henry Ford's 19th century assembly line. Unlike manufacturers who had modernized their
production with the introduction of new technologies, our schools—
these authors claimed—appeared frozen in time with outdated
curricula, worn-out instruction, and inadequate tools for assessing
the quality of what teachers produced (Bellanca & Brandt, 2010).

As several essays in this book note, little in the U.S. education scene appears to have changed since 2010. Barbara Chow's preface points to the data from the 2012 international PISA results as one clue to the inaction. Several of the authors in this volume add fuel to this fire, while others report on the attempts made to change the scene.

Since OECD's first PISA results in 2000 highlighted the mediocrity of U.S. test scores on the international stage (OECD, 2000), strong accountability pressures have headed attempts to improve U.S. students' performance. First came the Common Core State Standards (CCSS). States also increased the number and rigor of tests, and districts added hours to test preparation. Some states and districts moved to match teacher evaluations with student performance. On the national front, the U.S. federal government funded two consortia, Smarter Balanced and PARCC, to develop national assessments that measure world-class standards. In spite of these intense accountability pressures, the 2012 PISA results show little change in U.S. fifteen-year-olds' international standing. *TIME International* called the United States "a nation of C students" (Rhodan, 2013). Their mathematics, science, and literacy scores continue to sit in the middle of the pack. Secretary of Education Arne Duncan (2013) notes the 2012 PISA results showed a picture of education stagnation.

The Good News

Yet the news is not all bad. As several contributors point out, there are hints of a significant and substantive new direction to replace the partial and sometimes superficial attempts to do little more than add a coat of paint to the old school factory. For instance, consider the following.

- Throughout the United States, individual teachers, school principals, district administrators, and state education officials are calling for deeper learning opportunities for all students. Collaborative efforts, such as the activist New York Performance Standards Consortium (http://performance assessment.org), are challenging high-stakes testing regimens not only in their own states but also across the United States.

Growing lists of major networks of schools—charter, public, and independent—focus specifically on deeper learning transformation. This trend points toward a re-establishment of world-class quality in U.S. education.

- Researchers are not only identifying new ways of learning; they are also pinpointing the best practices in instruction, curriculum, assessment, and leadership that show the highest promise for transforming learning from the superficial recall and regurgitation of facts, figures, and procedures to the intentional development of crucial cognitive skills (News from the National Academies, 2012).

- The drive toward more substantive 21st century learning in the United States gives special credence to the emerging superhighway that goes by the name *deeper learning*. Much is already possible in terms of meaningful systems of assessment in states, districts, and classrooms. Exemplar assessment practices that reflect the rigorous PISA exam process—but also transform formative assessments into instructional guides— are developing (Fairfax County School District, n.d.).

Definitions of Deeper Learning

In this book's preface, Hewlett's Barbara Chow defines deeper learning as "the ability to master rigorous academic content through the application of higher-order skills, including critical thinking and problem solving, communication, collaboration, learning to learn, and the development of an academic mindset." The Hewlett Foundation (n.d.) has also provided a succinct starter list of six key attributes of deeper learning. Hewlett arrived at these attributes:

> based upon the best available evidence of the skills, knowledge and dispositions, students will need for success in 21st century career and civic life. We were also most interested in competencies that are measurable and malleable—for example there are a number of personality traits that are highly correlated with future success but may be harder to teach. (Chow, 2014)

Because the chosen attributes are essential elements of deeper learning, an exposition of each is warranted.

1. **Mastery of core academic content:** School curricula consist of well-defined subjects. In the elementary grades, the curricula highlight language arts, mathematics, science, and social studies through facts, concepts, terms, and basic principles. In the upper grades, these expand into sub-areas with more in-depth treatment of literature (American, English, world), science (biology, chemistry, physics, environmental studies, technology and engineering), U.S. and world history, and various arts. Some students qualify for more rigorous advanced placement courses, and some schools link topics for interdisciplinary study. The deeper learning emphasis in the content is marked by a student's understanding of the core ideas in each curriculum and how he or she can connect them, use skills gained for more advanced study in the same or other content areas and apply the knowledge to solving outside-of-school problems.

2. **Critical thinking and problem solving:** In alignment with the Common Core, WIDA, NETS and Next Generation Science Standards, and the Partnership for 21st Century Skills framework, the skills of critical- and creative-thinking are essential to enable students to solve the loose and tightly structured problems that have become a priority across curriculum areas. To facilitate deeper learning, it is important that students not only develop these skills by engaging in more rigorous examination of course content but that they receive explicit, formal, structured and consistent preparation that develops these skills within each content area. The standards serve as guides to identify subject-specific critical- and creative-thinking competencies that lead to problem-solving proficiency in each subject and can be applied to looser, outside-the-curriculum challenges (Bellanca, Fogarty, & Pete, 2012).

3. **Collaboration:** The research on collaboration notes that it is one of the most powerful instructional strategies for raising student achievement (Hattie, n.d.; Marzano, n.d.). Cooperative

learning is the most researched method on the creation of collaborative classroom climates (Johnson & Johnson, 2009; Slavin & Cooper, 2009) via the explicit development of collaborative skills. These are the skills that undergird teamwork—social skills ranging from active listening of other points of view to conflict resolution in situations where multiple minds are more effective in reaching a shared goal than a single mind working alone.

4. **Communication in writing and speaking:** Many schools have dropped writing from the curriculum, because states, strapped for funds, have dropped writing tests. However, valuing communication as a key element that links the other attributes of deeper learning, many teachers have continued on their own to blend writing and speaking skill development into their lessons and projects. Project-based learning (PBL) makes it easier to integrate tasks that develop writing skills with digital media skills, as well as with the Partnership's 4Cs (critical thinking and problem solving, creative thinking and innovation, collaboration, and communication) via "need to know" instruction and large doses of feedback using guiding assessments. PBL also provides the chance for teachers to join the Speaking and Listening strand of ELA with the Writing and Reading strands to weave large doses of informal and formal communication through authentic and meaningful student work, increasingly using digital media (Bellanca, 2010).

5. **Self-directed learning:** In a time of teacher-controlled instruction under the guise of preparing students for high-stakes tests, new modes of instruction are recognizing the need for increased student voice in decision making. In its narrowest sense, student voice is associated with engaging students in answering teacher questions. However, if self-directed learning means little more than increased amounts of classroom discussion or increased student choice of topics for book reports, then its meaning is very shallow. Following the description of self-directed learning advanced by Malcolm Knowles (1975), self-directed learning is when an individual "takes the

initiative, with or without the assistance of others, in diagnosing their own learning needs, formulating learning goals,
identifying their human and material resources for learning,
choosing and implementing appropriate learning strategies,
and evaluating learning outcomes" (p. 18). In the deepest learning classrooms, teachers facilitate deeper self-directed learning
by *intentionally* promoting students' self-directed academic
goal setting; definition of learning issues; development of
study, work, and project plans; selection of learning strategies,
including independent internships and project-based learning;
self-monitoring; and student self-assessment of academic performance (Knowles, 1975).

Although Knowles believes self-directed learning is the
prerogative of adult learners, others see its value in K–12 classrooms and advocate for its inclusion in the school curriculum
in order to better promulgate deeper learning practices and
outcomes. In these cases, teachers "guide on the side," and
students are free to choose what and how they study and to
add their voices to their own and their peers' development of
the salient characteristics of highly self-directed learners. The
greater the freedom given over to student choice, the greater
the self-directed outcomes (Guglielmino, 1978).

6. **Academic mindset:** This is an essential attribute of successful
   21st century deeper learners. The learner has formed a deep
   commitment to learning as a lifelong process. Such learners
   feel comfortable with their abilities to solve academic problems and overcome hurdles as they apply their 21st century
   thinking, collaborating, and communicating talents. They
   have a deeply rooted feeling of competence that motivates
   them to regulate their cognitive behavior, find meaning, share,
   plan, assess, and change themselves inside and outside the
   classroom. As described in the theories of Lev Vygotsky and
   Reuven Feuerstein, these learners tend to be precise, accurate,
   logical, systematic, focused, intrinsically motivated, committed to problem solving and self-directed in their learning
   (Feuerstein, Feuerstein, & Falik, 2010).

In addition to these six attributes, the definition of deeper learning has another dimension.

The Transfer Element

In his foreword to this book, researcher James Pellegrino extends the definition of deeper learning to highlight the element of transfer: "Deeper learning can be understood as the process through which a person becomes capable of taking what was learned in one situation and applying it to new situations—in other words, learning for transfer." His statement helps us understand that teachers with a deeper learning agenda do more than ask students to memorize facts and procedures, practice skills for rote recall over and over on worksheets, and fill in the blanks on quizzes and tests. Such obsolete practices may help students at the recall level of Bloom's taxonomy, but they don't ask students to do the more rigorous thinking that comes from the upper stories of the intellect and is demanded more and more in the 21st century work world.

When teachers teach for transfer, they call on students to use the six attributes identified by Hewlett that lead to problem solving and deeper learning outcomes. In the process, students learn how to move facts, concepts, and values into other lessons and courses across the curriculum and apply those lessons to solving the many varied problems they face and will face outside school walls for the remainder of their lives. In short, they learn how to learn more efficiently and effectively. With the attributes as their tools, students learn faster and better, but more importantly, deeper, competently taking on not only what is prescribed to learn in the curriculum, but an expanding curriculum built on their own interests.

A Twofold Split

Using Hewlett's attributes as the first road signs and Pellegrino's clarification of the transfer element, I have framed two starter definitions to guide the discussion of deeper learning and connect it to 21st century skills. Although supporters of deeper learning can trace their origin back to Socrates and Confucius, these two definitions—a process and an outcome definition—highlight the special worth deeper learning has for contemporary students, who must become college and career ready in a global, high-tech, high-information age. In truth, deeper learning is both a process and an outcome, and all of the authors contributing to this volume have accepted one or both of these definitions as a frame for their own work. This has allowed all of them to speak the same language and focus on the how-to that has become one of the driving questions in education.

The Process Definition

Deeper learning is a process that enables students to become more proficient at developing the fullest possible insights into the meaning of curricular content relevant to college and careers in this century. This process is made possible by students' increased proficiency as self-directed, critical thinkers who apply their thinking, problem solving, collaborating, and communicating skills so they become more effective masters of the curricular content. The more skilled students become at learning how to apply the 4Cs, the more confident they become, the more ready they are to continue acting with this confident mindset, and the more able they are to deepen their understanding of the content. In short, their sharpened cognitive processes help grow the 4Cs. Sharpened critical thinking, for instance, leads to deeper understanding on a spiraling stairway.

Although the voices in this book do not all agree about which of the 4Cs is the most crucial, it's clear that it is important from the earliest grades that teachers attend to the development of these process skills through explicit instruction, ample opportunities to transfer knowledge and skills, and guiding assessments to drive their instruction.

As called for in the Common Core standards, a first-grade student learns to count to one hundred by memory and deepens her understanding by learning how to group numbers into sets of two, ten, and twenty-five. She also learns how to arrange physical objects like buttons and shells by grouping these items according to the same number sets. At a later stage, she is helped to create the same and new groupings using other objects. Similarly, a fifth-grade student memorizes five vocabulary words that are used to describe light and its effects as called for in the Next Generation Science Standards. That student deepens his understanding by explaining each term in his own words, notes examples, then figures out how to use the terms to design a light source for use in his closet. A tenth-grade student memorizes the parts of the plant from the bold vocabulary words of a botany textbook, deepening her understanding by examining a variety of flowers and vegetables in the lab and using the recalled terms to label samples. While walking home with a friend, the tenth grader notices flowers by the path, names the parts of each plant to a friend, and makes sketches in her notebook.

In each of these very simple examples, students were moved to deeper understandings via a more complex or higher-order thinking skill (grouping, explaining why, classifying) before transferring that understanding into a fresh situation in a new way. Ultimately, a highly competent teacher will decide how to take off the training wheels of her facilitating instruction and prompt the student to invent and design his or her own applications (transfer). No Child Left Behind with its low-expectations mandates, which stop at the recall step, made it difficult for teachers to carry out this kind of deeper learning.

The Outcome Definition

Deeper learning is an outcome that results from the self-directed transfer of the 4Cs to the student's understanding of a concept's meaning. The deeper learning outcome is made evident by (1) the mastery of core and complex content, (2) the construction of academic and entrepreneurial mindsets, and (3) increased proficiency in the 4Cs.

For several decades, there have been increasing pleas to add performance assessments to the assessment mix. Performance assessments investigate how students can apply (make use of, or transfer) the knowledge they have gained about a subject (for example, fractions, metaphors, marsupials) by showing skill. Can the student add one and one? Can the student write a sentence? The proof is in the correct action. However, as performances become higher order (analyze a poem, graph an equation) or tasks more complex (complete an architectural dig, write a narrative poem, keep a portfolio of sketches), teachers need different tools to assess them. To add consistency to what students were showing they knew or could do, teachers added performance tasks so that students could demonstrate that they were able to transfer knowledge and skills to a fresh task that matched what they learned but would not resemble the exact problem solved or product made. For these unique tasks, more effort was needed.

PISA has pushed performance tasks to new heights. PARCC and the Smarter Balanced have already posted by grade on their website sample performance items that show the level of digital skill students will need to take the tests, the type of thinking and problem solving they must be able to do, and what it means to learn how to think with real-world examples that lack answers to memorize.

In this volume, you will have the opportunity to hear what leading voices have to say about the effort it will take to transform the landscape, to shift the paradigm from shallow to deeper learning that includes both outcome and process. You will read about the theory and research that supports these exemplar practices as well as how well schools and teachers are succeeding in ways that go far beyond the limits of No Child Left Behind ([NCLB], 2002).

Outline of the Book

Although it is customary in a collection such as this to start with a big-picture article that describes the theory and delineates the rationale before closing with chapters that focus on practical how-to applications, this volume is structured in reverse, in three parts. The first part covers best practices; the second covers changes in curriculum, instruction, and assessment; and the third consists of paradigm-shift exemplars.

Part I: How Does Deeper Learning Look and Sound?

First, we give attention to what teachers do and say that promotes deeper learning; thus, part I includes exemplary deeper learning practices that illustrate the how-to in a classroom. From these examples, you will progress to read about what major voices are recommending based on their intensive in-the-field research so that all students have access to such opportunities.

Chapter 1: Deeper Learning for Students Requires Deeper Learning for Educators

This essay advocates for changing teachers' minds. Richard DuFour and Rebecca DuFour not only explicate the reasons for this priority attention, but they also go into depth about what teacher renewal should entail, why it is such an important first step, and how professional learning communities can provide the best practice for accomplishing the task of enabling teachers as deeper learners. As the DuFours see it, teacher transformation must precede student transformation.

Chapter 2: Dispositions—Critical Pathways for Deeper Learning

Since their active leadership in the thinking skills movement of the 1970s and '80s, Arthur L. Costa and Bena Kallick have advocated for the explicit development of critical and creative thinking in daily classroom instruction. Their innovative and world-recognized leadership model, Cognitive Coaching, has provided educators around the globe with the belief system and the practical tools to keep the essential flame of thinking alive in the battle against the myopia of No Child Left Behind (2002). Today, their voices are no less silent. In this chapter, they link their prior knowledge to the present need for advancing the skills of creative and critical thinking to their fullest development as *dispositions.* Providing practical how-to examples with illustrations from exemplar schools, Costa and Kallick show how it is possible to shift teaching and learning into a mindful curriculum that highlights thinking pathways in tomorrow's classrooms.

Chapter 3: Paradigm Shift—Educating Creative and Entrepreneurial Students

Yong Zhao's essay may surprise those who misconstrue the paradigm shift of deeper learning as the sole domain of critical thinking and tightly structured analytic problem solving. After framing the argument for a creative thinking paradigm as an antidote to the employee-driven paradigm of the industrial past, Zhao builds a strong case for creative, innovative thinking and the entrepreneurial mindset as the driving forces of a student-centered, personalized paradigm in *all* classrooms. Such an education will focus on development of individual talents so that learners go from adequate to great.

Chapter 4: Powering Up Learning With PBL Plus Technology

Suzie Boss, long-term champion of project-based learning (PBL), shows how the synthesis of project-based learning with the ever-expanding array of digital tools can take deeper learning instruction to greater heights than either tool alone. She notes the special power of easily accessible technology tools that help students develop skills for accessing, analyzing, and organizing information; connect learners with peers and experts; create new content; and facilitate the sharing of results with authentic audiences. Her examples show transfer in action as students use tools such as Skype to research their responses with peers around the globe. Boss ends by pointing readers toward future possibilities with blended learning, maker spaces, and rapid prototyping.

Chapter 5: Developing Teachers for Deeper Learning

Rob Riordan and High Tech University colleagues Stacy Caillier and Ben Daley bring the discussion of 21st century teacher preparation back to the teacher-first theme initiated by the DuFours in chapter 1. They show how graduate preparation can shift from the obsolete and ineffective teacher preparation theory to expanding teachers' professional practical expertise in order to align it with deeper learning research. With multiple concrete examples selected from High Tech University's theory and practice repertoire, the authors describe in detail a revolutionary pathway to deeper learning preparation that could well become a model for all institutions.

Part II: What Will Drive the Shift?

The essays in part II address the systemic application challenges presented by the deeper learning paradigm shift in the broader school, district, and state domains of curriculum, instruction, and assessment. What issues in these areas require attention from district decision makers so that classroom teachers can have the permission, the moral support, the encouragement, and the resources to implement the deeper learning agenda?

Chapter 6: The Worst of Times, The Best of Times

Here, Tony Wagner recalls his first foray into the global achievement gap. This essay on "the worst of times" also traces the "educational reforms that aren't," such as flipped classrooms, increased time, and even the Common Core. Quickly, however, he moves into promising practices that promote true innovation.

Chapter 7: Road Maps to Deeper Learning

Bernie Trilling brings his deep understanding of school change, intensive research on what is working in schools across the United States, and his ability to synthesize the principles and practices of deeper learning to this profound and comprehensive how-to essay. This chapter could easily serve as a step-by-step guide for recreating any public, private, or charter school into an exemplar of 21st century teaching and learning. Highlighting a new 21st century change model, the PRISM, Trilling provides example after example to guide any willing school or district leader through the transformation process to deeper learning for all.

Chapter 8: 21st Century Curriculum—A Global Imperative

Although most literature about 21st century skills and deeper learning has focused on instruction, in this chapter, long-time advocate for 21st century skills Charles Fadel examines the other side of the coin. He not only calls for a deep curriculum revamp, but using examples from pilot projects around the globe, he also outlines what it must look like to ready students for the 21st century world.

Chapter 9: Assessment Systems for Deeper Learning

Linda Darling-Hammond and David T. Conley take on the most difficult challenge that comes with the current drive toward deeper learning schools—assessment. These researchers note how a decade of test-based accountability targeted narrowly on reading and mathematics failed to help schools focus on the importance of these subjects. With a plea for new means of assessment "to gauge the full range of knowledge and skills that comprise readiness for college and careers," they propose new systems of national, state, district, and classroom assessments that can generate information for a variety of purposes without distorting classroom instruction. These systems are highlighted by the authors' new, tripartite definition of *accountability*.

Part III: What Lessons Will Work?

In this section, long-time advocates of school change address what is happening now and what must occur in the next decades to advance the 21st century paradigm shift to deeper learning for all. We first look at a school that is completely deeper learning driven and has the achievement results to back that up; second, we look at lessons learned from leading school districts in the change process. Finally, we examine what exemplar states are doing to lead districts through the paradigm shift.

Chapter 10: Breakthrough Learning

Packed with research and exemplars that reveal the power of deeper learning best practices, Michael Fullan's insightful essay promises "a potential breakthrough in terms of both learning conditions and the level of change, the likes of which we have not seen since the industrial factory model of public schooling was established in the 19th century." He challenges school leaders to find a sense of urgency and quicken the slow pace toward the goals of deeper learning for all students.

Chapter 11: All or Nothing—A Deeper Learning Experience

Steven Zipkes, a National Distinguished Principal, paints an in-depth picture of a total school change. He shows how adoption of the New Tech Model in one school seeded needed changes throughout a non-affluent, rural district with a substantial minority and impoverished population. Manor New Tech's story is very concrete, showing the dramatic shift in college and career readiness, low absenteeism, and high college acceptance.

Chapter 12: Ears to the Ground—School Leadership in the New Millennium

Deborah Rosalia Esparza provides school leaders with an easy-to-adapt change template for advancing 21st century skills and deeper learning and describes how she and her team used such a plan in an urban school district to produce demonstrable results. This chapter describes a collective journey of professional educators who undertook a relentless pursuit for excellence in instructional delivery for multicultural-multilingual student populations, highly relevant and rigorous curriculum paradigm shifts, and optimal restructuring of basic school operational practices. Four key organizational elements are introduced as the 4Cs of 21st century school leadership—*context, culture, conditions,* and *competencies.* These elements are examined through a systemic school and district change process for preparation toward a 21st century transformation.

Chapter 13: The Pivotal Role of the District

Ken Kay and Valerie Greenhill, a dynamic duo who planted early seeds in the 21st century skills garden with the establishment of the Partnership for 21st Century Skills—and who now water that garden through EdLeader21—use the all-district change efforts occurring in EdLeader21's coast-to-coast network as their exemplars. The authors connect their seven-step district implementation model to the theory and practice of deeper learning. Recognizing the uniqueness of each district, Kay and Greenhill conclude with specific recommendations to help district leadership teams focus on this pathway to deeper learning.

Chapter 14: Levers for Change—The Role of the States

Helen A. Soulé and Steven Paine build on Paine's tenures as state superintendent of West Virginia's Department of Education and president of the Council of Chief State School Officers, when he led the development of the Common Core State Standards, as well as on Soulé's work with Partnership for 21st Century Skills states. Here, they focus on what state offices of education have done to advance efforts to enrich education with 21st century skills and deeper learning. They identify six levers used by exemplar states, note key questions state offices need to raise as they prepare statewide actions to advance the 21st century skill agenda, and cite best-practice examples. Their chapter is not only a road map, it is also is a document showing what is already working that can assist newcomers as they move forward.

Glossary

The book ends with a glossary that defines key terms from the language and literature of 21st century skills and deeper learning theory and practice.

Conclusion

In the end, the contributing authors have created a more powerful tool than I could have anticipated when I first envisioned this collection. After reading these chapters, I find it difficult to believe that anyone could say "but we don't know how." Just as *21st Century Skills: Rethinking How Students Learn* that Ron Brandt and I presented focused on the *what* and *why* of 21st century skills, this volume provides a gold mine of what, why, and how examples of deeper learning—as both a means and an end for teachers' attention to 21st century skills.

It is now time for us all to accept the challenge, to wade into the fray, and to advance the re-construction not just of individual schools but of American education, so that deeper learning is available to all. As Effective School's champion Ronald Edmonds (1979) wrote, "Whether or not we do it must finally depend on how we feel about the fact that we haven't so far" (p. 23).

References and Resources

Bellanca, J. A. (2010). *Enriched learning projects: A practical pathway to 21st century skills.* Bloomington, IN: Solution Tree Press.

Bellanca, J. A., & Brandt, R. (Eds.). (2010). *21st century skills: Rethinking how students learn.* Bloomington, IN: Solution Tree Press.

Bellanca, J. A., Fogarty R. J., & Pete, B. M. (2012). *How to teach thinking skills within the Common Core: 7 key student proficiencies of the new national standards.* Bloomington, IN: Solution Tree Press.

Duncan, A. (2013). *The threat of educational stagnation and complacency: Remarks of U.S. Secretary of Education Arne Duncan at the release of the 2012 Program for International Student Assessment (PISA).* Accessed at www.ed.gov/news/speeches/threat-educational -stagnation-and-complacency on July 26, 2014.

Edmonds, R. (1979, October). Effective schools for the urban poor. *Educational Leadership.* Accessed at www.midwayisd.org/cms/lib/TX01000662/Centricity /Domain/8/2.%20Edmonds%20Effective%20Schools%20Movement.pdf on May 14, 2014.

Fairfax County School District. (n.d.). *OECD test for schools (based on PISA) Pilot in 2012–13* [Newsletter]. Accessed at www.fcps.edu/pla/ost/pisa/pisa_2012_13_index.shtml on July 26, 2014.

Feuerstein, R., Feuerstein, R. S., & Falik, L. H. (2010). *Beyond smarter: Mediated learning and the brain's capacity for change.* New York: Teachers College Press.

Guglielmino, L. M. (1978). *Development of the self-directed learning readiness scale.* (Doctoral dissertation, University of Georgia, 1977). Dissertation Abstracts International, 38, 6467A.

Hattie, J. (n.d.). *Visible learning, tomorrow's schools, the mindsets that make the difference in education* [PowerPoint slide 7]. Accessed at www.treasury.govt.nz/publications/media speeches/guestlectures/pdfs/tgls-hattie.pdf on August 11, 2014.

Hewlett Foundation. (n.d.) *Deeper learning.* Accessed at www.hewlett.org/programs /education/deeper-learning accessed on July 27, 2014.

Johnson, R., & Johnson, D. (2009). *An educational psychology success story: Social interdependence theory and cooperative learning.* (AERA Document.) Accessed at http://edr .sagepub.com/cgi/content/abstract/38/5/365 on August 1, 2014.

Kahler, A. (2014, August). My TED connection: Little people's big world. *P21 Blogazine.* Washington, DC: Partnership for 21st Century Skills.

Knowles, M. S. (1975). *Self-directed learning: A guide for learners and teachers.* Chicago: Association Press.

Marzano Research Labatory. (2014). *Meta analysis data base of instructional strategies.* Accessed at www.marzanoresearch.com/research/database on August 12, 2014.

News from the National Academies. (2012, July 10). *Transferable knowledge and skills key to success in education and work: Report calls for efforts to incorporate 'deeper learning' into curriculum.* Accessed at www8.nationalacademies.org/onpinews/newsitem.aspx? RecordID=13398 on July 28, 2014.

No Child Left Behind (NCLB) Act of 2001, Pub. L. No. 107-110, § 115, Stat. 1425 (2002).

Organisation for Economic Co-operation and Development. (2000). *Literacy skills for the world of tomorrow.* Accessed at www.oecd.org/edu/school/programme forinternation-alstudentassessmentpisa/33690591.pdf on July 31, 2014.

Performance Assessment. (n.d.). *New York Performance Standards Consortium.* Accessed at www.performanceassessment.org on July 26, 2014.

Rhodan, M. (2013, December 16). A nation of C students. *TIME International, 182*(25), 12.

Slavin, R., & Cooper, R. (1999). Improving intergroup relations: Lessons learned from cooperative learning programs. *Journal of Social Studies Center for Research on the Education of Students Placed at Risk.*

PART I

How Does Deeper Learning Look and Sound?

Richard DuFour

Richard DuFour, EdD, was a public school educator for thirty-four years, serving as a teacher, principal, and superintendent. During his nineteen-year tenure as a leader at Adlai E. Stevenson High School in Lincolnshire, Illinois, Stevenson was one of only three schools in the nation to win the United States Department of Education Blue Ribbon Award on four occasions and the first comprehensive high school to be designated a New American High School, a model of successful school reform. He received his state's highest award as both a principal and superintendent. A prolific author and sought-after consultant, he is recognized as one of the leading authorities on helping school practitioners implement the Professional Learning Communities at Work™ process in their schools and districts. Richard was named one of the Top 100 School Administrators in North America by *Executive Educator* magazine, and was the 2004 recipient of the National Staff Development Council's Distinguished Service Award.

Rebecca DuFour

Rebecca DuFour has served as a teacher, school administrator, and central office coordinator. As a former elementary principal, she helped her school earn state and national recognition as a model professional learning community. Rebecca is one of the featured principals in the 2001 Video Journal of Education program "Leadership in an Age of Standards and High Stakes" and is the lead consultant and featured principal in the 2003 program, "Elementary Principals as Leaders of Learning." She is coauthor of numerous books, articles, and video series on the topic of PLCs. Serving as a consultant for more than a decade, Rebecca brings over thirty years of professional experience to her work with educators around the world who are implementing the Professional Learning Communities at Work™ process in their own organizations.

Chapter 1

Deeper Learning for Students Requires Deeper Learning for Educators

Richard DuFour and Rebecca DuFour

Pundits and politicians are increasingly strident in portraying the public schools of the United States in a negative light. Their references to American schools inevitably include derogatory descriptors, such as *declining* or *failing*. Yet, 2013 was arguably the greatest year in the history of American education. The American workforce is more educated than ever before (Carnevale, Smith, & Strohl, 2013). The nation's high school graduation rate was the highest in forty years (*Education Week*, 2013). Student achievement on the National Assessment of Educational Progress continued its two-decade trend of slowly improving scores in reading and mathematics. More students than ever pursued the challenging curriculum of college-equivalent advanced placement (AP) courses, and more students than ever were successful in scoring an honor grade of three or higher on those exams. In fact, far more students earned honor grades in 2012 than even attempted AP exams a decade earlier (College Board, 2013). Parent satisfaction with their local school was at an all-time high (Bushaw & Lopez, 2013).

The American system of education has not declined but has actually improved. Furthermore, this improvement has occurred in the face of an increasing number of students living in poverty, dramatic cuts in education funding in most states, and demographic groups who have traditionally struggled in school. The system is doing a better job than ever of preparing students . . . *for the 1960s.*

Preparing Students for Their Future Rather Than Our Past

Throughout the 1960s, the United States was the leading industrial nation in the world. Teenagers who found schooling to be tedious could drop out of high school and find high-paying jobs that offered benefits and security in factories, mills, and mines. Those conditions no longer exist in 21st century America.

In 1970, 74 percent of the middle class was made up of high school graduates and dropouts. By 2007, only 31 percent of the middle class was composed of these groups, with only 8 percent of the middle class composed of high school dropouts. In the same period, the percentage of the middle class with postsecondary education increased from 26 percent to 61 percent. By 2020, two out of every three jobs in the economy will require postsecondary training. Only 7 percent of the 55 million job openings in the United States between 2010 and 2020 will be available to high school dropouts, and those jobs are limited to three job classifications that are either low paying or declining in numbers—sales and office support, blue-collar jobs, and food and personal services (Carnevale et al., 2013).

As the Center on Education and the Workforce reports, "High school graduates and dropouts will find themselves largely left behind in the American economy. Postsecondary education and training is no longer just the preferred pathway to the middle and upper income classes—it is increasingly the only pathway" (Carnevale, Smith, & Strohl, 2010). The Center for Public Education came to a similar conclusion. In its analysis of demographic and economic factors impacting the United States, it states that "increasingly, some postsecondary education or technical training is essential for an opportunity to support a family or secure a middle-class lifestyle" (Jerald, 2009, p. 23).

In light of these facts, contemporary American educators must strive to accomplish something that has never been done in the history of the United States—to ensure all students acquire the deeper learning that, so far, has been expected of only the best and brightest students. The most promising strategy for meeting this challenge is to develop the capacity of educators to function as members of collaborative teams within a high-performing professional learning community (PLC). To address the major changes to curriculum, pedagogy, and assessment that deeper learning requires, schools must function as powerful PLCs.

Recognizing That Clarity Precedes Competence

A basic premise of the PLC process is that before educators can become competent at any aspect of that process, they must be crystal clear as to what it entails. As organizational theorists Jeffrey Pfeffer and Robert Sutton (2000) note, "It is hard enough to explain what a complex idea means for action when you understand it and others don't. It is impossible when you use terms that sound impressive but you don't understand what they mean" (p. 52). Therefore, we begin with an exploration of the meaning of two key terms—*professional learning community* and *deeper learning*.

What Is a Professional Learning Community?

Urging educators to create schools and districts that function as professional learning communities is pointless without a clear understanding of what this term means. The PLC concept represents *"an ongoing process in which educators work collaboratively in recurring cycles of collective inquiry and action research to achieve better results for the students they serve"* (DuFour, DuFour, Eaker, & Many, 2010, p. 11). The following three big ideas drive the PLC process.

1. The fundamental purpose of the school is to ensure that *all* students learn at high levels. To address that fundamental purpose, systems are in place to engage all of the school's educators in the consideration of four critical questions.

   + What is it we expect all students to know and be able to do as a result of each essential standard we teach?

+ How will we know when each student has learned?

+ How will we respond when, at the end of a unit, some students have not learned?

+ How will we enrich and extend the learning for students who have demonstrated proficiency?

2. To ensure all students learn requires a collective effort. The fundamental structure of the school is collaborative teams of educators who work interdependently to achieve shared goals for which members are mutually accountable.

3. Educators have a results orientation that fosters both student and adult learning. They are hungry for evidence of student learning and use that evidence to inform and improve their professional practice and to better meet the needs of individual students.

What Is Deeper Learning?

Few would oppose the idea that students should learn at deeper rather than shallower levels. However, unless educators have developed a common language with a shared understanding of key terms, calls for deeper learning will remain morally impeccable but impossible to translate into purposeful classroom practice. The National Research Council's Committee on Defining Deeper Learning (2012) concludes that deeper learning "is the process through which an individual becomes capable of taking what was learned in one situation and applying it to new situations (i.e. transfer) . . . by developing cognitive, interpersonal, and intrapersonal competencies" (p. 5).

Norman Webb has modified Bloom's taxonomy to classify Depth of Knowledge (DOK) criteria into the following four levels, with levels 3 and 4 representing deeper learning (Herman & Linn, 2013). The levels are as follows:

DOK 1—Recall of a fact, term, concept, or procedure—basic comprehension

DOK 2—Application of concepts or procedures involving some mental processing

DOK 3—Applications requiring abstract thinking, reasoning, or more complex inferences

DOK 4—Extended analysis or investigation that requires synthesis and analysis across multiple contexts and non-routine applications

The Hewlett Foundation (2012) defines *deeper learning* as

the skills and knowledge students will need to succeed in a world that is changing at an unprecedented pace. Deeper learning prepares students to master core academic content, think critically and solve complex problems, work collaboratively, communicate effectively, and learn how to learn (for example, self-directed learning).

While these definitions and descriptions may vary somewhat, there is general agreement that deeper learning must prepare all students for continued learning beyond the K–12 system. *Every* student must be prepared to attend college or engage in the ongoing learning after high school that is necessary for success in a career.

Creating the Curriculum to Develop Deeper Learning

In 2008, the National Governors Association, the Council of Chief State School Officers, and Achieve issued a report urging states to adopt "a common core of internationally benchmarked standards in mathematics and language arts for grades K–12 to ensure that students are equipped with the necessary knowledge and skills to be globally competitive" (p. 6). The following year, the National Governors Association began the process of creating robust standards in curriculum areas that would reflect the skills and knowledge students need to succeed in college and careers.

Two long-standing assessment programs intended to monitor the ability of students to apply their learning are the National Assessment of Educational Progress (NAEP) and the Programme for International Student Assessment (PISA). The former was created in the 1960s to assess the progress of American students in a variety of subject areas by testing a small sampling of students from around the country. NAEP was initially funded by the Carnegie Foundation; however, by 1972, the federal government had assumed full responsibility for funding the program. The test has continued through several iterations since that time. The PISA exam was developed by the Organisation for Economic Co-operation and Development to assess the learning of fifteen-year-old students in countries around the world in mathematics, science, and reading. It, too, relies on a random sampling of students rather than testing all students. It was first administered in 2000 and is designed to assess a student's ability to apply his or her knowledge.

The task of creating the assessments for the new Common Core State Standards (CCSS) fell to two state-led consortia, the Partnership for Assessment of Readiness for College and Careers (PARCC) and the Smarter Balanced Assessment Consortium. Although they differ somewhat in their approach, both plan to assess deeper learning and will be much more rigorous than the assessments that states have used under No Child Left Behind. Table 1.1 demonstrates the projected increase in rigor using Webb's DOK criteria.

Table 1.1: Projected Increase in Rigor Using Webb's Depth of Knowledge Criteria

State Assessments	Consortia Assessment Specifications
No students were assessed with items at DOK 3 or 4 in mathematics.	All students will be assessed with items at DOK 3 and 4.
None of the items were at DOK 3 or 4 levels in mathematics.	Seventy percent of items in mathematics will be assessed at DOK 3 or 4 levels.
Sixteen percent of students were assessed at DOK 3 or 4 in language arts.	All students will be assessed at DOK 3 and 4 in language arts.
Fourteen percent of selected-response items in reading were at DOK 3, none at DOK 4.	Sixty-eight percent of items in reading will be assessed at DOK 3 and 4.
Forty-nine percent of items were at DOK 3, and 11 percent were at DOK 4 on open-ended reading items.	

Fully 100 percent of students in tested grades using consortia tests will be held accountable for deeper learning beginning with the

2014–2015 school year. These assessments reflect a "dramatic upward shift in intellectual rigor and toward deeper learning" (Herman & Linn, 2013, p. 17).

Addressing the Common Core Challenge Through PLCs

In a professional learning community, educators address the challenge of helping all students demonstrate deeper learning by working in collaborative teams rather than in isolation. Members of these collaborative teams are provided with time to work together as part of their routine practice. Teams will typically be organized by grade level or content (for example, all third-grade teachers or all algebra teachers), because those structures have the greatest impact on improving student learning (Gallimore, Ermeling, Saunders, & Goldenberg, 2009; Little & Barlett, 2010). The deeper learning of the CCSS certainly lends itself to interdisciplinary efforts that cut across subject areas, but we recommend that these efforts come later in the process. In the initial stages of teaching and assessing for deeper learning, job-alike teams represent the best structure for collective inquiry.

Members of a *learning* community will recognize that every step they take in implementing the Common Core will begin with *learning* together. This collective inquiry begins with the question of *why* before addressing the issue of *how*. Before asking educators to implement the new Common Core curriculum and prepare students for the rigorous assessments that will accompany it, members of a PLC will build shared knowledge as to why the initiative is warranted. An objective analysis of three areas—(1) the importance of preparing students for learning beyond high school, (2) the failure of our current system of education to provide that preparation, and (3) the serious implications for students who are unsuccessful in the K–12 system—provides a compelling rationale for deeper learning.

Student Preparation for Learning Beyond High School

Earlier we referenced the need for all students to master deeper learning in order to have access to higher education. This need for deeper learning is not, however, limited to college-bound students. A study by ACT (2006) finds that the levels of readiness that high-school graduates need for college and workforce training programs are comparable. For example, the mathematics skills required by electricians, construction workers, and plumbers match what is necessary to do well in college-level courses (ACT, 2006). As the ACT report concludes,

> The results of this study underscore the importance of having a *common expectation for all students* when they graduate from high school, one that prepares all high school graduates for both credit-bearing entry-level college courses and workforce training programs associated with jobs that are likely to offer both a wage sufficient to support a small family and the potential for career advancement. (p. 8; italics added)

All students must be able to continue growing and learning beyond the K–12 system if they are to have access to opportunity in 21st century America.

The Failure of the Current System

It is undeniable that the current educational system fails to prepare all students for ongoing learning beyond K–12 schooling. Consider the following:

- Approximately one of every four students who enter high school in the United States will drop out of school (*Education Week*, 2013).

- Only one in four high school students graduates ready for college in all four core subjects—English, mathematics, science, and social studies (ACT, 2013a).

- Thirty-seven percent of students who enter college require remedial courses (College Board, 2013).

- Only 12 percent of students who take a remedial reading course in college will earn a bachelor's degree (Strong American Schools, 2008).

- Thirty-three percent of students who enter college will drop out by the end of their first year (ACT, 2012).

- Only 42 percent of American students who enter college (public or private) will earn a bachelor's degree within five years (ACT, 2013b).

Einstein described insanity as doing the same thing over and over and expecting to get better results. It would indeed be insane for American educators to work harder at maintaining a system that was never designed to help all students learn at high levels and to expect different results. The assumptions about the purpose of schooling, the responsibilities of educators, and the capabilities of students must all change, and the PLC process promotes those changes in a very intentional way.

Implications for Students Unable to Succeed in the K–12 System

The educational system that served the baby boomer generation so well will not prepare students for success in the 21st century. Even though the United States achieved its highest graduation rate in forty years in 2013, over 5500 students dropped out of high school every school day, or one student every thirty-one seconds (Swanson & Lloyd, 2013). Consider the prospects for those students. A high school dropout in the United States:

- Is three times more likely to be unemployed than a college graduate (Breslow, 2012).

- Makes twenty-five cents for every dollar a college graduate makes and sixty-three cents for every dollar a high school graduate makes, and the gap is widening (U.S. Census Bureau, 2009). This is the highest earning discrepancy of any industrialized nation. Put another way, the negative impact of dropping out of high school is greater in the U.S. than anywhere in the world (OECD, 2009).

- Will live in poverty with an average annual salary of $20,241. For 2013, the federal guideline defining poverty was an annual income of $23,550 for a family of four (Breslow, 2012).

- Is more prone to ill health (OECD, 2009) and four times more likely to be without health insurance (Olshansky, 2012).

- Will live a shorter life. The difference in life expectancy between dropouts and college graduates is ten and a half years for women and thirteen years for men. The difference in life expectancy is growing (Tavernise, 2012).

- Is sixty-three times more likely to be incarcerated than a college graduate (Breslow, 2012).

- Will end up costing taxpayers $292,000 over his or her lifetime compared to a high school graduate (Breslow, 2012).

This collective examination of the need for schools to prepare students for learning beyond the K–12 system creates a moral imperative for changing the traditional practices of schooling. As Daniel Pink (2011) notes, the most powerful motivator for knowledge workers is a common cause or shared purpose larger than themselves. So in a professional learning community, the effort to begin helping all students learn at deeper levels will not begin with distribution of new curriculum materials or workshops explaining the CCSS. The process will begin at the starting point for all aspects of the PLC process—learning together about why the initiative warrants the full commitment and collective efforts of every member of the community.

Recognizing That Moral Purpose Is Not Enough

Even if a staff embraces a common cause based on a moral imperative and even if its members burn with a fiery zeal to help all students develop mastery of deeper learning, there is no guarantee that they have the capacity to bring students to higher levels of learning. A study of the world's best school systems finds that these systems recognize that "the quality of an education system cannot exceed the quality of its teachers. The only way to improve outcomes is to improve teaching" (Barber & Mourshed, 2007, p. 4). We would broaden that observation from "teachers" to "educators" and concur with the study's conclusion that "one cannot give what one does not have" (p. 16). Good intentions aren't enough. So like the world's best school systems, the United States must recognize that if students are to learn at deeper levels, schools must create the conditions that allow for the ongoing, deeper learning of the educators who serve those students in each of the three critical areas—(1) curriculum, (2) pedagogy, and (3) authentic assessment.

Curriculum: What Must All of Our Students Learn?

Although most schools and school districts have created mission statements that proclaim a commitment to help all students learn, they often fail to specify exactly what knowledge, skills, and dispositions all students must acquire in each course, each grade level, and each unit of instruction. It is only when members of a collaborative teacher team can answer the question "learn what?" with a consistent voice for each unit they teach that students will have access to a guaranteed and viable curriculum.

The idea that students will learn more when those who are called on to teach them are crystal clear about exactly what students must learn is certainly not counterintuitive and is a consistent finding in research on factors that impact student learning (Hattie, 2012). The challenge that faces educators is how to best ensure that each teacher is clear about and committed to teaching the essential standards.

A truly guaranteed curriculum that supports deeper learning requires more than the district office providing teachers with copies of the Common Core standards for their grade level, a curriculum framework, a pacing guide, and a textbook—and then leaving it to each teacher to figure out the details. Districts that use this approach to implementing curriculum conveniently overlook the fact that teachers can and do interpret the documents differently, assign different levels of priority to recommended content, may lack the skill to teach particular standards, or may simply ignore the documents. In short, it is not unusual to see a huge gap between the *intended* curriculum established by a national committee, the state, or the district office, and the *implemented* curriculum that is taught when teachers close their classroom doors (Marzano, 2003). Distributing documents and hoping for the best is not a viable strategy for implementing the CCSS.

Other districts will be more directive. Central office administrators will assume responsibility for translating the Common Core into a prescribed curriculum that dictates exactly what will be taught and when. These districts may go so far as to script lessons, so that teachers are also told exactly how to teach each lesson. Administrators in these districts monitor teachers closely to ensure they are teaching the right content on the right day and using the right strategies with "fidelity." This top-down approach fails to generate the clarity, coherence, or commitment to the curriculum among the very people who are asked to implement it (DuFour & Fullan, 2013). As Stephen Covey (1989) writes, "without involvement there is no commitment. Mark it down, asterisk it, circle it, underline it. *No involvement, no commitment*" (p. 143).

In *Leaders of Learning*, Rick DuFour and Robert Marzano (2011) emphasize that a guaranteed and viable curriculum requires much more than distributing the same documents to educators or dictating every aspect of instruction. As they write,

> The only way that the curriculum in a school can truly be guaranteed is if the teachers themselves, those who are called upon to deliver the curriculum, have worked collaboratively to do the following:
>
> - Study the intended curriculum.
> - Agree on priorities within the curriculum.
> - Clarify how the curriculum translates into student knowledge and skills.
> - Establish general pacing guidelines for delivering the curriculum.
> - Commit to one another that they will, in fact, teach the agreed-upon curriculum. (p. 91)

Educators must understand that we are not suggesting they ignore the CCSS, their district curriculum frameworks, or pacing guides for their grade level. We are saying that these documents are so significant they are worthy of the collective study of the teacher teams who will ultimately interpret and implement the standards in their classrooms.

In the final analysis, it is each team's commitment to help all students acquire the essential knowledge, skills, and dispositions that will determine whether a school is providing students with access to a guaranteed curriculum. When team members commit to one another ("So we have agreed to teach this specific skill in the next unit"), the likelihood of a guaranteed curriculum increases exponentially. When done well, a team will regard the essential skills of a guaranteed curriculum not as a list of topics to be covered but as a promise they are making to students and to one another about what each student will learn.

Pedagogy: How Can We Teach for Deeper Learning?

The idea that curriculum reform will result in students learning at higher levels did not suddenly emerge with the CCSS initiative. Since the Sputnik era of the late 1950s, there have been calls to improve student achievement through developing more rigorous curriculum. If there is a single lesson to be learned from this history, it is that simply adopting new curriculum standards does not improve student learning. As Dylan Wiliam (2011) asserts, "a bad curriculum well taught is invariably a better experience for students than a good curriculum badly taught: pedagogy trumps curriculum" (p. 13). Unless attention is paid to helping teachers develop instructional skills that elicit deeper learning, student achievement may actually regress under the CCSS.

Linda Darling-Hammond (2008) identifies the following as some of the keys to teaching for deeper learning:

- Students actively engage in well-designed, inquiry-based projects, problems, and design tasks that call on them to apply what they have learned. These real-world issues focus students on central questions of the disciplines and engage students in doing the work.

- Teachers build on students' prior knowledge and progress. They scaffold instruction so that it helps students systematically build on their knowledge and skills.

- Teachers develop clearly defined standards of proficiency with specific examples of different levels of proficiency available to teachers and students alike.

- Students receive formative feedback as they advance toward the well-defined learning standards through self-, peer, and teacher assessment. Students learn to reflect on their work, evaluate it against a standard, and improve it.

- Students engage in frequent, small-group collaboration with their peers so that their learning takes place in a social context and relies on communication and interaction with others.

- Teachers develop students' metacognitive skills so that they learn to reflect on what they know, what they need to know, and processes for solving problems.

The NRC Committee on Defining Deeper Learning (2012) concludes that effective teachers of deeper learning expect students to access, evaluate, and explain competing information about issues; develop and respond to probing questions as they investigate an issue; work collaboratively with peers; establish norms for questioning each other; and justify their answers.

Teachers may confront several potential obstacles as they attempt to use an inquiry-based approach to foster deeper learning. Educators have often mistakenly assumed that inquiry-based learning is "unstructured," allowing students to construct their own meaning. But as a summary of the research on unstructured learning concludes, "The past half century of empirical research on this issue has provided overwhelming and unambiguous evidence that minimal guidance during instruction is significantly less effective and efficient than guidance specifically designed to support the cognitive processing necessary for learning" (Kirschner, Sweller, & Clark, 2006, p. 75). Teachers must thoughtfully and purposefully design instruction to illustrate key subject-matter concepts, balance students' need for direct instruction with opportunities to inquire, provide extensive scaffolding of the learning, model effective strategies for inquiry, give frequent feedback, and develop and use assessment to guide the learning process (Barron & Darling-Hammond, 2008).

Educators also face the challenge of establishing new approaches to classroom management that support student-to-student communication and collaboration—key elements of inquiry-based learning and essential 21st century skills (Partnership for 21st Century Skills [P21], 2013). The inquiry-based tasks and projects must foster cooperative work, shared learning goals, interdependence, and mutual accountability to ensure that students are not only working in a group but also as a team. Students must be explicitly taught norms and structures that support effective teamwork. They must also learn group-processing skills so that members can frequently assess the effectiveness of their team and identify ways to improve their ability to work together. Accountability structures must be in place for the entire team as well as for each member, so that individual students can't shirk their responsibilities (Johnson & Johnson, 1994). Teachers accustomed to having students sit silently in rows and speaking only when they are called on will need help in developing new approaches to classroom management.

Finally, effective teaching is not an algorithmic activity in which one follows a prescribed road map for arriving at the desired destination. For example, Robert J. Marzano (2009) identifies instructional strategies that have a high probability of enhancing student achievement. He cautions, however, that no instructional strategy is guaranteed to work and that for every "high-probability" strategy he has found, there are research studies concluding that these strategies are ineffective.

Teaching is a heuristic activity that requires enlightened trial and error. No one can script instruction that is guaranteed to result in deeper learning. As DuFour and Marzano (2011) contend, "Instruction is a means to an end—student learning—and thus the ultimate test of effective instruction is actual evidence that students have learned. . . . The most important criterion in assessing the success of a lesson is whether or not students have learned" (p. 142). This fact brings us to the third element of deeper learning—authentic assessment.

Authentic Assessment: How Will We Know They Have Learned?

Once a team has identified the knowledge and skills each student must acquire as a result of a particular unit of instruction and the amount of time it will devote to that unit, members must turn their attention to how students will demonstrate their learning. Clarifying standards might answer the question of what students must know and be able to do, but assessments clarify how students will demonstrate they have met the standards.

There is widespread agreement that assessments must undergo a dramatic change if they are to promote and measure deeper learning. The Alliance for Excellent Education asserts that changing the way students are assessed is "the most urgent priority" in the effort to help students master deeper learning (Rothman, 2011, p. 1). The NRC Committee on Defining Deeper Learning (2012) cites the lack of quality assessments for deeper learning as a major obstacle in the effort to help students demonstrate higher levels of learning and concludes, "In particular, new types of assessment systems, capable of accurately measuring and supporting acquisitions of these competencies, will be needed" (p. 14). The Center for K–12 Assessment and Performance Management at ETS (2012) concludes that major changes in traditional methods of assessment are needed to determine if students can complete the complex tasks required of the CCSS. Each of these organizations argues that high-quality assessments could serve as a catalyst for improved instruction because if "assessments measure deeper learning abilities, teachers are more likely to teach the relevant skills" (Rothman, 2011, p. 1).

One important aspect of assessment that members of a collaborative team will consider is how to integrate formative assessment of deeper learning into their routine teaching practice so that they are checking for student understanding almost minute by minute. They will help one another develop, share, and practice new techniques for monitoring student learning during classroom instruction. They will also engage in collective inquiry regarding how to expand their instructional strategies, so that when a favored teaching practice is ineffective for some students, they can access other strategies from their pedagogical toolbox.

When done well, these formative assessments will make learning goals more clear to students, continuously monitor and respond to students' learning needs, provide feedback to students regarding their progress, and involve students in self- and peer assessment (NRC Committee on Defining Deeper Learning, 2012). Dylan Wiliam's (2011) *Embedded Formative Assessment* is an excellent resource to assist teams with this learning.

A second area of inquiry for collaborative teams in assessment will be how to design more formal assessments of deeper learning that can be administered multiple times throughout the year. Although many educators have been persuaded that creating a quality assessment is a process shrouded in mystery that can only be deciphered by psychometricians and statisticians, W. James Popham (2005) insists that quality assessments rely on "commonsense ideas, not numerical obscurities." He suggests that teachers can learn what they need to know about good assessments by reading an article or an introductory text on the topic (Popham, 2001).

Teams will also build their assessment literacy by investigating the high-stakes assessments their own students will take to demonstrate proficiency in the CCSS. PARCC, Smarter Balanced, the NAEP, and PISA provide excellent resources that are worthy of the collective study of teams committed to developing assessments that challenge their students to demonstrate deeper learning. When teams identify items or projects from these organizations that align with a skill or concept they are teaching, they can incorporate the items and projects into their own assessments. More importantly, as the teams become familiar with the assessments created by these organizations, they can create their own items and projects that simulate the rigor and format of those models. We provide a brief summary of each.

PARCC

The Partnership for Assessment of Readiness for College and Careers has created task prototypes and sample items to provide educators with a snapshot of what its 2014–2015 assessments look like. The language arts performance tasks include (PARCC, 2013):

- **Type I (Literary analysis tasks)**—Students will be asked to carefully consider literature worthy of close study and compose an analytic essay.

- **Type II (Narrative tasks)**—Students may be asked to write a story, detail a scientific process, write a historical account of important figures, or describe an account of events, scenes, or objects.

- **Type III (Research simulation tasks)**—Students will analyze an informational topic presented through several articles or multimedia stimuli, the first text being an anchor text that introduces the topic. Students will engage with the texts by answering a series of questions and synthesizing information from multiple sources in order to write two analytic essays.

The mathematics performance tasks include (PARCC, 2013):

- **Type I**—Tasks assessing concepts, skills, and procedures

- **Type II**—Tasks expressing mathematical reasoning

- **Type III**—Tasks asssessing modeling or applications

PARCC provides sample language arts and mathematics assessment items for grades 3 through 11 as well as scoring rubrics on its website (www.parcconline.org). PARCC also intends to create a series of professional development modules to help teachers, counselors, school leaders, and school and district testing coordinators understand the new assessment system. The first five of these online modules will address an overview of the PARCC assessment, the optional midyear assessment, diagnostic assessments, assessments for speaking and listening, and PARCC's (2013) accessibility system.

Smarter Balanced

This consortium also provides sample items in language arts and mathematics intended to give educators "clear benchmarks to inform their instruction" (Smarter Balanced Assessment Consortium, 2013). The format includes:

- Selected-response items that prompt students to select one or more responses for a set of options

- Technology-enhanced items that take advantage of computer-based administration to assess a deeper understanding of content and skills than would otherwise be possible with traditional item types; technology-enhanced items capitalize on technology to collect evidence through a nontraditional response type, such as editing text or drawing an object

- Constructed-response items that prompt students to produce a text or numerical response in order to collect evidence about their knowledge or understanding of a given assessment target

- Performance tasks that measure a student's ability to integrate knowledge and skills across multiple standards—a key component of college and career readiness; performance tasks will be used to better measure capacities such as depth of understanding, research skills, and complex analysis, which cannot be adequately assessed with selected- or constructed-response items

Each sample item includes an "about this item" link that connects it to a particular grade level and the specific standard or standards that the item addresses. The site also provides rubrics to assist with scoring the item. Visit www.smarterbalanced.org/sample-items-and-performance-tasks to access the sample items.

Smarter Balanced (2013) also provides practice tests in language arts and mathematics for different grade levels but cautions that these tests "do not encompass the full range of content that students will encounter on the spring 2014 Field Test or on the operational assessments, and should not be used to guide instructional decisions." The practice tests provide performance-task writing rubrics for argumentative, informative-explanatory, narrative, and opinion tasks. Scoring guides are also provided. Visit http://sbac.portal .airast.org/practice-test/resources to access both the rubrics and scoring guides. Smarter Balanced promises to create online professional development resources and research-supported instructional tools.

NAEP

The National Assessment of Educational Progress is a congressionally mandated project administered by the National Center for Education Statistics (2013) within the Institute of Education Sciences of the U.S. Department of Education. The NAEP Questions Tool (www.nces.ed.gov/nationsreportcard/itmrlsx/default.aspx) provides access to over three thousand released questions from NAEP assessments. (Visit **go.solution-tree.com/21stcenturyskills** to access all live links in this book.) Unlike the PARCC and Smarter Balanced assessments that focus on language arts and mathematics, the NAEP also offers assessments in U.S. history, economics, civics, geography, and science.

NAEP assessments are administered at grades 4, 8, and 12 and include multiple-choice, short-constructed, and extended-constructed items. The site indicates the particular skill being assessed, the degree of difficulty of each item (easy, medium, or hard), and the percentage of students who answered the item correctly. It also provides a scoring guide using actual student responses that illustrate different levels of proficiency.

The National Assessment of Educational Progress has been criticized by assessment experts for failure to establish the validity of the tests and for establishing a proficiency level that is unrealistic. Diane Ravitch (2012) contends that "proficient" on the NAEP is equivalent to a grade of A in a course while the "basic" level is the equivalent of a grade of B or C. If, however, educators are looking for extremely rigorous assessments that include constructed responses in addition to multiple-choice items, this free resource is one they might consider.

PISA

The Programme for International Student Assessment aims to evaluate education systems worldwide by testing the skills and knowledge of fifteen-year-old students in reading, mathematics, and science. Every three years, a test in one of these three areas is administered to randomly selected students in countries around the world. These tests are designed to determine the extent to which students can apply their knowledge to real-life situations and thus could serve as useful tools for assessing high school students in the CCSS.

PISA provides released items from their past assessments with a scoring guide that identifies the intent of the item, the skill it is assessing, and a rubric for scoring each item. Visit www.oecd.org/pisa /pisaproducts to view released items from mathematics as well as the

ELA reading passages and released items based on those passages. In addition, go to www.oecd.org/pisa/38709385.pdf to view released items for science.

Since the PARCC and Smarter Balanced assessments and PISA will all be administered via computer, collaborative teams should structure their assessments to give students lots of practice on computer-based assessments. A useful tool to help teams become familiar with different kinds of computer-based assessments of varying complexity is the interactive chart available at http://pages .uoregon.edu/kscalise/taxonomy/taxonomy.html (Scalise, 2012). You can also visit www.parcconline.org for technology guidelines.

Digging Deeper Into Deeper Learning

A team's analysis of the deeper learning required of students must also establish the rigor of the standard and what students must do to demonstrate proficiency. For example, PARCC's language for tasks is the same for students at all grade levels. Both third graders and high school students are expected to complete tasks expressing mathematical reasoning, though clearly the levels of rigor would vary greatly in completing the tasks. One CCSS writing standard (W.4.2.A) asks fourth graders to "introduce a topic clearly and group related information in paragraphs and sections; include formatting (e.g., headings), illustrations, and multimedia when useful to aiding comprehension" (NGA & CCSSO, 2010a, p. 20). Six years later, as tenth graders, those students must meet a writing standard with language that is almost identical.

It should be evident that merely reading the standard will not give teachers much insight regarding different levels of expectations for students in different grade levels. For standards to be meaningful, teachers need to establish agreed-on criteria for members to use when judging the quality of student work and to ensure that every teacher can apply the criteria consistently. PARCC attempts to address this need by offering a general rubric to apply to student work, but again, the language is exactly the same for grades 6 through 11. The terms of the rubric—*inaccurate, minimally accurate, generally accurate, mostly accurate*, and *accurate*—lack specificity and will be of little use in terms of helping teachers or students assess the quality of student work.

Therefore, collaborative teams need to translate the CCSS into student-friendly language that clarifies for both teachers and students the expected level of performance all students will achieve. They also need to create examples of the different levels of proficiency that clearly delineate the standard of performance for each level. They need to practice applying their agreed-on criteria to real examples of student work until they establish the inter-rater reliability that ensures students are receiving consistent, accurate feedback.

In their collective effort to create high-quality assessments of deeper learning, educators must always be cognizant of one essential fact: the effort will have no impact on student learning unless they use the results to respond to the learning needs of individual students and to inform and improve their professional practice. Team-developed common assessments are a means to an end rather than the end itself. If the assessments do not lead to more learning on the part of both students and educators, the time it takes to create and administer them is wasted. Even worse, a powerful opportunity to improve instruction is wasted.

Responding When Students Don't Learn

Any school that asserts its mission is to help all students learn at deeper levels must confront the grim reality that not all students will learn in the same amount of time or with the same amount of support. Team-developed common assessments, therefore, must be an instrument for identifying students who are unable to demonstrate proficiency, for helping both teachers and students identify the problems students are experiencing, and for providing struggling students with immediate intervention until they become proficient. Educators must do more than teach, test, hope for the best, and then move on to the next unit. The assessments they create must be formative, that is, part of "a planned process in which assessment-elicited evidence of students' status is used by teachers to adjust their ongoing instructional procedures or by students to adjust their current learning tactics" (Popham, 2008, p. 6).

In a PLC school, collaborative teams of educators analyze the evidence of student learning from frequent common formative assessments to ensure that students who are struggling receive additional time and support for learning that extends beyond the individual classroom teacher to include a schoolwide plan of intervention. This intervention must be:

- **Timely**—Responding to student needs as soon as they become apparent

- **Diagnostic**—Providing evidence of the specific problem the student is experiencing rather than generic statements, such as, "He is not doing well in math"—the school monitors each student's learning by name and by need, by the student and by the standard

- **Directive**—In that students are not *invited* to seek additional time and support but rather are required to continue to keep working at a skill or concept until they can demonstrate proficiency

- **Fluid and flexible**—Allowing students to move easily in and out of intervention; they are not assigned to intervention for specific periods of time but rather receive this extra time and support until they can demonstrate proficiency

- **Systematic**—Since the response to students who are not learning is not left to each teacher to resolve; rather, it is part of a coordinated, schoolwide plan to ensure that struggling students receive the benefit of additional time and support for learning in a way that does not remove them from new direct instruction

For an excellent, in-depth analysis of how systematic interventions work in a PLC, we recommend *Simplifying Response to Intervention* by Austin Buffum, Mike Mattos, and Chris Weber (2012). We emphasize, however, that effective systems of intervention depend on educators who use common assessments in a formative way. Common assessments must be used not merely to give students a chance to prove what they have learned, but to *improve their learning.*

Using Common Formative Assessment as a Catalyst for Professional Learning

Educators in a PLC also use the evidence of student learning from common formative assessments as a feedback loop to analyze and impact their professional practice. The results of a team assessment are transparent among members of the team and enable them to support one another's ongoing learning. If the assessment reveals that a member has exceptional results in teaching a particular skill or concept, that member shares his or her strategies with colleagues. If the results demonstrate that a teacher has been unable to help large numbers of his or her students reach proficiency, the entire team can brainstorm ways that teacher can integrate new instructional practices for the skill or concept.

Using evidence of student learning to inform and improve professional practice is the *sine qua non* of a PLC. Michael Fullan (2011), who has examined the practices of school systems around the world, reports that "in every case" of significant improvement, "leaders focused on common assessment frameworks linked to individualized instructional practices. Progress and problems were also transparent . . . with corresponding discussion of how to improve results" (p. 45).

John A. C. Hattie (2012) concludes that schools should have systems in place to ensure that:

- Educators are working as members of a team rather than in isolation

- There is a shared understanding of the knowledge, skills, and dispositions all students must acquire

- Evidence of student learning is collected in a regular and dependable way

- Students are provided with multiple opportunities to demonstrate their learning

- Educators use the evidence of student learning to examine their teaching

As Hattie writes (2012),

> Within a school we need to collaborate to build a team working together to solve the dilemmas in learning, to collectively share and critique the nature and quality of evidence that shows our impact on student learning, and cooperate in planning and critiquing lessons, learning intentions, and success criteria on a regular basis. (p. 151)

Collaborative teams are not fully engaged in the PLC process until members are using evidence of student learning to inform and improve their professional practice.

Supporting Adult Learning

The key to helping students demonstrate deeper learning is investing in the ongoing professional learning that builds the capacity of teachers and principals to develop and implement more powerful curriculum, instruction, and assessments. So how do educators learn to apply more effective teaching strategies? By removing teaching from its "cloak of privacy and autonomy" (Goodlad, 1983, p. 557) and developing a new culture in which what and how teachers teach becomes the ongoing focus of peer analysis, discussion, and improvement.

Once again, educators must assess the quality of their instruction on the basis of actual evidence of student learning and then use that evidence to share their strengths and seek the support of their colleagues in addressing weaknesses.

When, however, a team discovers that none of its members are being effective in helping students acquire a skill or concept, the team must seek assistance from others—both inside and outside of the school—in developing new strategies. Its members must then engage in action research to learn, apply, and assess the impact of the new strategies. They must be supported in this ongoing learning at the same time that they are held accountable for sustaining their collective inquiry, until there is tangible evidence of improved results (Gallimore et al., 2009). This iterative process of educators working together with others—both inside and outside of their schools—to use evidence of student learning to improve their individual and collective practice is vital to improved pedagogy.

How do teachers develop the assessment literacy that can serve as a catalyst for improved pedagogical practice? Here again, assessment experts agree that the best way for educators to build their capacity to create quality assessments is to address the challenge as members of collaborative teams rather than as individuals. The collaborative team structure is described as "essential" in any effort to build the assessment literacy of educators (Stiggins, 1999, p. 198), the "best hope" to support teachers in learning how to use powerful classroom assessments (Wiliam, 2007, p. 197), and "the best way to accomplish a schoolwide implementation of formative assessment" (Popham, 2008, p. 119).

And what is the best strategy for delivering the professional development that builds the capacity of educators to improve their instructional and assessment practice? Researchers from throughout the world have offered consistent advice: ensure that schools operate as professional learning communities. As Judith Warren Little (2006) summarizes this research,

> No matter how well designed a structured program of professional development, its track record of success will depend on the strength of the professional learning community . . . professional learning communities provide fertile ground for good professional development. (p. 20)

The process of developing professional learning communities in which educators work collaboratively to improve both student and adult learning does not happen by accident. School leaders must be intentional in:

- Establishing the moral imperative of helping all students acquire deeper learning

- Assigning teachers into meaningful teams that share a collective responsibility for helping all students to demonstrate deeper learning

- Providing time for teachers to work together on curriculum, instruction, and assessment as part of their routine practice, which includes—

  + Ensuring teams have a deep understanding of the knowledge and skills students must acquire in each course, each grade level, and each unit of instruction

  + Helping teams monitor student learning on an ongoing basis through the use of frequent, team-developed common formative assessments that prepare students for the format and rigor of new assessments for deeper learning

  + Creating systems of intervention and enrichment that guarantee students will receive the time and support that enable them to succeed in deeper learning

  + Creating a climate and culture in which educators use evidence of student learning to enhance adult learning rather than assign blame

The Partnership for 21st Century Skills (2013) concludes that schools *must* (our emphasis) operate as professional learning communities if students are to learn at the deeper levels necessary for success in the 21st century. But to transform traditional schools into PLCs, educators must recognize that transformation is not a program to be purchased; it is a process, and moreover, one that can be pursued but never quite perfected. Nor is it an appendage to existing structures and cultures; on the contrary, it profoundly impacts structure and culture. It does not ask educators to work harder at what they have always done. Instead, it calls on teachers, counselors, principals, central office staff members, and superintendents to redefine their roles and responsibilities. In short, schools must create the conditions that result in deeper learning for educators if they hope to foster deeper learning in their students.

References and Resources

ACT. (2006). *Ready for college or ready for work: Same or different?* Iowa City, IA: Author. Accessed at www.act.org/research/policymakers/pdf/ReadinessBrief.pdf on April 2, 2014.

ACT. (2012). *2012 Retention/completion summary tables.* Accessed at www.act.org /research/policymakers/pdf/12retain_trends.pdf on December 1, 2013.

ACT. (2013a). *The condition of college and career readiness 2013.* Iowa City, IA: Author. Accessed at www.act.org/research/policymakers/cccr13/pdf/CCCR13-National ReadinessRpt.pdf on April 2, 2014.

ACT. (2013b). *2012 retention/completion summary tables.* Iowa City, IA: Author.

Barber, M., & Mourshed, M. (2007). *How the world's best-performing school systems come out on top.* Accessed at http://mckinseyonsociety.com/how-the-worlds -best-performing-schools-come-out-on-top/ on April 2, 2014.

Barron, B., & Darling-Hammond, L. (2008). How can we teach for meaningful learning? *In Powerful learning: What we know about teaching for understanding* (pp. 11–70). San Francisco: Jossey-Bass.

Breslow, J. (2012). *By the numbers: Dropping out of high school.* Accessed at www.pbs . org/wgbh/pages/frontline/education/dropout-nation/by-the-numbers -dropping-out-of-high-school/ on October 21, 2014.

Buffum, A., Mattos, M., & Weber, C. (2012). *Simplifying response to intervention: Four essential guiding principles.* Bloomington, IN: Solution Tree Press.

Bushaw, W., & Lopez, S. (2013). Which way do we go: The 45th annual PDK/Gallup poll of the public school's attitudes toward the public schools. *Phi Delta Kappan, 95*(1), 8–25.

Carnevale, A., Smith, N., & Strohl, J. (2010). *Help wanted: Projections of jobs and education requirements through 2018.* Washington, DC: Center on Education and the Workforce, Georgetown University. Accessed at www9.georgetown.edu/grad/gppi/hpi/cew/pdfs /HelpWanted.ExecutiveSummary.pdf on August 18, 2013.

Carnevale, A., Smith, N., & Strohl, J. (2013). *Recovery: Job growth and education requirements through 2020.* Washington, DC: Center on Education and the Workforce, Georgetown University. Accessed at www9.georgetown.edu/grad/gppi/hpi/cew/pdfs/Recovery2020. ES.Web.pdf on August 18, 2013.

Center for K–12 Assessment and Performance Management at ETS. (2012). *Coming together to raise student achievement: New assessments for the Common Core State Standards.* Accessed at www.k12center.org/rsc/pdf/Coming_Together_April_2012_Final.PDF on October 18, 2013.

College Board. (2013). *9th annual report to the nation.* Accessed at http://media.college board. com/digitalServices/pdf/ap/rtn/9th-annual/9th-annual-ap-report-single-page.pdf on October 10, 2014.

Covey, S. (1989). *The seven habits of highly effective people: Powerful lessons in personal change.* New York: Fireside.

Darling-Hammond, L. (2008). Conclusion: Creating schools that develop understanding. In *Powerful learning: What we know about teaching for understanding* (pp. 193–211). San Francisco: Jossey-Bass.

Darling-Hammond, L., Barron, B., Pearson, P. D., Schoenfeld, A. H., Stage, E. K., Zimmerman, T. D., et al. (2008). *Powerful learning: What we know about teaching for understanding.* San Francisco: Jossey-Bass.

DuFour, R., DuFour, R., Eaker, R., & Many, T. W. (2010). *Learning by doing: A handbook for professional learning communities at work* (2nd ed.). Bloomington, IN: Solution Tree Press.

DuFour, R., & Fullan, M. (2013). *Cultures built to last: Systemic PLCs at work*. Bloomington: IN: Solution Tree Press.

DuFour, R., & Marzano, R. J. (2011). *Leaders of learning: How district, school, and classroom leaders improve student learning*. Bloomington, IN: Solution Tree Press.

Education Week. (2013). Diplomas count 2013: Second chances. Accessed at www.ed week.org/ew/articles/2013/06/06/34execsum.h32.html?intc=EW-DC13-LNAV on October 10, 2013.

Fullan, M. (2011). *The moral imperative realized*. Thousand Oaks, CA: Corwin Press.

Gallimore, R., Ermeling, B., Saunders, W., & Goldenberg, C. (2009). Moving the learning of teaching closer to practice: Teacher education implications of school-based inquiry teams. *Elementary School Journal, 109*(5), 537–551.

Goodlad, J. (1983). A study of schooling: Some implications for school improvement. *Phi Delta Kappan, 64*(8), 552–558.

Hattie, J. A. C. (2012). *Visible learning for teachers: Maximizing impact on learning*. New York: Routledge.

Herman, J., & Linn, R. (2013). *On the road to assessing deeper learning: The status of Smarter Balanced and PARCC assessment consortia* (CRESST Report 823). Accessed at www.hewlett.org/uploads/documents/On_the_Road_to_Assessing_DL-The_Status_of_SBAC_and_PARCC_Assessment_Consortia_CRESST_Jan_2013.pdf on October 4, 2013.

Hewlett Foundation. (2012). *Deeper learning*. Accessed at www.hewlett.org/deeperlearning on September 24, 2013.

Jerald, C. D. (2009, July). *Defining a 21st century education*. Alexandria, VA: Center for Public Education. Accessed at www.centerforpubliceducation.org/Learn-About/21st-Century/Defining-a-21st-Century-Education-Full-Report-PDF.pdf on October 10, 2013.

Johnson, R. T., & Johnson, D. W. (1994). *An overview of cooperative learning*. Accessed at http://clearspecs.com/joomla15/downloads/ClearSpecs69V01_Overview%20of%20Cooperative%20Learning.pdf on December 1, 2013.

Kirschner, P. A., Sweller, J., & Clark, R. E. (2006). Why minimal guidance during instruction does not work: An analysis of the failure of constructivist, discover, problem-based, experiential and inquiry-based teaching. *Educational Psychology, 41*(2), 75–86.

Little, J. W. (2006). *Professional community and professional development in the learning-centered school*. Washington, DC: National Education Association. Accessed at www.nea.org/assets/docs/mf_pdreport.pdf on April 2, 2014.

Little, J. W., & Bartlett, L. (2010). The teacher workforce and problems of educational equity. *Review of Research in Education, 34*(1), 285–328.

Marzano, R. J. (2003).*What works in schools: Translating research into action*. Alexandria, VA: Association for Supervision and Curriculum Development.

Marzano, R. J. (2009). Setting the record straight on "high-yield" strategies. *Phi Delta Kappan, 91*(1), 30–37.

National Center for Education Statistics. (2013). *NAEP questions tool.* Accessed at http://nces.ed.gov/nationsreportcard/itmrlsx/default.aspx on October 10, 2013.

National Governors Association Center for Best Practices & Council of Chief State School Officers. (2009). *Implementing the common core state standards.* Accessed at www.corestandards.org on October 10, 2013.

National Governors Association Center for Best Practices & Council of Chief State School Officers. (2010a). *Common Core State Standards for English language arts and literacy in history/social studies, science, and technical subjects.* Washington, DC: Authors. Accessed at www.corestandards.org/assets/CCSSI_ELA%20Standards.pdf on April 2, 2014.

National Governors Association Center for Best Practices & Council of Chief State School Officers. (2010b). *Common Core State Standards for mathematics.* Washington, DC: Authors. Accessed at www.corestandards.org/assets/CCSSI_Math%20Standards.pdf on April 2, 2014.

National Governors Association, Council of Chief State School Officers, & Achieve. (2008). *Benchmarking for success: Ensuring U.S. students receive a world-class education.* Accessed at www.corestandards.org/assets/0812BENCHMARKING.pdf on October 10, 2013.

National Research Council Committee on Defining Deeper Learning. (2012). *Education for life and work: Developing transferable knowledge and skills in the 21st century.* Accessed at www.hewlett.org/uploads/documents/Education_for_Life_and_Work.pdf on August 1, 2014.

Olshansky, S. J. (2012). Differences in life expectancy due to race and educational differences are widening, and many may not catch up. *Health Affairs, 31*(8), 1803–1813.

Organisation for Economic Co-operation and Development. (2009). *Education at a glance.* Paris: Author.

Organisation for Economic Co-operation and Development. (2012). *Education at a glance: Table D4.1.* Paris: Author.

Organisation for Economic Co-operation and Development. (2013a). *Programme for International Student Assessment: PISA released items—Mathematics.* Accessed at www.oecd.org/pisa/pisaproducts/pisa2012-2006-rel-items-maths-ENG.pdf on October 20, 2013.

Organisation for Economic Co-operation and Development. (2013b). *Programme for International Student Assessment: PISA released items—Reading.* Accessed at www.oecd.org/pisa/pisaproducts/pisa2009/PISA%202009%20reading%20test%20items.pdf on October 20, 2013.

Organisation for Economic Co-operation and Development. (2013c). *Programme for International Student Assessment: PISA released items—Science.* Accessed at www.oecd.org/pisa/38709385.pdf on October 20, 2013.

Partnership for Assessment of Readiness for College and Careers. (2013). *Task prototypes and sample items.* Accessed www.parcconline.org/samples/item-task-prototypes on October 20, 2013.

Partnership for 21st Century Skills. (2013). *21st century learning environments.* Accessed at www.p21.org/overview/skills-framework/831 on August 19, 2013.

Pellegrino, J. W., & Hilton, M. (Eds.). (2012). *Education for life and work: Developing transferable knowledge and skills in the 21st century.* Washington, DC: National Academies Press.

Pfeffer, J., & Sutton, R. (2000). *The knowing-doing gap: How smart companies turn knowledge into action.* Boston: Harvard Business School Press.

Pink, D. H. (2011). *Drive: The surprising truth about what motivates us.* New York: Riverhead Trade.

Popham, W. J. (2001). *The truth about testing: An educator's call to action.* Alexandria, VA: Association for Supervision and Curriculum Development.

Popham, W. J. (2005). Standardized testing fails the exam. *Edutopia Magazine.* Accessed at www.edutopia.org/standardized-testing-evaluation-reform on August 8, 2009.

Popham, W. J. (2008). *Transformative assessment.* Alexandria, VA: Association for Supervision and Curriculum Development.

Ravitch, D. (2012). *What do NAEP scores mean?* Accessed at http://dianeravitch.net/2012/05/14/what-do-naep-scores-mean on October 20, 2013.

Rothman, R. (2011). *Assessing deeper learning: Policy brief.* Washington, DC: Alliance for Excellent Education. Accessed at http://all4ed.org/wp-content/uploads/2013/06/AssessingDeeperLearning.pdf on October 9, 2013.

Scalise, K. (2012). *Computer-based assessment: "Intermediate constraint" questions and tasks for technology platforms.* Accessed at http://pages.uoregon.edu/kscalise/taxonomy/taxonomy.html October 20, 2013.

Smarter Balanced Assessment Consortium. (2013). *Sample items and performance tasks.* Accessed at www.smarterbalanced.org/sample-items-and-performance-tasks on October 10, 2013.

Stiggins, R. (1999). Assessment, student confidence, and school success. *Phi Delta Kappan, 81*(3), 191–198.

Stiggins, R., & DuFour, R. (2009). Maximizing the power of formative assessments. *Phi Delta Kappan, 90*(9), 640–644.

Strong American Schools. (2008). *Diploma to nowhere.* Washington, DC: Author.

Swanson, C., & Lloyd, S. (2013). Nation's graduation rate nears a milestone. In *Education Week: Diplomas count 2013: Second chances.* Accessed at www.ed week.org/ew/articles/2013/06/06/34analysis.h32.html on October 15, 2013.

Tavernise, S. (2012, February 9). Education gap grows between rich and poor, studies say. *New York Times.* Accessed at www.nytimes.com/2012/02/10/education/education-gap-grows-between-rich-and-poor-studies-show.html?_r=1&nl=todaysheadlines&emc=tha2 on February 10, 2012.

U.S. Census Bureau. (2009). *What's it worth: Field of training and economic status in 2009, Table 2b*. Accessed at www.census.gov/hhes/socdemo/education/data /sipp/2009/tables.html on April 2, 2014.

Wiliam, D. (2007). Content then process: Teacher learning communities in the service of formative assessment. In D. B. Reeves (Ed.), *Ahead of the curve: The power of assessment to transform teaching and learning* (pp. 183–225). Bloomington, IN: Solution Tree Press.

Wiliam, D. (2011). *Embedded formative assessment*. Bloomington, IN: Solution Tree Press.

Arthur L. Costa

Arthur L. Costa, EdD, is an emeritus professor of education at California State University, Sacramento. He is cofounder of Habits of Mind International and the Center for Cognitive Coaching. Art has served as a classroom teacher, curriculum consultant, assistant superintendent for instruction in the Office of the Sacramento County Schools, and the director of educational programs for the National Aeronautics and Space Administration. He has made presentations and conducted workshops in all fifty states as well as on six of the seven continents.

Active in many professional organizations, Art served as president of the California Association for Supervision and Curriculum Development and was the national president of the Association for Supervision and Curriculum Development from 1988 to 1989. He was the recipient of the prestigious Lifetime Achievement Award from the National Urban Alliance in 2010.

Bena Kallick

Bena Kallick, PhD, is a private consultant providing services to school districts, state departments of education, professional organizations, and public agencies throughout the United States and abroad. She is the cofounder of Habits of Mind International, which provides services and products to support bringing the habits of mind into the culture of schools and the communities they serve. Bena is also the program director for Eduplanet21, a company dedicated to offering online professional development as a model for the kind of thinking that will engage 21st century learners.

Chapter 2

Dispositions: Critical Pathways for Deeper Learning

Arthur L. Costa and Bena Kallick

What makes learning "deeper"? Is it adding content to an already overcrowded curriculum? Is it giving more time to learning by extending the school day or school year? Is it deliberately ensuring that instructional strategies are used to develop students' understanding? Is it posing questions to cause students to think at higher levels of Bloom's taxonomy? Is it ensuring that students justify their answers by citing evidence and references from the text? Is it making the curriculum more interdisciplinary? Is it "toughening" the achievement tests to measure a student's increasing depth of understanding of the content being taught? Perhaps it is all the above. It is clear that something more is needed.

We must all think anew about the important outcomes of education as we prepare students for a vastly different future than that we have known in the past. The first task is to identify what we believe to be the critical dispositions of deeper learners and then suggest ways to design instructional and assessment strategies intended to cultivate the growth of deeper learners over time. This will require a reframing of our mental maps about what education is for, what the attributes of deeper learners are, and what needs to go on in dispositionally oriented schools and classrooms. It will require a new language with which we communicate about educational purposes, assessments of student progress, and excellence in teaching and learning.

Heightened Thinking About Deeper Learning

Education for deeper learning is an adaptive shift, which requires a change of paradigm or mental model, rather than a technical shift such as installing new computers, changing time schedules, adopting new textbooks, or other educational tinkerings. It is not simply another innovative intervention such as flipped classrooms, 360-degree classrooms, problem-based learning, or standardized curriculum. Although each of those technical changes may lead to significant opportunities for student engagement and learning, they will not bring about a deeper commitment to the development of minds essential for both the present and future.

We are at a crossroads in education. One path suggests that we continue to do what we have always done but with more rigor and relevance. Another path is to adopt a new premise—a new view of what schooling is for.

While we need to prepare our students for success in school today, given the rate of change that is occurring, we know that they will face a vastly different future. We are somewhat weary of the term *21st century*, because we are already more than one-tenth of the way through this century and with better health care, it is very likely that today's kindergartners will be living well into the 22nd century! Furthermore, as technology continuously changes our world and our cultures, deeper learning is needed today, not sometime in the future.

Deeper learning must require educators, parents, and politicians to think and talk differently about the goals of education. We believe that this will necessitate transforming the educational process from a content-oriented, subject-centered, test-driven frame to a view of education being *dispositional* in nature.

Why Dispositions?

Authoritative futurists, neuroscientists, educators, and sociologists cite the need for problem solving, creating, innovating, and communicating to sustain the democratic and capitalistic society in which we live. These authors use different terms, but they all reference dispositions that are necessary to lend oneself to learning. In the absence of these dispositions, students will be unable to become productive, innovative, problem solvers for our economy and for our democracy. Paul Tough (2012) and the U.S. Department of Education's Office of Educational Technology (2013) advocate grit, tenacity, and perseverance as critical factors for success in the 21st century. Daniel H. Pink (2010) refers to the keys to internal motivation as autonomy, mastery, and purpose. Harvard University's Tony Wagner (2008) calls for seven essentials for all our youth:

1. Problem solving and critical thinking

2. Collaboration across networks and leading by influence

3. Agility and adaptability

4. Initiative and entrepreneurship

5. Effective written and oral communication

6. Accessing and analyzing information

7. Curiosity and imagination

Advocating for college and career readiness, David Conley (2010) refers to a set of key cognitive strategies. He identifies such dispositions as:

- Open-mindedness

- Inquisitiveness

- Analyzing the credibility and relevance of sources

- Reasoning, argumentation, and explaining proof and point of view

- Comparing, contrasting ideas, analyzing, and interpreting competing or conflicting evidence

- Knowing how to arrive at an accurate answer

- Finding many ways to solve problems

The Partnership for 21st Century Skills (www.p21.org) lists essential attributes and abilities for functioning successfully in the future, shown in table 2.1.

Table 2.1: Essential Attributes and Abilities for Successful Future Functioning

Critical Thinking	Creative Thinking
Analysis	Inventive and intuitive thinking
Precision and accuracy	Innovation
Managing complexity	Adaptability
Inductive and deductive reasoning	Problem solving
Information development	Curiosity
Communication	**Collaboration**
Professional and technical writing	Small-group dynamics
Information development	Management of outcomes
Rhetoric and persuasion	Networking skills
Confidence	Interpersonal
Credibility and charisma	
Responsibilty and Leadership	
Ethics, initiative, persistence, accountability, endurance and sustainability	
21st Century Model	
Global awareness, financial responsibility, civic duty, global economic principles, information communication, technology literacy, thematic integration	

Source: Partnership for 21st Century Skills, 2007.

Furthermore, we are living in an era of increasing uncertainty, complexity, and ambiguity in which we are bombarded with conflicting models of what to value, what to believe, how to decide, and how to live. Ron Ritchhart (2002) of Harvard University challenges us to think differently when he states:

> What if education were less about acquiring skills and knowledge and more about cultivating the dispositions and habits

of mind that students will need for a lifetime of learning, problem solving and decision making? What if education were less concerned with the end-of-year exam and more concerned with who students become as a result of their schooling? What if we viewed smartness as a goal that students can work toward rather than as something they either have or don't? (p. xxii)

What Are Dispositions?

A disposition is a habit, preparation, state of readiness, or tendency to act in a specified way. When we use the term *dispositions*, we are referring to thinking dispositions—tendencies toward particular patterns of intellectual behavior. Israeli psychologist Gavriel Salomon (1994, as quoted in Tishman & Andrade, n.d., p. 2) suggests that

> dispositions do more than describe behavior; they assume a causal function and have an explanatory status. A disposition is a cluster of preferences, attitudes, and intentions, plus a set of capabilities that allow the preferences to become realized in a particular way.

Skillful thinkers, therefore, have both thinking abilities *and* thinking dispositions. Critical thinkers who seek balanced reasons in an argument, for example, have both the ability and the disposition to do so. Good listeners not only have the skills and abilities to listen well but are also inclined to do so and are alert to situations in which skillful listening presents itself.

Ron Ritchhart's (2002) definition helps us understand that dispositions are under our control; we can consciously, intentionally choose to employ them rather than being mindlessly on autopilot. Dispositions, Ritchart says, are

> acquired patterns of behavior that are under one's control and will as opposed to being automatically activated. Dispositions are overarching sets of behaviors, not just single specific behaviors. They are dynamic and idiosyncratic in their contextualized deployment rather than prescribed actions to be rigidly carried out. More than desire and will, dispositions

must be coupled with the requisite ability. Dispositions motivate, activate, and direct our abilities. (p. 21)

Sixteen Dispositions of Deeper Learners

We have identified sixteen dispositions that are characteristic of
skillful, efficacious problem solvers in many walks of life (Costa &
Kallick, 2009). We call them *habits of mind*. They are what intelligent
people do when confronted with problems, dilemmas, paradoxes,
polarities, and confusing situations for which answers and reso-
lutions are not immediately apparent. No one is ever perfect at all
times in all situations, nor do people achieve mastery of these dispositions. These habits of mind are journeys of continuous learning.
We believe that they are the dispositions that deeper learners continue to draw upon and develop throughout a lifetime. The habits of
mind are described in the following sections.

1. Persisting

Deeper learners don't give up easily. They have a goal in mind
and persevere on a task until it's completed. They remain focused
toward goal attainment. Paul Tough (2012) refers to this as "grit":
they stick to a task until it is completed. They analyze a problem
and develop a system, structure, or strategy to attack. They have a
repertoire of alternative strategies for problem solving. They search
for evidence to indicate their problem-solving strategy is working,
and if one strategy doesn't work, they know how to back up and
try another. They recognize when a theory or idea must be rejected
and another employed. They have systematic strategies for problem
solving that include knowing how to begin, knowing what steps
must be performed and what questions to ask, and what data need
to be generated or collected. Because they are able to sustain a problem-solving process over time they are comfortable with ambiguity.

2. Managing Impulsivity

All humans are innately impulsive. It is a survival mechanism
that gave our primate ancestors the means to survive attacks from
wild beasts or enemies. In contemporary society, however, the dan-
gers are often not physical but social. The brain doesn't differentiate

between the two; the same mechanisms are at play no matter what the source of real or perceived threat.

While we are all impulsive, deeper learners have strategies for managing and inhibiting impulses (Rock, 2009). They think before they act, having a sense of deliberativeness. They delay gratification and intentionally form a vision of an end product or a plan of action. They have formulated a goal or destination before they begin. They strive to clarify and understand directions and withhold making immediate value judgments before fully understanding an idea. They consider the alternatives and consequences of several possible directions. They decrease their need for trial and error by taking time to reflect on an answer before giving it.

3. Listening With Understanding and Empathy

Highly effective people spend a lot of their time and energy listening to others. The ability to listen attentively and to understand another's point of view requires concentration, self-control, flexibility, empathy, and a certain amount of selflessness. Such people have developed the capacity to take turns talking, to paraphrase the other person's ideas, and to respond nonjudgmentally, even though their own ideas may differ. Deeper learners' listening behaviors include alertness to indicators (cues) of emotional states in oral language (pitch, volume, rapidity of speech, tonality, and so on), body language (gestures and posture, for example), and facial expression (frowns, smiles, eye movements, and so on), and they can accurately express another person's concepts, emotions, and problems. They are able to see through the diverse perspectives of others. They gently attend to the other person by demonstrating their understanding of and empathy for an idea or feeling by paraphrasing it accurately, building upon it, clarifying it, or giving an example of it.

Listening fully also means being aware of whom a person is behind or beneath the words—listening not only for what someone says but also for what he or she is trying to say and represent. Listening requires the art of developing deeper silences in oneself, of keeping the focus on the listener rather than shifting the response to a personal (autobiographical) reference (Derber, 1979).

4. Thinking Flexibly

Flexible thinkers are open-minded. They have the capacity to change their minds based on additional information, data, or reasoning, which may contradict their beliefs. They have the capacity to engage in multiple and simultaneous outcomes and activities. They draw upon a repertoire of problem-solving strategies and can practice style flexibility, knowing when it is appropriate to be broad and global in their thinking and when a situation requires detailed, analytical precision. They seek novel approaches and have a well-developed sense of humor. They can envision a range of consequences and can approach a problem from various angles using novel approaches. Edward De Bono (1970) refers to this as *lateral thinking*. They consider alternative points of view or deal with several sources of information simultaneously. Flexible people develop options and alternatives to consider. Flexible thinkers are able to shift at will, through multiple perceptual positions—past, present, future, egocentric, allocentric, macrocentric, visual, auditory, kinesthetic. The flexible mind is activated by knowing when to shift perceptual positions.

Egocentrism means perceiving from our own point of view; *allocentrism* refers to perceiving through the orientation of others— empathizing with feelings, predicting how others are thinking, and anticipating potential misunderstandings.

5. Thinking About Your Thinking (Metacognition)

Metacognition is the unique human capacity for "inner language," our ability to talk to our self. It is our ability to plan a strategy for producing what information is needed, maintaining that plan in mind over a period of time, being conscious of our own steps and strategies during the act of problem solving, and reflecting on and evaluating the productiveness of our own thinking. Planning a strategy before embarking on problem solving assists in keeping track of the steps in the sequence of planned behavior at the conscious level for the duration of the activity. It assists in making temporal and comparative judgments, assessing the readiness for more or different activities, and monitoring interpretations, decisions, and alternatives.

Metacognition means becoming increasingly aware of one's actions and the effect of those actions on others and on the environment. It means posing internal questions (interrogative talk) as one searches for information and meaning, developing mental maps or plans of action. We engage in metacognition when we mentally rehearse prior to performance, monitoring those plans as they are employed—being conscious of the need for midcourse correction if the plan is not working, then, upon completion, reflecting on the plan for the purpose of self-evaluation, and editing mental pictures for improved performance (Dunlosky & Metcalf, 2009; Hacker, Dunlosky, & Graesser, 2009).

6. Striving for Accuracy and Precision

Deeper learners have a desire for truth, exactness, accuracy, correctness, precision, fidelity, and craftsmanship. They check over their products, review the rules by which they are to abide; hold in their heads the models and visions they are to follow, review the criteria they arc to employ and confirm that their finished product matches the criteria. Craftsmanship means rejecting mediocrity, knowing that one can continually perfect one's craft by working to attain the highest possible standards. Deeper learners pursue ongoing learning in order to bring a laser-like devotion of their energies to task accomplishment. They take pride in their work and have a desire for accuracy, evidence, and truth.

7. Questioning and Problem Posing

Deeper learners are inquirers, are curious, have an inclination and ability to find problems to solve, and enjoy the problem-solving process (Barell, 2013). They are alert to and recognize discrepancies and phenomena in their environment and probe into their causes. Deeper learners know how to ask questions to fill in the gaps between what they know and what they don't know. They are inclined to ask a range of questions. For example:

- What data do you have to support this finding?

- How do you know that's true?

- On what assumptions are you basing your conclusions?

- How reliable is this data source?

They pose questions about alternative points of view:

- From whose viewpoint are you perceiving this?

- From what perspective are we viewing this situation?

They pose questions like the following to establish causal connections and relationships:

- How are these (events/situations) related to each other?

- What produced this connection?

They pose hypothetical problems characterized by "iffy"-type questions:

- What do you think would happen if . . . ?

- If that is true, then what might happen if . . . ?

8. Applying Past Knowledge to Novel Situations

Deeper learners learn from all their experiences, not only their successes, and see failures as learning opportunities. They access prior knowledge and apply it beyond the situation in which it was learned. When confronted with new and perplexing problems they often draw forth experience from their past and say to themselves, "This reminds me of . . ." or "This is just like the time when I . . ." They explain that they are using analogies or references to previous experiences calling upon their storehouse of knowledge and experiences as sources of data and use intuition to support theories and processes to solve each new challenge. They are able to derive meaning from one experience, carry it forth, and apply it in a new and novel situation.

9. Thinking and Communicating With Clarity and Precision

Deeper learners take care to use precise language. They define terms and use correct names, universal labels, and analogies. They strive to avoid overgeneralizations, deletions, and distortions. They support their statements with explanations, comparisons, quantification, and evidence.

10. Gathering Data Through All Senses

Deeper learners know that all information gets into the brain through our external sensory pathways (gustatory, olfactory, tactile, kinesthetic, auditory, and visual) as well as internal data sources (emotions, pain, balance, thirst, and hunger). Linguistic, cultural, and physical learning is derived from the environment by observing or taking in data through the senses. Learners whose sensory pathways are open, alert, and acute absorb more information than those whose pathways are withered, immune, and oblivious to sensory stimuli.

11. Creating, Imagining, and Innovating

Deeper learners have a well-developed capacity to generate novel, original, clever, or ingenious products, solutions, and techniques. They conceive problem solutions differently, examining alternative possibilities from many angles. They tend to project themselves into different roles using analogies, starting with a vision and working backward. Deeper learners push the boundaries of their perceived limits (Perkins, 1985). They are intrinsically rather than extrinsically motivated—they work on the task because of the aesthetic challenge rather than the material rewards. Creative people are open to criticism, holding up their products for others to evaluate, and seek feedback in an ongoing effort to refine their technique, knowledge, and skills.

12. Responding With Wonderment and Awe

Deeper learners find the world mysterious. They are intrigued, astonished, and mesmerized with phenomena and beauty. They have a passion and compulsion for what they do. They seek problems to solve for themselves and to submit to others. They delight in making up problems to solve on their own and request enigmas from others. They enjoy figuring things out by themselves and continue to learn throughout their lifetimes. They seek and practice being amazed.

13. Taking Responsible Risks

Deeper learners have an almost uncontrollable urge to go beyond established limits. They "live on the edge of their incompetence" and place themselves in situations where the outcomes are unknown. They accept confusion, ambiguity, and the higher risks of failure as part of the normal process of learning. They view setbacks as interesting, challenging, and growth-producing opportunities to learn. However, they do not behave impulsively—their risks are educated. They draw on past knowledge, are thoughtful about consequences, have a well-trained sense of what is appropriate, and gather relevant data before embarking. They know that all risks are not worth taking. Deeper learners take risk only if they know that there is either scientific or past history that suggests that what they are doing is not going to be life threatening or harmful to others or if they believe that there is enough support in the group to protect them from harm. Their learning is deepened because they are far more able to take actions than they previously believed.

14. Finding Humor

Engaging in the mystery of humor, deeper learners perceive situations from original and often interesting vantage points. They initiate humor more often, place greater value on having a sense of humor, appreciate and understand others' humor, and are verbally playful when interacting with others. Having a whimsical frame of mind, deeper learners thrive on finding incongruity and perceiving absurdity, irony, and satire; finding discontinuities; and being able to laugh at situations and themselves.

15. Thinking Interdependently

Present-day problem solving has become so complex that no one person can go it alone. No one has access to all the data needed to make critical decisions; no one person can consider as many alternatives as several people can. One of the foremost dispositions needed for success and survival in the 21st century is the heightened ability to think in concert with others and to find ourselves increasingly more interdependent and sensitive to the needs of others.

Working in groups requires the ability to justify ideas and to test the feasibility of solution strategies on others. Deeper learners, therefore, contribute their time and energy to tasks on which others would quickly tire when working alone. They realize that all of us are more powerful, intellectually or physically, than any one of us.

Effective collaboration requires the development of a willingness and openness to accept the feedback from critical friends. Through this interaction the group and the individual continue to grow (Vygotsky, 1978). Listening, consensus seeking, giving up an idea to work with someone else's, empathy, compassion, group leadership, knowing how to support group efforts, altruism—all are behaviors of deeper learners (Costa & O'Leary, 2013).

16. Remaining Open to Continuous Learning

Deeper learners are in a continuous learning mode. Their confidence, curiosity, and persistence allow them to constantly search for new and better ways. With this disposition, deeper learners are always striving for improvement, always growing, always learning, always modifying themselves. They seize problem situations, conflicts, and difficult circumstances as valuable opportunities to learn.

A great mystery about humans is that many seem complacent in knowing rather than learning. They confront learning opportunities with fear rather than mystery and wonder. Defending their status quo, they are complacent with their existing biases, beliefs, and storehouses of knowledge rather than inviting the unknown, the creative, and the inspirational. Being certain and closed gives them comfort while being doubtful and open gives them fear. Deeper learners exhibit humility when admitting they don't know but want to find out.

While this list of dispositions is extensive and may seem overwhelming, other authors identify still more additional dispositions. (See Claxton, Chambers, Powell, & Lucas, 2011; Meier, 2011; Sizer, 1992; Tishman, Perkins, & Jay, 1995.) We believe that deeper learning means embarking on a continuous life journey of internalizing these dispositions deeper and deeper in one's body, mind, and spirit.

Why Are Thinking Dispositions Considered Deeper Learning?

Dispositions are drawn forth in response to problems, the answers to which are not immediately known. We believe, therefore, that these dispositions are vastly more challenging than such cognitive skills as recalling and understanding information, because they require self-awareness, inhibition of impulses, management of internal thought processes, being alert to situational cues, skillfully employing capacities, and gathering feedback about results—all of which are deep inside the mind. Learning these dispositions takes time, practice, self-monitoring, and reflection. Indeed we believe that employing these dispositions opens the pathways for deeper learning. When confronted with problematic situations, these dispositions serve as an internal compass. Mindful human beings use their executive processes to consciously and metacognitively employ one or more of these dispositions by asking themselves, "What is the most thought-full thing I can do right now?" We might refer to this as *inner self-coaching*. The deeper learner might ask:

- How might I learn from this? What are my resources? How can I draw on my past successes with problems like this? What do I already know about the problem? What resources do I have available or need to generate?

- How might I approach this problem flexibly? How might I look at the situation in another way, how can I draw on my repertoire of problem-solving strategies, or how can I look at this problem from a fresh, divergent perspective?

- How might I analyze this problem to make it clearer, more precise? Do I need to check out my data sources? How might I break this problem down into its component parts and develop a strategy for understanding and accomplishing each step?

- What do I know or not know? What questions do I need to ask? What strategies are in my mind now? What am I aware of in terms of my beliefs, values, and goals with regard to this problem? What feelings or emotions am I aware of that might be blocking or enhancing my progress?

Deeper learners, who think interdependently, might turn to others for help. They might search for how this problem affects others; how it might be solved collaboratively, and what can be learned from others that would help them become better problem solvers (Costa & Kallick, 2014).

Cultivating Deeper Learning With Dispositions in Mind

We suggest that dispositions become the goals of the curriculum and that teachers deliberately teach and assess them. Fostering growth in dispositional learning affects the design of teachers' instructional activities, their selection of content, and their range of assessments.

To be successful, students must come to own the dispositions. Following are seven strategies that individual teachers and the entire school staff might use to cause students to internalize dispositions.

1. Making Dispositions Explicit by Establishing Expectations

Students need to have an opportunity to explore the meaning of the habit. Therefore, the habit may need to become the center of a lesson. For example, to start a lesson on metacognition, the teacher might say, "Today we're going to think about how we think. I want you to become more mindful about what's going on inside your head when you solve the problems we will encounter. As a way of learning about your thinking, we will solve a problem together. We will talk about what you observe about your thinking as you work. You may want to write down, draw a graphic, or talk with someone about the steps and strategies you are employing."

Or, "Today in our mathematics lesson, we're going to examine questioning. I'm going to give you a problem, and I want you and your partner to generate as many questions as you can about the problem. I do not want you to answer any of the questions, just think, generate, and write down as many questions as you can. Afterward, we'll examine and classify the list."

Or, "Yes, we are going to focus on listening with understanding and empathy again during our class meeting today. I know we did this during our last class meeting as well. But we agreed that listening without interrupting was difficult, and you said that several times you forgot and responded impulsively without thinking.

Today, let's become even more aware of our listening and pay attention to what we tell ourselves when we are tempted to interrupt."

As we are coaching for growth, we need to offer positive, descriptive feedback (not praise) when the desired behavior is observed. For example, "You described the steps you were taking and what you planned to do next to solve the problem" or, if persistence were the goal, "Your persistence paid off! You stuck with it until you completed your task. You really remained focused!" (Dweck, 2006).

2. Developing a Common and Consistent Vocabulary Throughout the Culture of the Classroom, the School, and the Community

It is much more likely that students will internalize the dispositions of deeper learning if they are heard and applied in all subject areas as well as on the playground, in the cafeteria, and at home. Names and labels of dispositions provide conceptual tools for students and staffs with which they can communicate, operationalize, define, and categorize behaviors.

3. Transferring and Applying the Disposition in Many Settings, Circumstances, Contexts, and Situations

Margie Martinez (2009), a physical education coach at Furr High School in Houston, Texas, invites students to apply what they've learned in P.E. to other classes. For example, she encourages students to think interdependently as they coach one another for better performance. She then asks, "Besides thinking interdependently in the weight room, when and where else might it be important to think interdependently? When you're in the science lab working in groups to conduct an experiment, how might you apply what you've learned about collaboration and interdependent thinking?"

Teachers often invite students to transfer their dispositional learning to potential future careers, to other settings, and to readings. "As you think about your future in technology, how might thinking interdependently benefit you? As you read in the newspaper about how our Congress makes decisions, how does thinking interdependently assist them in their decision-making processes?" (See Costa & O'Leary, 2013.)

4. Operationalizing Dispositions as Actions

To make the dispositions come alive in their mind, students must explore their meaning, build their capacities for performing the disposition, become sensitized to situations in which it would appropriately be used, see the value and benefits of using the disposition, and build their commitment to improvement. Defining the disposition as actions creates a more vivid picture inside the mind of the learners as to what they will be doing, saying, or feeling if they are performing the disposition. It is more likely that we can agree on actions than on definitions. Teachers, therefore invite students to translate the labels of the dispositions into actions and tactics by inviting them to envision what they would see people doing or hear them saying if they are, for example, accurate and precise, empathic or curious. "So while you are working through this problem together, what might it look like and sound like if you are communicating with clarity and precision?"

For insights to be useful, they should not be given to individuals as conclusions. Rather insights must be generated from within. Humans experience the adrenaline-like rush of insight only if they go through the process of making connections themselves. This would be true for breaking an old habit as well. When students envision what a disposition looks and sounds like, it makes possible the elimination of undesirable habits. Change requires observing the pattern that we presently have and then making a conscious decision to break that pattern. We can begin to attend to changing our dispositions and seeing the benefit when we do so (Davidson, 2013).

5. Building the Vocabulary of Deeper Learning

To think and talk about thinking dispositions, students must have a vocabulary of thinking words and phrases. One way to help develop and expand their vocabulary is to build a collection of key terms, synonyms, and phrases that convey similar meanings. This builds fluency with the terms, elaborates their meaning, and enhances flexibility by providing alternatives rather than restricting someone to use of a single term. Such a collection expands the range of questioning and paraphrasing, and it allows students and teachers to communicate with others using common terminology.

Teachers ask many questions. If teachers model questions that deliberately engage students' cognitive processing and let students know why the questions are being posed in this way, it is more likely that students will become aware of and engage their own mental processes. They become spectators of their own thinking.

Table 2.2 shows how behavioral questions can be transformed into questions that invite thinking dispositions.

Table 2.2: Changing Behavioral Into Dispositional Questions

Questions That Invite a Behavioral Response	Questions That Invite Cognitive Responses	Disposition
Why did you do that?	What was going on inside your head when you did that?	Managing impulsivity
Why do you say that . . .?	From whose perspective are you seeing that?	Empathy, thinking interdependently
Was that a good choice?	What criteria did you have in mind as you made that choice?	Accuracy and precision, metacognition, thinking about your thinking
What are you going to do next time?	What will you be aware of next time?	Metacognition/thinking about your thinking

6. Reflecting on the Use of the Dispositions and Setting Goals for Improvement

Time should be devoted for students to reflect on, discuss, and journal their thoughts about their own growth in deeper, dispositional learning. Students become spectators of their own thinking when they are invited to monitor and make explicit the internal dialogue that accompanies the dispositions. "What goes on in your head when you think creatively?" Or, "What did you hear yourself saying inside your brain when you were tempted to talk but your job was to listen?"

During a reflective time, not only do students become spectators of their behavior, they also are invited to make a commitment to constantly improve the performance and apply the disposition in an ever-widening set of circumstances. (This capacity is known as self-directed neuroplasticity [Rock & Schwartz, 2006].)

Because dispositions are never fully mastered in the same way that understanding content and concepts are mastered, the purposes of reflection on dispositions are to have learners monitor themselves, confront themselves with self-generated data, and reveal to others how they have coped with adversity. It means setting goals for themselves to constantly improve their decisions and actions and making commitments to pursue those goals in future situations. It means being alert to feedback by self-observation, seeking feedback from others, and modifying their actions to become even more efficient in the execution of their dispositions. It means self-modification—building your own new neural pathways.

7. Modeling

Because imitation is the most basic form of learning, the significant adults in a child's life—teachers, parents, and administrators—should strive to become deeper learners themselves and to provide models of dispositional behavior in the day-to-day operation of the school and classroom. Teachers often and easily find examples of deeper learning in our respected leaders, heroes, and heroines. When they bring these characters to the attention of the students, they provide opportunities to model reasoning. This structured modeling offers students a way to model reasoning for themselves, and helps students identify reasoning behavior (or the lack of it) in everyday situations.

Teachers realize the importance of their own display of desirable dispositions in the presence of learners. The purpose of the modeling is to ensure that students see and hear examples of thinking dispositions in action. Without this consistency, there is likely to be a credibility gap.

How Might We Determine If Learners Are Growing Deeper Over Time?

We are proposing a theory of change that keeps dispositional thinking at the center. We make these assumptions for real school reform—a reformulation of what the focus should be as we prepare our students for the present and future. Our assumptions, based on both formal and informal research over the past thirty years, are as follows:

- When students are aware of the significance and benefits of getting in the habit of entering situations with the habits of mind in mind, they become more successful as learners. They are more willing to go deeper and resist the desire to have someone rescue them from learning.

- When assessment does not depend on a number or a score but rather as student-generated descriptions of behaviors that are scaffolded, ongoing, and formative, the opportunities for growth increase exponentially.

- When an entire school embraces the habits of mind as a part of their vision and mission, the likelihood of building and sustaining the habits is increased enormously.

- When an entire system recognizes that the habits of mind are a part of the curriculum, instruction, and assessment rather than "soft skills" that one can easily put aside, the likelihood of the students developing the habits is greatly enhanced.

- When the school community embraces the habits for themselves as well as for the students, there is a greater chance of sustaining this commitment as boards of education, administrators, and teachers come and go.

- As one district at a time understands and behaves with the habits of mind in mind, the world gradually becomes a more thought-full place.

Given those assumptions, assessment methods and measures would follow. As you read the descriptions for each habit, you may have recognized the indicators for the individual.

Transforming these descriptions into a checklist, rubric, or journal prompt for self-reflection is fairly easy. Each of these formats elicits different ways of learning about student growth as an ongoing, formative process.

Checklists

The value of using checklists is that each indicator is accessible and can serve as a means of checking up. It is a list of behaviors that is observable either to the student or to others. We suggest, therefore, that the checklist be used, not as a means of scoring with a point count—rather, that it be used as a way for students to do some self-reflection, for a teacher to offer some observations as feedback, as an opportunity for students to do some peer observations that strengthen their knowledge of the meaning of the habits through action.

Rubrics

Most people associate rubrics with a range that moves from *not so good* to *awesome*. We would propose that rubrics could also be developmental. Rather than scoring a student on the basis of whether he or she is there yet, we suggest that "there" be set up as a series of milestones or benchmarks that are ongoing. This would lead to rubrics that focus on ways to identify indicators, based on the targets suggested in each descriptor above, in a developmentally appropriate way. So, for example, remaining open to continuous learning as highlighted above, change might look like this for a first-grade student:

- Looks for new ways to extend learning

- Sees feedback about work as a means of learning rather than as a final judgment

- Asks questions when uncertain about knowing

Notice that as you move through developing these indicators and checklists, there is often repetition. For example, the description of Remaining Open to Continuous Learning is also reinforcing the habit of Striving for Accuracy and Precision. As teachers and students develop rubrics and checklists, they will begin to see the inter-related indicators and will be able to reduce the number of rubrics and checklists so that they have a more consolidated picture than the sixteen suggest. We have learned that the entire landscape of the sixteen establishes meaning that can be accompanied by specific behaviors. However, once the sixteen are introduced, teachers make choices as to which are most significant for their students at this particular time. As they work with the students to develop indicators, they consolidate some of the behaviors from the habits they have chosen.

Portfolios

Portfolios offer a different option for assessing growth. As students become familiar with the Habits, they are able to identify which of the habits was most helpful as they were learning. For example, if they were working on a project, they might identify which of the habits they used in the planning stage, which in the process of developing the project, which in the evaluation of their final product, and finally, which in their reflection of the learning process as a whole. This process reinforces the inner self-coaching referenced above. As students begin to consciously think of those questions, they can also begin to document that thinking specifically tied to phases of their work process. The most significant value of the portfolio is its representation of growth over time through the artifacts of product.

As is clear from all of these methods, self-assessment is as significant as the assessment from others. This relationship between the internal and the external measures of growth build the inner compass for becoming a contributing global citizen who has the disposition for deeper learning and thinking.

Does It Work?

By now many readers may be asking, "All this sounds ideal, but is it pie in the sky? How do we know it works? Are we talking about an ideal state, or is it possible that schools are putting their attention to this work in deep and meaningful ways?"

A number of years ago we established Habits of Mind International with an eye toward helping schools network and learn together. At this point, there are many schools around the world that embrace the habits of mind: New Zealand, Australia, South Africa, Scandinavia, the United Kingdom, Hong Kong, Singapore, Saudi Arabia and, of course, schools throughout the United States and Canada.

Two examples, a high school (Community High School of Vermont) and an elementary school (Waikiki Elementary in Honolulu) tell us the results. (For additional research, see Hargett & Gayle, 2008.)

Community High School of Vermont designed a life skills program called the Workforce Development Program to teach students in corrections fundamental life skills using a holistic approach focusing on living, learning, and working. The habits of mind were selected as the framework and benchmark behaviors that would be taught to students and role modeled by the teachers and program staff.

The Workforce Development Program began in three correctional facilities, and by 2007, the habits of mind were being taught and integrated into all seventeen campuses of the Community High School of Vermont. Students throughout corrections were now learning how to develop successful dispositions through the habits of mind and successfully using the Habits in many areas of their lives.

Since 2003 the habits of mind have helped Community High School of Vermont develop a culture of teaching students how to think effectively through challenging situations. The research demonstrated that the people who participated in the habits of mind program were less likely than the control group to return to prison and were more likely to acquire and retain employment than the control group. Evidence has taught that it takes a common vision and language to create a positive culture of learning that can be sustained in a school operating within a corrections department (www.chsvt .org/wdp.html).

Waikiki Elementary, a Mindful School, on the slopes of Diamond Head Crater in Honolulu, has embraced the habits of mind for over twenty years. The results have been remarkable. More than instructional strategies, the habits of mind are infused into the organizational norms and are shared by the instructional and support staff, the students, and the community—they live the habits of mind. They have endured through three changes in principals and numerous new additions to the faculty. Waikiki Elementary was one of three schools selected as a 2013 Hawaii Blue Ribbon School and has gone on to be awarded the title of a 2013 National Blue Ribbon School. These achievements are a result of consistent state proficiency test scores in the top 10 percent while serving a student population with 38 percent economically disadvantaged, 30 percent English language learners, and 40 percent from nontraditional families. On school quality surveys, parent satisfaction measures are a whopping 94.4 percent. On *Honolulu Magazine*'s yearly school ranking, Waikiki School has consistently placed in the top 5 out of 267 state public schools, receiving an overall grade of A+. Additionally, on October 25, 2013, Waikiki Elementary was honored by having one of its teachers selected as the 2013 State Teacher of the Year (Tabor, Brace, Lawrence, & Latti, 2008).

Summary

Deeper learning means deeper thinking; deeper thinking means that one must develop the dispositions that foster such thinking. It is important to be skillful as a thinker—to be able to think creatively and critically. Being skillful, however, is not enough. One must also have the dispositions, the habits of mind, that foster deeper thinking. We explicitly call them habits because we know that when thinking becomes complex, rigorous, and demanding, we need to be able to call upon those habits that will help us struggle through new learning. Too often, teachers try to teach skillful thinking by assignment. They design incredibly rich units of study and assign creative projects or tasks. They are then disappointed when the students remain apathetic—not willing to engage. We are suggesting that building the habits of mind help students become more aware of the significance of their attitudes toward learning. They realize that it is not that they cannot do the deeper work; it is that they have not been willing to do the deeper work. They also realize which habits they may need to call upon to help them through the tough spots—is it persisting, is it learning how to work interdependently, is it questioning? Which of these habits, when called upon, will serve as a motivator for deeper learning?

Deeper learners are expansive learners. Habits are built upon a consistent pattern of behaviors. Those patterns should be explicitly a part of the work of the individual student, the work of groups of students, the work of the classroom, the work of the school, and the work of the system. Every single fractal of the school community should be a microcosm of the whole. This worldview can translate into a more thought-full place for each of us to be able to live interdependently.

References

Barell, J. (2013). Fostering curiosity here, there and everywhere [Web log post]. Accessed at https://smartblogs.com/education/2012/11/20/fostering-curiosity-here-there-everywhere-john-barell on April 1, 2014.

Bloom, B. S. (1984). *Taxonomy of educational objectives: Book 1 cognitive domain.* New York: Addison-Wesley.

Claxton, G., Chambers, M., Powell, G., & Lucas, B. (2011). *The learning powered school: Pioneering 21st century education.* Bristol, England: TLO Limited.

Costa, A. L. (2001). Habits of mind. In *Developing minds: A resource book for teaching thinking* (3rd ed., pp. 80–85). Alexandria, VA: Association for Supervision and Curriculum Development.

Costa, A. L., & Kallick, B. (2004). *Assessment strategies for self-directed learning.* Thousand Oaks, CA: Corwin Press.

Costa, A. L., & Kallick, B. (Ed.). (2009). *Learning and leading with habits of mind: 16 essential characteristics for success.* Alexandria, VA: Association for Supervision and Curriculum Development.

Costa, A. L., & Kallick, B. (2014). *Dispositions: Reframing teaching and learning.* Thousand Oaks, CA: Corwin Press.

Costa, A. L., & O'Leary, P. W. (Eds.). (2013). *The power of the social brain: Teaching, learning, and using interdependent thinking.* New York: Teachers College Press.

Conley, D. T. (2010). *Redefining college readiness.* Eugene, OR: Education Policy Improvement Center.

Davidson, C. N. (2013). *Now you see it: How the brain science of attention will transform the way we live, work, and learn.* New York: Viking.

De Bono, E. (1970). *Lateral thinking: A textbook of creativity.* London: Ward Lock Educational.

De Bono, E. (1991). The Cort thinking program. In A. L. Costa (Ed.), *Developing minds* (Rev. ed.; pp. 27–32). Alexandria, VA: Association for Supervision and Curriculum Development.

Derber, C. (1979). *The pursuit of attention: Power and ego in everyday life* (2nd ed.). New York: Oxford University Press.

Dunlosky, J., & Metcalf, J. (2009). *Metacognition.* Thousand Oaks, CA: SAGE.

Dweck, C. S. (2006). *Mindset: The new psychology of success.* New York: Ballantine Books.

Hacker, D. J., Dunlosky, J., & Graesser, A. C. (Eds.). (2009). *Handbook of metacognition in education.* New York: Routledge.

Hargett, M. P., & Gayle, M. E. (2008). Habits of mind in North Carolina: Increasing intellectual capacity of disadvantaged students. In A. L. Costa & B. Kallick (Eds.), *Learning and leading with habits of mind: 16 essential characteristics for success* (pp. 319–332). Alexandria, VA: Association for Supervision and Curriculum Development.

Martinez, M. (2009). Notes from the gym: Using habits of mind to develop mind and body. In A. L. Costa, & B. Kallick (Eds.), *Habits of mind across the curriculum: Practical and creative strategies for teachers* (pp. 145–150). Alexandria, VA: Association for Supervision and Curriculum Development.

Meier, D. (2011). *5 habits of mind: Deborah Meier* [Web log post]. Accessed at http://21centuryschools.wordpress.com/2011/06/28/5-habits-of-mind-debroah-meier/ on March 27, 2014.

Partnership for 21st Century Skills. (2007). *Framework for 21st century learning.* Washington, DC: Author.

Perkins, D. (1985). What creative thinking is. In A. L. Costa (Ed.), *Developing minds: A resource book for teaching thinking* (pp. 85–88). Alexandria, VA: Association for Supervision and Curriculum Development.

Pink, D. H. (2010, June 9). *'Can we fix it' is the right question to ask.* Accessed at www.telegraph.co.uk/finance/7839988/Can-we-fix-it-is-the-right-question-to-ask.html on April 4, 2014.

Ritchhart, R. (2002). *Intellectual character: What it is, why it matters, and how to get it.* San Francisco: Jossey-Bass.

Rock, D. (2009). *Your brain at work: Strategies for overcoming distraction, regaining focus, and working smarter all day long.* New York: Harper Business.

Rock, D., & Schwartz, J. (2006, May 30). The neuroscience of leadership: Breakthroughs in brain research explain how to make organizational transformation succeed. *Strategy + Business.* Accessed at www.strategy-business.com/article/06207?gko=6da0a on August 4, 2014.

Salomon, G. (1994). *Interaction of media, cognition and learning: An exploration of how symbolic forms cultivate mental skills and affect knowledge acquisition* (2nd ed.). Mahwah, NJ: Erlbuam.

Sizer, T. (1992). *Horace's school: Redesigning the American high school.* New York: Houghton Mifflin.

Tabor, B., Brace, S., Lawrence, M., & Latti, A. (2008). The mindful culture of Waikiki School. In A. L. Costa & B. Kallick (Eds.), *Learning and leading with habits of mind: 16 essential characteristics for success* (pp. 348–361). Alexandria, VA: Association for Supervision and Curriculum Development.

Tishman, S., & Andrade, A. (n.d.). *Thinking dispositions: A review of current theories, practices, and issues.* Accessed at https://learnweb.harvard.edu/alps/thinking /docs/Dispositions.htm on August 4, 2014.

Tough, P. (2012). *How children succeed: Grit, curiosity, and the hidden power of character.* New York: Houghton Mifflin Harcourt.

Tishman, S., Perkins, D., & Jay, E. (1995). *The thinking classroom: Learning and teaching in a culture of thinking.* Boston: Allyn and Bacon.

U.S. Department of Education, Office of Educational Technology. (2013, February). *Promoting grit, tenacity, and perseverance: Critical factors of success in the 21st century.* Accessed at http://pgbovine.net/OET-Draft-Grit-Report-2-17-13.pdf on August 4, 2014.

Vygotsky, L. (1978). *Society of mind.* Cambridge, MA: Harvard University Press.

Wagner, T. (2008). *The global achievement gap: Why even our best schools don't teach the new survival skills our children need—And what we can do about it.* New York: Basic Books.

Yong Zhao

Yong Zhao, PhD, is an internationally known scholar, author, and speaker whose works focus on the implications of globalization and technology on education. He has designed schools that cultivate global competence, developed computer games for language learning, and founded research and development institutions to explore innovative education models. He has published over one hundred articles and twenty books, including *Catching Up or Leading the Way* and *World Class Learners*, which won the Society of Professors of Education Book Award, the Association of Education Publishers' (AEP) Judges' Award, and a Distinguished Achievement Award in Education Leadership.

Yong received his doctorate at the University of Illinois at Urbana-Champaign.

To learn more about Yong Zhao's work, visit zhaolearning.com, or follow him on Twitter @YongZhaoUO.

Chapter 3

Paradigm Shift: Educating Creative and Entrepreneurial Students

Yong Zhao

Today's education is inadequate for preparing tomorrow's citizens. That is the consensus around the world. International organizations, national and local governments, educational institutions, businesses, and the public all have put forth tremendous efforts with unprecedented courage to improve education. But as former U.S. president John F. Kennedy once said, "Efforts and courage are not enough without purpose and direction."

The purpose is clear—a better education capable of preparing our students to live successfully in the future—but the direction is not. There are so many paths before us. Some are a waste of time, and others move us even further away. In fact, the path most countries have chosen does both, because it has been infected with the GERM.

The GERM, short for the Global Education Reform Movement, is a term coined by Pasi Sahlberg (2011), Finnish education scholar and author of *Finnish Lessons: What Can the World Learn From Educational Change in Finland*, to summarize education reform efforts undertaken by many nations around the world. In his view, one pattern is being copied too widely:

Curricula are standardized to fit to international student tests, and students in different nations study learning materials from the same global providers. . . . So visible is this common way of improvement that I call it the *Global Educational Reform Movement or GERM*. It is like an epidemic that spreads and infects education systems through a virus. It travels with pundits, media and politicians. Education systems borrow policies from others and get infected. As a consequence, schools get ill, teachers don't feel well, and kids learn less. (Sahlberg, 2012)

Countries infected with the GERM push schools and teachers to compete with each other, using parental choice of schools as the motivator, with standardized testing scores as the selection criterion. The purpose is, of course, to improve education in order to better prepare students for the future.

However, these efforts will not usher in a better tomorrow. Instead they take us further from where we want to go, because they are geared toward strengthening the traditional education paradigm aimed at producing employee-minded workers needed in the past (Zhao, 2012), while the future needs innovators, creators, and entrepreneurs (Hoffman & Casnocha, 2012; Rizvi, Donnelly, & Barber, 2012; Wagner, 2012; Zhao, 2012).

The Employee-Oriented Paradigm of Education

The GERM reform efforts undertaken by many countries are aimed at improving an obsolete education paradigm that is dominating modern schooling. This paradigm aims to prepare individuals to find gainful employment in the current economy and to fit into the existing society. It was designed to produce workers for the mass-production economy that came with the Industrial Revolution. The mass-production economy needed a large workforce with similar skills and knowledge but at very basic levels. There was no need for the majority of individuals to be inventors or entrepreneurs. The few great inventors and entrepreneurs could arise by accident, as long as society permitted them to thrive.

To educate the masses with similar basic knowledge and skills required a common curriculum, a prescription for the skills, knowledge, talents, and abilities that were to be taught in schools to prepare students to function well in society. Since schools cannot possibly teach everything, the task to define what to teach is basically an exercise in making choices about what to include and what to exclude. It is also an exercise in placing value on different human talents and abilities. Once the prescription is complete, it governs students' learning experiences. It dictates what students are exposed to in the form of textbooks, classroom instructions, assessments, and homework. The prescription also serves as the basis on which local, national, and international assessments are built. The extent to which students master the prescribed skills and knowledge becomes the measure of their readiness for a career, the quality of their schools, and even the quality of their national education systems.

Governments, educational authorities, parents, and educators are responsible for ensuring that students master this prescribed, look-alike curriculum. Curriculum standards, textbooks, and supplemental materials are developed to make sure the prescribed content is prominent in the students' school life. Teachers are trained to dispense the prescribed content effectively. Tests are administered to assess to what degree students have acquired the prescribed content. And based on the extent to which they master the prescribed curriculum, students are then sorted into different tracks at the end of their basic education—some going to vocational school, some going to community colleges, some to four-year colleges, and a few to prestigious universities. The different tracks correspond to different careers that offer different returns in terms of social status and economic resources. The type of school and the number of years attended thus have a direct correlation with the jobs people can have and how much money they will make.

This paradigm chalks a clear path toward life's success, often defined externally by society as a good college, a decent job, and a handsome income. It has a set of clearly defined learning objectives and multiple regular checkpoints—that is, tests—to ensure that the objectives are met. If a student meets the objectives, he or she is rewarded and recognized. Otherwise, the student may be given a bad grade, retained for one more year, or given remediation lessons.

In essence, the employment-oriented paradigm is about reducing human diversity into a few desirable skills. When executed well, this paradigm is most effective in producing people with similar skills, classified by test scores or academic performance.

This well-educated, employment-oriented education in the process of forcing conformity and imposing uniformity is also very successful in weeding out those unwilling or unable to conform. They become outcasts and dropouts and are rendered to low-status, lower paying jobs, or even no jobs. While most of them are not rewarded with high social status or high income, a few may nevertheless become successful. Think Albert Einstein, Richard Feynman, Lady Gaga, Steve Jobs, and Bill Gates.

A Necessity That No Longer Works

The employee-oriented paradigm has been necessary and has worked well for a society that no longer exists, at least in most of the developed world. Globalization has made all societies open to outside influences. Jobs can easily be sent to other countries. People cross national boundaries in vast numbers. Ideas travel around the globe at the speed of light. Technological changes continue to accelerate. All evidence suggests that Alvin Toffler was right: we have entered the *third wave* society (Toffler, 1980), where the industrial-era creed of standardization is no more.

As a result, it has become increasingly difficult to predict the future, to know what jobs will be available in a given society due to outsourcing or replacement by technology, and to even know where and for whom our students will be working. As recognized by many, it is no longer possible to prescribe the knowledge and skills students must master for future careers and employment. "Career ready" is but a fancy dream when one does not know what careers will exist when a student leaves school. Furthermore, teachers or schools are no longer the only, or even primary, sources of knowledge or opportunities to develop skills. More importantly, the opportunities for different types of talents and skills deemed "valuable" have dramatically expanded (Pink, 2006). As evidence, consider occupations like TV chefs, social media managers, bloggers, and environmental scientists.

The Need for Entrepreneurship

Youth unemployment has become an urgent challenge facing the global society. In 2011, nearly 75 million youth aged fifteen to twenty-four were unemployed worldwide. The majority of the world's youth (87 percent) living in developing countries "are often underemployed and working in the informal economy under poor conditions," according to the *World Youth Report* of the United Nations (2011). But the situation is not much better in the developed countries. In the thirty-four member countries of the Organisation for Economic Co-operation and Development, which include the world's wealthiest and most developed countries, "22.3 million young people—were inactive in the fourth quarter of 2010, neither in jobs nor in education or training" (United Nations, 2011).

Entrepreneurs are what the world needs to solve the unemployment problem. Numerous international organizations have produced reports about the importance of entrepreneurship and issued calls for countries to develop entrepreneurship (Schoof, 2006; World Economic Forum, 2011). The World Economic Forum, for example, has identified entrepreneurship education as the core of its Global Education Initiative (World Economic Forum, 2009, 2011), because "innovation and entrepreneurship provide a way forward for solving the global challenges of the 21st century, building sustainable development, creating jobs, generating renewed economic growth, and advancing human welfare" (World Economic Forum, 2009, p. 7). Entrepreneurs are important drivers of economic and social progress, and the enterprises they run are important sources of innovation, employment, and growth (World Economic Forum, 2012).

The Redefinition of Entrepreneurship

While traditional entrepreneurship refers to the ability to start a business, the meaning of entrepreneurship has expanded significantly in the current times. The World Economic Forum (2009) defines entrepreneurship as:

a process that results in creativity, innovation and growth. Innovative entrepreneurs come in all shapes and forms; its benefits are not limited to startups, innovative ventures and new jobs. Entrepreneurship refers to an individual's ability to turn ideas into action and is therefore a key competence for all, helping young people to be more creative and self-confident in whatever they undertake. (p. 9)

Entrepreneurs are thus no longer limited to those who start a business and try to maximize profits. There are social entrepreneurs who recognize a social problem and apply entrepreneurial principles to achieve social change (Martin & Osberg, 2007). There are *intrapreneurs* who bring significant innovative changes from within an organization, such as Post-it notes inventors Art Fry and Spencer Silver of 3M (Swearingen, 2008). There are also policy entrepreneurs whose enterprise is to bring innovative improvement in policy from within public and government institutions (Harris & Kinney, 2004).

Entrepreneurs, in this expanded sense of the term, have more power to solve the complex problems facing human beings and bring prosperity to humanity than governments and international organizations. Philip Auerswald (2012), senior fellow in entrepreneurship of the Kauffman Foundation and associate professor at George Mason University argues in his book, *The Coming Prosperity*, that "the vast majority of alleged threats to humanity are, in fact, dwarfed by the magnitude of opportunities that exist in the twenty-first century" (Kindle loc. 136). These opportunities, he writes, will be harnessed by entrepreneurs, more than by governments, and will transform human society:

If anything is more naïve than an unquestioning belief in the transformative power of entrepreneurs, it is an unquestioning belief in the power of national governments, international organizations, and multinational corporations to address complex twenty-first century challenges. In many parts of the world where change is most urgently needed, governments are as likely to be a part of the problem as a part of the solution. In such environments, all institutions structured to work through national governments face serious handicaps.

> The relevance, much less effectiveness, of the UN and the World Bank—the two institutions most clearly tasked in the post-World War II order with addressing global challenges—is less assured today than that of entrepreneurs (Auerswald, 2012, Kindle loc. 136–139).

Thus, entrepreneurs are no longer a select few. Everyone needs to be entrepreneurial in the 21st century. Entrepreneurs are now the "black-collar workers," a termed coined by Auerswald (2012) and inspired by the black turtlenecks Steve Jobs always wore. He continues:

> From where we sit now, it seems improbable that an entire economy could be built of such workers. Where are the drones in this picture? Where are the undifferentiated masses of the unfulfilled? Try asking yourself this question instead: from the standpoint of a 15th-century peasant, how likely is the reality of the present day? . . . Just as former farmers were compelled to convert themselves into blue-collar workers to realize their potential in the economy of the 20th century, so will former factory workers (and retooling economic drones of all types) convert themselves into black-collar workers to realize their potential in the economy of the 21st century. (Auerswald, 2012)

It is evident the world needs more entrepreneurs. Some may even be great, like Henry Ford, Thomas Edison, Oprah Winfrey, Steve Jobs, Richard Branson, J. K. Rowling, and Mark Zuckerberg—people who are remembered, celebrated, or envied. Why don't we have more people who can think like they do?

A Modern Missing Link

Today's missing link is "an entrepreneurial mindset—a critical mix of success-oriented attitudes of initiative, intelligent risk-taking, collaboration, and opportunity recognition," says a report by the Aspen Youth Entrepreneurship Strategy Group (2009, p. 7). It is hard to imagine someone without an entrepreneurial mindset engaging in entrepreneurship activities. Moreover, the entrepreneurship mindset, as defined by the Aspen Institute, is also needed for working in existing businesses and organizations. It is a frustrating and sad irony that with so many unemployed in the world, business leaders are complaining that they cannot find qualified workers (Auerswald, 2012; Zhao, 2009). "The number of workers with adequate skills has decreased," says the Manpower Group (2012, p. 7), a global consulting firm with offices in over eighty countries.

The real problem, Auerswald (2012a) says, is that our employee-oriented "educational system continues to push students through career services offices around the U.S. toward the same pathways followed by their parents, rather than encouraging students to map out new pathways that correspond to current realities" (p. 186).

"Our education system is designed to turn out 'good employees,' not 'good entrepreneurs,'" Tom of Dayton, Ohio, writes to Steve Strauss, a *USA Today* columnist who specializes in small business and entrepreneurship (Strauss, 2006). And Strauss agrees, adding,

> We have an education system that was created around the time of the Industrial Revolution, when we needed to turn rural kids into urban employees capable of working in assembly line, mass-market factories. As a result, we ended up with a school system focused on rote memorization and measurable, predictable results.

In contrast, entrepreneurship is fundamentally about the desire to solve problems creatively. The foundation of entrepreneurship—creativity, curiosity, imagination, risk-taking, and collaboration—is, just like the ideas of engineering, "in our bones and part of our human nature and experience" (Petroski, 1992, p. 2). Human beings are born with the desire and potential to create and innovate, to dream and imagine, and to challenge and improve the status quo. We are also born with the propensity to be social, to communicate, and to collaborate. For thousands of years, bees have kept the same design of their dwellings, the honeycomb, but the design of human buildings has been changing constantly. "It is the human tastes, resources, and ambitions that do not stay constant," says Henry Petroski (1992, p. 2).

Some experiences enhance our creativity, while others suppress it. Some experiences encourage risk-taking, while others make us risk-averse. Some experiences strengthen our desire to ask questions, while others instill compliance. Some experiences foster a mindset of challenging the status quo, while others teach us to follow orders. People are adaptable, and our nature is malleable. The experiences we have play a significant role in what we become.

Besides family, schools are the primary institution for our students and therefore the primary place that shapes the experiences our students have. Because of the differences in definitions and measures of creativity and differences in the experiences schools offer, there is no definitive research to show to what degree school experiences in general increase or decrease creativity and entrepreneurial capacities (Claxton, Pannells, & Rhoads, 2005). That said, one well-known longitudinal study by George Land and Beth Jarman finds a decline in creativity as students became older. In their 1992 book, *Breakpoint and Beyond*, Land and Jarman describe a longitudinal study on creativity beginning in the 1960s. Land administered eight tests of divergent thinking, which measure an individual's ability to envision multiple solutions to a problem. When the tests were first given to sixteen hundred three- to five-year-olds, Land found that 98 percent of them scored at a level called "creative genius." But five years later, when the same group of students took the tests, only 32 percent scored at this level, and after another five years, the percentage of geniuses declined to 10 percent. Figure 3.1 (page 92) illustrates the sharp decline in one measure of creativity as students get older.

By 1992, over two hundred thousand adults had taken the same tests, and only 2 percent scored at the genius level. The Harvard psychologist Howard Gardner (1982) also notes a decline in artistic creativity once children enter school. In addition, Tony Wagner (2008) observes that "the longer our children are in school, the less curious they become" (p. xxiii).

These findings are not surprising. In fact, they are the intended consequence of the traditional education paradigm designed to produce employees. Good employees, in the traditional economy, are those who have homogenized skills, follow directions, and obey orders. Creativity—that is, the ability and desire to do things differently or do different things—makes one a poor employee or disobedient citizen and must be suppressed.

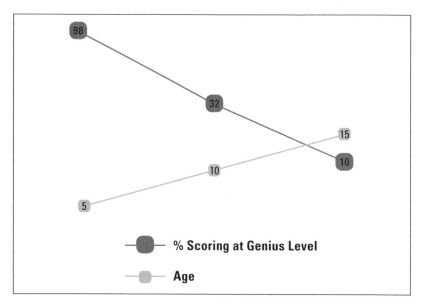

Source: Land & Jarman, 1992.

Figure 3.1: Changes in divergent thinking with age.

No Free Lunch

Others disagree that tradition and creativity are mutually exclusive. Among the most prominent features of the GERM, the effort to strengthen the traditional paradigm of education, is that it begins with standardization and ends with accountability as the most effective way to execute the prescription. In defense of standardization and accountability, the influential education leader Michael Barber and associates at the global education publishing giant Pearson write that "the road to hell in education is paved with false dichotomies" (Rizvi et al., 2012). They denounce "the belief that systems that ensure high standards in reading, writing and arithmetic inevitably do so at the expense of creativity, thinking, individuality and so on" (Rizvi et al., 2012). They also note that this oppositional statement is a "devastating" point of view, "because it is so thoroughly misleading." He suggests that this is a false dichotomy, and that the pursuit of high standards should not come at the cost of creativity (Rizvi et al., 2012).

This argument may be theoretically true and very appealing, but in practice, the problem persists. Depending on how they are implemented, the standards and accountability measures can certainly cause the decline of creativity and entrepreneurial thinking. This is akin to the side effects of medicine. All medicine has side effects. That is, when it cures, it can cause harm as well. In other words, every gain comes at a cost. Education is no exception for a number of reasons:

- **Time is a constant.** When it is spent on one thing, it cannot be spent on others. As a result, when all time is devoted to classroom studies, it cannot be spent on visiting museums. Similarly, when time is spent on non-academic activities, the same time is not available for school subjects and preparing for exams.

- **Certain human qualities may be antithetical to each other.** Conformity is the opposite of creativity. Thus, when one learns to conform, it will be difficult for him to be creative. When one is frequently punished for making mistakes, it is hard for her to be a risk-taker. When one is told he is inadequate all the time, it is difficult for him to maintain confidence. When students are granted freedom to explore, they may question what they are asked to learn and may decide not to comply.

- **Resources are finite.** Resources a society or school has are limited. When all resources are devoted to certain things, they cannot be used for others. For instance, when more resources are spent on teaching mathematics and language, schools have to spend less on other programs such as the arts. When more money is spent on testing students, less will be available for actually helping them learn.

These side effects are rarely mentioned in education, but they explain the discrepancy between test scores and entrepreneurship. The annual Global Entrepreneurship Monitor (GEM) survey, which tracks various aspects of entrepreneurship activities in over fifty countries, shows significant differences in terms of entrepreneurial capabilities and activities across different countries of similar economic conditions (Bosma, Wennekers, & Amorós, 2012; Kelley, Bosma, & Amorós, 2010). The number of patents per capita, an indicator of a nation's innovation endeavors and innovative talents, also varies a great deal across different nations (World Intellectual Property Organization [WIPO], 2007).

What is intriguing about these results is that countries that show a low level of entrepreneurship are countries that have consistently high performers on international tests. For example, countries that scored high on PISA and Trends in International Mathematics and Science Study (TIMSS) , such as Singapore, Japan, Finland, Korea, and Taiwan, scored much lower than Australia, the United Kingdom, and United States in the category of perceived entrepreneurship capabilities of the GEM survey in 2011 (Bosma et al., 2012). Correlational analyses show a statistically significant negative relationship between test scores in mathematics, reading, and sciences and aspects of entrepreneurship. Figure 3.2 shows the ranking of twenty-three countries (regions) that participated in both the 2009 PISA and 2011 GEM survey in PISA mathematics performance and reported entrepreneurial capabilities. All twenty-three countries are considered developed economies and thus are categorized as "innovation-driven economies" by the GEM study.

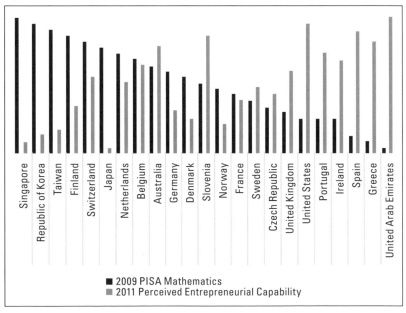

■ 2009 PISA Mathematics
■ 2011 Perceived Entrepreneurial Capability

Source: Bosma et al., 2012; OECD, 2010

Figure 3.2: Countries participating in the 2009 PISA and 2011 Global Entrepreneurship Monitor survey in PISA mathematics performance.

This inverse relationship between test scores and entrepreneur-ship does not necessarily mean high test scores caused the loss of entrepreneurial capabilities or vice versa, but it does suggest that education systems that produce good test scores more often than not have lower entrepreneurship activities and capabilities.

It also suggests the possibility that the mechanisms that lead to higher test scores could lead to lower levels of entrepreneurship. There is other evidence to support this suspicion. For example, the TIMSS has consistently found a significant negative correlation between a nation's scores and students' self-reported confidence (Loveless, 2006; Zhao, 2012). That is, nations with higher scores tend to have lower confidence. And confidence is one of the major attributes underpinning entrepreneurship. PISA has also shown a negative correlation across nations between scores and student inter-ests (Sjøberg, 2012). If students lack the interest in certain subjects, it is less likely that they would pursue them with the passion required for creative and entrepreneurial work in that area.

The possibility becomes even more certain when other evidence, such as differences in educational policy, curriculum, pedagogical practices, and student activities are taken into consideration. For example, the United States has seen a significant decline in creativity among its youth over the past two decades, which coincides with waves of educational changes to boost student test scores.

In July 2010, *Newsweek* published "The Creativity Crisis," an article about the decrease in creativity in the United States (Bronson & Merryman, 2010). The article cites research by Kyung Hee Kim, an educational psychology professor at the College of William and Mary, who analyzed the performance of adults and children on a commonly used creativity measure known as the Torrance Test of Creative Thinking. The results indicate a creativity decrease in the last twenty years in all categories. Fluency scores (a measure of the ability to produce a number of ideas) decreased by 7 percent from 1990 to 2008, while Originality scores (ability to produce unique and unusual ideas) decreased by 3.74 percent from 1990 to 1998. Although they remained static between 1998 and 2008, Kim says "originality scores have actually significantly decreased, but the decrease has been deflated through the use of outdated scoring lists" (Britannica Editors, 2010a). Creative strengths (creative personality traits) decreased by 3.16 percent from 1990 to 1998 and by 5.75 percent from 1990 to 2008. Elaboration scores (the ability to develop and elaborate on ideas, detailed and reflective thinking, and motivation) decreased by 3.68 percent from 1984 to 2008. Scores in abstractness of titles (ability to produce the thinking process of synthesis and organization, to know what is important) increased until 1998, but decreased by 7.41 percent from 1998 to 2008. Scores in resistance to premature closure (intellectual curiosity and open-mindedness) decreased by 1.84 percent from 1998 to 2008 (Britannica Editors, 2010a).

When asked to explain this decline, Kim proposed several societal, home, and school factors. For example, "contemporary parenting styles may create overly programmed lives for children, by over-protecting them and over-scheduling them, which has the effect of denying children opportunity to discover for themselves" (Britannica Editors, 2010b). Kim told editors of the Encyclopedia Britannica that schools certainly play a significant role: "Teachers claim to value creativity in children, but in fact it is proven that they generally dislike creative behaviors and characteristics in the classroom because they are inconvenient and hard to control" (Britannica Editors, 2010b). Speaking about the impact of No Child Left Behind on creativity, Kim notes, "NCLB has stifled any interest in developing individual differences, creative and innovative thinking, or individual potential" (Britannica Editors, 2010b).

She also says,

Teaching to this test discourages purposeful creativity development and stifles children's creativity in schools. Standardized testing forces emphasis on rote learning instead of critical, creative thinking, and diminishes students' natural curiosity and joy for learning in its own right. Further, NCLB may stifle teachers' creativity because the high pressure to cover the content required to produce passing test scores override the desire (and time) to stimulate children's imagination and curiosity. (Britannica Editors, 2010b)

The picture may even be more ominous. She continues,

The standardized testing movement created by NCLB has led to the elimination of content areas and activities, including gifted programs, electives, arts, foreign languages, and elementary science and recess, which leaves little room for imagination, and critical and creative thinking. This may eliminate the opportunities for creative students to release their creative energy in school. . . . Those who preserve and develop their creative abilities despite the odds will be adversely affected. . . . Further, research shows, high school students who exhibit creative personalities are more likely to drop out of school. (Britannica Editors, 2010b)

Kim's research seems to substantiate the concept of side effects in education. When NCLB forced schools to reduce time for arts, music, science, and even recess in order to focus more on literacy and numeracy, it took away opportunities for students to explore, imagine, and create.

Entrepreneur-Oriented Education: A New Paradigm

There is another paradigm of education. This paradigm does not presuppose or predefine what knowledge or skills are worthwhile. In this paradigm, the "curriculum" follows the student. It begins by asking students what they are interested in, what excites them, what they are capable of, and how they learn. This paradigm does not assume all students are the same. Therefore it does not impose artificial standards or age-based, grade-level expectations. It helps students move forward from where they are. Furthermore, it does not believe students are simply empty vessels ready to be filled with knowledge; rather, it assumes that each is a purposeful agent who interacts with the outside world.

The great American educator and philosopher John Dewey (1938) summarizes the differences between this paradigm and the factory paradigm in *Experience and Education*.

To imposition from above is opposed expression and cultivation of individuality; to external discipline is opposed free activity; to learning from texts and teachers, learning through experience; to acquisition of isolated skills and techniques by drill, is opposed acquisition of them as means of attaining ends which make direct vital appeal; to preparation for a more or less remote future is opposed making the most of the opportunities of present life; to static aims and materials is opposed acquaintance with a changing world. (pp. 5–6)

Education following Dewey's student-centered paradigm aims to guide, support, and celebrate individual students rather than reducing human diversity into a few employable skills. It is designed to enhance and expand human talents and exceptionality instead of standardizing them. Outcasts are the new normal in this paradigm. Great creative people are not accidents but are deliberately cultivated and supported.

It would be a mistake to say that this new paradigm denies the importance of common and essential knowledge and skills required of all citizens in order for a society or community to function. By promoting student-centered learning, this paradigm places the responsibility of learning on the student, instead of external agencies. By following the students' passions and interests, this paradigm capitalizes on their intrinsic motivation and natural curiosity to learn. When students have a reason to learn, they will seek the basics, rather than have the basics imposed on them. If they are true basics, they are hard to avoid.

This new paradigm also recognizes the arrival of the era of globalization. Students no longer live in isolated societies, and thus their context of learning and living should not be confined to a physical location. They must become citizens of their local community, their nation, and also the world. Hence the new paradigm suggests that education should make the global society the default context of learning.

Essential Ingredients of a World-Class Education

Education must be designed around the student and be student-centered. A world-class education should aim to meet each student's unique needs, capitalize on each student's strengths, and grant the student autonomy so he or she can take the responsibility for learning. Thus, a world-class education now includes three essential ingredients: (1) autonomy (the what), (2) product-oriented learning (the how), and (3) globalized campus (the where).

Autonomy

Following and supporting students' passions and interests produces competent, responsible, passionate, productive, and happy citizens (Posner, 2009). Granting students their deserved autonomy in choosing what to learn rather than imposing already-made decisions on them is necessary when cultivating creative entrepreneurs in the age of globalization, because it fills several needs.

- **The need to develop unique and diverse talents.** In a globalized world crowded by more than seven billion individuals, we cannot all have the same talent and compete for the same job. Likewise, in a world in which human needs are diverse, a standardized set of talents cannot possibly meet all the needs. Furthermore, in a world that is changing constantly and rapidly, a predetermined set of standardized skills and talents are not good bets for jobs that have not yet been invented. More important, in a world in which human interests, backgrounds, living conditions, and abilities are diverse, it is ethically wrong and economically disastrous to reduce all the diversity into a few skills. Granting and supporting individual students' pursuit of learning enables the development of unique and diverse talents.

- **The need to move talent from adequate to great.** While the agricultural and mass production industrial economy needs many workers with similar skills, these skills are routine, standard, and basic. As technology and economic globalization render the traditional lines of jobs obsolete and the economy is increasingly driven by knowledge and creativity (Florida, 2002; Goldin & Katz, 2008), we will need individuals with different talents and skills—beyond what can be standardized and basic. They need to be great—adequate is not enough. But greatness does not come from standards. Best-selling author Daniel Coyle (2009) suggests in his book *The Talent Code* that greatness comes from deep practice—that is, tens of thousands of hours of practice with master coaching. He writes, "Deep practice isn't a piece of cake: it requires energy, passion, and commitment. In a word, it requires motivational fuel" (Coyle, 2009, p. 93). That motivational fuel comes from inside, not outside, of an individual. Thus, only when students have autonomy do they feel the drive to become great.

- **The need to develop confident, curious, and creative talents.** The world needs creators: creators of more jobs, better products, more sensible policies, more effective business models, and more meaningful human services. Creators are curious people who keep wondering and imagining. They are confident people who are courageous and think and act outside the box. Creators are, well, creative and can come up with novel ideas and solutions. Creative individuals cannot be planned, predetermined, or standardized. They must be allowed the freedom and encouraged to wonder and wander, to explore, and to experiment. They must not be judged against others, a standard norm, or an external assessment. They need autonomy.

Product-Oriented Learning

Product-oriented learning changes the orientation of the learner from recipient and consumer to creator and provider. It changes the relationship between the teacher and the learner as well. The teacher no longer serves as the sole source of knowledge or disciplinary authority, but rather as a motivator, a reviewer, a facilitator, and an organizer. The learner becomes owner of his or her learning and is responsible for seeking and securing the necessary guidance, knowledge, skills, and support to make high-quality products. These changes facilitate the cultivation of creative entrepreneurs who have the following.

- **The ability to view problems as opportunities.** Entrepreneurs seek to solve—not avoid—problems. They ask more questions rather than find ready-made answers. They challenge the status quo with the belief they can always make it better. Product-oriented learning asks the learner to consider problems as opportunities for actions. It inspires them to create solutions, which then motivates them to acquire the knowledge, skills, and resources necessary for creating the solutions.

- **The ability to respond to other people's needs.** Product-oriented learning compels the learner to care about others, because in order to make meaningful and useful products and services, the learner must first know what is needed by and meaningful to different people in different situations. It helps the learner develop an empathetic perspective on others and the necessary skills to learn about other people's conditions and needs. An acute sense of other people's needs helps entrepreneurs develop alertness to opportunities, which is a common trait of successful entrepreneurs.

- **The ability to see strengths and weaknesses.** No one can be good at everything. Thus, knowing what one is good at or wants to be good at is essential. Successful entrepreneurs know their strengths and limitations. They stick to what they are good at and outsource their weakness to other able people. Product-oriented learning provides learners with the opportunities to try out their interests and talents so they can decide what to pursue and what they need help with.

- **The ability to show perseverance and disciplined creativity.** Entrepreneurship is not a smooth journey without bumps. It requires perseverance to go through the ups and downs. Unbounded creativity or a flash moment of enthusiasm does not lead to meaningful products or successful enterprises. Great ideas lead to great results only when sustained and disciplined efforts are applied over a long period of time. As I note in *World Class Learners*, "Product-oriented learning, through multiple drafts and peer reviews, helps the learner to develop resilience and perseverance before failure and learn about the importance of discipline and commitment" (Zhao, 2012, p. 241).

Globalized Campus

There is a sad irony in education reforms around the world today. While the reformers intend to prepare their students to be globally competitive by admiring and adopting international standards and practices, they are, in reality, closing their school doors to the outside world because they want their students to focus on the core academics and raise test scores on international tests. To prepare students for the globalized world, schools need to consider themselves as global enterprises, making the world their campus in order to help students develop the competency that enables them to benefit from helping and working with others. In order to do so, schools need the following.

- **Global perspective.** In a globalized world in which all aspects of human life are interconnected, the schools need to see their work as part of the global economic and political network. They need to know how their work affects and is affected by people in other places. Such a perspective is most effectively developed through engaging in experiences with people from around the world.

- **Global networks.** In a globalized world, innovators and entrepreneurs need friends for fresh ideas, different perspectives, local knowledge, and a variety of resources. A global network of friends and partners is thus a tremendous asset. But friends and partners do not just fall from a tree in one's backyard. They become friends and partners only through interactions on the various occasions when mutual interests, respect, and understanding are uncovered and developed. Therefore, expanding the campus—the learning environment—beyond the physical boundaries is key to developing global partners.

- **Global competency.** A global campus cannot avoid interacting with people and organizations in other countries. To be effective in international settings requires a level of global competency that ideally includes fluency in a foreign language and a high level of cultural intelligence. Schools intending to cultivate global entrepreneurs must provide opportunities for students to learn foreign languages and become culturally intelligent.

The End of Education

The title of this final section comes from the late cultural critic Neil Postman's (1996) book *The End of Education*. In explaining the book's purpose, he says:

> I write this book in the hope of altering, a little bit, the definition of the "school problem"—from means to ends. "End," of course, has at least two important meanings: "purpose" and "finish." Either meaning may apply to the future of schools, depending on whether or not there ensures a serious dialogue about purpose. By giving the book its ambiguous title, I mean to suggest that without a transcendent and honorable purpose schooling must reach its finish, and the sooner we are done with it, the better. With such a purpose, schooling becomes the central institution through which the young may find reasons for continuing to educate themselves. (p. xi)

Postman would be disappointed with what's happening so far in this century's education arena. The dominant discourse remains about the means of employee-oriented schooling: curriculum standards, teacher effectiveness, better assessment, charter schools, data-driven instruction, and a host of other factors that may or may not affect student achievement—and there is little questioning whether the achievement itself is meaningful.

Politicians, businessmen, and to some degree the public and educators, have been working hard to make better *schools*, not necessarily better *education* for students. A former teacher and doctoral student at Harvard Graduate School of Education laments the loss of the human dimension in some schools that may be deemed successful:

> Over the last two years I have visited public schools of many varieties, and many seem to share some level of this ruthless intensity around "on-task" and "forward-driving" work. In all of them I recognize the image of the achievement-hungry school where I spent four years teaching. There, the rhetoric

of urgency and seriousness loomed above all of us like a shadow. On the one hand, it cast our practices in a new light, allowing us to become more focused and driven. On the other hand, it clouded our vision, making us feel desperate to make sure that we were meeting goals and closing gaps. It was all too easy sometimes to lose track of the human dimensions that underpin the best teaching and learning: Respect, dignity, curiosity. (Fine, 2011)

The new education paradigm is really about the human dimensions. It is about respecting students as human beings and about supporting, not suppressing, their passions, curiosity, and talents. If schools can do just that, our students will become global, creative, and entrepreneurial. There needs to be a strong link between the future and the past. What is needed in the future is the enhancement of what comes with us as human beings, our natural curiosity, creativity, and passion for learning.

References and Resources

Aspen Youth Entrepreneurship Strategy Group. (2009). *Youth entrepreneurship education in America: A policy maker's action guide.* Washington, DC: The Aspen Institute.

Auerswald, P. (2012). *The coming prosperity: How entrepreneurs are transforming the global economy.* New York: Oxford University Press.

Australian Curriculum Assessment and Reporting Authority. (2010). *A curriculum for all young Australians.* Accessed at www.acara.edu.au/verve/_resources/Information_Sheet_A_curriculum_for_all_young_Australians.pdf on December 2, 2011.

Booher-Jennings, J. (2006). Rationing education in an era of accountability. *Phi Delta Kappan, 87*(10), 756–761.

Bosma, N., Wennekers, S., & Amorós, J. E. (2012). *Global entrepreneurship monitor: 2011 extended report—Entrepreneurs and entrepreneurial employees across the globe.* London: Global Entrepreneurship Research Association.

Breakspear, S. (2012). *The policy impact of PISA: An exploration of the normative effects of international benchmarking in school system performance.* Paris: Organisation for Economic Co-operation and Development.

Britannica Editors. (2010a, April 20). The decline of creativity in the United States: 5 questions for educational psychologist Kyung Hee Kim [Web log post.]. Accessed at www.britannica.com/blogs/2010/10/the-decline-of-creativity-in-the-united-states-5 -questions-for-educational-psychologist-kyung-hee-kim/ on April 1, 2014.

Britannica Editors. (2010b, April 20). Explaining the decline of creativity in American children: A reply to readers [Web log post]. Accessed at www.britannica.com

/blogs/2010/12/explaining-the-decline-of-creativity-in-american-children-a-reply-to-readers/ on April 1, 2014.

Bronson, P., & Merryman, A. (2010, July 10). The creativity crisis. *Newsweek*. Accessed at www.newsweek.com/creativity-crisis-74665 on April 11, 2014.

Bureau of Labor Statistics. (2011, December 21). *International comparisons of hourly compensation costs in manufacturing, 2010*. Accessed at www.bls.gov/news .release/pdf/ichcc.pdf on January 2, 2012.

Claxton, A. F., Pannells, T. C., & Rhoads, P. A. (2005). Developmental trends in the creativity of school-age children. *Creativity Research Journal, 17*(4), 327–335.

Common Core State Standards Initiative. (2009). *Why we are behind: What top nations teach their students but we don't*. Washington, DC: Author.

Common Core State Standards Initiative. (2010, June 2). *National Governors Association and State Education Chiefs launch common state academic standards*. Accessed at www.nga .org/cms/home/news-room/news-releases/page_2010/col2-content/main-content-list /title_national-governors-association-and-state-education-chiefs-launch-common -state-academic-standards.html on July 28, 2014.

Coyle, D. (2009). *The talent code: Greatness isn't born. It's grown. Here's how*. New York: Bantam Dell.

Department for Education. (2011, November 16). *Remit for review of the national curriculum in England*. Accessed at www.education.gov.uk/schools/teachingand learning/curriculum/b0073043/remit-for-review-of-the-national-curriculum -in-england on May 19, 2014.

Dewey, J. (1938). *Experience and education*. New York: Collier Books.

Education Commission of the States. (2008). *From competing to leading: An international benchmarking blueprint*. Denver, CO: Author.

Fine, S. M. (2011, October 26). School "urgency" and the loss of the human dimension. *Education News Colorado*. Accessed at www.ednewscolorado.org /2011/10/26/27253-school-urgency and-the-loss-of-the-human-dimension on April 5, 2012.

Florida, R. (2012). *The rise of the creative class: Revisited* (2nd ed.). New York: Basic Books.

Freeman, H., & Auerswald, P. (2012, March 11). Bliss is on the way: Black-collar workers and the case for economic optimism. *Good*. Accessed at http://m.good.is/post/bliss-is-on -the-way-the-case-for-economic-optimism on April 5, 2012.

Gardner, H. (1982). *Art, mind, and brain: A cognitive approach to creativity*. New York: Basic Books.

Goertz, M. E. (2010). National Standards: Lessons from the past, directions for the future. In B. Reys, R. Reys, & R. Rubenstein (Eds.), *Mathematics curriculum: Issues, trends, and future direction, 72nd Yearbook* (pp. 51–64). Washington, DC: National Council of Teachers of Mathematics.

Goldin, C., & Katz, L. F. (2008). *The race between education and technology*. Cambridge, MA: Belknap Press of Harvard University Press.

Harris, M., & Kinney, R. (Eds.). (2003). *Innovation and entrepreneurship in state and local government*. Lanham, MA: Lexington Books.

Hoffman, R., & Casnocha, B. (2012). *The start-up of you: Adapt to the future, invest in yourself, and transform your career.* New York: Crown Business.

Kane, T. (2010). *The importance of startups in job creation and job destruction.* Kansas City, MO: Kauffman Foundation.

Kelley, D. J., Bosma, N., & Amorós, J. E. (2010). *Global entrepreneurship monitor.* London: Global Entrepreneurship Research Association.

Korea Institute for Curriculum and Evaluation. (2011). *College scholastic ability test.* Accessed at www.kice.re.kr/en/contents.do?contentsNo=149&menuNo=405 on August 2, 2014.

Land, G., & Jarman, B. (1992). *Breakpoint and beyond: Mastering the future today.* Carlsbad, CA: Leadership 2000.

Loveless, T. (2006). *The 2012 Brown Center report on American education: How well are American students learning?* Washington, DC: Brookings Institute.

Manpower Group. (2012). *How to navigate the human age: Increasing demand for better skills assessment and match for better results.* Milwaukee, WI: Author.

Martin, R. L., & Osberg, S. (2007). Social entrepreneurship: The case for definition. *Stanford Social Innovation Review,* 29–39.

Mathis, W. J. (2010, July). *The "Common Core" standards initiative: An effective reform tool?* East Lansing, MI: The Great Lakes Center for Education Research & Practice.

McGaw, B. (2010, December 9). *A historic moment: The first Australian curriculum endorsed.* Accessed at www.acara.edu.au/default.asp on December 12, 2010.

Ministry of Education. (2011). *What will primary education like for my child?* [Video file]. Accessed at www.primaryeducation.sg on December 2, 2012.

National Governors Association, Council of Chief State School Officers, & Achieve. (2008). *Benchmarking for success: Ensuring U.S. students receive a world-class education.* Washington, DC: Authors.

National Governors Association Center for Best Practices & Council of Chief State School Officers. (2010a). *Common Core State Standards initiative.* Accessed at www.core-standards.org on November 11, 2011.

National Governors Association Center for Best Practices & Council of Chief State School Officers. (2010b). *Mission statement.* Accessed at www.corestandards.org on May 20, 2011.

National Research Council. (1999). *Global perspectives for local action: Using TIMSS to improve U.S. mathematics and science education.* Washington, DC: National Academy Press.

Oates, T. (2010). *Could do better: Using international comparisons to refine the National Curriculum in England.* Cambridge, UK: Cambridge Assessment.

Organisation for Economic Co-operation and Development. (2010). *Programme for International Student Assessment.* Accessed at www.pisa.oecd.org/pages /0,2987,en_32252351_ 32235731_1_1_1_1_1,00.html on January 10, 2010

Petroski, H. (1992). *To engineer is human: The role of failure in successful design.* New York: Vintage Books.

Pink, D. H. (2006). *A whole new mind: Why right-brainers will rule the future.* New York: Riverhead.

Posner, R. (2009). *Lives of passion, school of hope: How one public school ignites a lifelong love of learning.* Boulder, CO: Sentient.

Postman, N. (1996). *The end of education: Redefining the value of school.* New York: Knopf.

Rizvi, S., Donnelly, K., & Barber, M. (2012). *Oceans of innovation: The Atlantic, The Pacific, global leadership and the future of education.* London: Institute for Public Policy Research. Accessed at www.ippr.org/publications/oceans-of-innovation-the-atlantic-the-pacific-global-leadership-and-the-future-of-education on May 16, 2014.

Sahlberg, P. (2011). *Finnish lessons: What can the world learn from educational change in Finland?* New York: Teachers College Press.

Sahlberg, P. (2012, November 20). How GERM is infecting schools around the world [Web log post]. Accessed at www.washingtonpost.com/blogs/answer-sheet/post/how-germ-is-infecting-schools-around-the-world/2012/06/29/gJQAVELZAW_blog.html on April 3, 2014.

Schleicher, A. (2010). *The case for 21st-century learning.* Accessed at www.oecd.org/document/2/0,3746,en_2649_201185_46846594_1_1_1_1,00.html on January 2, 2011.

Schoof, U. (2006). *Stimulating youth entrepreneurship: Barriers and incentives to enterprise start-ups by young people* (Working paper no. 76). Geneva, Switzerland: International Labour Organization.

Singapore Examinations and Assessment Board. (2011). *Primary school leaving examination.* Accessed at www.seab.gov.sg/psle/psle.html on August 2, 2014.

Sjøberg, S. (2012). *PISA: Politics, fundamental problems and intriguing results.* Accessed at www.recherches-en-education.net/spip.php?article140 on April 2, 2014.

Spring, J. (2008). *Globalization of education: An introduction.* London: Routledge.

Strauss, S. (2006, June 26). *Education for entrepreneurs.* Accessed at www.usatoday.com/money/smallbusiness/columnist/strauss/2006-06-26-education_x.htm on April 8, 2012.

Swearingen, J. (2008, April 10). *Great intrapreneurs in business history.* Accessed at www.cbsnews.com/8301-505125_162-51196888/great-intrapreneurs-in-business-history January 14, 2012.

Tienken, C. H., & Zhao, Y. (2010). Common Core national curriculum standards: More questions . . . and answers. *AASA Journal of Scholarship and Practice, 6*(4), 3–14.

Toffler, A. (1980). *The third wave.* New York: Morrow.

United Nations. (2011, November 24). *The world youth report.* Accessed at www.unworldyouthreport.org/index.php?option=com_k2&view=itemlist&layout=category&task=category&id=1&Itemid=67 on April 8, 2012.

Wagner, T. (2008). *The global achievement gap: Why even our best schools don't teach the new survival skills our children need—And what we can do about it.* New York: Basic Books.

Wagner, T. (2012). *Creating innovators: The making of young people who will change the world.* New York: Scribner.

World Economic Forum. (2009). *Educating the next wave of entrepreneurs: Unlocking entrepreneurial capabilities to meet the global challenges of the 21st century.* (A report of the Global Education Initiative.) Geneva, Switzerland: Author.

World Economic Forum. (2011, June). *Unlocking entrepreneur capabilities to meet the global challenges of the 21st century: Final report on the entrepreneurship education work stream.* Geneva, Switzerland: Author.

World Intellectual Property Organization. (2007). *WIPO patent report: Statistics on worldwide patent activity (2007 edition).* Geneva, Switzerland: Author.

Zhao, Y. (2009). Comments on the Common Core standards initiative. *AASA Journal of Scholarship and Practice, 6*(3), 46–54.

Zhao, Y. (2012). *World class learners: Educating creative and entrepreneurial students.* Thousand Oaks, CA: Corwin Press.

Suzie Boss

Suzie Boss is a writer and consultant who focuses on the power of teaching and learning to empower others to improve their lives and transform their communities. A member of the National Faculty of the Buck Institute for Education, she is coauthor of *Reinventing Project-Based Learning* and *Thinking Through Project-Based Learning*. Suzie is the lead author of *PBL for 21st Century Success* and *Bringing Innovation to School* and is a regular contributor to *Edutopia*, the *P21 Blogazine*, and the *Stanford Social Innovation Review*. Her work has appeared in a wide range of other publications, including *Educational Leadership*, *Principal Leadership*, the *New York Times*, *Education Week*, and the *Huffington Post*.

To learn more about Suzie's work, visit www.edutopia.org/suzie-boss, or follow her on Twitter @suzieboss.

Chapter 4

Powering Up Learning
With PBL Plus Technology

Suzie Boss

A creative agency headquartered in the Atlanta area has no trouble recruiting professional talent to work on award-winning films, animations, and other projects for the entertainment industry. For a 2013 PBS documentary about a global health issue, the agency outsourced 3-D modeling work to a team of local high school students. Risky?

Not according to the agency's creative director. Before enlisting "the kids," as he calls them, Walter Biscardi Jr. toured the Center for Design and Technology (CDAT), a project-based learning program at Lanier High School in Sugar Hill, Georgia. He was impressed not only by the professional-grade tools that students were using to produce high-quality work but also by their passion for tackling challenging projects. Students' contributions to the documentary—ninety seconds of scientifically accurate 3-D animations that help explain the spread of a disease known as river blindness—"have simply blown away all expectations," says Biscardi (as cited in Reilly, 2013).

For CDAT teacher Mike Reilly, this is the kind of real-world learning experience that he strives to offer his students on a regular basis. By incorporating technology into project-based learning, he is able to address rigorous academic standards while also encouraging what he calls *digital creativity*. The ability to solve problems creatively—while using digital tools and collaborating with others—has value in today's economy and will be an asset for tomorrow's job creators and engaged citizens (Wagner, 2012; Zhao, 2012).

Project-Based Learning Plus Technology: A Digital-Age Combination

The combination of project-based learning plus technology (PBLT) brings a proven instructional strategy into the digital age. Across diverse contexts—from elementary through high school—PBLT provides teachers and students with a framework for in-depth inquiry and tools for authentic problem solving. This powerful combination also reflects how important work gets accomplished in the world outside the classroom.

Project-based learning has a long track record as a strategy to prepare students for college, careers, and citizenship. When students take on meaningful projects and share their work with authentic audiences, they find learning more relevant and school more engaging (Thomas, 2000). Along with producing academic gains, well-designed projects help students develop problem-solving skills (Finkelstein, Hanson, Huang, Hirschman, & Huang, 2010; Mergendoller, Maxwell, & Bellisimo, 2006). PBL also gives students expanded opportunities to practice and hone 21st century skills, such as collaboration, effective communication, and critical thinking (Ravitz, Hixson, English, & Mergendoller, 2012).

Infusing projects with technology has the potential to amplify and even transform the learning. Consider what happens when students have access to collaborative tools while engaged in a project: using Skype, they can consult with remote content experts as part of their research. They can team up with peers—from their own school or from halfway around the world—on a wiki to brainstorm possible solutions and consider diverse perspectives. Using Google Docs, they can get real-time feedback to improve their work at the formative stage. When they're ready to share their final products, they can use publishing tools to interact with everyone from local community members to global stakeholders.

Access to technology is a must for this kind of experience, but access alone is no guarantee of deeper learning. What matters is how the tools are used in PBLT to help students accomplish important learning goals.

Learning by Doing and Then Some

Learning by doing is hardly a new idea. A century ago, John Dewey and other progressive thinkers were advocating for experiential education to replace traditional schooling that kept students in a passive role. In the 1950s, medical schools began pioneering a teaching approach intended to transform book-smart students into competent clinicians. Rather than being drilled on medical facts without context, medical students were now challenged to apply their understanding to arrive at a diagnosis and treatment plan for someone role-playing a patient. This shift from knowledge acquisition to problem solving has taken hold in many other disciplines, from engineering to business to K–12 education.

Across content areas and levels, PBL starts with an open-ended question that has many potentially correct answers. (For example: How can we keep pollutants out of the creek at our local park? How might we improve the lunch experience in our school cafeteria? How should we advise the United Nations to meet the U.N. Millennium Development Goals?) Students can't google their way to solutions. Rather, they must engage in extended inquiry to arrive at their own understanding and develop defensible arguments for their positions. Projects typically conclude with student teams applying what they have learned to produce something original, such as a product, demonstration, or exhibition that they share with an authentic audience. As John Mergendoller (2012), executive director of the Buck Institute for Education, writes: "In Project Based Learning, in order for students to *learn something*, they must *do something*."

When done well, PBL delivers a range of benefits for diverse learners. Yet it's not without challenges. Most teachers have never been students themselves in a project-based setting. That means educators may need extensive professional development to get comfortable teaching in a more student-centered way (Hmelo-Silver, Ravit, & Chinn, 2007).

Incorporating technology—adding the "T" in PBLT—introduces another layer of complexity. Teachers who have limited experience using technology in the classroom may need support to effectively integrate digital tools into projects.

What's Essential in PBLT?

When PBLT works as intended, students meet important learning goals and also develop 21st century skills, such as collaboration and critical thinking. They incorporate technology not as an afterthought to a project, but because specific digital tools are critical to their inquiry experience. To help students stay on track and accomplish meaningful results, teachers need to focus on what's essential for project success.

The Buck Institute for Education (BIE), a nonprofit organization that focuses on project-based learning as a strategy for school reform, has been a driver of PBL expansion, both in the United States and internationally. Through research, professional development, and consultations with thousands of teachers, schools, and districts, BIE has synthesized best practices for PBL into a set of eight essential elements (see figure 4.1).

When teachers incorporate these eight elements across the arc of projects, they set the stage for high-quality PBL experiences in which projects are the "main course" of learning, not the dessert (Mergendoller & Larmer, 2010). Other researchers have reached similar conclusions about the need for careful attention to project design, student collaboration, and comprehensive assessments that support student success in PBL (Darling-Hammond et al., 2008; Vega, 2012).

Technology is not explicitly listed as one of the essential ingredients for project success, although opportunities to integrate technology can be found at all stages of the learning experience. For example, students might use online libraries or collections of primary source documents for in-depth inquiry, digital publishing tools to share work with audiences, and project-management tools to keep team efforts organized.

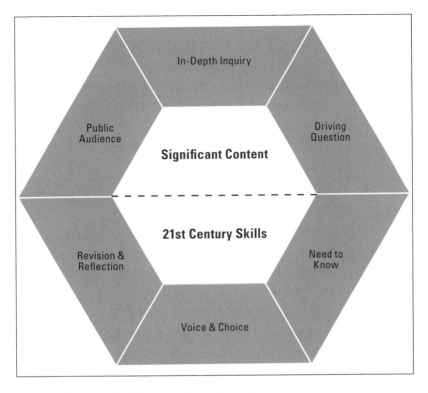

In-Depth Inquiry

Public
Audience

Significant Content

Driving
Question

21st Century Skills

Revision &
Reflection

Need to
Know

Voice & Choice

Figure 4.1: Eight essential elements of project-based learning.

In PBLT, teachers and students deliberately leverage these opportunities, using digital tools to accomplish results that might not be achievable otherwise. During the 2012 U.S. election season, for instance, students from several states used YouTube and video-conferencing to debate issues during a virtual political convention. Technology enabled students to produce and publish original videos about the issues they had researched, interact with peers in diverse locations, and find out (via polling) if their arguments had swayed others' opinions.

For teachers who are new to PBLT, it helps to see technology-infused learning in action. Pioneering school models such as High Tech High, Expeditionary Learning, and New Tech Network open their doors to visitors and share project resources. Similarly, websites such as Edutopia (www.edutopia.org) provide video case studies illustrating PBLT in diverse contexts—charters, independent schools, and traditional public schools spanning the K–12 range.

Despite an explosion of interest in the project approach, only an estimated 1 percent of schools in the United States use PBL as their central approach to instruction (Merrow, 2013). Increasingly, however, individual teachers, schools, and entire districts are incorporating project-based instruction into at least part of the school year. In the Vail (Arizona) School District, teachers are collaborating to design grade-level projects that address Common Core State Standards and incorporate performance assessments. West Virginia has encouraged PBL through a statewide professional development initiative and created an online library of project plans that integrate technology. To encourage projects that have an authentic community focus, Metropolitan Nashville (Tennessee) Public Schools recruit local nonprofits, government agencies, and other organizations to serve as PBL partners for school projects.

Widespread adoption of the Common Core State Standards is adding more urgency to the PBLT movement. The new standards call for students to think critically, solve problems, work collaboratively, use technology to communicate, and be able to apply what they learn. These are natural outcomes of well-designed projects. Michigan teachers Pauline Roberts and Rick Joseph, for example, see their students meeting rigorous, interdisciplinary learning goals through projects that develop what they call *sciracy*, or scientific literacy. In a project that won international honors in the Microsoft Partners in Learning Global Forum in 2012, their fifth- and sixth-graders from Birmingham Covington School conducted an educational campaign to encourage more sustainable business practices among local merchants. They also ranked business according to a "green" scale and published their evidence-based analysis of sustainability practices online.

For PBL practitioners, the higher expectations of the Common Core are nothing new; they align with necessary elements of high-quality project work, including performance-based assessment. Researchers have also long understood the value of learning experiences that call on students to transfer knowledge to new situations

(Bransford, Brown, & Cocking, 2000). Discussions of deeper learning that have been underway since the early 2000s build on this foundation, bringing into sharper focus the strategies that lead to application of knowledge, such as engaging students in challenging tasks. As James Pellegrino and Margaret Hilton (2012) note, "While other types of learning may allow an individual to recall facts, concepts, or procedures, deeper learning allows the individual to transfer what was learned to solve new problems" (p. 6).

Technology as a Turbo-Boost for Learning

The integration of technology sets PBLT apart from experiential learning initiatives of previous eras. With access to digital tools, students can overcome limitations of geography and take inquiry into the wider world. They can also accomplish professional-quality results, using the same tools that experts use to apply the strategies associated with specific disciplines.

Indeed, researchers note that this convergence of interest in PBL use and new technologies has led to many interventions that intentionally incorporate technology as a key component of PBL use (Ravitz & Blazevski, 2010). Some digital tools, such as the following, are uniquely able to open new windows onto student thinking, thus setting the stage for more productive classroom conversations.

- ChronoZoom (www.chronozoom.com), an interactive timeline tool, enables students to zoom in and out of different eras as they explore and discuss the visual history of the cosmos.

- Tuva Labs (https://tuvalabs.com) is a platform that curates open data sets so that students can analyze, visualize, and interpret statistical information about issues relevant to their communities and interests.

- Modeling software like SketchUp (www.sketchup.com) facilitates the process of 3-D drafting and refining. It also supports the rapid prototyping typical of project work.

- QuadBlogging (www.quadblogging.com) is a simple platform for connecting four classrooms of writers—from anywhere in the world—to comment on each other's blogs, providing students with an authentic audience and real-world feedback.

Many of these online tools allow for instant global connections, redefining the meaning of a learning community (Boss & Krauss, 2014). Of course, simply adding computers, tablets, or other digital devices to classrooms is no guarantee that high-quality PBLT will happen. In many schools, technology is still used primarily for test prep or for an online version of traditional instruction. Harnessing the power of technology to reach deeper learning goals requires a wholesale shift in what students and teachers do with these tools. Tom Vander Ark and Carri Schneider (2013) write that "technology-enabled instruction must be the linchpin of this evolution, and not just casually layered on top of an outdated, industrial-era system" (p. 6).

When fully integrated into projects, technology becomes a powerful tool for accessing, analyzing, and organizing information; connecting learners with peers and experts; personalizing learning; creating new content; and sharing results with authentic audiences. Digital tools, made accessible in a student-centered learning context, can also lead to what researchers have defined as "connected learning" (Ito et al., 2013). Connected learning "draws on the power of today's technology to fuse young people's interests, friendships, and academic achievement through experiences laced with hands-on production, shared purpose, and open networks" (Digital Media and Learning Research Hub, 2012).

Such results can happen from a young age. In a project that connected students with peers around the world, fourth graders in Baltimore, Maryland, took up the issue of girls' right to education. The project was sparked by news reports about Malala Yousafzai, a teenager from Pakistan who was attacked by the Taliban because of her outspoken support for girls' education.

Teacher Heidi Hutchison, in a reflective post about the evolution of the #MalalaProject, cited a number of digital tools that were integrated into the learning experience (Hutchison, 2013). In each instance, specific technologies were used because they were essential for students to extend their learning: a wiki to organize the project and share content from participating classes in multiple countries, the Internet for research and critical analysis of cultural barriers to girls' education, and digital media to produce advocacy pieces (such as brochures or public service announcements) that were shared at public events. Hutchison herself used Twitter to think through the project with colleagues from her personal learning network as well as a blog to reflect publicly on the outcomes of the project.

In an environment that fosters deeper learning, technology needs to be "like oxygen—ubiquitous, necessary, and invisible" (Lehmann, 2010). That's the oft-repeated mantra of Chris Lehmann, founding principal of the Science Leadership Academy (SLA) in Philadelphia. At SLA, a highly regarded public high school that teaches entirely through PBL, all students have laptops plus access to the social media tools that many other schools routinely block. Ninth graders use these tools for a year-long project called You and the World. Students conduct in-depth research about an issue of personal interest, exploring questions such as, "How can I be a global citizen?" They use blogs and social media to share their passions with others, leveraging their digital fluency to take civic action or lead advocacy efforts to support specific causes.

Technology to Scaffold Instruction

The student-centered learning that is a hallmark of PBLT does not happen without careful teacher planning and facilitation. Across the arc of projects, digital tools can help teachers scaffold instruction, gather formative feedback, and make adjustments to address the needs of diverse learners.

Consider these opportunities to integrate digital tools to support instruction:

- At the project planning stage, online surveys can help identify student interests that may connect with content standards.

- At the launch of projects, compelling videos or immersive online experiences can engage student interest.

- Primary sources and rich data sets help students access, evaluate, and discuss online information throughout the project to answer their own research questions.

- Student blogs, podcasts, and video interviews can encourage reflection throughout a project and provide insights into understanding and opportunities to adjust instructional plans as needed.

- Collaborative tools allow students to cocreate content with team members, connect with content experts, manage the flow of project work, and receive formative feedback throughout the learning process.

- Digital tools allow for rapid prototyping, leading to iterative cycles of feedback, testing, and product improvement.

- Online publishing tools enable students to document and present their work in a compelling way of their choosing, sharing results with authentic audiences.

The instructional strategies essential to PBLT—questioning, formative assessment, and engaging learners in challenging tasks—help put students on the path to deeper learning (Pellegrino & Hilton, 2012). Thoughtful technology use can support all these strategies. Having a backchannel for conversations, via Twitter or TodaysMeet (https://todaysmeet.com), provides a forum for quieter students to pose questions or respond to whole-class discussions. Screenshots of student work in progress allow for quick formative assessments and also create artifacts for deeper discussions. Photo diaries and blogs enable students to document their work over time, encouraging thoughtful reflection when they look back at the completion of a project.

The integration of PBL with technology also helps students take on the role of experts—such as journalists, historians, or scientists—and apply the lenses of these authentic disciplines (Krauss & Boss, 2013). Even projects that require scaffolding to make the work "right sized" for learners can still put students into authentic roles. Middle school students preparing to conduct oral history interviews, for example, might benefit from having teachers model questions that prompt them to think like historians.

Access to technology means students use the same tools that the pros use—whether for gathering and analyzing scientific data, producing a documentary, or making an infographic to represent information visually. Students at the Science Leadership Academy, for example, worked alongside scientists from the Franklin Institute in Philadelphia to locate and photograph anomalies on the surface of the sun; they then used photo-editing software to create a composite picture from hundreds of individual shots. When it was time to present their research about solar flares at a scientific conference, co-presenters included the planetarium director and a high school student (Schachter, 2013).

Trends to Watch for in PBLT

Digital tools that offer promise in the context of PBL are in almost constant flux. As new tools emerge in beta versions and yesterday's favorites fall by the wayside, teachers may find it challenging to settle on an ideal tech toolkit for the PBL classroom. Rather than gravitating to the latest shiny object, teachers are wise to focus first on the essential learning goals they seek to accomplish in a project and then integrate digital tools that support those goals (Boss & Krauss, 2007).

Four trends are worth watching because of their potential for deeper learning in PBLT: (1) PBLT anywhere, anytime; (2) personalization of PBLT; (3) blended and online learning; and (4) maker spaces, rapid prototyping, and PBL.

PBLT Anywhere, Anytime

The latest *Horizon Report*, an annual forecast of emerging technologies and their effects on education globally, predicts that cloud computing and mobile learning will be key drivers of K–12 education change. Indeed, the report notes that both trends have already gained traction; earlier barriers to adoption are being quickly overcome (Johnson et al., 2013). In the PBLT context, both trends have potential to help students go deeper with collaboration, inquiry, and creativity.

The ability to store and access information in the cloud rather than on a single computer expands opportunities for collaboration. With access to cloud-based platforms such as Google Apps for Education and Microsoft Office 365, students can team up on projects with classmates or remote collaborators from anywhere in the world.

Cloud-based computing also enables formative assessment throughout a project. The iterative nature of project work means that a product will likely go through several cycles of review and revision en route to a final version. With 24-7 access to project materials, team members are able to work simultaneously (rather than waiting for a handoff from a peer). They also benefit from faster feedback. For example, a teacher who has her students use Google Docs for journalism projects says being able to see their work at the early draft stage allows her to offer more timely feedback, which leads to faster revisions and more polished work when it's time to publish. The teacher is not the only one who offers critiques—as part of their project work, peers are expected to give each other critical feedback. The teacher also can look at document history to see students' comments and revisions.

Mobile devices, including mobile phones and tablets, also enable users to gather data and create content, anywhere, anytime, at a fraction of the cost of yesterday's computers. Increasingly, schools are adopting bring-your-own-device (BYOD) policies that allow students to use their own technology tools at school. Essentially, mobile devices put tools for inquiry and creativity into students' hands, equipping them to be more self-directed learners. In PBLT, students often need to leave the physical setting of school to conduct real-world research, and mobile devices allow them to take their digital toolkit with them. On a science project about water quality, for example, students might use mobile devices to analyze test samples in the field, take photos of stream conditions, and add precise GPS location information. This makes their learning environment more like the world beyond the classroom, where access to information and digital tools is ubiquitous.

To appreciate how online collaboration can be the springboard for global learning, consider the Flat Classroom Project. Cofounded by educators Vicki Davis and Julie Lindsay in 2006, their project model used Web 2.0 tools to connect students and teachers from schools around the world. Middle and high school students from different cultures studied and discussed topics raised in Thomas Friedman's (2005) bestseller, *The World Is Flat*. These geographically dispersed teams then collaborated to create digital stories and other multimedia products that represented what they learned.

A similar project was underway in 2012 when Superstorm Sandy hit the East Coast, knocking out power to some households for weeks. Students from the affected region used their mobile phones to update their project partners. Davis says,

> In the middle of the storm, these kids were worried about their partners' depending on them. When a kid cares enough to get on a smart phone and leave a message for a partner halfway around the world, then you have fundamentally transformed that student. (as cited in Boss & Krauss, 2014)

Online content management systems are a related trend with specific benefits for PBLT. For instance, the New Tech Network, which includes more than 120 schools using PBLT as a core instructional strategy, has built its own proprietary learning management system, called Echo. The system gives students, teachers, and parents a real-time window into PBLT (including ongoing project work, upcoming assignments, and grades). It's a walled garden, accessible only to those within the network. Other platforms, such as fee-based Project Foundry (www.projectfoundry.org) and Edmodo (www.edmodo.com), which is a free social network for educators, incorporate content management and assessment tools that help teachers and students organize the moving parts of PBLT and keep learning on track.

Personalization of PBLT

Personalizing education is a goal that cuts across camps, according to Justin Reich, a fellow at Harvard's Berkman Center for Internet and Society. Reich (2012) states,

> Whether you are a market-based reformer, an open education advocate, or a 21st-century Dewey partisan, everyone agrees

that learning should be personalized: learning experiences should be tailored to each individual student. We also agree that personalization is made feasible by new technologies.

Heightened student engagement has long been identified as a key benefit of project-based learning (Thomas, 2000). Not surprisingly, engagement increases when projects have personal significance for students. Driving questions that frame the inquiry experience in PBLT are intentionally open ended, so that students can direct their own learning and decide how they will demonstrate their understanding. BIE calls this essential element "student voice and choice."

What do student voice and choice look like in action? Consider a project about heroism that begins with students reading literature or analyzing films that introduce the hero's journey theme. From there, the teacher has students form teams based on the hero they choose to celebrate—real or fictional, contemporary or historic, well known or unsung. Similarly, students are offered a wide range of options for how to honor their selected heroes, such as video documentary, museum-style exhibit, or community presentation. At this stage in the project, students are likely to have different needs for instructional support. To personalize the learning experience, the teacher provides a range of resources, such as curated content for deeper research, mini-lessons about nonfiction narrative writing, or YouTube videos about using specific technology applications. Based on formative assessment and the questions students are asking, the teacher matches students with instructional supports that meet their immediate needs.

At CDAT, the PBL program described at the start of this chapter, teacher Mike Reilly uses a version of the flipped classroom approach to personalize instruction for his digital media students. The flipped classroom idea is deceptively simple: instead of delivering lectures in class, a teacher records them, using video or screen-capture software, then posts lessons online for students to watch as homework (Bergmann & Sams, 2012). Reilly's approach offers a good illustration of how the flipped classroom concept can mesh with PBLT. Many projects in his program involve using the same software or editing equipment that the pros use. Rather than teaching the whole class about software that only one or two students may be using; however, Reilly directs individual students to online tutorials to learn new applications. He checks in informally to assess their proficiency. For some students, the just-in-time tutorials provide all they need to get going. Others need more instruction from Reilly or perhaps help from peers who are already proficient with a particular tool or software. By differentiating instruction and inviting his students to share their expertise, Reilly helps all learners make progress at the speed that makes sense to them.

Content from other sources can be added to the flipped classroom approach, as well, such as Khan Academy lectures or, in Reilly's case, technical tutorials. In the PBLT classroom, such content is not necessarily assigned as homework; it's available "just in time"—whenever students need it to deepen or expand their inquiry.

Blended and Online Learning

Blended and online learning is another trend on the fast track to influence not only PBLT but education globally, according to the *Horizon Report* (Johnson et al., 2013). Early efforts are underway to combine project-based learning with online learning. Even for teachers who use projects often, bringing this approach to virtual spaces raises new challenges along with the opportunities.

For the New Tech Network, the initial motivation to consider online learning was to expand course offerings beyond what students might find on their own campuses, without jettisoning the PBLT approach used in face-to-face courses across the network. Lydia Dobyns, CEO of New Tech Network, explains, "It seemed that students were taking online courses [from other providers] more for expedience than for the learning experience. We didn't think students were being served as well when it came to learning to learn" (L. Dobyns, personal communication, March 5, 2013).

Convinced that online or blended learning "is the way of the future," Dobyns said, New Tech moved ahead with its first two pilot courses in 2012–2013. The first courses attracted students from across the United States, and online offerings are expected to expand in the future.

What's the potential for deeper learning with PBL online? Consider the design of an online statistics class. In a project called "The 'Mean' Truth About Unemployment," students used the concepts of mean, median, and mode to analyze monthly unemployment rates in their respective regions and then worked together (virtually) to produce a 20/20-style news segment in which they presented their analysis to a public audience (New Tech Network, 2013). The project launched with a video introduction from a real broadcast journalist, challenging students to produce video content to document their own investigations of local unemployment trends.

Having students collaborate on a project like this from different parts of the country set the stage for critical thinking as they compared and contrasted local information and observations. "What's more," Dobyns said, "students are building relationships with people from different backgrounds, people they would not have had opportunities to meet otherwise. The student feedback has been phenomenal. They're looking honestly at how much they have had to grow to learn this way" (L. Dobyns, personal communication, March 5, 2013).

Similarly, students who enroll in an advanced placement U.S. government class through the Online School for Girls, a virtual institution created by a consortium of independent schools, are navigating their first online PBL experience. In an interview, social studies teacher Mike Gwaltney explained the challenges and opportunities of combining online learning with the project approach (M. Gwaltney, personal communication, October 19, 2013):

- A significant challenge with online PBL seems to be that the nature of online education allows learners the ability (right?) to do work on their own pace and at the times that they prefer. Since PBL is naturally (or at least in my class, intentionally) collaborative, that presents a challenge for students: they have to at least think about their online work as being at the same pace and time as their project partners.

- To facilitate this, and in part to create a willingness to collaborate, I spend a good amount of time putting students in situations where they have to share back-and-forth and collaborate in smaller ways. Examples are online discussions and small collaborative presentations on some piece of content. That helps all of them build rapport and a desire to work together.

- From there, students have to get good at using digital tools. Because my students are in every American time zone, digital collaborating requires they are good with Google Docs, Hangouts, VoiceThread, as well as email. Students have to determine for themselves how to use all these tools to bridge the time and space challenges. We've done quite a bit with PBL and VoiceThread, resulting in online presentations for our classes and for public use. As well, students have made short videos by sharing clips in Google Drive that they have recorded individually, then one student does some editing, and they share the files back around for further editing before a final version is made.

Within this digital context, Gwaltney also thinks hard about the relationship side of the learning experience. He describes what it means to get to know students online:

Do I think I get to know the students well? I get to know them *differently.* With my face-to-face students, I learn plenty about them through non-verbal communication, and by just being around them. With the online students, I only ever see their intentional participation in class activities. But since their participation is so much more robust—they have to be constantly using their "voice" in class for daily discussions—I learn more about what they think than in the traditional brick-and-mortar classes. (M. Gwaltney, personal communication, October 19, 2013)

One student post on the class blog underscores the importance of feedback—in this case, delivered virtually—to promote deeper learning in PBLT:

The discussion activities seemed to me less like assignments that we had to do, but rather a platform for each of us to raise our opinions and view what others hold as their thoughts on

an issue. Whenever I saw people commenting on my post, no
matter if the comment is agreeing or disagreeing with my opinion, I always found it beneficial to me. (chanchan0207, 2013)

Clearly, this new way of learning requires both students and teachers to hone their communication, collaboration, and problem-solving
skills.

Maker Spaces, Rapid Prototyping, and PBL

Maker spaces are reinvented workshops that are equipped with
both old-school construction tools and digital fabrication tools, such
as 3-D printers, useful for producing prototypes or scale models. In
school settings, maker spaces are gaining popularity, in part because
they foster the creative thinking and innovation strategies that go
hand in hand with PBLT.

The maker movement began outside of education, with people
of all ages using a range of tools (from jigsaws and soldering irons
to laser cutters and 3-D printers) to unleash grassroots creativity
and collaborative problem solving. The make-to-learn idea is rapidly
making its way into K–12 settings as a strategy to build students' creative confidence, encourage collaboration, and spark interest in the
science, technology, engineering, and mathematics (STEM) fields.
In 2012, the first ten pilot sites of an anticipated one thousand high
school maker spaces opened in California. Funding is coming from
the Defense Advanced Research Projects Agency.

Recognition of the potential of making to learn goes far beyond
STEM fields. Make-to-learn environments include not only workshops, but also libraries and community recording studios that foster
digital creativity.

The make-to-learn movement also has implications for the
teaching of writing. As Elyse Eidman-Aadahl of the National
Writing Project explains (Boss, 2013):

Every writer is trying to make something—some new knowledge with language, some new framing or understanding.
We write to inquire about something we don't fully know at
the beginning, and we use making (with text and sometimes

images) as a way to push that inquiry forward. Then we share it with the world . . . Now we have colleagues saying this is what engineering is, this is what the arts are, this is what civic engagement and the design of communities can be. We're seeing a common belief about the kind of learning environments where people do serious and creative work.

Sylvia Martinez and Gary Stager (2013), coauthors of *Invent to Learn*, see maker spaces as ideal settings for student-driven learning in the constructivist tradition: "This 'maker movement' overlaps with the natural inclinations of children and the power of learning by doing. The active learner is at the center of the learning process, amplifying the best traditions of progressive education" (Kindle loc. 172 of 5629). Having a dedicated workspace in a school that puts tools and materials into students' hands, they note, offers a strategy to "reinvigorate project-based learning" (Kindle loc. 191 of 5629).

To imagine the benefits of maker spaces, picture a class of ninth graders in an interdisciplinary class that combines environmental science and geography. These students tackled an engineering question that could have far-reaching benefits: How can we design the most efficient, solar-powered mango dehydrator for Haiti? Their question was not theoretical. They were developing a design that would actually be tested in Haiti. It's a poor country where new sources of revenue from agriculture, such as producing dried mangoes, could help lift farming families out of poverty.

Science teacher Leah Penniman designs such real-world projects at Tech Valley High School in Rensselaer, New York, to give her students opportunities to apply their understanding of engineering and environmental science. A previous class of ninth graders developed a comprehensive reforestation plan for an environmentally distressed region of Haiti, and a team of Tech Valley students traveled to the country to work alongside Haitians to implement the plan.

A variety of supports are in place to set the stage for such ambitious projects, including schoolwide use of PBLT for instruction and a culture that encourages teacher collaboration. For instance, Penniman has developed working relationships with professional engineers who consult at the project design stage and also give students critical feedback at key times throughout the project.

The school is one of a growing number that are introducing design workshops or maker spaces to complement PBLT. Students have access to high- and low-tech tools and materials that allow for rapid prototyping and collaborative problem solving. Along with laptops, they have a workspace adjacent to the science classroom equipped with tools and materials for building prototypes. Students use the workspace to make their thinking visible, improving solutions through iterative cycles of rapid prototyping, testing, feedback, and revision. "Until students get their hands on materials, sometimes they don't understand how to design," Penniman observes in an interview (L. Penniman, personal communication, September 5, 2012).

During a project, students will typically cycle through multiple learning experiences: workshop-style lessons or mini-lectures to explain concepts, online research and analysis with project teams, sketching and online modeling, hands-on exploration of materials, and building, testing, and improving prototypes. "It's not necessarily linear," Penniman said. Student teams may cycle through the workshop several times as they test and fine-tune prototype designs. Teams collaborate on end-of-project presentations to formally present their findings.

Technology to Support PBL Teachers

The shift from traditional teaching to project-based learning is challenging and requires teachers, students, and administrators to develop new ways of working together. In shifting to PBL, teachers must reconsider how they design curriculum, how they scaffold instruction, and how they assess learning outcomes. Through project experiences, students are expected to acquire deep understanding of content while also applying 21st century skills that may be new to them. Incorporating technology into this mix can add more confusion, especially if there is no coherent vision of why the shift to a new pedagogy, with new tools, is worth all the effort (Park & Ertmer, 2008). Administrators need to encourage this shared vision through their leadership and also remove systemic barriers—such as poor technology access or inadequate teacher planning time—that can interfere with PBLT.

Yet technology can also provide a lifeline for teachers who might otherwise be struggling alone with the shift to PBL. Teachers who make progress with PBL use technology to build their understanding of this instructional approach (Ravitz & Blazevski, 2010). They access online resources such as project libraries to help with project design. They also use technology tools to connect with peers for feedback, mirroring in their professional networks the collaboration that they want to see students practicing during projects (Ravitz & Blazevski, 2010).

During project implementation, PBLT teachers may use digital tools to scaffold instruction, encourage collaboration, provide students with feedback, and manage the flow of project work. Indeed, the more teachers use online features, the better prepared they feel to handle project challenges. As Jason Ravitz and Juliane Blazevski (2010) note, "online tools may provide an important way for teachers and schools to help address the challenges of PBL use" (p. 9).

Schools doing PBLT wall to wall, such as those that are part of the Deeper Learning Network, allow generous time for collaborative professional development as part of their models. For teachers who do not have that sustained support on site, online communities of practice may help fill at least some of the gaps. Connected educator activities, such as #PBLChat on Twitter or Google Hangouts to discuss PBL best practices, make use of social media tools to support ongoing professional learning and foster peer collaboration.

Implications for Practice

A number of factors are aligning to encourage the wider acceptance of PBLT. Digital tools are becoming more affordable, powerful, and accessible. Educators are gaining appreciation for project-based learning as an effective, engaging instructional strategy. Expectations for what learners need to know and be able to do are becoming increasingly rigorous. Together, these factors have four implications for practice:

1. Consider technology integration and PBL goals together as part of an overall vision of deeper learning through PBLT.

2. Focus on deeper learning goals first; then consider appropriate technology tools to help meet them.

3. Be authentic—as students take on the roles of professionals, have them use the tools of the discipline (scaffolding the experiences as needed to be right-sized to fit the learning needs and abilities of students).

4. Leverage technology to support teachers as they build confidence and competence with PBLT, and provide professional development that champions their continued learning and collaboration with peers.

If PBLT continues its rapid expansion, we may finally realize the vision of more authentic, student-centered learning that has been on the horizon for decades. Twenty years ago, researchers identified a then-promising school reform model calling for

> lengthy multidisciplinary projects, cooperative learning groups, flexible scheduling, and authentic assessments. In such a setting, technology is a valuable tool. It has the power to support students and teachers in obtaining, organizing, manipulating, and displaying information. These uses of technology will, we believe, become an integral feature of schooling. (Means & Olson, 1994)

That model was rare in the 1990s. It's still far from the norm for most U.S. students. But when the right pieces are in place, we see benefits for both students and teachers. We need to watch, learn from, and celebrate pioneers who are leading the way with deeper learning through PBLT. Their results show what is possible when technology is ubiquitous and pedagogy is student centered.

References and Resources

Bergmann, J., & Sams, A. (2012). *Flip your classroom: Reach every student in every class every day.* Eugene, OR: International Society for Technology in Education.

Boss, S. (2013, May 15). Gearing up for a summer of making, connecting and learning by doing [Web log post]. Accessed at http://learning.blogs.nytimes.com/2013/05/15 /guest-lesson-gearing-up-for-a-summer-of-making-connect ing-and-learning-by -doing/?_r=0 on May 20, 2014.

Boss, S., & Krauss, J. (2007). *Reinventing project-based learning: Your field guide to real-world projects in the digital age.* Eugene, OR: International Society for Technology in Education.

Boss, S., & Krauss, J. (2014). *Reinventing project-based learning: Your field guide to real-world projects in the digital age* (2nd ed.). Eugene, OR: International Society for Technology in Education.

Bransford, J. D., Brown, A. L., & Cocking, R. R. (2000). *How people learn: Brain, mind, experience, and school.* Washington, DC: National Academy Press.

chanchan0207. (2013, October 7). Together or not together? That is a question [Web log post]. Accessed at http://osgapusgov.wordpress.com/2013/10/07/together-or-not-together-that-is-a-question/ on May 20, 2014.

Darling-Hammond, L., Barron, B., Pearson, P. D., Schoenfeld, A. H., Stage, E. K., Zimmerman, T. D., et al. (2008). *Powerful learning: What we know about teaching for understanding.* San Francisco: Jossey-Bass.

Digital Media and Learning Research Hub. (2012). *The essence of connected learning.* Accessed at http://dmlcentral.net/resources/5000 on October 19, 2013.

Finkelstein, N., Hanson, T., Huang, C.-W., Hirschman, B., & Huang, M. (2010). *Effects of problem based economics on high school instruction* (NCEE 2010–4002). Washington, DC: National Center for Education Evaluation and Regional Assistance, Institute of Education Sciences, U.S. Department of Education.

Friedman, T. L. (2005). *The world is flat: A brief history of the twenty-first century.* New York: Picador.

Hmelo-Silver, C., Ravit, D., & Chinn, C. (2007). Scaffolding achievement in problem-based and inquiry learning: A response to Kirshner, Sweller, and Clark (2006). *Educational Psychologist, 42*(2), 99–107.

Hutchison, H. (2013, April 1). Project based learning . . . I think we really did it! [Web log post]. Accessed at http://communicateconnectsupport.com/2013 /04/01/project-based-learning-i-think-we-really-did-it/ on March 27, 2014.

Ito, M., Gutiérrez, K., Livingstone, S., Penuel, B., Rhodes, J., Salen, K., et al. (2013). *Connected learning: An agenda for research and design.* Irvine, CA: Digital Media and Learning Research Hub.

Johnson, L., Becker, S. A., Cummins, M., Estrada, V., Freeman, A., & Ludgate, H. (2013). *NMC Horizon report: 2013 K–12 edition.* Austin, TX: The New Media Consortium.

Krauss, J., & Boss, S. (2013). *Thinking through project-based learning: Taking inquiry deeper.* Thousand Oaks, CA: Corwin.

Lehmann, C. (2010). *TEDxNYED* [Video file]. Accessed at www.youtube.com/watch?v=6FEMCyHYTyQ on May 20, 2014.

Martinez, S., & Stager, G. (2013). *Invent to learn: Making, tinkering, and engineering the classroom.* Torrance, CA: Constructing Modern Knowledge Press.

Means, B., & Olson, K. (1994, April). The link between technology and authentic learning. *Educational Leadership, 51*(7), 15–18. Accessed at www.ascd.org/publications/educational-leadership/apr94/vol51/num07/The-Link-Between -Technology-and-Authentic-Learning.aspx on October 17, 2013.

Mergendoller, J. (2012). Teaching critical thinking skills through project based learning [Web log post]. Accessed at www.p21.org/news-events/p21blog/1097 -teaching-critical-thinking-skills-through-project-based-learning on December 29, 2013.

Mergendoller, J. (2013, April 11). Does project based learning teach critical thinking? [Web log post]. Accessed at http://biepbl.blogspot.com/2013/04/does -project-based-learning-teach-critical-thinking.html?spref=tw on October 17, 2013.

Mergendoller, J., & Larmer, J. (2010). Seven essentials for project-based learning. *Educational Leadership, 68*(1), 34–37.

Mergendoller, J. R., Maxwell, N. L., & Bellisimo, Y. (2006). The effectiveness of problem-based instruction: A comparative study of instructional methods and student characteristics. *Interdisciplinary Journal of Problem-Based Learning, 1*(2), 49–69.

Merrow, J. (2013, April 3). *School district uses project based learning over testing* [Video file]. Accessed at http://video.pbs.org/video/2364990349/ on March 27, 2013.

New Tech Network. (2013). Digital learning @ New Tech Network: A glimpse into a project [Web log post]. Accessed at www.newtechnetwork.org/about/video /digital-learning-new-tech-network-glimpse-project on December 29, 2013.

Park, S. H., & Ertmer, P. A. (2008). Impact of problem-based learning (PBL) on teachers' beliefs regarding technology use. *Journal of Research on Technology in Education, 40*(2), 247–267.

Pellegrino, J. W., & Hilton, M. L. (Eds.). (2012). *Education for life and work: Developing transferable knowledge and skills in the 21st century.* Washington, DC: The National Academies Press.

Ravitz, J., & Blazevski, J. (2010, October 28). *Assessing the impact of online technologies on PBL use in US high schools.* Paper presented at Annual Meetings of the Association for Educational Communications and Technology, Anaheim, CA. Accessed at www.bie. org/research/study/online_supports_for_pbl_use on October 17, 2013.

Ravitz, J., Hixson, N., English, M., & Mergendoller, J. (2012, April 16). *Using project based learning to teach 21st century skills: Findings from a statewide initiative.* Paper presented at Annual Meetings of the American Educational Research Association, Vancouver, BC. Accessed at www.bie.org/research/study/PBL_21CS_WV on October 17, 2013.

Reich, J. (2012, June 25). Battling over the meaning of personalization [Web log post]. Accessed at http://blogs.edweek.org/edweek/edtechresearcher/2012/06 /battling_over_the_meaning_of_personalization.html on October 17, 2013.

Reilly, M. (2013). Creating animation for PBS—in high school [Web log post]. Accessed at http://library.creativecow.net/reilly_michael/CDAT-History-Videos/1 on December 29, 2013.

Schachter, R. (2013, December). Schools embrace project-based learning 2.0. *District Administration.* Accessed at www.districtadministration.com/article /schools-embrace-project-based-learning-20 on December 29, 2013.

Thomas, J. W. (2000). A *review of research on project-based learning.* San Rafael, CA: Autodesk Foundation. Accessed at www.bobpearlman.org/BestPractices /PBL_Research.pdf on April 4, 2014.

Vander Ark, T., & Schneider, C. (2013). *How digital learning contributes to deeper learning.* Seattle, WA: Getting Smart. Accessed at http://gettingsmart.com /2012/12/how-digital-learning-contributes-to-deeper-learning/ on April 4, 2014.

Vega, V. (2012). *Project-based learning research review.* Accessed at www.edutopia.org /pbl-research-learning-outcomes on December 29, 2013.

Wagner, T. (2012). *Creating innovators: The making of young people who will change the world.* New York: Scribner.

Zhao, Y. (2012). *World class learners: Educating creative and entrepreneurial students.* Thousand Oaks, CA: Corwin.

Rob Riordan

Rob Riordan, EdD, is a cofounder of High Tech High (HTH) and president of the HTH Graduate School of Education. A public school teacher, trainer, and program developer for over forty years, he has worked with teams to develop fourteen new schools (eleven at High Tech High) spanning the K–12 years.

Rob holds a master of arts in teaching and a doctorate from the Harvard Graduate School of Education and a bachelor of arts from Haverford College.

Stacey Caillier

Stacey Caillier, PhD, is the director of the Teacher Leadership MEd program in the HTH Graduate School of Education, where she also advises graduate students and teaches courses in action research and leadership for school change. Stacey began her career as a high school physics and mathematics teacher and is currently investigating intersections between teacher identity, teacher leadership, and school culture.

She holds degrees from Willamette University and the University of California, Davis.

Ben Daley

Ben Daley began at High Tech High as a founding physics and robotics teacher. His role evolved to school director and then to chief academic officer and chief operating officer. Ben works closely with school directors and teachers to provide leadership for hiring, curriculum, and professional development for HTH schools as well as with other staff on the nonteaching side of the organization.

Ben has a bachelor of arts degree in physics from Haverford College as well as teaching credentials in physics and mathematics. He holds a master's in education with a focus on teaching and learning from the University of California, Santa Barbara, and is currently pursuing a doctorate in educational leadership at the University of California, San Diego.

Chapter 5

Developing Teachers for Deeper Learning

Rob Riordan, Stacey Caillier, and Ben Daley

It's Monday. Carla is on a visit to San Ysidro, a port of entry on the border between the United States and Mexico. She is part of a small group of new teachers at the High Tech High (HTH) schools in San Diego County (www.hightechhigh.org). Earlier that morning, her first day on the job, she met with forty other teachers new to HTH and several veteran HTH teachers to embark on the HTH New Teacher Odyssey addressing the essential question, How do we honor the experiences and meet the needs of all our students? The first day is a "project slice" focused on the Mexico-U.S. border; the goal is for these new teachers to experience project-based learning as learners, while investigating an issue relevant to their local community.

Carla and her colleagues began by examining brief texts as well as photos of the border area, some showing the border crossing as it looked in 1920. They viewed and shared interpretations of maps, which are in Spanish, showing the paths illegal migrants take across forbidding terrain, the location of water stations, and the sites of migrant deaths. They also looked at statistics on legal and illegal immigration and raised questions. Then they split up into groups of five to ten to go out to sites near the border—Carla's group to San Ysidro, others to a Mexican American artist's studio, a soup kitchen for day laborers, or a youth center across the border in Tijuana.

In San Ysidro, Carla's group visits sites managed by Casa Familiar (www.casafamiliar.org), a comprehensive community services center that runs a variety of learning and arts programs and mobilizes local organizations to address community issues. A Casa Familiar leader describes the organization's approach of creating cross-organizational and cross-neighborhood think tanks and action groups on issues of concern to the community—for example, the increased health risk from auto pollution that has resulted from increased border surveillance and longer lines at the San Ysidro border crossing, affecting nearby elementary schools and residences in the area.

At the end of the day, Carla's group members reflect together on their learning. Using paper, markers, Popsicle sticks, glue, and other typical classroom art supplies, group members design and create a representation of their experience and their findings. They display their work the following morning for the other slice groups in a gallery-walk format, in which each group views and responds to the disparate and differentiated work of the others using sticky notes to respond to the questions, What strikes you? What can you celebrate? and What questions does this work raise?

This is just the beginning of Carla's fifteen-day entry into the world of teaching and learning at High Tech High, a school where projects drive the curriculum. On the second morning, she is asked to reflect on her own experiences with significant learning as a student, in or out of school. She and her colleagues get to know each other as they share their stories in small groups, extracting the elements of significant learning. They ask questions they will return to time and again in their work at HTH: What is significant learning? How can I provide significant learning experiences to my own students? What would a place look like where significant learning is happening all the time?

On the second afternoon, veteran HTH teachers bring in draft project designs and ask for help. Each veteran presents his or her project to a group of new teachers, who offer reactions and suggestions following a project-tuning protocol. (Visit **go.solution-tree .com/21stcenturyskills** to download the full protocol.) On day three, participants choose from a range of workshops on topics such as writing to learn, differentiated instruction, inclusion, motivation, peer critique, and cooperative learning. By day four, Carla is tuning her own project design with a group of peers. On day five, she constructs a digital portfolio with help from a team of HTH sixth graders who have come in for that purpose. The sixth day is devoted to the first day of class and the importance of establishing a supportive learning community early on in which all students feel known and heard. Finally, on the seventh day, Carla shares artifacts of and reflections on her learning in a presentation to an audience of peers, veteran teachers, and students, who provide her with feedback on her work and suggest next steps. Here again, as with the project slice, Carla experiences as a learner the kind of event she will be orchestrating and facilitating for her students before long. After this seven-day odyssey, Carla is off to her HTH school site for eight more days of preparation for the opening of school.

Carla emerges from the New Teacher Odyssey with tools and products for immediate use: a project design, a digital portfolio, and a draft syllabus. More important, the odyssey is the first step in a process of acculturation, as Carla and her colleagues experience the key features of adult learning at HTH: reflective practice, collaboration, and co-design.

It Starts With the Adults

When we started High Tech High in September 2000, we knew we wanted visitors to be unable to tell if it was a technical school or a college preparatory school. We were particularly interested in the integration of hands-on technical pedagogy with academic content, aiming to develop the skills articulated in the education secretary's Commission on Achieving Necessary Skills (SCANS) report (1991) and Richard Murnane and Frank Levy's (1996) book *Teaching the New Basic Skills*. (For a discussion of the school-to-work roots of HTH, see *The New Urban High School* [Big Picture, 1998].) When you walk down the hallway, you see students wearing safety goggles and using power tools, but it's not shop class—it's ninth-grade mathematics, physics, art, or humanities. This project-based approach, allowing many entry points for students and many ways to shine, serves a larger purpose of equity: to show that when students from very different backgrounds and academic experiences sit side by side in classrooms and work side by side on projects, everyone benefits, and no one is hurt. Data from the class of 2012–2013 indicate that 92 percent of ninth graders entering High Tech High graduated from one of the HTH schools, with a 0 percent dropout rate (others move, transfer, and so on) (California Department of Education, 2014). National Student Clearinghouse (2011) data show that of HTH graduates, 98 percent go on to college and 75 percent go to four-year schools. Eighty-two percent of graduates have either graduated college or are still enrolled.

We also knew that we would be asking teachers—including recent college graduates, midcareer transfers to teaching, and veteran teachers—to facilitate learning in a way that many had never themselves experienced in school. To construct an integrated learning environment of the kind we envisioned for our students, we would have to start by developing a deep learning environment for the adults.

This chapter represents field notes about our efforts to develop that environment. We discuss our design principles, the structures and practices we have put in place, and the tools we have employed in the service of teacher development. In the end, we offer suggestions for educators and program designers interested in developing and supporting a culture of adult learning in schools.

Design Principles

We began High Tech High as a single public charter high school near downtown San Diego. Now the organization includes twelve schools in San Diego County—three elementary schools, four middle schools, and five high schools. HTH students are admitted via a blind zip-code-based lottery, which yields a student population that roughly mirrors the demographics of the San Diego school-age population. Moreover, once inside the school, there is no tracking. There are no AP courses and no separate honors classes. Instead, each core class during the junior and senior years offers an honors option within the class, which any student may elect to complete.

High Tech High ignores the axioms that schools use to separate students by perceived academic ability, divide knowledge into discrete subjects, and isolate students from the adult world of work and learning. In contrast, HTH integrates students, the curriculum, and school itself with the world beyond. The subtext for all of this is social-class integration and equity, based on HTH design principles of personalization, common intellectual mission, adult-world connections, and teacher as co-director. These principles are drawn from two distinct reform initiatives: (1) the Coalition of Essential Schools and (2) the school-to-career movement of the 1990s. (See Steinberg, Cushman, & Riordan, 1999, for a discussion of the complementarity of these initiatives.)

The HTH design principles permeate every aspect of the program. HTH personalizes the learning by ensuring that students are known well (each student has a faculty advisor who conducts a home visit and monitors the student's progress) and by encouraging students to pursue their interests and passions through projects. The schools establish adult-world connections through internships and other fieldwork in the community. They develop a common intellectual mission by not tracking students, by developing a common language (for example, habits of heart and mind) for intellectual work across the academic disciplines, and by establishing a culture of presentation and exhibition for all students. These principles also drive the design of High Tech High facilities, which feature flexible spaces for projects, community events, and exhibitions and are configured to allow teacher teams to function effectively.

Finally, the four principles trigger questions about our own practice, as we examine our project designs and student work:

1. **Personalization**—Where do we see evidence in this project design or in this student work that students are exercising voice and choice?

2. **Common intellectual mission**—Where in this work do we see evidence of access and challenge for all learners?

3. **Adult-world connections**—Where in this work do we see evidence that students are making authentic connections with adults in the world beyond school?

4. **Teacher as co-designer**—What structures and practices are in place to support the co-design work of teachers?

The fourth design principle, teacher as co-designer, gets to the heart of adult work and learning. HTH teachers do not follow a prescribed curriculum. Instead, they work in teams and with their students to design units and projects that offer opportunities for choice and voice, that have students working in teams, and that connect with the world beyond school. This is challenging work that requires teachers to take risks, solicit feedback from students and colleagues, and make adjustments to ensure that all students are engaged and learning deeply. The curriculum tends to evolve as students live it and as teachers respond to their students' needs, interests, and questions. The teacher as co-designer principle pushes us to ask ourselves, What are the structures and practices that support teachers' work and learning?

Structures for Teacher Learning and Development

The great irony in schools is that we expect teachers to model and foster 21st century competencies, but they themselves are not working in a 21st century work environment. Many high school teachers carry a teaching load of 150 students or more, with little or no common planning time and infrequent professional development. Growing teachers' capacity for deeper learning means changing the structure of schooling not only for students but also for adults. In addition to the New Teacher Odyssey just described, High Tech High has designed several other structures to support teacher development, including the daily schedule, the teacher hiring process, formal structures for new and veteran teacher development, and development of teacher leadership for deeper learning.

The Daily Schedule

From the beginning, HTH built time for teacher collaboration into the daily schedule. By contract, teachers arrive at school an hour before the students each day to meet in teaching teams, academic departments, study groups, or whole-faculty sessions. These meetings serve as a theoretical context for veteran and new teachers to address the issues and needs they identify in their work. A study group may design an inquiry into students' perceptions of equity in the school. Mathematics teachers may meet to co-construct or share open-ended problems aligned with the Common Core mathematics. The whole faculty may meet in general session to tune projects or look at student work together, using protocols for those purposes. Each HTH faculty decides how it will use these days.

In addition, whole days are allocated to teacher planning and development. For example, all staff members return to work eight days before the first day of school. There are also typically four staff days throughout the year plus two additional staff days at the end of the year. Again, teachers play a significant role in planning and facilitating these days. They are co-designers, not only of student learning, but also of each other's learning.

High Tech High integrates the subjects. For example, ninth-grade teachers teach interdisciplinary courses like mathematics-science and English–social studies (humanities). This subject-matter integration avoids the overcompartmentalization of knowledge, allowing a multidisciplinary focus on big questions. (For a brief description of this integrated approach, with examples from HTH projects, see Riordan & Rosenstock, n.d., 2013, a flash animation.) Just as important, from a structural point of view, it allows for a teacher load of fifty to sixty students in the core areas; each humanities teacher, for example, teaches two double blocks of humanities instead of four blocks of English or social studies.

In a related structural feature, HTH students take their academic courses as a cohort or team. Team teachers share students, which enables the efficient use of staff resources as the teachers work together not only to plan the curriculum and engage in joint projects but also to discuss the strengths, interests, and needs of the students they share.

The Teacher Hiring Process

The process of teacher development begins with hiring. HTH invites as many as forty candidates at a time to attend full-day bonanzas, which allow candidates to tour the site, observe classes, interview with faculty members and students, and teach a one-hour demonstration lesson in their preferred grade level or subject area. Toward the end of the day, candidates participate in small-group discussions in which they are asked, as a group, to create a hypothetical project together or come to a deeper understanding of a brief, provocative text, such as Peggy McIntosh's (2003) piece on white privilege.

Candidates are observed throughout the day, and all teachers can submit their opinion on a potential faculty member to a director or attend the end-of-day faculty debrief. Students provide input from their interviews and from candidates' sample lessons, filling out forms that include the questions, Do you think this individual is ready to teach at HTH? Why, or why not?

In the end, we're looking for individuals who are curious to know what and how students think, who are able to engage multiple perspectives and reflect on their own experiences, and who are ready and eager to collaborate with other adults. Bonanzas were designed to illuminate these qualities and to let candidates know what we care about as an organization.

The Formal Structures for Teacher Development

In the beginning, we hired engineers from the industry who held PhDs and were qualified to teach at the university level but who were not certified to teach in a public high school. We also hired talented recent college graduates who had deep content knowledge but little or no experience in teaching, and we wanted to conduct their training on site and in accordance with our design principles. Therefore, we applied for and received approval from the California Commission on Teacher Credentialing to run teacher internship programs for the single subject, multiple subject (for elementary school teachers), and special education credentials. (High school credentials for academic subjects are for a single subject. A teacher who teaches both mathematics and science, for example, needs to be certified in both subject areas.)

The upshot is that we can hire talented individuals with a range of experiences we value, offer them training in the summer at the New Teacher Odyssey, and put them in the classroom as teachers of record. They enter the profession while simultaneously pursuing their teaching credential and enjoying the support of a full salary, morning meetings with colleagues, weekly evening seminars with their credentialing cohort, and consultation with veteran teachers who serve as mentors. The weekly seminar experience focuses on a series of put-it-to-practice exercises around themes like equity, assessment, and technology. The goal is to support new teachers in connecting theory to practice and making sense of their teaching experience as they live it.

Development of Teacher Leadership for Deeper Learning

Offering our own credential programs was a significant step in developing a wall-to-wall adult learning community at High Tech High. In 2007, we introduced a further formal structure for teacher development and leadership by opening the HTH Graduate School of Education (GSE). The GSE (http://gse.hightechhigh.org) is fully embedded within the HTH K–12 schools and offers MEd programs in teacher leadership and school leadership for educators from within and beyond HTH. Both programs integrate theory and practice, emphasizing the design of equitable learning environments, reflective practice, and leadership for school change (Caillier & Riordan, 2009).

The GSE provides support for teachers to grow as designers of learning environments and curricula, as well as support for teachers' own inquiries into teaching and learning (Caillier, 2008). Within the credentialing and MEd programs, teachers conduct action research projects to explore "fierce wonderings" from their practice. They pursue questions such as, How do students experience open-ended mathematics problems? What happens when I co-design projects with students? How can we use critique to create a culture of collaboration and improve the quality of student work? What do social networks reveal about the ability of peer relationships to support learning in integrated settings? How do teachers experience their first year in HTH schools? Each of these projects involves collecting, analyzing, and reflecting on data from various sources to develop a richer understanding of how we, as educators, can improve our practice and better meet the needs of students and colleagues. (See http://gse.hightechhigh.org for full program descriptions and GSE student digital portfolios.) Most significant, each of these projects serves as a catalyst for engaging students and colleagues in change efforts at both the classroom and school levels.

Such inquiry challenges distinctions between theory and practice, between knower and doer. It positions teachers as active contributors to the knowledge base of teaching and learning and as active participants in school transformation. The work of the graduate students, inside HTH or in other area schools, tends to percolate through their settings as they step up to exercise leadership within or outside the classroom.

Tools to Support Teacher Learning and Development

Structures such as those just delineated may be a precondition, but they offer no guarantee of teacher development. Time together is not enough. Now that we've secured the time, how do we use it well?

High Tech High has developed personalized learning plans to help teachers build on their strengths, explore their interests, and attend to areas of potential growth. Teachers may engage in activities throughout the year as outlined in the plan—observe colleagues' classrooms, serve as a mentor, collaborate with an outside organization, bring a dilemma or example of student work to a faculty meeting for consultation, co-teach a credential seminar, participate in an action group, share their work with an audience beyond HTH, and so on. (Visit **go.solution-tree.com/21stcenturyskills** to download the High Tech High Personalized Teacher Learning Plan.) We recognize, however, that teacher development is social as well as personal. It is a matter of building a culture of collaboration and mutual support. For this broader agenda, we have found the use of protocols and collegial coaching to be vital to the growth of new and veteran teachers.

Protocols

At High Tech High, the use of protocols for teacher (and student) interaction has proven invaluable, both for enabling productive conversations and for developing teacher expertise in group facilitation. Joseph McDonald, Nancy Mohr, Alan Dichter, and Elizabeth

McDonald (2007) offer a helpful guide, and the School Reform Initiative (www.schoolreforminitiative.org) has been a rich source of material, providing protocols for nearly every imaginable issue and occasion. In particular, we have adapted three protocols for our use—(1) for project tuning, (2) for looking at student work, and (3) for discussing dilemmas of practice. These protocols foster equitable conversation, ensuring that all voices are heard. They unleash energy and encourage diverse ideas and help democratize our professional conversations, reinforcing that we are each other's resources and that we collectively benefit from making our thinking and our work public. A typical protocol for project tuning or examining student work begins with norm-setting (see the following paragraph), after which the presenter offers a brief description of the work at hand. Clarifying and then probing questions follow, as the audience attempts to better understand the work. Then the presenter steps aside, still within earshot, as the audience conducts a discussion— raising questions, discussing possible new perspectives, and offering suggestions. The great benefit here is that the presenter is free to absorb the feedback, relieved of the pressure of responding point by point. Finally, the presenter returns to the group to say what he or she now thinks about the work, having heard the discussion.

Protocols support the creation of professional communities of practice focused on teaching and learning, collaboration, and dialogue. One crucial component of these communities, and of the protocols we use, is the development of shared norms and values. When a colleague presents a project design, an example of student work, or a dilemma, we typically start with four bedrock HTH norms and build from there as needed:

1. **Share the air**—If you are someone who tends to speak often and at length, we encourage you to step back so that all voices can be heard. If you are someone who tends to not contribute to the conversation as readily, we encourage you to step up so that we can benefit from your ideas.

2. **Go hard on the content, soft on the people**—Presenters wish to have their thinking pushed but also want to hear constructive feedback; they also need to feel understood and valued.

3. **Be kind, specific, and helpful**—The more specific we can be with our affirmations and our constructive feedback, the more helpful our comments will be.

4. **Resist the urge to deviate from the protocol**—It can be tempting to just talk, especially when we know each other well, but remember that the protocol will help us take risks, share our thinking and work, and stay focused on the topic at hand.

To support teachers' growth as facilitators, we attempt to model effective facilitation and collaboratively unpack the approaches that strong facilitators take. We encourage facilitators to be courageous and confident. We are also careful to debrief the process at the end of each protocol: What worked well? What didn't? Did we stay focused on the presenter's question? Was there a turning point in the conversation that helped us get closer to the presenter's dilemma? Reflecting on the process together solidifies our collective learning about how to engage in these conversations effectively. It also ensures that the facilitator learns more about his or her strengths and possible areas for growth.

We've found that the more teachers experience protocols with colleagues, the more likely they are to engage students in protocols as well. Teachers might conduct a project tuning with their students to gather feedback and ideas to drive the final design or exhibition. In turn, their students may use—and facilitate—protocols to provide feedback to each other on project ideas, drafts of their work, and dilemmas they are experiencing. In short, protocols have helped us move toward collegial pedagogy, student ownership, and equitable participation in our classrooms.

Collegial Coaching

Every teacher in our credentialing program has an assigned mentor, but we supplement that structure with peer collegial coaching for all teachers for two reasons. First, everyone can benefit from observation and coaching. Second, we want to democratize coaching as a process in which even new teachers can add value by observing closely and asking good questions. We've found that effective coaching is less about the advice teachers offer to one another and more about how we can ask good questions and engage in reflective conversations. In fact, two students in the High Tech High Graduate School of Education studied collegial coaching at High Tech High and have created a website to serve as a resource for educators (http://collegialcoaching.weebly.com).

Collegial coaching typically takes place in pairs and occurs several times throughout a semester, with teachers meeting to discuss the focus for the observation, to observe each other's teaching, and then to debrief the observations. Some of the preparation, as well as postobservation debriefing, may take place in morning meetings. Teachers use a variety of tools for observation, including the continua in HTH teacher practice (figure 5.1, page 150), which articulates dimensions of classroom culture that an observer might attend to. As seen in the figure, some of these dimensions are unidirectional. With respect to coherence, for example, we are trying to move from isolated activities to connectedness—of one activity to another, and one day or week to the next. Other dimensions are context dependent—for the dimension of presentation, a range of activities from pair and share to public presentation may be appropriate (hence, in the figure, the arrow points both ways). Two common lenses that teachers bring to these observations are: (1) Where do I see evidence of student thinking? and (2) Where do I see evidence of student engagement?

A key component of collegial coaching, particularly as practiced in our credentialing and graduate programs, is video consultancy. Teachers videotape themselves teaching a lesson, select a short clip that represents a moment or an issue they want help thinking through, and then pose a question to guide the group's feedback. In small groups—which may include teachers, faculty from our credentialing and graduate programs, and high school students—participants watch the video clip together and provide feedback to the presenting teacher using a video consultancy protocol. (Visit **go.solution -tree.com/21stcenturyskills** to download the full protocol.)

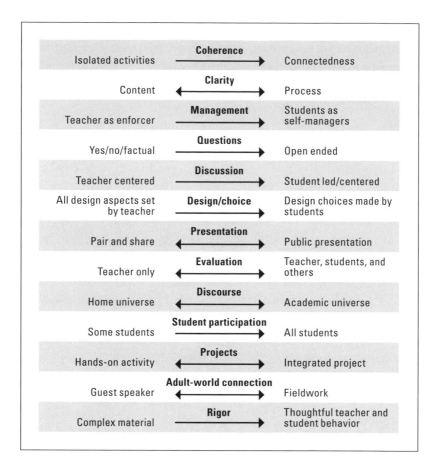

Figure 5.1: Continua in HTH teaching practice.

It's one thing to observe well and another to have a productive conversation about teaching. To this end, HTH directors and teachers view clips of teaching and role-play conversations about what they are seeing and how they might approach a collegial conversation with the teacher in the video. We encourage the observer to focus on three questions while watching the clip:

1. What can I celebrate?

2. What questions emerge?

3. What suggestions might I offer?

We have found that the first question requires repeated emphasis, as teachers are often their own harshest critics. As observers, our first aim should be to celebrate what is going well and help the teacher build from his or her strengths. The order of the second and third questions is also important; it prioritizes the posing of questions that draw out the teacher's thinking so that the teacher might generate his or her own solutions and next steps, making our suggestions unnecessary. Our use of video does not end with the role plays; we also record our conversations with colleagues about their teaching and use a similar protocol to unpack our effectiveness as coaches.

Suggestions for Educators and Program Designers

The premise of this chapter has been that deeper learning in schools starts with the adults. Here we offer suggestions for educators and program designers who are committed to building a culture of adult learning in schools.

1. **Change the schedule:** Set aside time during the school day for teachers to engage in reflection, collaboration, and co-design. Provide opportunities for teachers to cross subject-matter boundaries, explore their passions, collaborate, lead, and grow as facilitators of each other's learning. Assign teachers to work in teams where they share students, so they can plan projects together and work together to meet the needs of the students they share.

2. **Foster teacher agency:** Bring teacher voice, choice, and agency into professional development and support. Too much of what passes for professional development is provided by external agents and is experienced by teachers as irrelevant to their needs. Aim to have every teacher engaged in adult learning in the K–12 environment in one way or another—for example, as a mentor, mentee, workshop provider, action researcher, facilitator, or collegial coach. (For a discussion of teachers' options in the kinds of support they receive from a school director, see Wilson, 2008.)

3. **Invite students into the dialogue about teaching and learning:** Engage students as co-presenters, facilitators, and teaching assistants in new teacher training and ongoing professional development, whether it be project tuning, looking

at student work, or discussions of dilemmas in teaching and learning.

4. **Make the work of teachers and students public:** Use digital portfolios, schoolwide exhibitions of learning, and the sharing of work through protocols. There are several benefits to such transparency. First, when all students exhibit their work, the work of the adults is on display as well. Second, regular sharing fosters the development of internal standards, both for teachers and students, not to mention a culture of continuous improvement.

5. **Assess teacher effectiveness through a variety of lenses:** With respect to student achievement, the National Research Council, professional assessment organizations, and even testing companies have long agreed that high-stakes decisions about who passes, who fails, who is retained, and who graduates are best made by those who know the student well, using a variety of assessments. (See, for example, Heubert & Hauser, 1999). The same wisdom applies to the assessment of teacher work. Assessment of teacher effectiveness begins by looking at student performance, particularly as indicated by student work products. But any comprehensive assessment should also include observation, video documentation and reflection, interviews with parents and students, evidence of work with colleagues, and contributions to the larger community.

At a time when educational policy is calling for schools, districts, and states to adopt research-based practices to reform schools and improve student achievement, it is ironic that those same policies ignore what research has shown us about what motivates human beings to do their best work. Many current policy initiatives—merit pay for performance, takeovers of low-performing schools (many of which serve our most disadvantaged students), and scripted curriculum—are based on carrot-and-stick models of motivation.

In short, holding out a carrot (or a bonus) may make people work hard in the short term, but it shifts their focus away from the work itself and their own learning. As James Stigler (2010) points out, such individual incentives undermine collaboration, which is essential to improving teaching and learning across entire schools. We can't expect to attract and retain creative, committed people in the profession if they have to follow scripted curricula and teach to a test for their pay—such a system stifles autonomy and motivation, prevents mastery from developing, and fails to provide a purpose that can engage the heart or mind.

Conclusion

Carla checks back in with new teacher colleagues at a daylong Winter Odyssey in December. There, she presents examples of student work that she has questions about and invites colleagues to consult with her in a looking-at-student-work protocol. Other colleagues engage in consultancies on dilemmas from their practice, asking questions such as, "How do I meet the needs of struggling readers in the youth radio project?" Even in these first months, Carla is learning to treat experience—her own, and that of her students, as a primary text. She unpacks that text through observation, dialogue, and reflection. In doing so, she is developing a reflex of consulting her students and colleagues when she has a question about planning or practice. In the end, her trajectory leads her to collegial pedagogy (Soep, 2008), where she and her students are working together on projects and addressing problems that have uncertain solutions.

What does it take to develop teachers for deeper learning? One thing is certain: it takes time. Preservice training, however effective, is only the beginning. Research shows that if we create schools in which teachers are continuously learning, students will learn, too. Nancy Latham and W. Paul Vogt (2007) find that teacher education programs that diminish the gap between theory and practice, while providing extensive school experience and mentoring, result in improved teaching practice and decreased attrition. Susan Moore Johnson (2004) finds that 50 percent of teachers who leave the profession do so within the first five years, but she also suggests that a supportive adult culture leads to increased retention. In a five-year study of three high-performing schools for at-risk students, Jacqueline Ancess (2000) discovers relationships between teacher learning, teacher practice, school culture, and student outcomes (for example, improved graduation rates, course pass rates, college admission rates, and academic course-taking rates). These schools were structured to support teacher learning and decision making, with the result of improved teacher practice and student learning. Schools can and should be powerful sites for adult learning.

The inescapable reality is that teacher development, for better or worse, takes place in schools. To develop effective teachers, schools must dedicate sufficient time to establish adult learning communities in which teachers plan lessons and projects together, share student work, discuss student and classroom dilemmas, use student data to inform practice, engage in collegial coaching, and refine their practice. In short, schools must become clinical sites so teachers can witness and practice effective approaches in the same way that a teaching hospital fosters adult learning for young and experienced physicians. The overall aim, for both new and experienced teachers, is to develop reflective practitioners who are themselves deep learners committed to continual growth. To accomplish this, it is both necessary and feasible to focus not only on classrooms but also on the adult culture in schools as the leverage point for transformation.

References

Ancess, J. (2000). The reciprocal influence of teacher learning, teaching practice, school restructuring and student learning outcomes. *Teachers College Record, 102*(3), 590–619.

Big Picture. (1998). *The new urban high school: A practitioner's guide.* Providence, RI: Author.

Caillier, S. (2008). Transforming schools one question at a time. *UnBoxed, 1*(1). Accessed at www.hightechhigh.org/unboxed/issue1 on November 1, 2013.

Caillier, S. L., & Riordan, R. C. (2009). Teacher education for the schools we need. *Journal of Teacher Education, 60*(5), 489–496.

California Department of Education (2014). Data accessed at http://data1.cde.ca.gov /dataquest on August 1, 2014.

Heubert, J., & Hauser, R. (1999). *High stakes: testing for tracking, promotion, and graduation.* Washington, DC: National Academy Press.

Johnson, S. M. (2004). *Finders and keepers: Helping new teachers survive and thrive in our schools.* San Francisco: Jossey-Bass.

Latham, N., & Vogt, W. P. (2007). Do professional development schools reduce teacher attrition? Evidence from a longitudinal study of 1,000 graduates. *Journal of Teacher Education, 58,* 153–167.

McDonald, J. P., Mohr, N., Dichter, A., & McDonald, E. C. (2007). *The power of protocols: An educator's guide to better practice* (2nd ed.). New York: Teachers College Press.

McIntosh, P. (2003). White privilege: Unpacking the invisible knapsack. In S. Plous (Ed.), *Understanding prejudice and discrimination* (pp. 191–196). New York: McGraw-Hill.

Murnane, R., & Levy, F. (1996). *Teaching the new basic skills: Principles for educating children to thrive in a changing economy.* New York: Free Press.

National Student Clearinghouse. (2011). *StudentTracker for high schools aggregate report: Prepared for High Tech High.* Herndon, VA: Author.

Pink, D. H. (2009). *Drive: The surprising truth about what motivates us.* New York: Penguin.

Riordan, R., & Rosenstock, L. (n.d.). *Changing the subject* [Monograph]. Accessed at http://gse .hightechhigh.org/Changing_the_Subject.pdf on May 20, 2014.

Riordan, R., & Rosenstock, L. (2013). *Changing the subject* [Video file]. Accessed at www.you tube.com/watch?v=KBW9ChKzkfQ on May 20, 2014.

Secretary's Commission on Achieving Necessary Skills. (1991). *What work requires of schools: A SCANS report for America 2000.* Washington, DC: U.S. Department of Labor.

Soep, E. (2008). Learning as production, critique as assessment. *UnBoxed*, 2. Accessed at www.hightechhigh.org/unboxed/issue2/learning_as_production/ on November 2013.

Steinberg, A., Cushman, K., & Riordan, R. (1999). *Schooling for the real world: The essential guide to rigorous and relevant learning.* San Francisco: Jossey-Bass.

Stigler, J. W. (2010, June 9). Rethinking teacher accountability—Before it's too late. *Education Week*, 29(33). Accessed at www.edweek.org/ew/articles /2010/06/09/33stigler_ep.h29.html?r=443553910 on November 20, 2013.

Wilson, K. (2008). Options for reflection: Building a faculty culture of reflection and conversation. *UnBoxed*, 1. Accessed at www.hightechhigh.org/unboxed/issue1/cards/7.php November 20, 2013.

PART II

What Will Drive the Shift?

Tony Wagner

Tony Wagner currently serves as an expert in residence at Harvard University's Innovation Lab. Prior to this appointment, Tony was the first Innovation Education Fellow at the Technology and Entrepreneurship Center at Harvard and the founder and co-director of the Change Leadership Group at the Harvard Graduate School of Education for more than a decade. His previous work experience includes twelve years as a high school teacher, K–8 principal, university professor in teacher education, and founding executive director of Educators for Social Responsibility. Tony is a frequent speaker at national and international conferences and a widely published author. His work includes numerous articles and five books. His recently published *Creating Innovators* has been received with wide acclaim and translated into ten languages. His 2008 book, *The Global Achievement Gap*, continues to be an international best seller and has a second edition. Tony also recently collaborated with noted filmmaker Robert Compton to create a sixty-minute documentary, *The Finland Phenomenon*.

Tony earned an masters of arts in teaching and a doctorate of education at the Harvard University Graduate School of Education.

Chapter 6

The Worst of Times, The Best of Times

Tony Wagner

In 2008, I published *The Global Achievement Gap*, which outlined the new skills all students need for work, learning, and citizenship in the 21st century. The global achievement gap is the disparity between these new skills versus what is taught in the overwhelming majority of our public and independent schools. One conclusion of that book is that a test-prep curriculum increasingly dominated classrooms around the United States.

Since the book was published, we have continued to see fundamental changes and disruptions in our economy, as well as a dramatic increase in the number of so-called education reforms. Frighteningly, these reforms have done nothing to close the gap between the skills that all students need more urgently than ever and what is tested and taught in even our best schools. But we have also seen the creation of new networks of schools and districts that are genuinely innovating in learning and teaching. They are working together to reimagine—not merely reform—schools for the 21st century. Borrowing from Charles Dickens, education today is experiencing the worst of times and the best of times.

The Worst of Times: A Rapidly Evolving Economy

The global economic meltdown that began in 2008 has accelerated the elimination of many kinds of jobs. Businesses have figured out how to use ever more automation to cut workers and increase profits. In their important book *Race Against the Machine*, MIT economists Erik Brynjolfsson and Andrew McAfee (2011) argue convincingly that even highly skilled jobs are increasingly at risk. In 2008, no one thought that unmanned machines could handle a task as complex as driving in heavy traffic. The Google driverless car has proved otherwise. Similarly, computers now compile and write complex financial reports and compete successfully against humans in chess and on *Jeopardy!*

The declining unemployment rate reported in the media does not capture the percentage of people who have given up looking for jobs or who have part-time jobs and are seeking full-time work. As I write this in the summer of 2014, the percentage of Americans working or seeking work—63 percent—is at the lowest point since women began entering the labor force in significant numbers in the late 1970s (Mui & Jayakumar, 2013). Nor does the unemployment rate say anything about the quality of jobs available. The vast majority of jobs created since the end of the recession in 2009 are minimum-wage service and sales jobs. The result of all of these trends, economists tell us, is that the gap between the rich and the rest of us in the United States is greater than at any time since 1917 (Greenwood, 2013).

Historically, college graduates have always had an easier time finding jobs, and they earn considerably more than high school graduates over the course of their work life. It is no surprise, then, that more young people are enrolling in college in response to this job crisis. Indeed, the mantra of many of our policymakers and educators is that all students should graduate from high school "college ready." As a result, the college attendance rate in the United States is the highest it has ever been. But there is a growing body of evidence that attending college might not be the sure investment it once was.

Since 2000, college tuitions have gone up 72 percent, while family income is down 10 percent. To close this gap, students and their families are borrowing more money than ever. College debt now exceeds credit card debt in the United States—topping $1 trillion. Students now graduate with an average combined family debt of over $33,000 (Izzo, 2014). That is, if they graduate at all. Colleges have done nothing to stem the horrible student attrition rate. Of the students who enroll in colleges, only about half complete any sort of degree. The completion rate of our community colleges—where many of our most disadvantaged students enroll—is only about 25 percent (Schneider, 2012).

Then there is the problem of job prospects for recent college graduates. The combined unemployment and underemployment rate since 2006 of college graduates in the United States is 52 percent. More than 36 percent of college graduates are finding that the only kinds of jobs they can get do not require a degree and certainly do not pay a college graduate wage. They are often earning 40 percent less than others with a degree (Luhby, 2013). In the United States, the talk is often about government debt, but the debt I worry about most is the debt of our college graduates. It is the only form of personal debt that cannot be eliminated by filing for bankruptcy.

This dismal employment picture for college graduates exists at a time when employers say they cannot fill available positions for highly skilled workers. There is a profound mismatch between what students learn in college versus what employers say they need. It is not merely a matter of students picking the wrong college major. Employers say they do not care what job applicants' college majors are. They care about skills. According to a survey of employers conducted on behalf of the Association of American Colleges and Universities, "nearly all those surveyed (93 percent) agree, 'a candidate's demonstrated capacity to think critically, communicate clearly, and solve complex problems is more important than their undergraduate major'" (Hart Research Associates, 2007, p. 1).

In *The Global Achievement Gap* I described what I called the Seven Survival Skills for work, learning, and citizenship (Wagner, 2008).

1. Critical thinking and problem-solving

2. Collaboration across networks and leading by influence

3. Agility and adaptability

4. Initiative and entrepreneurialism

5. Effective oral and written communication

6. Accessing and analyzing information

7. Curiosity and imagination

In numerous discussions with business leaders since I wrote the book, I have discovered that these employers want something more from new hires now. Over and over, business leaders have been telling me that they want employees who can "just go figure it out"— employees who can be creative problem solvers or innovators. In my book *Creating Innovators*, I explore what parents and teachers can do to develop these capacities (Wagner, 2012). One of my most striking findings in interviews with young creative problem solvers in their twenties is that many became innovators in spite of their excellent schools, not because of them. Students who went to Harvard, MIT, Stanford, and Carnegie Mellon all told me that it was the rare outlier teacher who truly made the difference in their development.

Sadly, many of our college graduates are not learning any of the skills that matter most. In a study that involved 2,300 undergraduates at twenty-four institutions, Richard Arum and Josipa Roksa (2011) analyzed data from the Collegiate Learning Assessment, a state-of-the-art test that measures students' critical thinking, problem solving, and writing skills. They found that after two years of college, 45 percent of the students tested were no more able to think critically or communicate effectively than when they started college. Their book, *Academically Adrift*, makes a compelling case for the need to fundamentally rethink the nature of a college education and to re-evaluate accountability for results.

Employers are beginning to wise up to the fact that students' college transcripts, GPAs, and test scores are a poor predictor of employee value. Google famously used to hire only students from name-brand colleges with the highest GPAs and test scores. However, according to several 2013 interviews with Laszlo Bock, senior vice president of people operations at Google, these data are "worthless" as predictors of employee effectiveness at Google. The company now looks for evidence of a sense of mission and personal autonomy and is increasingly hiring people who do not have a college degree. Even the interview questions they pose have changed. In the past, Google interviewers asked prospective employees brain teaser questions like "How many ping-pong balls can you get into a 747?" or "How many cows are there in Canada?" Now they want them to talk about a complex analytic problem they have tried to solve (Bryant, 2013; Lohr, 2013).

Education Reforms That Aren't

In the midst of all this economic turmoil, education "reform" efforts have gained momentum. The number of charter schools has expanded exponentially, even though research shows that, on average, these schools are no more effective than comparable public schools (Center for Research on Education Outcomes [CREDO] at Stanford University, 2013). Salman Khan's work has spawned another educational reform that has continued to grow in popularity. According to its website, the Khan Academy now boasts more than 4,300 short video lessons that have been seen on YouTube 283 million times. These videos are widely used in so-called flipped classrooms, in which teachers assign specific videos as homework, freeing up class time for other activities. MOOCs, short for *massively open online courses*, have also grown exponentially. An increasing number of university consortia are offering these courses for free and are supplying certificates of completion for a nominal fee.

While current research shows less than a 7 percent completion rate for online courses, the move to various forms of online learning will have a profoundly disruptive influence on schools and colleges over time (Parr, 2013). Increasingly, knowledge is being commoditized—available to anyone around the world who has an Internet connection. The growth of MOOCs will be especially disruptive to the college market. In 2013, the prestigious Georgia Institute of Technology announced its intention to offer an online master's degree in computer science for only $6,600. Some experts, like Harvard's Clayton Christensen, are predicting that in fifteen years half of U.S. universities may be in bankruptcy (Suster, 2013), because they will be unable to compete with inexpensive online education programs.

Perhaps the most significant educational reform of the last five years is the development of a common set of academic standards for all K–12 public schools—the Common Core State Standards. The U.S. Department of Education, through its Race to the Top competition, made grants available to states on the condition that they adopt the Common Core. As of 2014, forty-six states have joined. The Department of Education has also funded two consortia of states to develop common assessments to accompany the new standards.

The new standards have become increasingly controversial as states have begun teaching and testing them. Conservatives claim that they represent an effort by the federal government to create a national curriculum. Educational leaders worry that teachers have not had sufficient time or training to be able to teach to the higher academic standards and that they lack the necessary new curriculum materials. Some argue that implementation of the tougher tests that will accompany the new standards should be delayed. I have a number of concerns about the Common Core that are different from these, however.

Should Minnesota, Massachusetts, and Mississippi have common academic standards? Of course! High-performing countries like Finland have had national curriculum guidelines for thirty years or more, though they are far briefer and less prescriptive than ours. But the first question that must be asked is this: Are these the right standards?

The Common Core standards have been designed to align quite specifically with college admissions requirements that have gone unquestioned. Because most colleges require all applicants to take advanced mathematics—at least algebra 2—this is the mathematics standard that all students in the United States will now have to meet. Very few students will ever have to solve a quadratic equation or factor a polynomial in their lives. In contrast, all students will need to know statistics, probability, computation, and estimation, and will need to be financially literate! Unfortunately, these are not significant elements of the Common Core because they're not requirements for college admission. I worry that we are creating a college-prep, one-size-fits-all curriculum that will not meet many students' interests and needs.

In 2010, I had an opportunity to spend time studying the education system of Finland, one of the highest-performing countries in the world. One of the many things that intrigued me is that when students begin tenth grade, they choose between an academic track that leads straight to the university and a career, technical, and vocational track that has been developed in close collaboration with businesses and leads straight to a good job. It also prepares students for postsecondary education. Nearly half of all Finnish high school students choose the career, technical, and vocational track.

In 2010, noted filmmaker Robert Compton and I collaborated to make a documentary film about Finland's education system titled *The Finland Phenomenon.* I visited a high school in Douglas County, Colorado, an upper-middle-class community with some of the highest test scores in the state, where I was invited to speak to a group of fifty twelfth graders who had just seen our film. First, I asked how many planned to attend college, and every hand in the room was raised in response. Then I asked, if a technical and vocational curriculum like the one in Finland had been available to them, how many would have chosen such a track? Half the hands in the room went up. A growing number of students worry that college is a risky bet, because it is increasingly expensive and does not necessarily lead to a high-paying job, as we've learned. Students need meaningful alternatives to an overly abstract, academic, college-preparatory curriculum. Many students would prefer not to go to a four-year college but do not think they have other options.

In the midst of all these efforts to improve education, there has been no real discussion about the goals of education in the 21st century or how best to prepare students for a rapidly changing job market and for active and informed citizenship. None of the education reforms I've discussed here challenge the nature of what is being taught. Whether they are charter schools or online courses or the Common Core, the academic content has been largely unchanged since the turn of the 20th century. The assumption of most adults seems to be that the only problem in education is how to ensure that all students get more of it. And yet, as we've seen, what matters most in getting and keeping a decent job today is not how much you know but rather what you can do with what you know.

When the Common Core was first being pushed by education leaders, promises were made about the creation of significantly improved standardized tests to accompany the higher academic standards. It was said that more critical thinking will be required as well as more writing. However, the two consortia developing the new tests have had to eliminate many performance tasks—where students apply what they've learned—in favor of the cheaper-to-grade multiple-choice test items. Even so, state education leaders continue to worry that they will not be able to afford the new tests. So long as we insist on testing every student every year, instead of testing only a sample of students every few years, we will be unable to afford the kinds of assessments, like the College and Work Readiness Assessment, that measure the skills that matter most.

Another reform that was pushed out by the Department of Education as a part of Race to the Top was the requirement that states begin assessing teacher effectiveness on the basis of students' standardized test scores. Thirty-five states currently use test scores as part of teacher evaluations. Teachers used to be under a great deal of psychological pressure to raise test scores and teach to the test. Now the pressure is economic. They worry that they will lose their jobs if their students do not produce good test results. I believe that this "reform" will only serve to accelerate the trend of teaching to the tests and to ensure that whatever good qualities that may exist in the Common Core will be lost in an increasingly test-prep-centered curriculum. And because there are only Common Core standards for language arts and mathematics, the time given to teaching other subjects will continue to decline—especially in the arts.

While many business leaders continue to push for increased use of standardized tests for measuring student achievement and teacher effectiveness, I have discovered that no corporations make important hiring or promotion decisions on the basis of a standardized test score. Even Google, the outlier, has given up the practice. What corporations rely on is collective human judgment, informed by evidence, as the 2013 interviews with Laszlo Bock, cited earlier, clearly show. While we in education are increasingly data driven, many in the business world are more evidence based—meaning that they rely on a combination of quantitative data and qualitative evidence. If this is good enough for our best businesses, then why isn't it good enough for our schools?

Finally, there is the question of whether the Common Core curriculum will result in students having work that is merely more difficult (and more frequently tested) or truly interesting to students. Will students be more actively engaged as learners with the new curriculum? I continue to worry about the impact of a test-prep curriculum on student motivation, as well as on teacher morale. A 2013 Gallup survey finds that while eight in ten fifth graders report being engaged in school, the number drops to four in ten by high school. Brandon Busteed (2013), executive director of Gallup Education, writes,

> The drop in student engagement for each year students are in school is our monumental, collective national failure. There are several things that might help to explain why this is happening—ranging from our overzealous focus on standardized testing and curricula to our lack of experiential and project-based learning pathways for students—not to mention the lack of pathways for students who will not and do not want to go on to college.

Student motivation remains a critical—and largely ignored—issue in education. My friends at Expeditionary Learning—a network of schools around the United States that has now surpassed the Knowledge Is Power Program (KIPP) in total number of students—focus on giving students work worth doing. In contrast to KIPP's carrot-and-stick approach to motivating students, Expeditionary Learning teachers strive to design inquiry lessons and projects that build on students' interests, knowing that this approach will result in higher-quality work. Research I conducted for *Creating Innovators* (2012) points to the importance of play, passion, and purpose in stimulating young people's intrinsic motivation.

The Best of Times: Real Innovation

The so-called education reforms I've just described have gar-
nered a great deal of media attention. Less well known but far more
important is the work being done by several new affiliations of
schools and districts. The Expeditionary Learning schools—along
with the High Tech High and New Tech High schools described in
The Global Achievement Gap—are active members of a growing network of K–12 schools and school districts across the United States
that are pursuing real innovation in education.

More than five hundred schools in ten school networks are
now part of the Deeper Learning Initiative, which is supported
by The William and Flora Hewlett Foundation and other funders.
According to the Hewlett website (www.hewlett.org), students
engaged in deeper learning

> are using their knowledge and skills in a way that prepares
> them for real life. They are mastering core academic con-
> tent, like reading, writing, math, and science, while learning
> how to think critically, collaborate, communicate effectively,
> direct their own learning, and believe in themselves. (Hewlett
> Foundation, n.d.)

(See also www.deeper-learning.org/resources.php for additional
resources.)

Another new effort, EdLeader21 supports teaching, learning,
and assessing the 4Cs: (1) critical thinking and problem solving,
(2) communication, (3) collaboration, and (4) creativity and innovation. Founded in 2010 and led by Ken Kay, who cofounded The
Partnership for 21st Century Skills in 2002, EdLeader21 now has 150
school districts in thirty-two states that are members and continues
to grow rapidly. They are organized as a professional learning community that works together to develop strategies for transforming
their districts, rubrics for assessing the 4Cs, and other vital resources
needed to transform classrooms. (See www.edleader21.com for more
information.)

Many business leaders decry the lack of innovation in education, not realizing how few schools, school districts, and states have

any kind of funding for educational research and development. In conversations with business executives over the last several years, I learned that Cisco Systems' research and development (R&D) budget is about 13 percent, Microsoft's 17 percent, Google's well over 20 percent. Even a manufacturing company, 3M, has a 6 percent R&D budget. When I ask school and education leaders what their R&D budget is, they laugh at me. I am proud to be an (unpaid) advisor to both the Hewlett Deeper Learning Initiative and EdLeader21 because I believe they are doing the essential educational R&D needed to transform education for the 21st century. They are creating existence proofs—models of what works—which show that schools and school districts can do a dramatically better job of preparing students for work, citizenship, and lifelong learning in the 21st century. Their inspiring work offers us a reason to be hopeful about the evolution of education in the United States.

Character

One of the questions I am frequently asked when I give talks to audiences familiar with *The Global Achievement Gap* (2008) is why I did not write about character as one of the essential survival skills. It is a good question, and one that I perhaps should have addressed in the book.

My main goal in writing that book was to understand the *new skills* all students must master for learning, citizenship, and work in the 21st century. The importance of character—of values—is not at all new to education or to human development. In the 1930s, the Swiss developmental psychologist Jean Piaget (1997) writes that the most important goal of education is to overcome egocentrism in two domains. Intellectually, overcoming egocentrism means replacing superstition or uninformed opinion with evidence and reason. Emotionally, overcoming egocentrism means developing what Piaget calls *reciprocity*, or what many of us might call *empathy*. I continue to believe that this is the best short summary of the aims of education that I have ever encountered.

Values also matter enormously as a vital part of the culture of a classroom and a school. Without trust and respect, neither students nor teachers will take intellectual risks or try new things. Without trust and respect—among students, between students and teachers, and among adults—there is no real learning or lasting change. The motto of the Finnish education system is "trust through professionalism." One of the reasons why our current education reform efforts are unlikely to produce real improvements is that they are compliance driven, punitive, and rooted, I believe, in a profound distrust of teachers.

Since writing *The Global Achievement Gap*, I have come to understand that there is a second meaning of *character* that is far more important than I had previously understood. MacArthur Foundation Award winner Angela Lee Duckworth's research and Paul Tough's (2012) excellent book *How Children Succeed* point to the importance of a set of character traits that can be best summed up as grit. Research shows that traits like perseverance, tenacity, and the ability to recover from setbacks and to self-regulate are more important to adult success than talent or IQ. Tough's book also reports on research that shows the extremely destructive effects of stress on the brain's capacity to develop these traits in infancy and early childhood. Poverty, he writes, causes more stress than any other single factor in childhood (Tough, 2012).

If we are serious about closing the achievement gap between our middle-class students and our most disadvantaged students, we must address the effects of childhood poverty in the United States. According to the National Center for Children in Poverty, the U.S. rate is more than 22 percent. I simply do not understand how our leaders can continue to perpetuate the belief that we can improve disadvantaged students' achievement by simply giving harder tests more frequently and by putting more pressure on teachers to teach to those tests.

When I first began my teaching career and worked with at-risk students in an alternative school-within-a-school, I learned that the most important thing I could do to keep students in school was to encourage them to discover their own reasons for learning. Students with whom I worked had very little hope for or belief in their future. I discovered that I had to help them connect their interests and passions with future possibilities. In addition to better understanding factors affecting early childhood brain development, I think it likely that future research will show the importance of intrinsic motivation in the development of grit. As a teacher and then as a researcher, I discovered that the intrinsic motivations of play, passion, and purpose are not just for young or privileged students. They are equally important for disadvantaged students and are reasons for them to acquire grit and to persist in learning and in life.

Genuine Innovation Scaling

It is increasingly true in the United States that what gets tested is all that gets taught. To scale innovation, we need broader agreement on the education outcomes that matter most, as well as an accountability system aligned with those outcomes. The key to accomplishing these two tasks, I believe, is for educators to more actively engage with business and community leaders and to work together to develop an Accountability 2.0 system.

It was business leaders, not policymakers, who generated the momentum for what I call Accountability 1.0. Nothing happened when *A Nation at Risk* was first published in 1983 until 1996, when Louis Gerstner, then CEO of IBM, called for a national summit on education. He was increasingly concerned that his company and others could not find enough skilled employees for their growing businesses. Most U.S. governors and the CEOs of major businesses attended. They applied pressure both to state legislatures and to the federal Department of Education to push for higher academic standards as well as accountability for meeting them.

Surprisingly, only a handful of educators were invited to that summit—and then only in the capacity of observers. I think the reason for this lack of inclusion is that many business leaders do not trust educators. In their eyes, teachers have jobs for life with no accountability. And teachers' unions have historically been far more protective than progressive. (The lack of trust goes both ways, as many educators see business leaders as only interested in profits.) Thus, the education accountability system had no real input from educators. Sadly, the dominant response of many educators to this problem has been merely to complain rather than to offer alternatives.

We urgently need education and business and community leaders to work together to fashion an accountability system that will incent much more powerful learning and teaching. It must be an accountability system based on performance standards—not content standards—and one that relies on both data and evidence.

First, we should use dramatically better assessments like the College and Work Readiness Assessment and the PISA-based test for schools. More information about the College and Work Readiness Assessment can be found online (http://cae.org/students /career-seeker/what-is-cla). Also visit www.americaachieves.org /oecd for more information on the PISA-based test for schools. Both assessments measure the skills that matter most—like critical thinking and problem solving—as well as students' ability to apply what they've learned previously to new questions or problems. We should also use an auditing strategy and test representative sample populations of students only every few years to reduce the testing frenzy that currently grips our schools. The substantial amounts of money that can be saved by reducing the frequency of testing could then be applied to the development of new curriculum materials and training programs for teachers.

Another essential part of an Accountability 2.0 system is requiring all students to have a digital portfolio in which they collect work that is evidence of progressive mastery of skills like critical thinking, oral and written communication, collaboration, and creative problem solving. Representatives from the business community should work with college teachers to audit random samples of these portfolios to ensure they meet the performance standards for college and work readiness. More than eight in ten business leaders have already indicated an interest in reviewing students' e-portfolios in a 2012 survey conducted by the Association of American Colleges and Universities (Hart Research Associates, 2013).

What about holding teachers accountable? The best educators and union leaders I know welcome accountability—not based on results of a single standardized test for which students have no accountability but rather on evidence of growth and effectiveness over time. All teachers should also have digital portfolios for initial licensure and recertification. These portfolios would include videos of their teaching, sample units of study, student work, and student course evaluations. I think teachers can and should be evaluated on the basis of evidence of improvement in their students' work over a school year, and school faculty can be held collectively accountable for attendance and graduation rates. Most teachers I've surveyed agree.

To scale innovations, we need courageous leadership at every level. We need business and community leaders who will advocate for the education outcomes that matter most in the 21st century and for an accountability system aligned with those outcomes. We need education leaders to advocate for higher, more professional standards for teacher licensure and recertification, and a dramatic overhaul of our schools of education. We need political leaders to address the devastating impact of childhood poverty on the ability to learn of a growing number of our young people. Finally, we need parents and students to demand better classrooms and schools in which what matters most is taught and assessed in ways that are both challenging and engaging.

References

Arum, R., & Roksa, J. (2011). *Academically adrift: Limited learning on college campuses.* Chicago: University of Chicago Press.

Bryant, A. (2013, June 19). In head-hunting, big data may not be such a big deal. *New York Times*, p. F6. Accessed at www.nytimes.com/2013/06/20/business/in-head-hunting-big-data-may-not-be-such-a-big-deal.html?pagewanted=all&_r=0 on March 27, 2014.

Brynjolfsson, E., & McAfee, A. (2011). *Race against the machine: How the digital revolution is accelerating innovation, driving productivity, and irreversibly transforming employment and the economy.* Lexington, MA: Digital Frontier Press.

Busteed, B. (2013, January 7). The school cliff: Student engagement drops with each school year [Web log post]. Accessed at http://thegallupblog.gallup.com/2013/01/the-school-cliff-student-engagement.html on November 2, 2013.

Center for Research on Education Outcomes at Stanford University. (2013). *National charter school study 2013.* Accessed at http://credo.stanford.edu/documents/NCSS%202013%20Final%20Draft.pdf on August 1, 2014.

Compton, R., & Wagner, T. (2010). *The Finland phenomenon: Inside the world's most surprising school system* [Documentary]. Accessed at www.2mminutes.com on August 1, 2014.

Duckworth, A. (2014). *The Duckworth lab: Publications*. Accessed at https://sites.sas.upenn.edu /duckworth/pages/research on August 1, 2014.

Greenwood, F. (2013, September 10.) Gap between US rich and poor reaches record width. *Global Post*. Accessed at www.globalpost.com/dispatch/news/regions/americas/united -states/130910/gap-between-us-rich-and-poor-reaches-record-width on August 1, 2014

Izzo, P. (2014, May 16). Congratulations to class of 2014, most indebted ever [Web log post]. *Wall Street Journal*. Accessed at http://blogs.wsj.com/numbers/congatulations-to-class- of-2014-the-most-indebted-ever-1368/ on August 1, 2014.

Hart Research Associates. (2007). *It takes more than a major: Employer priorities for college learning and student success—An online survey among employers conducted on behalf of the Association of American Colleges and Universities*. Washington, DC: Author. Accessed at www.aacu.org/leap/documents/2013_EmployerSurvey.pdf on October 20, 2013.

Hewlett Foundation. (n.d.). *Deeper learning*. Accessed at www.hewlett.org/programs /education/deeper-learning on November 2, 2013.

Lohr, S. (2013, April 20). Big data, trying to build better workers. *New York Times*. Accessed at www.nytimes.com/2013/04/21/technology/big-data-trying-to-build-better-workers .html on October 3, 2013.

Luhby, T. (2013, June 25). Recent college grads face 36 percent 'mal-employment' rate. *CNN Money*. Accessed at http://money.cnn.com/2013/06/25/news/economy/malemploy ment-rate/ on December 11, 2013.

Mui, Y. Q., & Jayakumar, A. (2013, September 6). Unemployment dips to 7.3 percent, but only 63 percent of Americans are in labor force. *Washington Post*. Accessed at http://articles .washingtonpost.com/2013–09–06/business/41816402_1_labor-force-labor-department -job-market on December 11, 2013.

National Center for Children in Poverty. (2014). *Basic facts about low-income children*. Accessed at www.nccp.org/publications/fact_sheets.html on August 13, 2014.

The National Commission on Excellence in Education. (1983, April). *A nation at risk: The imperative for educational reform*. (A report to the nation and the secretary of educa- tion United States Department of Education.) Accessed at http://datacenter.spps.org /uploads/sotw_a_nation_at_risk_1983.pdf on September 24, 2014.

Parr, C. (2013, May 10). *Not staying the course*. Inside higher education. Accessed at www .insidehighered.com/news/2013/05/10/new-study-low-mooc-completion-rates on August 1, 2014

Piaget, J. (1997). *The moral judgment of the child*. New York: Free Press.

Schneider, M., & Yin, L. (2012, April 3.) *Completion matters: the high cost of low community college graduation rates*. Washington, DC: American Enterprise Institute. Accessed at www.aei.org/outlook/education/higher-education/community-colleges/completion -matters-the-high-cost-of-community-college-graduation-rates on August 1, 2014

Suster, M. (2014, February 20). Clayton Christensen interview with Mark Suster at Startup Grind [Video file]. Accessed at www.youtube.com/watch?v=KYVdf5xyD8I on August 1, 2014.

Tough, P. (2012). *How children succeed: Grit, curiosity, and the hidden power of character.* Boston: Houghton Mifflin Harcourt.

Wagner, T. (2008). *The global achievement gap: Why even our best schools don't teach the new survival skills our children need—and what we can do about it.* New York: Basic Books.

Wagner, T. (2012). *Creating innovators: The making of young people who will change the world.* New York: Scribner.

Bernie Trilling

Bernie Trilling is a 21st century learning expert, advisor, author, founder and CEO of 21st Century Learning Advisors, and former global director of the Oracle Education Foundation, where he directed the development of education strategies, partnerships, and services and the foundation's ThinkQuest programs. He has served as board member for the Partnership for 21st Century Skills (P21), co-chaired the committee that developed the highly regarded rainbow learning framework, and is currently a P21 senior fellow.

Bernie has developed pioneering educational products and services and is an active member of a variety of organizations dedicated to bringing 21st century learning methods to students and teachers across the globe. He coauthored the widely acclaimed book *21st Century Skills: Learning for Life in Our Times* and has also written dozens of articles for educational journals and magazines. He is a featured speaker at numerous educational conferences and a contributor to the *Huffington Post* and the Partnership for 21st Century Skills' blogs.

To learn more about Bernie's work, visit www.21stcenturyskillsbook.com.

Chapter 7

Road Maps to Deeper Learning

Bernie Trilling

A different future, both confounding and full of hope, is already appearing in our daily lives. With a button click, shiny screens stored in pockets and on laps and desktops become instant portals to vast libraries and storerooms of media-packed information, knowledge, and online learning—along with distracting advertising, enticing entertainment, and persuasion masquerading as facts. Live news clips and round-the-clock, up-to-the-minute developments from every global corner flash on our digital panels and widescreens, keeping us instantly and perpetually informed—as streams of gripping images transfix our attention, leaving little room for reflection or deep analysis. With a screen tap, we instantly connect with friends, helpers, and experts from nearly anywhere, mingling and learning together, exploring and sharing insights and possible solutions to common concerns and issues—as well as droves of gossip, crowds of celebrity chatter, and flocks of clever tweets from a vast, global, public, social media network.

For learners and educators alike, it is truly an exciting, confounding, and hopeful time, as we all innovate our way through a rather bumpy transition toward a renewed learning landscape—one that may eventually empower all students for success in learning, in work, and in building a better world.

Winston Churchill is reported to have once said, "You can always count on the Americans to do the right thing . . . after they've tried everything else." Fortunately in the United States (and in part from witnessing the results of "everything else" attempted in education reform), a large number of classrooms, schools, and school networks have been hard at work repaving student pathways to modern success. Over the years, these repavers have been developing similar sets of learning practices, principles, and school cultures that all seem to fit together, forming an integral ecosystem for deeper, more compelling and meaningful learning for all students.

The ongoing implementation of the Common Core State Standards and their assessments is adding further motivational fuel for a shift toward this way of learning—from shallow memorization and recall to deeper understanding and creative applications of knowledge—a shift these deeper learning schools instituted early on in their history. It turns out that "Common Core and more" is what many of these school networks have been doing and refining for a long time.

Deeper Learning Schools

In 2010, the Hewlett Foundation initiated an informal study of eight networks of schools representing over four hundred schools in thirty-eight states. The eight networks consisted of the Asia Society, Big Picture Learning, ConnectED, EdVisions Schools, Envision Schools, Expeditionary Learning, High Tech High, and New Tech Network. Since 2010, two additional school networks have been added: Internationals Network for Public Schools and New Visions for Public Schools. This brings the total to more than five hundred schools in forty-one states serving 227,000 students, most of whom are low-income minority students. Recent reports and analyses that cover schools in these networks and others include *Time for Deeper Learning* (Traphagan & Zorich, 2013), "Learning From Leaders" (Cervone & Cushman, 2013), *Deeper Learning* (Martinez & McGrath, 2014), and "Deeper Learning for Every Student Every Day" (Schneider & Vander Ark, 2014).

These school networks were early adopters in developing the competencies identified to be most important for student success in the 21st century: critical thinking and problem solving, effective communications, productive collaboration, and the ability to learn how to learn, all applied to rigorous academic content.

The study first looked at each school network's guiding principles—the core values and goals for an education that they firmly believe (with convincing evidence) can regularly produce high levels of student success. A Wordle—a graphic representation of the most common words—of all these education principles (figure 7.1) revealed some preliminary insights.

Figure 7.1: Deeper learning principles Wordle.

A more comprehensive analysis of shared principles and practices based on surveys and interviews of network leaders, as well as multiple visits and conversations with teachers and students in these schools, uncovered common sets of practices (figure 7.2, page 180), which together formed what appeared to be a coherent, self-reinforcing learning system.

These common sets of practices can be summarized by six common themes:

1. **School culture**—For both students and educators, a professional culture of high expectations, responsibility, ownership, and self-direction along with a highly personal culture of caring, respect, trust, cooperation, community, and a common commitment to helping each other succeed

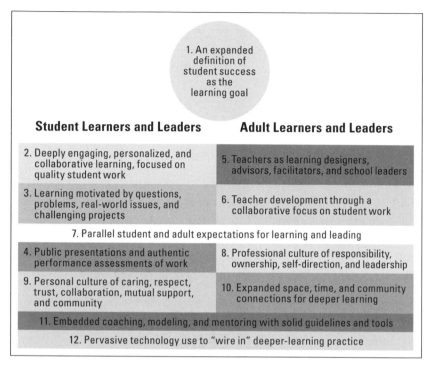

Source: Adapted from Hewlett report findings.

Figure 7.2: Deeper learning "ecosystem."

2. **Learning**—Active, deeply engaging, personalized, and collaborative approaches to learning motivated by relevant questions and problems, developed through deep inquiry, problem solving, and issue-based evidence gathering; the design of both rigorous and creative solutions and answers to real-world concerns in challenging projects, all with a focus on high-quality student work refined through reflection, supportive feedback, iteration, and continuous improvement

3. **Teaching**—Teachers as learning designers, model learners, mentors, guides, advisors, resource facilitators, project managers, and leaders all while expertly applying and modeling the same methods and skills their students are developing

4. **Assessment**—Student work evaluated through public presentations, demonstrations, and exhibitions by a variety of regular, authentic, performance-based assessments

incorporated into everyday learning activities and through reflective writing, feedback, and revision

5. **Development**—Teacher and student development focused on continually improving the quality of students' work and students' ability to reflect on and articulate their learning progress through portfolio presentations, collaborative evaluations, guidance, coaching, modeling, mentoring, and leadership

6. **Learning tools**—Pervasive access and use of technology and a variety of other learning resources, including opportunities to learn in communities, real and virtual, beyond school, all in support of deeper learning practices and outcomes

Research supported by the Raikes Foundation on the critical importance of motivational, social, and emotional factors for success in school (Farrington et al., 2012)—often called *student mindsets*—has led the Hewlett Foundation to add an additional set of student outcomes to its core list of desired deeper learning competencies, calling them *academic mindsets*. Seven key mindsets and learning strategies having a significant positive effect on student performance (measured by course grades) were identified from this thorough review of the related research. Based on this research, these seven factors can be grouped into three types of character qualities or student agency factors, which are all learnable and improvable if a school culture actively promotes them.

- Personal character qualities
   + Growth mindset—"I can learn."
   + Self-efficacy and confidence—"I can do this."
   + Purpose and relevance—"This is important to me."
- Performance character qualities
   + Goal setting and managing—"I can reach my goals."
   + Reflection and metacognition—"I know myself and what I need to do."
- Social character qualities

+ Social belonging—"I belong here."

+ Social capital—"I can get the help I need."

Recent research (Fanscali, Walter, & Dessein, 2013) on the use of these student agency factors in both deeper learning classrooms and in other network schools with a focus on high levels of student achievement indicates that certain learning practices promote positive improvements in specific character qualities. Three of these learning practices (highlighted in figure 7.3) promote all seven factors—suggesting that these powerful learning strategies, if done well, can dramatically boost the development of all agency factors, and can lead to deeper and wider learning achievements for all students.

The link between teaching and learning practices and the development of character qualities is clear—student agency is not something that just happens; it is the result of intentional learning strategies, programs, and school culture. What do these schools do to enhance student agency?

- They use *project-based learning approaches* for which students take increasing ownership of their learning goals and roles and work in teams to create learning products that they proudly present to the public, sharing the twists, turns, and final results of their learning explorations.

- They reach out beyond their walls in *community partnerships*, working on real-world issues and service projects in internships, apprenticeships, and mentored work experiences guided by working professionals with practical expertise in their fields.

- They rely on strong *advisory programs*, which allow students to belong to an ongoing family of support with at least one consistent adult advisor, plus a trustworthy group of caring students.

The results of these practices—intensively, artfully, and consistently applied for the benefit of all students—are schools that produce high levels of student agency. By genuinely engaging and motivating students to achieve beyond their expectations; by cultivating the grit and self-direction to persist and persevere through the

Practices	Growth Mindset	Self-Efficacy and Confidence	Relevance, Purpose	Social Belonging	Goal Setting and Managing	Reflection and Meta-cognition	Social Capital
Project-Based Learning	✓	✓	✓	✓	✓	✓	✓
Encouragement of a Growth Mindset	✓	✓					
Relevant, Personalized Instruction			✓		✓		
Alternative Grading Policies	✓	✓			✓		
Advisory Programs	✓	✓	✓	✓	✓	✓	✓
Community Meetings	✓	✓		✓			
Interdisciplinary Teams			✓	✓			
One-to-One Access to Technology		✓	✓	✓			
Character Education	✓	✓	✓				
Common Intellectual Mission	✓	✓	✓		✓		✓
Schoolwide 21st Century Learning Goals			✓		✓	✓	
Reflection Protocols				✓	✓	✓	
Restoration Room		✓		✓	✓		
Community Partnerships and Presentations of Work	✓	✓	✓	✓	✓	✓	✓

Figure 7.3: Student agency factors and practices.

Source: Fancsali, Walter, & Dessein, 2013.

many challenges of high school, postsecondary education, and on to securing productive and creative work; by building resilient families; and by engaging students in local community life as active local and global citizens, these schools motivate their students and help them develop the can-do mindsets needed for success.

A Prism for Deeper Learning

By assembling all the common components that make up this deeper learning ecosystem—the core competencies of *essential skills*, rigorous *content understandings*, the *mindsets and learning strategies* that positively motivate student achievement, and the *deeper learning practices* that build the capabilities most valued in today's world—we can construct a prism model (figure 7.4) based on research findings of the National Academy of Sciences (Pellegrino & Hilton, 2012) in their analysis of 21st century deeper learning.

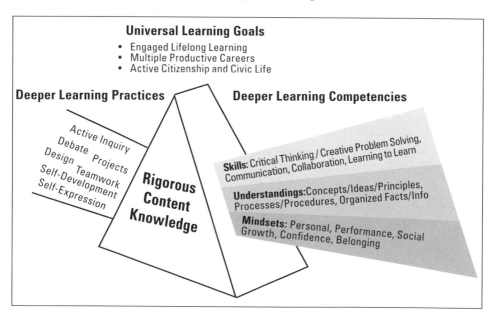

Figure 7.4: The prism model for deeper learning.

In this new model, under the banner of three broad universal goals, the sunlight of common deeper learning practices illuminates the many-hued prism body of rigorous content knowledge, producing a rainbow of increasing competencies—the skills, understandings, and mindsets (the learning "SUM") needed for 21st century success:

- Essential skills
    + Critical thinking—Critical and creative problem solving and systems thinking
    + Communication—Oral, written, and media literacy
    + Collaboration—Teamwork and leadership
    + Learning to learn—Reflecting on and applying appropriate learning strategies
- Rigorous understandings in a variety of content knowledge areas
    + Organized facts in well-structured knowledge schemes
    + Core concepts, ideas, and principles
    + Core procedures and processes
- Motivational mindsets
    + Personal qualities—Growth mindset, self-efficacy/confidence, purpose/relevance
    + Performance qualities—Goal setting/managing, reflection/metacognition
    + Social qualities—Social belonging, social capital

With this foundational prism as a guide, evaluations of the work students create in their learning programs can be devised to help gauge the levels of deeper learning achieved in ways that current assessments of surface work do not.

One attempt to create such a deeper learning student work evaluation was prompted by a 2013 Hewlett Foundation gathering of deeper learning thought leaders, practitioners, researchers, policymakers, public relations experts, and students. Mixed teams representing all of the backgrounds, led by high school student facilitators, examined and discussed rich examples of student work assembled from across the deeper learning network of schools. A checklist was used to help design this collaborative activity of evaluating deeper learning work.

The deeper learning student-work review checklist provides an example of a structured review protocol that, when combined with facilitated discussions, can offer substantial opportunities for deep, reflective "learning about learning" for those seeking to better understand what makes deeper learning "deeper" in practice. Visit **go.solution-tree.com/21stcenturyskills** to download this checklist.

More importantly, student-work reviews—especially of complex assignments and real-world projects—can give teachers and parents an invaluable window into the thinking, skills, understandings, and mindsets developing within each student.

A wide spectrum of other more rigorous evaluation methods, both summative (at the end of learning units) and formative (during learning activities), are being used to measure student gains in many of the desired deeper learning outcomes, with further refinements and new evaluation tools and rubrics now under development. In addition to the Common Core assessments that so far include items measuring critical thinking, written communication skills, and content knowledge in English language arts and mathematics, other larger scale evaluation options in place—or soon to be available— include the following:

- School-based assessments

    + PISA-based test for schools—Also known in the United States as the OECD Test for Schools, this is a student assessment tool geared for use by schools and networks of schools to support research, benchmarking, and school-improvement efforts. It provides descriptive information and analyses on the skills and creative application of knowledge of fifteen-year-old students in reading, mathematics, and science, comparable to the international PISA.

    + The College and Work Readiness Assessment Plus (CWRA+)—This high school assessment measures critical thinking, analysis and problem solving, scientific and quantitative reasoning, writing, critical reading and evaluation, writing effectiveness and mechanics, and the ability to critique and construct arguments.

+ ACT's WorkKeys Assessments and the National Career Readiness Certificate Plus (NCRC+)—This series of work-readiness skills assessments is available to high school students as well as employees. It includes measures of problem solving, critical thinking, applied mathematics, locating and analyzing information, reading for information, work discipline, teamwork, service orientation, and management skills and is administered through a wide network of ACT testing centers throughout the United States.

+ The American Institute for Research (AIR) Study of Deeper Learning Opportunities and Outcomes—A research study funded by the Hewlett Foundation designed to examine the ways in which twenty exemplary schools from the deeper learning network and similarly matched schools near them provide opportunities for deeper learning, and the impact these opportunities have on the development of five deeper learning dimensions as well as on a wide variety of other student outcomes, including postsecondary achievements. Results from this study will be released throughout 2014.

• Classroom-based assessments and evaluations

+ The Deeper Learning Student Assessment System (DLSAS)—This joint development of the Stanford Center for Assessment, Learning and Equity (SCALE) and Envision Schools is actively used in four of the deeper learning networks. The DLSAS is designed as a series of performance-based tasks and rubric assessments aligned with Common Core and college- and career-ready standards, all administered online.

+ EdLeader21 Master Rubrics—These are developed by EdLeader21 staff with collaborative guidance from over seventy U.S. school districts for grades 3–4, 7–8, and 11–12.

+ Local effort—Schools and districts create their local versions of evaluative rubrics to measure 21st century deeper learning competencies. Having teachers and administrators design and develop their own rubrics builds strong ownership and commitment to implementing and sustaining deeper learning practices.

Efforts underway to create wide-scale, comparable evaluation rubrics, allowing students from different districts and states to be evaluated on similar criteria, are a sign of movement toward a broader system of assessments and a maturing deeper learning movement, gathering ever-wider support for 21st century student competencies and more sustainable implementations of deeper learning approaches.

A Road Map to Deeper Learning: The Transformation Approach

How does a school, or an entire school district, prompted by the adoption of Common Core standards and the new demands of a rapidly shifting world, go from traditional to deep? What are the steps, stages, and phases they must undergo to transform all the interlocked parts of a deep-rooted, resistant-to-change system? Michael Fullan (2013) writes,

In education we have just about reached the end of squeezing good out of an outdated school system. The current system is too costly, too ineffective, and as any kid will tell you, deadly boring. This can be changed and it will turn out to be easier than we think—easier because the new alternatives are incredibly less expensive and immensely more engaging. (p. 5)

Transforming traditional education systems into 21st century deeper learning systems can seem like a challenge more daunting than ending world hunger, stopping climate change, and achieving world peace, all at the same time. In the United States alone, this challenge involves 130,000 public and private preK–12 schools in fifty different state-run education systems, managed by 13,600 school districts, all shifting over to new and expanded educational goals, and inspiring over 3.8 million teachers to bring deeper teaching and learning practices to over 55 million students (National Center for Education Statistics, 2013)!

Two Change Models

The EdLeader21 organization and its professional learning community of over one hundred pioneering U.S. school districts has recognized seven key steps (figure 7.5) along the transformational road to 21st century deeper learning.

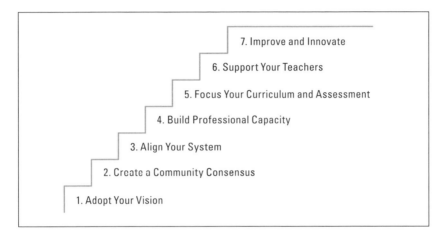

Source: *Kay & Greenhill, 2013.*
Figure 7.5: EdLeader21's seven steps for schools and districts.

Other experts with deep experience in the challenges of transforming school systems have outlined similar high-level frameworks, such as Michael Fullan and Maria Langworthy's (2013) five key transformational implementation steps (see also Fullan, 2013):

1. Forge deep commitment to the common purpose among partners.

2. Design a small number of ambitious goals defined by the common purpose.

3. Develop measures, tools, and feedback systems aligned to those goals.

4. Invest in focused capacity-building programs.

5. Continually measure and analyze what is working, learning from the work.

From empirically based change models such as these and from early results of ongoing research and analyses of the successful shifts to new models, a clearer picture of the common stages and phases of education systems transformation, especially at the district level, is slowly emerging.

Deeper Learning District-Transformation Model

Two approaches to change can be found in organizations and institutions. The common one is *improving* what's not working well; the more difficult, rarer, one is shifting and *transforming* what is now being done to something quite different and new—new goals, new rules of the game, shifts in what everyone does each day, and changes in how everyone thinks of what they are doing and why. This second type of change, the more challenging transformational one, is now staring many education systems in the face.

The good news is that transformation doesn't need to be done all at once. Transformations (like learning) can happen in well-chunked, well-planned stages, where the shifts in both thinking and doing can be phased in over time. Only in looking backward does it seem like a huge renovation. Of course the process can go much faster if one can visit, watch, interact, and discuss over time with help from expert coaches.

The deeper learning district-transformation cycle, shown in figure 7.6, offers a high-level navigational road map to deeper learning based on lessons learned from successful and, especially, not-so-successful experiences in transforming traditional, conventional schools and districts into deeper learning ones. The most important feature of this cycle is that it is iterative—each new wave of change follows a circular path that leads back to the top of the next round with opportunities to deepen and improve the changes gained in the previous cycle and to add new methods, practices, protocols, tools, and supports.

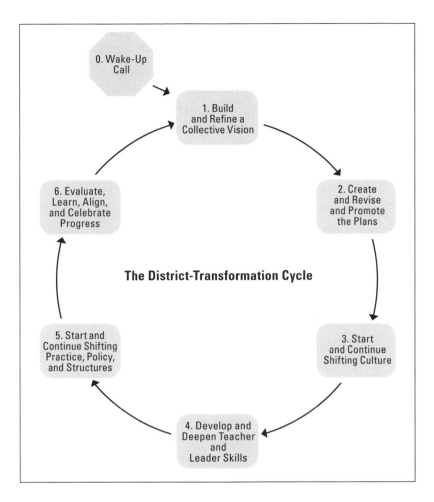

Figure 7.6: The deeper learning district-transformation cycle.

Every stage in the cycle, including the initial wake-up call, brings challenges and changes that eventually result in shifting all the interlocking parts of the original education system to a newly integrated learning ecosystem. The features, actions, and priorities for each stage of the cycle (and the instigating wake-up call) are as follows.

Stage 0: The Wake-Up Call

The wake-up call can come from any number of directions: from parents who want their students to be more engaged in their learning, from teachers who want to rebalance teaching for assessment performance with more applied learning that better answers the perennial question of why do we have to learn this, from students, from administrators frustrated with trying everything else and still not putting a big enough dent in the dropout rate or whole-school yearly performance, or from the business community not really seeing the level of work skills they need from the graduates of the school system.

Part of being a good transformational leader is to seize these moments of dissatisfaction, concern, and demands; embrace the wake-up call; and set the stage for the transformative journey to come.

Stage 1: Build and Refine a Collective Vision

If there is a single lesson to be learned from past transformational efforts in hundreds of schools, it is this: the stakeholder group you leave out in the early stages of forming your new collective vision will likely be the group that most resists your change efforts down the road.

It is critical in a long-term, multi-stakeholder change process to make sure every important group—parents, teachers, administrators, students, union leaders, school board members, elected officials, nonprofit organizations, the business community, and more—is represented at the collective table as soon as possible, so that the newly forming goals and mission are fully owned by everyone who cares about education. Those with the power to support or thwart education transformation must feel they are adding their colors to the collective painting of what a 21st century student must learn to be successful. It is also essential to keep all stakeholders engaged throughout the long transformation journey and to revisit and reinforce the new vision at least annually, celebrating successes, adding refinements to the collective vision from lessons learned along the way, and deepening the collective support for the next round of changes.

Stage 2: Create, Revise, and Promote the Plans

Once there is a shared vision of the new learning goals and desired student outcomes for the district schools, it's time to enlist a core leadership team to create a phased, strategic plan on how to get there. Incorporating feedback from stakeholder groups on drafts of this plan helps ensure that red flags are avoided or resolved before the plan is launched. It is also crucial to develop an implementation plan in close coordination with the strategic plan, making sure the necessary financial, organizational, political, and instructional supports are in place, or will be when needed, before going live with the plan.

In the first phase of the plan, it's also a good idea to focus on a small set of achievable changes that have the potential to signal a visible shift in learning practice and school culture, such as implementing project-oriented teacher professional development and having students begin to present their project work to the community in evening exhibitions.

Stage 3: Start and Continue Shifting Culture

In many ways, the shift to a learning culture of trust, collaboration, caring, respect, and mutual support—as well as a professional culture of high expectations, personal responsibility, and a commitment to constant learning and improving—has to start with the adults in the education system. This is often the most challenging of all the early shifts needed, given the isolated and competitive environments that can exist in traditional educational institutions.

There is convincing evidence that without the adults in the system able to embrace and adopt a collaborative learning culture among themselves and then model these mindsets and behaviors for students, the chances for a successful transformation are significantly diminished.

Of course, this culture shifting can be done in phases too, but there needs to be early indications that the adults are transformation ready and are willing to move toward increased collaboration, personal and collective responsibility, and a learning culture of continually finding and doing what it takes to help all students learn what they need to be successful.

It takes strong leadership and effective professional development to shift an entire school or organizational culture. Stages 3 and 4 must work hand in hand to share training and development in new practices, mindsets, and new ways of relating to each other, as well as to establish a learning community that can help make the changes down the road more of a learning adventure, similar to the engaging learning explorations students will be experiencing.

Stage 4: Develop and Deepen Teacher and Leader Skills

Throughout the many stages of the transformation cycle, the largest investments of time, funding, and other resources will most likely be in the form of professional development, which will continually build and enhance the deeper learning practices of teachers and the distributed leadership skills of the leadership team. Transformational change is hard work that demands constant learning—new teaching skills and methods, new ways of engaging students and teachers, new policies and shifts in community practices, new programs and initiatives that need careful stewarding, and most importantly, leaders who can continuously communicate the benefits of staying the course through thick and thin.

For teachers, training in project-based and student-centered learning practices, performance-based assessment methods, and effective use of technology to support deeper learning are all important early priorities. For administrators, the important challenges to tackle in the first few transformative cycles include devising creative ways of shifting schedules, configuring space, altering school policies, creating new learning opportunities outside of school, and making sure that the coaching and professional development resources are in place to support everyone through all the changes.

Stage 5: Start and Continue Shifting Practice, Policy, and Structures

All the common functions of an education system—curriculum and standards, instruction, assessment, the learning environments, leadership and teacher capacity, technology infrastructure, community partnerships, and much more—have to change in a coordinated way, one phase at a time. One of the trickiest parts of this process is coordinating the timing and sequencing of sets of changes so their implementation makes sense and goes well. For instance, when enough teachers have been sufficiently trained and have begun implementing project learning and performance-assessment approaches that require longer periods of classroom time, it makes sense to shift the school schedule to a block schedule with additional time for teachers to collaborate and plan their learning projects. This will also require administrators to work out all the accompanying infrastructure and resource issues to successfully implement the change.

The sequencing of specific changes in the interlocking operations of an education system must be carefully worked out in the implementation plan, with plenty of time built in for handling unforeseen consequences. It is important to set an expectation along the way that each new wave of change will no doubt be a bit rough at first and will get better with adjustments and alignments to all the other changes going on.

Stage 6: Evaluate, Learn, Align, and Celebrate Progress

In a long-term, transformative process that asks a great deal from everyone involved, it is essential to regularly evaluate what is going well and what isn't, and readjust.

The key questions to be answered in this stage of the transformative cycle are:

- Are we getting better at helping all students build the essential skills, understandings, and mindsets for success?

- What can we do to get even better at this?

And most importantly, it's now time to celebrate successes—even small ones—especially in the first few cycles of change. This gives confidence and hope that the benefits of further changes to come will be worth the effort.

Assessment of Transformation Results

One of the challenges of evaluating the results of early transformation work is that legacy measures may still be in place that can't capture all the benefits gained from recent changes in a school or district—they may not show any significant gains, and may even show declines during a period of rapid change. Also, brand-new assessment measures won't have enough historical data to indicate solid improvements yet. This has been the experience with some of the early implementations of the new Common Core assessments.

To overcome these challenges, it is critical to set an expectation among all stakeholders that it may take a while for the results of a long-term transformation process to clearly show all the benefits of the changes. These expectations must be set well before any official evaluation or assessment results come out, especially for parents, elected officials, and the press. This may be one more reason to have students exhibit their project work to the public early in the process, as this can serve as an alternative form of authentic assessment that can give community members a sense of pride in the accomplishments students are already achieving in the new initiative.

Ensuring resources, learning practices, organizational structures, school culture, learning tools, and all the rest make sense and are aligned with each other through each transformation cycle is challenging. The promise of fixing things in the next cycle may not be sufficient, so planning for extra time to make necessary adjustments before embarking on the next cycle may be essential.

Having a regular, year-end cycle of evaluating, aligning, and readjusting plans; recognizing lessons learned; and celebrating all the hard work and accomplishments of students, teachers, administrators, parents, and stakeholders involved will help keep motivation levels up for the challenges yet to come.

The Napa Journey

Nestled within the rolling hills and valleys of the wine country of northern California, Napa holds a rich mix of farm workers; small-business owners; vineyard and specialty food growers; government and service workers; retirees who have come for the quieter pleasures of a more small-town, rural lifestyle; and a pioneering education system committed to preparing all students for 21st century success.

In 1991, a gathering of Napa business and education leaders, called the Business Education Partnership, voiced deep worries that graduates from Napa schools were not prepared for the challenges of the new global, high-tech economy. A year later, they formed a community planning group to reinvent learning in one public high school to hopefully provide a model for surrounding schools. In 1997, Napa New Technology High School opened its doors to its first class of one hundred students, with an expanded set of education goals; a different approach to teaching and learning centered on project-based, student-centered learning; collaborative technology access for every student; and a culture of trust, respect, control, and responsibility. Napa New Tech quickly became a showcase for 21st century deeper learning, attracting visitors from all over the globe to see real education innovation in action.

In 2000 and 2003, grants from the Bill and Melinda Gates Foundation helped establish and fund the work of the New Tech Foundation, a nonprofit organization created with the goals of deepening learning at Napa New Tech and expanding this model of learning to many more schools nationwide. In 2009, New Tech Foundation became a subsidiary of KnowledgeWorks, an educational foundation dedicated to readying all students for college and careers, adding new investments for scaling and spreading the model even further, and renaming its rapidly growing collection of schools the New Tech Network (as of this writing there are well over 134 New Tech schools in the United States and two in Australia). In October 2014, New Tech returned to being an independent education organization separate from KnowledgeWorks.

In 2008, Napa Valley Unified School District (NVUSD), encouraged by the increasing success of Napa New Tech High School, adopted NVUSD 2015—a plan to move other district schools to the New Tech approach. In 2010, fourteen years after the first Napa New Tech school opened, a brand-new comprehensive high school, American Canyon High School, opened its doors with the intent of fully adopting the New Tech model. As of 2013, a total of ten NVUSD schools—four elementary, four middle, and two high schools—are now part of the New Tech 21st century deeper learning bandwagon, and even schools in other Napa County districts beyond Napa Valley Unified are making plans to adopt the New Tech model in the near future.

What were the factors that tipped the Napa District to finally commit to transforming its schools to a deeper learning model? And what are the lessons learned that can help other districts go about their own transformations? There were at least eight key strategies, mostly intentional, some serendipitous, that came together over time to enable a whole district to take on the deeper learning transformation challenge. They can be called the eight I's of innovation and education reinvention:

1. **Involvement of all stakeholders**—Ongoing engagement with community stakeholders from education, business, community organizations, parents, and so on creates increasingly deeper commitments to support education transformation. Since the first meeting of the Napa Business Education Partnership in 1991 to the current district commitment to transform a total of ten schools to the New Tech model, community support—with help from community organizations like NapaLearns, a strong local education foundation—continues to grow and gather momentum for deeper learning throughout the Napa region.

2. **Interactions with existing deeper learning schools**—Visits, dialogues, and discussions that grow more frequent and focused over time help make the seemingly impossible changes real and clearly achievable. In the Napa case, there were valuable educator and community interactions with the pioneering New Tech High School right in the backyard, including ongoing school visits and walkthroughs, student-guided tours, classroom observations, teacher and administrator panel discussions, presentations and discussions of student projects, and so on.

3. **Intentional leadership**—Transformational leadership incorporates a strong vision captured in clear strategic plans and carefully crafted implementation guides. This type of leadership requires leaders who are deeply committed to the everyday changes needed to build school cultures and operational supports that make these shifts easier and more rewarding for everyone. It also requires continual impactful

communications focused on instilling a common vision. In the Napa district, the vision and the steps to achieve it are continually communicated through a wide variety of community meetings, school and district trainings, fundraising events, conferences, professional development opportunities, and catchy posters (figure 7.7) visually portraying the essence of the transformations ahead.

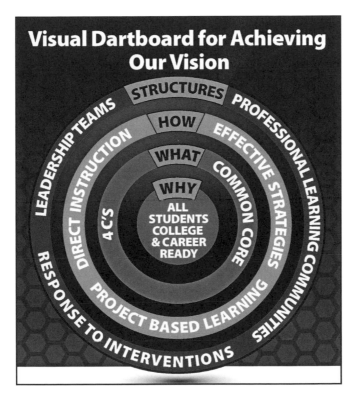

Source: Napa Valley Unified School District. Used with permission.

Figure 7.7: Napa Valley Unified School District transformation poster.

4. **Implementation capacity**—With clear, strategic implementation plans in place, the ability to carry out schoolwide transformations requires widespread capacity building and deep resource support for leaders to effectively manage all the steps in the implementation plans. These plans should inspire and support the development of new skills for both teachers

and administrators. One significant reason the Napa district transformation went into high gear was the fact that a founding New Tech High School principal, deeply versed in the daily ins and outs of what it takes to make a successful New Tech school, joined the Napa district team as director of secondary education and began to work closely with a new superintendent whose stated mission is to make sure all students in the entire district have the advantages of a 21st century deeper learning education.

5. **Investments of resources**—Schools need to invest any financial, physical, and professional resources gifted from foundations, donors, local businesses, and parents, so that when needed, there is adequate support available to transform learning and schooling practices. Napa is especially fortunate to have a number of local school-supporting foundations, such as the longstanding Napa Valley Education Foundation, and NapaLearns, which was established in 2010 to raise funds and support capacity building specifically in the Napa district and county schools to help them move to project-based learning approaches and the New Tech model.

6. **Infiltration**—Bringing the expertise and coaching support right into classrooms—from educator-coaches who have "lived the transformation," know how to make the dozens of small educational decisions that arise each day add up to moving one day closer to a deeper learning model, and know how to sustain these changes—is vital for successful transformation work. In the Napa schools that wanted to adopt the New Tech model, this "infiltration" was accomplished in part by putting at least one enthusiastic and expert New Tech–trained teacher in a classroom at the target school with release time to spend hours in an embedded model classroom observing and learning from the expert teacher. This made it easier for teachers to experience real and doable teaching transformations in their own school with their own students.

7. **Intensive professional development**—Such professional development is especially important in the new practices and

learning methods most needed to make the transformation happen, as well as in the types of distributed leadership skills essential to having everyone own and manage the major shifts to deeper learning. In Napa, this was brought about through the professional development efforts of the expanding New Tech Network of trainers and coaches, as well as through a close relationship with the Buck Institute for Education (BIE), a northern California nonprofit that has led the move to project-based learning methods through its wide network of PBL coaches and trainers. As of 2013, well over six hundred of the thousand Napa district teachers have received at least forty hours of PBL training, and in the last two years, Napa New Tech has hosted BIE's PBL World annual conference, bringing wonderful opportunities for Napa teachers to learn PBL methods from the best and most experienced coaches, teachers, and leaders. Recently, thanks to fundraising by the NapaLearns organization, a half-tuition reduction is being offered to any Napa county teacher who wants to enroll in a master's degree program with a focus on project-based learning and technology integration at a nearby university— adding one more powerful and intensive professional development incentive.

8. **Improvisation and continuous improvement**—This journey to become a 21st century deeper learning system is transformational. It is one of the greatest challenges any school, district, state, or country can take on. Although there are lots of common ordeals along the way that offer opportunities to learn from those who have gone down similar bumpy roads before, each educational institution has unique challenges that must be solved with creative improvisation and a steadfast commitment to learning and improving what works. The journey, as we've seen in this Napa case profile, can be a long and winding one that takes persistence, constant communication of the vision and its benefits, and a focus on each important step. It involves continually bringing along new supporters and cheerleaders, learning from mistakes and setbacks, and always deepening the resolve and widening the circle of

commitment to the goals of preparing all students for success in lifelong learning, productive careers, and an active civic life.

With these eight strategies gleaned from a real district's transformation-in-action story, a more grounded and operational road map to 21st century deeper learning can be outlined. This is in no small part due to the guidance provided by proven transformation leaders such as Michael Fullan and EdLeader21 pioneers, by research on school district transformation challenges (Levin, Datnow, & Carrier, 2012), and by well-tested models of transformational change and leadership in the business world (Anderson & Anderson, 2010a, 2010b).

Mapping all the stages in the transformation cycle against the eight I's provides a useful transformative energy investment chart (table 7.2). Highlighting in progressively darker shades denotes which strategies are more important to apply in each transformative stage.

There is clearly much more research and detail to be added to each of the stages in this proposed deeper learning transformation road map. Hopefully, this overview can begin to provide some of the helpful guidance and encouragement needed for more districts and schools to embark on their deeper learning transformation journeys, knowing that many others have successfully navigated similar roads to the brighter shores of a 21st century deeper learning education system.

The Prospects for a Deeper Learning Climate Change

There is much to celebrate in the movement toward deeper learning and 21st century competencies. Education leaders, practitioners, researchers, policymakers, and funders are increasingly gathering and learning from each other, meeting and working together to sketch the next steps in syncing the learning landscape with the opportunities and demands of our times.

As the 21st century deeper learning movement grows and matures, opportunities are expanding for all students everywhere to learn what is now needed for success in further schooling, in multiple productive careers, in raising strong and resilient families, in active community involvement and global citizenship, and in deep and rich lifetimes of enjoyable learning.

Table 7.1: Levels of "Energy Investments" in Strategies Applied to the Stages of the Transformation Cycle

Strategies	Stage 0. Embrace the Wake-Up Call	Stage 1. Build and Refine a Collective Vision	Stage 2. Create and Revise, and Promote the Plans	Stage 3. Start and Continue Shifting Culture	Stage 4. Develop and Deepen Teacher and Leader Skills	Stage 5. Start and Continue Shifting Practice, Policy, and Structures	Stage 6. Evaluate, Learn, Align, and Celebrate Progress
Involvement of all stakeholders							
Interactions with existing deeper learning schools							
Intentional leadership							
Implementation capacity							
Investments of resources							
Infiltration							
Intensive professional development							
Improvisation and continuous improvement							

References

Anderson, L. A., & Anderson, D. (2010a). *Beyond change management: How to achieve break-through results through conscious change leadership* (2nd ed.). San Francisco: Pfeiffer.

Anderson, L. A., & Anderson, D. (2010b). *The change leader's roadmap: How to navigate your organization's transformation* (2nd ed.). San Francisco: Pfeiffer.

Cervone, B., & Cushman, K. (2013). Learning from leaders: Core practices of six schools. In R. E. Wolfe, A. Steinberg, & N. Hoffman (Eds.), *Anytime, anywhere: Student-centered learning for schools and teachers* (pp. 15–53). Cambridge, MA: Harvard Education Press.

Fancsali, C., Walter, R. J., & Dessein, L. (2013). *Student agency practices in the Middle Shift Learning Networks.* Columbia, MD: IMPAQ International.

Farrington, C. A., Roderick, M., Allensworth, E., Nagaoka, J., Keyes, T. S., Johnson, D. W., et al. (2012). *Teaching adolescents to become learners: The role of noncognitive factors in shaping school performance.* Chicago: University of Chicago, Consortium on Chicago School Research.

Fullan, M. (2013). *Stratosphere: Integrating technology, pedagogy, and change knowledge.* Toronto: Pearson Canada.

Fullan, M., & Langworthy, M. (2013). *Towards a new end: New pedagogies for deep learning.* Seattle, WA: Collaborative Impact.

Kay, K., & Greenhill, V. (2013). *The leader's guide to 21st century education: 7 steps for schools and districts.* New York: Pearson Education.

Levin, B., Datnow, A., & Carrier, N. (2012). *Changing school district practices.* Boston: Jobs for the Future.

Martinez, M., & McGrath, D. (2014). *Deeper learning: A blueprint for schools in the twenty-first century.* New York: The New Press.

National Center for Education Statistics. (2013). *Digest of Education Statistics: 2010–11 data and projections for 2013–14 school year.* Washington, DC: Author.

Pellegrino, J., & Hilton, M. L. (2012). *Education for life and work: Developing transferable knowledge and skills in the 21st century.* Washington, DC: National Research Council.

Schneider, C., & Vander Ark, T. (2014). *Deeper learning for every student every day.* Accessed at http://cdno.gettingsmart.com/wp-content/uploads/2013/12/DLForEveryStudent_FINAL.pdf on August 5, 2014.

Traphagan, K., & Zorich, T. (2013). *Time for deeper learning: Lessons from five high schools.* Boston: National Center on Time and Learning.

Charles Fadel

Charles Fadel is a global education thought leader and expert, author, and inventor, with several affiliations. He is founder and chairman of Center for Curriculum Redesign (www.curriculumredesign .org), a nonprofit dedicated to answering the seminal question, What should students learn for the 21st century? and looking at redesign as a deeply substantial, ambitiously incremental (but not radical, so as to be realistically feasible) rethinking of knowledge, skills, character, and metacognition needed to prosper in life.

Charles is also the founder of the Fondation Helvetica Educatio (Geneva, Switzerland), visiting practitioner at Harvard Graduate School of Education, chair of the Education Committee of the Business and Industry Advisory Committee of the Organisation for Economic Co-operation and Development (BIAC), and coauthor of the best-selling book *21st Century Skills: Learning for Life in Our Times*. Charles is also senior fellow, human capital, at The Conference Board, and senior fellow, Partnership for 21st Century Skills. Formerly, he was board member at Innovate/Educate; angel investor with Beacon Angels in Boston; and Global Education Lead at Cisco Systems.

He has worked with a wide variety of education ministries and organizations and has contributed to education projects in more than thirty countries. He has been featured by media such as National Public Radio (NPR), the Canadian Broadcasting Corporation (CBC), the *Huffington Post*, and others.

Charles holds a bachelor of science in electronics and physics with a minor in neuroscience, and a master's in business administration. He has been awarded five patents.

Chapter 8

21st Century Curriculum: A Global Imperative

Charles Fadel

How do we prepare our students to thrive in a rapidly changing world? In the 21st century, humanity is witnessing remarkable changes that affect our societies, economies, and personal lives: international mobility, shifts in family structures, increasing diversity in populations, globalization and its impact on economic competitiveness and social cohesion, new and emerging occupations and careers, rapid and continued advances in technology and its increased use, and new knowledge about learning. This reconfiguration of our world is forcing us to explore ways to redesign *what* is being taught in schools, not just *how* we teach.

Acceptance and integration of technology and access to information have become integral components of our societies. The pervasiveness of technology creates learning opportunities never seen before. Expectations of employers are also changing: in addition to hiring workers who harness the power of digital tools, employers are demanding that workers be skilled in thinking critically and creatively to generate original solutions, solve problems, and have the confidence to bring about positive change. Moreover, new research from the learning sciences has revealed vast new insights on how people learn (Bransford, Brown, & Cocking, 2000). The role of students in their own learning is at the heart of these new ideas, and student engagement is a key priority of the 21st century learning agenda. These changes have made clear the need to reposition education systems to ensure that learners have the skills necessary to learn, live, and work in this century.

Several key bodies of work have recently explored the implications of emergent trends on current and future demands on traits of individuals and education systems at large. These resources include the following.

- *Beyond Current Horizons* program (Futurelab, 2014)

- *The Next 25 Years? Future Scenarios and Future Directions for Education and Technology* (Facer & Sandford, 2010)

- *Think Scenarios* and *Trends Shaping Education* publications (OECD, 2006, 2013)

- *Future Work Skills 2020* (Davies, Fidler, & Gorbis, 2011)

- *Forecast 3.0* (KnowledgeWorks Foundation, 2012)

These bodies of work, along with other more general analyses of current and emerging trends and futures models, serve as the foundation for the discussion that follows. While such analyses have tremendous implications for education, they are often not applied to the existing structures in education. Thus, we are faced with *redesign* scenarios, in which the implications of these bodies of work force us to reconsider, rethink, and ultimately redesign our current curricula in order to ultimately reach a desired outcome of personal and societal prosperity.

The 21st century world is facing substantial and substantive challenges. We look at four of those challenges: (1) living in a 21st century world, (2) factoring in technological growth, (3) defining demands on education, and (4) deciding on key aspects of a 21st century curriculum.

Challenge 1: Living in a 21st Century World

The increasing speed of change is the true hallmark of our time. We are experiencing a massive revolution in communication in the form of the Internet, the first truly global, interactive communication medium that is accessible to a significant number of the world's people. Ideas, images, and sounds fly around the world at the speed of light, disrupting industries, governments, and cultures along the way. As a result, the speed of change today is not the same as it was even several years ago: technological change is exponential in scope.

As an example, fifty sponsored workshops around the world, which formed the core of the Vodafone Forecast 2020 program (Vodafone, n.d.) dialogue, identified four certainties for our future:

1. A continued imbalance in the demographics of population (aging in developed countries, growing in developing ones)

2. More constraints on key resources

3. An accelerating shift of economic power to Asia

4. Universal data access

The changes afoot are leading to increased, perhaps unprecedented, challenges. The acronym VUCA (volatility, uncertainty, complexity, and ambiguity) has emerged to describe this general condition. The common usage of *VUCA* began in the late 1990s and springs from military vocabulary. It has been subsequently used in emerging strategic leadership ideas that apply in a wide range of organizations, including everything from for-profit corporations to educational institutions and systems. *Thus, the ultimate challenge for societies becomes defining the future we want rather than being reactive to a number of highly disruptive forces.*

The pushes (negative forces) and pulls (positive forces) of this new paradigm are described in table 8.1 (page 210). The resulting view relates to the consequence of living in a VUCA world while simultaneously embracing an aspirational and inspirational rather than a merely defensive objective.

Challenge 2: Factoring in Technological Growth

There is significant evidence that the impact of technology on our societies is not factored into policy discourses sufficiently, as general human understanding of the power of exponentials lags far behind their impact. See, for example, John Smart's (2011)

Table 8.1: Pushes and Pulls of the New Paradigm

Pushes	Pulls
Anxiety about the future	Promise of security and solidarity
Concern that policy adjustments are insufficient to avoid crises	Ethics of taking responsibility for others, nature, and the future
Fear of loss of freedom and choice	Participation in community, political, and cultural life
Alienation from dominant culture	Pursuit of meaning and purpose
Stressful lifestyles	Time for personal endeavors and stronger connection to nature

Source: Tellus Institute Report, 2002.

presentation "Evolutionary Development, Accelerating Change, Our Digital Future, and Values of Progress." In particular, the commoditization of knowledge is having an unfathomed impact on societies, both positive (spread of ideas) and negative (spread of weaponizable knowledge such as 3-D printed guns, biological warfare, and so on). The top ten technological breakthroughs transforming life over the next twenty to thirty years are, according to the World Future Society (as cited in Napier, Nichols, & Roscorla, 2009):

1. Alternative energy

2. Desalination of water

3. Precision farming

4. Biometrics

5. Quantum computers

6. Entertainment on demand

7. Global access

8. Virtual education

9. Nanotechnology

10. Smart robots

Critically, the interactions between various technologies make future predictions as hazardous as ever. For instance, in the early 1980s, teleshopping was forecast as a television experience, which missed the emergence and interactions between the following:

- The advances in semiconductor technology and algorithmic research, yielding the cloud servers and smartphones of today, with their inclusion of GPS

- The improvements in graphical user interfaces and operating systems

- The growth and popularization of the Internet and cloud-based services

- The birth of online shopping, coupled with location services

When combined, these factors may result in someone being lured by a discount coupon that arises on a smartphone when passing a merchant's location!

Challenge 3: Defining Demands on Education

The future agenda (Vodafone, n.d.) report, in its section on differentiated knowledge, states that

> in a world of commoditized knowledge, the returns go to the companies who can produce non-standard knowledge . . . While clear at a company level, the story is less strong at a national level: this view suggests that at a large/global scale, the competition is on to be the differentiated sources of insight. At a national economy scale, where one cannot have everyone producing non-standard knowledge, the challenge is more about speed and efficiency of knowledge development and sharing at a broader scale.

According to economists, educational institutions and systems are falling behind the curve (Goldin & Katz, 2008), as happened during the Industrial Revolution. As such, ensuring the relevance of curriculum is one way to redress the imbalances between what the modern world requires and students' preparedness for it. But, one might ask, "Is a baseline curriculum an obsolete concept in the 21st century?" To answer, we need to reexamine what a curriculum is for. A curriculum should do the following:

- Enhance the chances of an individual's success and fulfillment in personal and professional life through a relevant body of knowledge, skills, and character abilities

- Provide a common base of understanding in society

It would be hard to argue that these fundamental requirements are no longer needed, particularly for younger students, and that somehow the ad hoc nature, or "adhocacy," of individual decisions might be sufficiently wise for the majority of students. That said, a 21st century curriculum should also incorporate a certain amount of personalization to gain the best of both prescription and choice (as will be discussed later).

As to whether education systems can adapt fast enough, it is an existential axiom of the Center for Curriculum Redesign (CCR) that they can do so to a large extent. It is essential to keep in mind that four purposes of formal educational systems are very hard to replace—all of which provide fundamental value, albeit sometimes tainted by poor implementation:

1. **"Babysitting"**—The necessity to aggregate students for safe offloading by working parents

2. **Socialization**—The criticality for students to interface with each other and learn through myriad self-guided interactions

3. **Standards and curricula**—A common, canonical toolkit (knowledge, skills, and so on) that anticipates a majority of students' core needs and binds societies together

4. **Accreditation**—The "seal of approval" of a system, which provides a form of quality control

In addition, there is a need to reexamine the function and levels of the curriculum in a global perspective. When considering recommendations for 21st century curriculum, a global framework approach provides advice and support for national decision making and varied development and adaptations in different jurisdictions. There are many globally agreed-on factors regarding curriculum design and much commonality among them (Darling-Hammond, 2010). Core subjects taught in schools offer remarkably little variation, nor do they allow for the defined nature of skills that global citizens require.

Challenge 4: Deciding on Key Aspects of a 21st Century Curriculum

A 21st century curriculum should be adaptive and flexible, fluid and evolving. Frequent tweaks should be made to the curriculum, so it remains current and dynamic and over time incorporates entirely new domains as needed. We must be mindful of the entire range of informal as well as formal curricular possibilities, from afterschool programs, to museums as a place of learning, to certifications.

It is wise to reserve a portion of the curriculum that is not pre-scribed, of which some is given to the teacher for local adaptability and some to the student for additional engagement and personal expression (including expertise in their *own* areas of interest) (Egan, 2008). There should be continuous learning throughout life, but the ratio of society-prescribed to individually chosen opportunities should have an inverse relationship (figure 8.1).

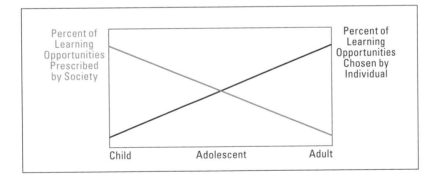

Figure 8.1: Inverse ratio of society-prescribed to individually chosen learning opportunities.

The curriculum should be free of false dichotomies, relying on the genius of *and* rather than the tyranny of *or* (Collins & Porras, 2002). There are many ways to provide this balance, such as:

- Focus on both STEM and humanities and arts; although a lot of demand exists for STEM-related jobs, versatility is a hedge against uncertainty. Humanities and arts, properly taught, can teach many required skills (critical thinking, creativity, and so on).

- Teach mind and body complementarity—a healthy mind in a healthy body.

- Expand the definition of an education to encompass not only knowledge (academic and competency based) but also skills, character, and metacognition.

- Nurture both process and outcome centricity.

- Focus on personal and individual needs and on societal goals.

- Impart global and local perspectives.

- Conceive of curriculum as a guiding as well as empowering document.

- Embed cultural diversity and respect of local norms.

- Develop technological savvy by learning about (for example, office applications, Web 2.0 apps, and programming), with (for example, applications such as GIS/GPS, mathematics modeling software), and through (for example, simulations and augmented technology).

While Web 2.0 technologies have brought changes to society, teachers and schools have made relatively little use of technology as an opportunity. And while technology by itself does not deliver educational success, it becomes useful if students, teachers, and schools can use it to learn in new and impactful ways. For technology to deliver educational success, important investments and efforts need to be made to adapt technological innovations—for example, the development of digital learning and teaching resources. For an excellent review, see the report *Inspired by Technology, Driven by Pedagogy* (OECD, 2010).

Ultimately, the curriculum should be lifelong and lifewide (Stevens, Bransford, & Stevens, 2005), as there is absolutely no reason to remain limited in our thinking during the first twenty-odd years of life.

Implications for What Students Should Learn

What should students learn for the 21st century? This question has served as the core driver of the strand of CCR's work that deals with future requirements, exploring global trends as well as their current and potential effects and their societal implications— resulting in a set of conclusions and recommendations for what knowledge, skills, and character traits will be critical in the 21st century. These trends are displayed and discussed in the following sections. To illustrate the trends and their implications, the CCR aligns the trends' attributes with potential responses (table 8.2). As some elements might correspond multiple times, there is not an exact one-to-one correspondence.

Table 8.2: Key 21st Century Attributes and Potential Responses

Key Attributes	Potential Responses (not exhaustive)
Versatility, broad knowledge	A robust spectrum of knowledge, including STEM and the humanities
	Multidisciplinarity (the capacity to be well developed in more than one domain, skill set, or profession) and thus the study of integrated disciplines which allow for a multidisciplinary approach (for example, robotics, biosystems, and business)
	Real-life contexts
	Futures studies (a branch of the social sciences that considers the future, parallel to history, which considers the past)
Critical thinking (including skeptical inquiry, logical reasoning, problem solving, and decision making)	Philosophy (includes several subtopics, such as ethics and social identity)

Continued →

Key Attributes	Potential Responses (not exhaustive)
Creativity and capacity for innovation	Interdisciplinarity (the ability to work between and with two or more traditional disciplines)
Entrepreneurial mindset and ability to execute decisions via ethical leadership	Entrepreneurship
Self-awareness and self-directedness, including the ability to direct one's own learning and development	Wellness education (that is, meditation, yoga, physical education, and so on)
Character traits such as curiosity, resilience, and courage	Civic participation and practices

The rapid increase in the rate of systemic change around the globe creates an increasingly VUCA world and thus is significantly more unpredictable. Such a context requires humans to engage with complex challenges and adapt to new situations. Following is a discussion of six factors—three human and three technological—that will require a diverse set of individual abilities and competencies and an increased collaboration among cultures.

Human Factors

The three human factors affecting our future are (1) increased human longevity, (2) global connectivity, and (3) environmental stresses.

Increased Human Longevity

The average human lifespan is lengthening, which will produce collective changes in societal dynamics, including better institutional memory and more intergenerational interactions, but it will also bring about increased resistance to change. This may also lead to economic implications, such as multiple careers over one's lifespan and conflicts over resource allocation between younger and older generations.

Such a context will require intergenerational sensitivity and a collective systems mindset in which each person balances his or her personal and societal needs. Table 8.3 describes the attributes of and responses to increased human longevity.

Table 8.3: Key Attributes of and Responses to Increased Human Longevity

Key Attributes	Potential Responses (not exhaustive)
Self-directedness (in one's own health, financial, and career pathways)	Well-being and health knowledge and practices (exercise, sports, and so on at all ages of life)
	Macroeconomics and financial planning
	Entrepreneurship, business (marketing and advertising), and sales (argument development, personal representation)
Social perspective taking (understanding the thoughts, feelings, and motivations of others) (Kohlberg, 1969)	Psychology, sociology, anthropology

Global Connectivity

The rapid increase in the world's interconnectedness has had many compounding effects, including exponential increase in the velocity of the dissemination of information and ideas, with more complex interactions on a global basis. Information processing has already had profound effects on how we work and think. It also brings with it increased concerns and issues about data ownership, trust, and the overall attention to and reorganization of present societal structures. Thriving in this context will require tolerance of a diversity of cultures, practices, and worldviews, as well as the ability to leverage this connectedness (table 8.4).

Table 8.4: Key Attributes of and Potential Responses to Global Connectivity

Key Attributes	Potential Responses (not exhaustive)
Global literacy	Macroeconomics
	Cultural studies (linguistics, geography, global history, anthropology, and so on)
	Political science
	Journalism and media
	Foreign languages / linguistics
Holistic mindset	Mathematics (complex systems)
	Integrated disciplines
Emotional intelligence	Practices (see page 227)
Deep awareness of one's digital footprints	Digital literacy

Environmental Stresses

Along with our many unprecedented technological advances, human society is using up our environment at an unprecedented rate, consuming more of it and throwing more of it away. So far, our technologies have wrung from nature an extraordinary bounty of food, oil, and materials. Scientists calculate that humans use approximately "40 percent of potential terrestrial [plant] production" for themselves (Global Change, 2008). What's more, we have been mining the remains of plants and animals from hundreds of millions of years ago in the form of fossil fuels in the relatively short period of a few centuries. Without technology, we would have no chance of supporting a population of one billion people, much less seven billion and climbing.

> A variety of factors, including population growth and current practices with natural resources, are placing significant stresses on our environment and planet. A continuation of these trends suggests an increased provoking of competition for resources and yet unknown effects with implications on daily life. However, this also brings with it an increased emphasis and effort on research and development of innovations targeting the alleviation of these problems and alternative technologies. This places emphasis not only on a society's ability to have the professional capacity to pursue these innovations, but it also means a collective need for more patience and tolerance for diffuse access to resources. (Global Change, 2008)

Changing dynamics and demographics will, by necessity, require greater cooperation and sensitivity among nations and cultures. Such needs suggest a reframing of notions of happiness beyond a country's gross domestic product (a key factor used in analyses of cultural or national quality of life) (Revkin, 2005) and an expansion of business models to include collaboration with a shared spirit of humanity for collective well-being. It also demands that organizations possess an ability to pursue science with an ethical approach to societal solutions (table 8.5).

Table 8.5: Key Attributes of and Potential Responses to Environmental Stresses

Key Attributes	Potential Responses (not exhaustive)
Systems thinking: in particular, sustainability and interrelatedness, delayed gratification and long-term thinking, social perspective-taking	Environmental literacy History (lessons from) System dynamics

Technology Factors

Three technology factors will also condition our future: (1) the rise of smart machines and systems, (2) the explosive growth of data and new media, and (3) the possibility of amplified humans.

The Rise of Smart Machines and Systems

While the creation of new technologies always leads to changes in a society, the increasing development and diffusion of smart machines—that is, technologies that can perform tasks once considered only executable by humans—has led to increased automation and offshorability of jobs and production of goods. In turn, this shift creates dramatic changes in the workforce and in overall economic instability, with uneven employment. At the same time, it pushes us toward an overdependence on technology—potentially decreasing individual resourcefulness. These shifts have placed an emphasis on nonautomatable skills (such as synthesis and creativity), along with a move toward a do-it-yourself (DIY) maker economy and a proactive human-technology balance—that is, one that permits us to choose what, when, and how to rely on technology (table 8.6).

The Explosive Growth of Data and New Media

The influx of digital technologies and new media has allowed for a generation of "big data" and brings with it tremendous advantages and concerns. Massive data sets generated by millions of individuals afford us the ability to leverage those data for the creation of simulations and models, allowing for deeper understanding of human behavioral patterns, and ultimately for evidence-based decision making.

At the same time, however, such big data production and practices open the door to privacy issues, concerns, and abuses. Harnessing these advantages, while mitigating the concerns and potential negative outcomes, will require better collective awareness of data, with skeptical inquiry and a watchfulness for potential commercial or governmental abuses of data (table 8.7, page 222).

The Possibility of Amplified Humans

Advances in prosthetic, genetic, and pharmacological supports are redefining human capabilities while blurring the line between disability and enhancement. These changes have the potential to create "amplified humans." At the same time, increasing innovation in virtual reality may lead to confusion regarding real versus virtual and what can be trusted. Such a merging shift of natural and technological requires us to reconceptualize what it means to be human with technological augmentations and refocus on the real world, not just the digital world (table 8.8, page 222).

Table 8.6: Key Attributes of and Potential Responses to New Technology

Key Attributes	Potential Responses (not exhaustive)
Technology quotient (fluency and self-direction over technology, such as computational thinking, data analysis, personal manufacturing, and so on)	Design and prototyping mindset (arts and technology) Simulation design (computer science and engineering) Technology and engineering (robotics, including programming and artificial intelligence; synthetic biology; 3-D printing; maker/DIY work; and so on)
Synthesis and integration	Literature (summarizing) Journalism
Imagination Creativity and innovation Leveraging technology when appropriate	Practices (see page 227)
Social resilience with and without technology	History and social sciences (to understand the impact of technologies on humans, societies, and communities) Linguistics (due to automatic translation) Diversification and archiving
Ethical mindset	Philosophy (ethics)

Table 8.7: Key Attributes of and Potential Responses to Growth of Data and New Media

Key Attributes	Potential Responses (not exhaustive)
Big data analysis	Statistics and probabilities
	Ethics
	History (global)
	Library studies
Media literacy	Integrated discipline (cinematography)
Self-identity and brand management	Marketing, advertising, and sales (persuasion)
	Anthropology (indigenous)

Table 8.8: Key Attributes of and Potential Responses to Enhanced Human Capability

Key Attributes	Potential Responses (not exhaustive)
Physical groundedness via hand and body skills	Practices (see page 227)
	Crafts, gardening, maker/DIY, and so on
	Integrated discipline (wellness)
Empathy Collective responsibility	Pet raising
	Ethics and civics
	Neuroscience, psychology, sociology, anthropology
	History (global)
	Comparative mythology
Mindfulness Maturity Wisdom	Practices (see page 227)

The Four Dimensions of an Education

Curricula worldwide have often been tweaked, of course, but they have never been completely redesigned for the comprehensive education of knowledge, skills, character, and metacognition—the four dimensions of education defined by the CCR (figure 8.2). The graphic shows the way in which adapting to 21st century needs means revisiting each of the four dimensions and their interplay: knowledge, skills, and character are all important to foster, but success in one has little to no bearing on success in others. As such, they are orthogonal to each other and are placed on three different axes. Metacognition is a higher-level awareness of one's place on the first three dimensions. In this way, all four are important to work toward, but not correlated to each other in terms of success.

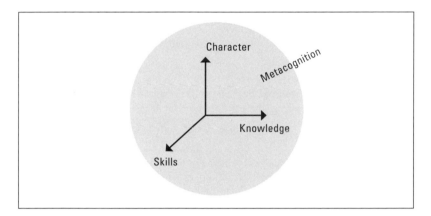

Figure 8.2: The four dimensions of an education.

Knowledge

Cortical plasticity is conditional upon relevance in humans as well as other primates (Ruytjens et al., 2006; Weinberger, 2008; Winer & Schreiner, 2011). Student lack of motivation and disengagement thus reflect the inability of education systems to connect content to real-world relevance. Relevance is also critically important not only to students' wishes but also to economic and societal needs. Traditional subjects must be augmented by modern disciplines, and tough choices must be made about what to pare back in order to allow for better-chosen areas of focus and concomitant depth that will cultivate the other three dimensions (skills, character, metacognition (figure 8.3, page 224).

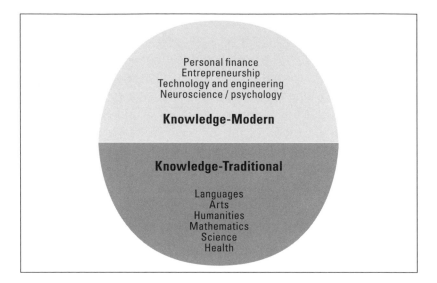

Figure 8.3: Traditional versus modern forms of knowledge.

Skills

Higher-order skills—such as the 4Cs of critical thinking and problem solving, communication, collaboration, and creativity and innovation—are essential for absorption of knowledge as well as for work performance As I noted on the blog *Education Today*, "the curriculum is already overburdened with content, which makes it much harder for students to acquire (and teachers to teach) skills via deep dives into projects" (Fadel, 2012). There is a global consensus on what the skills are at the broadest level and how teaching methods using projects can affect the acquisition of skills, yet in spite of this consensus, there are two major barriers that prevent building deep dives into curriculum:

1. Overwhelming amounts of prescribed content for each school year allow little time to address skills.

2. Little teacher expertise exists for combining knowledge and skills into various nondidactic practices.

Both traditional approaches of directly addressing these two barriers and new approaches of alternative paradigms are attempting to achieve the goal of effectively teaching higher-order skills.

Character

There is no perfect word that covers all meanings of *character* in all languages; by *character*, the CCR means all of agency, attitudes, behaviors, dispositions, mindsets, personality, temperament, and values. Note that the CCR objects to the use of the improper *non-cognitive* and much prefers the OECD's use of *social and emotional skills* (although it is a mouthful). Students need strong character to face an increasingly challenging world and to benefit civil and civic society (Ryan & Bohlin, 1999).

- Inevitability through the education system
- Intellectual authorities' call through history
- Generally widespread public support
- Laws (many countries have supportive laws and codes)
- Cultural indicators of need, and the impact of the media (Lickona, 2004)
    + Societal and personal challenges (violence, divorce, and so on)
    + Global challenges such as greed (global warming, financial meltdown, and so on) and intolerance (fundamentalism, absolutism)

As yet another important voice, United Nations Educational, Scientific and Cultural Organization (1996) states: "There is every reason to place renewed emphasis on the moral and cultural dimensions of education . . . this process must begin with self-understanding through . . . knowledge, meditation and the practice of self-criticism" (p. 19).

Character development is also becoming an intrinsic part of the mission of public schools, just as it has been for private schools, but this character learning is more likely to happen in out-of-school settings such as sports, scouts, adventure trips, and so on.

Metacognition

Metacognition is essential for activating transference among contexts, building expertise, fostering creativity via analogies, and establishing lifelong learning habits and, most importantly, is the best bet against continuous changes (Paris & Winograd, 1990). Because of its abstract nature, while knowledge, skills, and character goals may change, metacognition will necessarily remain relevant, since it is aiding in the process of achieving one's goals, whatever those goals may be. CCR's framework for metacognition consists of learning how to learn and self-directed learning.

Interdisciplinarity is viewed as a strong binding mechanism for many modern disciplines and the practices they require for the learning of the skills, character, and metacognition dimensions. For example, new interdisciplinary fields relevant to tomorrow's world include those listed in figure 8.4.

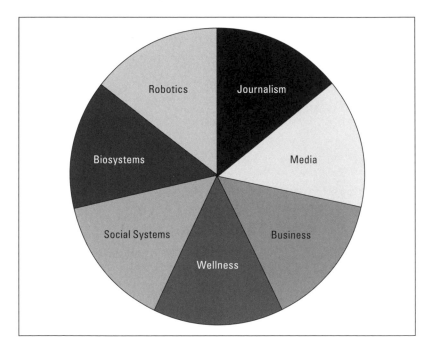

Figure 8.4: Integrated disciplines.

Education needs to be both broad in a *relevant* way, as well as deep in judiciously chosen areas, where the three dimensions of skills, character, and metacognition are taught through traditional and modern knowledge with interdisciplinary lenses. The visual representation in figure 8.5 attempts to clarify that knowledge, realistically, remains the medium through which the other dimensions are acquired.

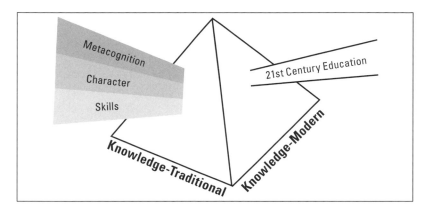

Figure 8.5: Knowledge as the medium through which education, metacognition, character, and skills are acquired.

The Role of Practices

Practices include pedagogical activities beyond didacticism in order to learn *skills, character, and metacognition,* and reinforce *knowledge* (table 8.9).

**Table 8.9: Pedagogical Activities (Practices)
as Related to Challenges and Goals**

Practice	Challenge	Goal
Play	Unstructured	Serendipity
Didactic	Engagement	Inspiration
Inquiry	Question	Answer
Debate	Issue	Position
Design	Problem	Solution
Performance	Perspective	Expression
Sport	Physical and mental fitness	Well-being
Contemplation		

Source: Trilling & Fadel, 2009.

Practices may feature characteristics such as:

- Growth mindset (à la Carol Dweck)

- Systems awareness

- "Co-opetition": competition (in sports, music, robotics, and so on) *and* collaboration (team structured)

- Fail-safely experimentation, with endeavors that stretch the student

- Processes, not just flat knowledge

- Systematic metacognition (reflection on processes)

- Longitudinal and multiyear span (in relation to projects and self [that is, career planning, metacognitive activity, and so on])

- Senior citizens involvement: for young plus old dynamics (wisdom, sensitivity, and so on)

- Global-cause involvement

- Internships and job training

- Embedding technology deeply and wisely

Major Impediments to Change

Historical inertia is a major factor in curriculum design, at both the policy and process level and the level of human dynamics. Four main factors can be identified:

1. **Policy**—At the system level, countries face political life-cycle instabilities that generally preclude the removal or addition of any major topic of study and make it hard for any system to innovate in an incrementally ambitious way.

2. **Dogma**—At the level of human dynamics, decisions are made by subject-matter experts in relative isolation from the demands of the real world, and such decisions often end up reaching incremental, often dogmatic, and overly consensual (groupthink) conclusions.

3. **Assessments**—Because systems tend to focus on what gets measured, there is a renewed imperative to vastly improve

assessments by designing ways to assess more than just knowledge (OECD's PISA [www.oecd.org/pisa] is a very good step in the right direction). Although assessments are not its focus, the CCR has called for the creation of a global assessment consortium, as has been done in other industries. This consortium would pool resources to share research and development of new assessments for skills, character, and metacognition. In the meantime, all of the following layers have a role to play in the assessment system.

+ Objective tests (direct tests)

+ Subjective tests (group, peers, 360-degree feedback from members of immediate work circle, self, and so on)

+ Behavior modeling without assessment

4. **College entrance**– College entrance requirements are the fourth reason why there is so much inertia in fresh curriculum thinking. While the requirements might have made sense from an academic standpoint in the 20th century, there has been a significant shift between what students need and what colleges require. Because curricula the world over are heavily reliant on traditional academics to drive requirement decisions, a significant adjustment is needed.

There are also other reasons for inertia; for instance, teacher preservice education and professional development will also need consideration. After these four priorities are properly addressed, educational leaders can attend to rethinking the rest as well.

Conclusion

Most global efforts to transform education are focused on the *how* with very little focus on the *what*. The status quo is hard to challenge, but education is in need of an innovative global curriculum adapted to 21st century students and society.

In a rapidly changing world, it is easy to get focused on current requirements, needs, and demands. Yet, adequately preparing for the future means actively creating it: the future is not the inevitable or something we are pulled into. There is a feedback loop between what the future could be and what we want it to be, and we have to deliberately choose to construct the reality we wish to experience. We may see global trends and their effects creating the ever-present future on the horizon, but it is up to us to choose to actively engage in co-constructing that future.

Future generations will have to think deeply about their own relation to nature, the benefits and the downsides of their technologies, and the corresponding lifestyles of choice. The synthesis presented here is the primary and foundational strand of work for the Center for Curriculum Redesign and will feed into subsequent curricular frameworks produced by the center. We invite you to continue to explore with us the seminal question, *What should students learn for the 21st century?*

References and Resources

Bransford, J. D., Brown, A. L. & Cocking, R. R. (2000). *How people learn: Brain, mind, experience, and school.* National Academy Press.

Collins, J. C., & Porras, J. I. (2002). *Built to last: Successful habits of visionary companies.* New York: HarperCollins.

Darling-Hammond, L. (2010). *The flat world and education: How America's commitment to equity will determine our future.* New York: Teachers College Press.

Davies, A., Fidler, D., & Gorbis, M. (2011). *Future work skills 2020* [White paper]. Phoenix: AZ: University of Phoenix Research Institute.

Dweck, C. S. (2010). *What is mindset?* Accessed at http://mindsetonline.com/whatisit/about on April 4, 2014.

Egan, K. (2008). *The future of education: Reimagining our schools from the ground up.* New Haven, CT: Yale University Press.

Facer, K. (2011). *Learning futures: Education, technology, and social change.* New York: Routledge.

Facer, K., & Sandford, R. (2010). The next 25 years?: Future scenarios and future directions for education and technology. *Journal of Computer Assisted Learning, 26,* 74–93.

Fadel, C. (2012, May 18). *What should students learn in the 21st century?* [Web log post] Accessed at http://oecdeducationtoday.blogspot.com/2012/05/what-should-students-learn-in-21st.html on May 22, 2014.

futureagenda. (n.d.). *Differentiated knowledge.* Accessed at www.futureagenda.org/pg/cx/view#327 on May 21, 2014.

Futurelab. (2014). *Beyond current horizons.* Accessed at www.beyondcurrenthorizons.org.uk on May 30, 2014.

Global Change. (2008, October 31). *The flow of energy: Primary production to higher trophic levels*. Accessed at www.globalchange.umich.edu/globalchange1/current/lectures/kling /energyflow/energyflow.html on April 4, 2014.

Goldin, C., & Katz, L. F. (2008). *The race between education and technology*. Cambridge, MA: Belknap Press.

Revkin, A. C. (2005). A new measure of well-being from a happy little kingdom. *New York Times: Science*. Accessed at www.nytimes.com/2005/10/04/science/04happ.html?page wanted=all on August 18, 2014.

Kohlberg, L. (1969). Stage and sequence: the cognitive developmental approach to socialization. In D. A. Goslin (Ed.), *Handbook of socialization theory and research*. Chicago: Rand-McNally.

KnowledgeWorks Foundation. (2012). *Forecast 3.0*. Accessed at http://knowledgeworks.org /futures-thinking on August 18, 2014.

Lickona, T. (2004). *Character matters: How to help our children develop good judgment, integrity, and other essential virtues*. New York: Simon & Schuster.

Manyika, J., Chui, M., Bughin, J., Dobbs, R., Bisson, P., & Marrs, A. (2013, May). *Disruptive technologies: Advances that will transform life, business, and the global economy*. Accessed at www.mckinsey.com/insights/business_technology/disruptive_technologies on April 4, 2014.

Napier, J. R., Nichols, R. Roscorla, T. (2009, April 24). *10 future forces*. Accessed at www .centerdigitaled.com/stem/Future-Forces.html on October 6, 2014.

Organisation for Economic Co-operation and Development. (2006). *Think scenarios, rethink education: Schooling for tomorrow*. Accessed at http://browse.oecdbookshop.org/oecd /pdfs/product/9606051e.pdf on April 4, 2014.

Organisation for Economic Co-operation and Development. (2010). *Inspired by technology, driven by pedagogy*. Accessed at www.oecd.org/edu/ceri/inspiredbytechnologydriven bypedagogyasystemicapproachtotechnology-basedschoolinnovations.htm on May 21, 2014.

Organisation for Economic Co-operation and Development. (2013). *Trends shaping education 2013*. Accessed at www.keepeek.com/Digital-Asset-Management/oecd/education /trends-shaping-education-2013_trends_edu-2013-en#page2 on April 4, 2014.

Organisation for Economic Co-operation and Development. (2014). *OECD better life index*. Accessed at www.oecdbetterlifeindex.org on April 4, 2014.

Paris, S. G., & Winograd, P. (1990). How metacognition can promote academic learning and instruction. *Dimensions of Thinking and Cognitive Instruction*, *1*, 15–51.

Raskin, P., Banuri, T., Gallopín, G., Gutman, P., Hammond, A., Kates, R., et al. (2002). *Great transition: the promise and lure of times ahead*. Accessed at http://tellus.org/documents /Great_Transition.pdf on April 4, 2014.

Ryan, K., & Bohlin, K. (1999). *Building character in schools: Practical ways to bring moral instruction to life*. San Francisco: Jossey-Bass.

Smart, J. (2011). *Evolution and development, accelerating change, our digital future, and values of progress* [PowerPoint]. Accessed at http://accelerating.org/presentations/EvoDevo ACDigitalFut&Progress-COSMOS2011(56).ppt on August 18, 2014.

Stevens, R., Bransford, J., & Stevens, A. (2005). *The LIFE Center's lifelong and lifewide diagram.* Accessed at http://life-slc.org on August 19, 2014.

Trilling, B., & Fadel, C. (2009). *21st century skills: Learning for life in our times.* San Francisco: Jossey-Bass.

United Nations Educational, Scientific and Cultural Organization. (1996). *Learning: The treasure within.* (Report to UNESCO of the International Commission on Education for the Twenty-first Century.) Accessed at www.unesco.org/education/pdf/15_62.pdf on August 18, 2014.

Vodafone. (n.d.). *Future agenda: The world in 2020.* Accessed at www.futureagenda.org/pg/cx /view#0 on August 18, 2014.

Wikipedia. (2014). *Roy Amara.* Accessed at http://en.wikipedia.org/wiki/Roy_Amara on April 4, 2014.

Linda Darling-Hammond

Linda Darling-Hammond, EdD, is Charles E. Ducommun Professor of Education at Stanford University, where she founded the Stanford Center for Opportunity Policy in Education and the School Redesign Network. A former public school teacher, she cofounded both a preschool / day care center and a charter public high school serving low-income students of color in East Palo Alto, California. She has worked with dozens of schools and districts on studying, developing, and scaling up new model schools, redesigning schools and district offices, and launching preparation programs for teachers and leaders. Linda was education advisor to Barack Obama's presidential campaign and headed his education policy transition team in 2008. Linda is author or editor of more than twenty books, and more than four hundred publications on education policy and practice. Her most recent is *Beyond the Bubble Test: How Performance Assessment Supports 21st Century Learning.*

She earned her doctor of education in urban education with highest distinction at Temple University.

To learn more about Linda's work, visit http://edpolicy.stanford.edu, or follow her on Twitter @LDH_ed.

David T. Conley

David Thomas Conley, PhD, has been a teacher and codirector of two public alternative schools and a secondary school, a central office administrator, and an executive in a state education agency. At the University of Oregon, he founded the Center for Educational Policy Research, which produced the first national set of college readiness standards. He is the founder and CEO of the not-for-profit Educational Policy Improvement Center, which conducts research on issues related to college readiness. His findings have been published in *Educational Administration Quarterly, Educational Policy, The Journal of the National Association of State Boards of Education, The Journal of College Admission, Principal Leadership, Educational Leadership, Education Week,* and other publications. David serves on numerous technical and advisory panels, including the Common Core State Standards Validation Committee and the Smarter Balanced Technical Advisory Committee. He is the recipient of the Innovation in Research Design Award and the Fund for Faculty Excellence Award at the University of Oregon, and is the author of *Getting Ready for College, Careers, and the Common Core.*

David earned his bachelor's degree from the University of California, Berkeley and his master's and doctorate degrees from the University of Colorado Boulder.

To learn more about David's work, visit www.collegecareerready.com.

Chapter 9

Assessment Systems for Deeper Learning

Linda Darling-Hammond and David T. Conley

Reform of educational standards and assessments has been a constant theme around the world. As part of an effort to keep up with countries that appear to be lengthening their educational lead over the United States, the nation's governors and the Council of Chief State School Officers issued a set of Common Core State Standards in 2010. Their purpose is to specify the concepts and skills needed for success in the modern world. These internationally benchmarked standards seek to create fewer, higher, and deeper curriculum goals that ensure more students are college and career ready.

This goal has profound implications for teaching and testing. Genuine readiness for college and 21st century careers, as well as participation in today's democratic society, requires, as U.S. President Obama has noted, much more than "bubbling in" answers on a test. Students need to be able to find, evaluate, synthesize, and use knowledge in new contexts; frame and solve nonroutine problems; and produce research findings and solutions. The rapidly evolving U.S. workplace increasingly requires students to demonstrate well-developed thinking skills, problem-solving abilities, design strategies, and communication capabilities. These are examples of so-called "21st century skills" that education reformers, business spokespeople, higher-education leaders, and others have been urging schools to pursue—skills that are increasingly in demand in a complex, technologically connected, and rapidly changing world. Yet college faculty have noted that first-year college students are often lacking these critical-thinking and problem-solving skills (Conley, 2005, 2014; Lundell, Higbee, & Hipp, 2005).

The Policy Challenge

As important as these skills are, the educational policy system and the larger political system are not functioning effectively enough to foster their development and implementation in U.S. schools. For example, a decade of test-based accountability targeted just on reading and mathematics helped focus schools on the importance of these subjects. However, in the process, the natural and necessary progression from basic skill acquisition to more complex application of these skills was disrupted.

Unfortunately, there are few incentives in the current policy system for educators to help students develop them. A side effect of No Child Left Behind's rapid increase in the frequency of testing (every student, every year from grade 3 on) was a narrowing of test methods and of the skills and abilities schools are encouraged to address. Current standardized tests mostly require students to recall or recognize fragmented and isolated bits of information. They rarely require students to apply their learning and almost never require students to exhibit proficiency in higher-order skills (Conley, Lombardi, Seburn, & McGaughy, 2009).

For example, a 2012 RAND Corporation study of tests in seventeen states, selected because they were reputed to have higher standards than many others, finds that fewer than 2 percent of mathematics items and only 21 percent of English language arts items reached the evaluated higher-level skills, such as analyzing, synthesizing, comparing, proving, or explaining ideas (Yuan & Le, 2012). This study finds that the level of cognitive demand was severely constrained by the extent of multiple-choice questions, which are unable to assess these higher-order skills.

New systems of curriculum, assessment, and accountability will be needed to ensure that students are given the opportunities to learn what they need to learn in order to be truly ready to succeed in college and careers. The advent of the Common Core State Standards provides an impetus for state legislators, governors, and educational leaders to rethink what they want from their public schools. This era of open thinking about how schools should be judged creates new opportunities to consider what students should be expected to know and be able to do, and how they can best be measured.

The two consortia of states designing the new assessment systems—the Partnership for Assessment of Readiness for College and Careers (PARCC) and the Smarter Balanced Assessment Consortium (Smarter Balanced)—have taken on the challenging task of trying to measure all of the Common Core standards (113 in ELA and literacy and 200 in mathematics) with one system. This task is particularly challenging given the standards' breadth and the range of cognitive complexity they represent. While they are a substantial step forward from the tests of the past, the consortia assessments are not able to assess Common Core standards such as oral communications, collaboration, and the capacity for extended investigations and problem solving.

And although the Common Core State Standards are designed to specify many of the skills students need to be college and career ready, they do not claim to address everything necessary for post-secondary success, such as interpersonal abilities, perseverance, resilience, and academic mindset, which have been found to be as important as academic skills. Therefore, other means of assessment will be needed to gauge the full range of knowledge and skills that comprise readiness for college and careers.

High-Quality System of Assessments

A carefully designed system of assessments takes into account the varied needs of all the constituents who use assessment data. They include students, parents, and teachers (most importantly); principals, superintendents, and boards of education; postsecondary officials and administrators in proprietary training programs; state education department staff, legislators, and governors; staff at the U.S. Department of Education and in Congress; members of education-advocacy groups; the business community; and many others. A system of assessments collates information from different sources to address a wider range of needs, and it does so in a way that results in a more holistic picture of students, schools, and educational systems. Such an approach does not waste or duplicate information or effort but also does not rely on a single source of data.

Assessment can also be instructive. While everyone agrees on this in principle, in practice we tend to create a distinction between teaching and testing. Students can learn a great deal from assessments beyond where they stand in comparison to other students or the teacher's expectations as expressed in a grade. A primary, though often forgotten, purpose of high-quality assessments is to help students learn how to improve their own work and learning strategies. Particularly in this era when "learning to learn" skills are increasingly important, it is critical that assessments help students internalize standards, become increasingly able to reflect on and evaluate their own work, be motivated and capable of revising and improving it, and seek out additional resources (human and other) to answer emerging questions.

Assessments can serve these purposes when they are clearly linked to standards reflected in the scoring rubrics; when these criteria are made available to students as they are developing their work; and when students are given the opportunity to engage in self- and peer assessments using these tools. In addition, students develop these skills when assessments ask them to exhibit their work in presentations to others, explain their ideas or solutions, answer questions that probe more deeply, and then revise the work to address these further questions.

Through the use of rubrics and public presentations, students can receive feedback that is concise and precise as well as generalizable. They end up with a much better idea of what to do differently next time, particularly in comparison to receiving an item analysis from a standardized test or generalized comments from a teacher on a paper, such as "nice job," or "good point." When students receive many different types of feedback from different sources, they are able to triangulate the results to identify patterns of strength and weakness beyond the specific questions they got right or wrong. This more comprehensive, holistic sense of knowledge and skills empowers the learner and builds self-awareness and self-efficacy.

This approach to assessment assumes that students are a primary consumer of the information they produce, and it designs assessment processes that explicitly develop students' metacognitive skills and give them opportunities for reflection and revision to meet standards. Not incidentally, these processes also support student learning by deepening teachers' learning about what constitutes high-quality work and how to support it—both individually and collectively as a staff.

Building a system of assessments opens the door to a much wider array of measurement instruments and approaches. Currently, states limit their assessment options, because almost all assessment is viewed through the lens of high-stakes accountability purposes and the technical requirements associated with these types of tests. Because of this, current assessments are not sufficient to bring about improvements in student readiness for college and careers, since readiness depends on more than what is measured by high-stakes tests. A *system* of assessments yields a wider range of actionable information, much of it low stakes, that students and their teachers can use to develop the broad range of knowledge and skills needed for postsecondary success.

Objectives of High-Quality Assessments

The 2013 report of the Gordon Commission on the Future of Assessment in Education, written by leading U.S. experts in curriculum, teaching, and assessment, describes the most critical objectives of new assessments this way:

> To be helpful in achieving the learning goals laid out in the Common Core, assessments must fully represent the competencies that the increasingly complex and changing world demands. The best assessments can accelerate the acquisition of these competencies if they guide the actions of teachers and enable students to gauge their progress. To do so, the tasks and activities in the assessments must be models worthy of the attention and energy of teachers and

students. The Commission calls on policy makers at all levels to actively promote this badly needed transformation in current assessment practice. . . . The assessment systems [must] be robust enough to drive the instructional changes required to meet the standards . . . and provide evidence of student learning useful to teachers. . . . Finally, it is also important that assessments do more than document what students are capable of and what they know. To be as useful as possible, assessments should provide clues as to why students think the way they do and how they are learning as well as the reasons for misunderstandings. (p. 7)

Following this report, a group of twenty assessment experts put forth a set of criteria for high-quality assessments (Darling-Hammond et al., 2013). Recognizing that no single assessment can evaluate all the kinds of learning we value for students, nor can a single instrument meet all of the goals held by parents, practitioners, and policymakers, these experts advocate for a coordinated system of assessment, in which different tools are used for different purposes (for example, formative and summative or diagnostic versus large-scale reporting). Such systems are defined by the following five major features.

1. **Assessment of higher-order cognitive skills:** Most of the tasks students encounter should tap the kinds of cognitive skills that have been characterized as higher order—skills that support transferable learning rather than just rote learning and the use of basic procedures. While there is a necessary place for basic skills and procedural knowledge, it must be balanced with attention to critical thinking and applications of knowledge to new contexts.

2. **High-fidelity assessment of critical abilities:** In addition to key subject-matter concepts, assessments should include the critical abilities articulated in the standards, such as communication (speaking, reading, writing, and listening in multimedia forms), collaboration, modeling, complex problem solving, planning, reflection, and research. Tasks should

measure these abilities directly as they will be used in the real world rather than through a remote proxy.

3. **Benchmarked to international standards:** With repsect to content, tasks, and performance standards, the assessments should be as intellectually challenging as those of the leading education countries.

4. **Instructionally sensitive and educationally valuable:** The tasks should be designed so that the underlying concepts can be taught and learned. Tasks should not rely on students' differential access to outside-of-school experiences (frequently associated with their socioeconomic status or cultural context) or depend on tricky interpretations that mostly reflect test-taking skills. Preparing for (and sometimes engaging in) the assessments should captivate students in instructionally valuable activities, and results from the tests should provide instructionally useful information.

5. **Valid, reliable, and fair:** In order to be truly valid for a wide range of learners, assessments should measure well what they purport to measure and accurately evaluate students' abilities and do so reliably across testing contexts and scorers. They should also be unbiased, accessible, and used in ways that support positive outcomes for students and instructional quality.

The rich instructional experiences and products that result from such efforts should be able to inform teaching and student improvement rather than merely produce scores that are determined outside of the school and sent back in as two-digit numbers that reveal little about what students have actually accomplished. Although these products might inform summative judgments, they should also serve formative purposes—helping teachers understand student thinking and performance and helping students understand how they can continue to revise and improve their work.

The new assessments present many opportunities as well as challenges. The process of developing and implementing new assessments on this scale offers a once-in-a-generation chance to rethink the way student learning is supported and evaluated within each state. A state will be able to consider moving beyond an *assessment system* composed of often overlapping, redundant, or disconnected tests, toward a *system of assessments* that is based on using a range of measures and methods that yield comprehensive, valid, and vital data for a variety of purposes. Among these, a critical priority is to enable teachers to improve instruction and students to improve their learning.

Many of these will be assessments that teachers use routinely in classrooms to guide instruction and evaluate learning. However, unlike currently, when classroom assessments are largely ignored in the formal assessment and accountability system—with nearly all the emphasis placed on a single end-of-the-year standardized test—they will be a meaningful part of the system. Rather than taking time *away* from instruction as many current tests are viewed as doing, these components of the assessment system will *contribute to* and be part of instruction.

As we have noted, a system of assessments is necessary to capture the wider range of skills that students must master to be successful in postsecondary school and beyond. Such a system can be critically important in a number of ways. A high-quality system of assessments can generate information for a variety of purposes without distorting classroom instruction. Assessment influences instruction, for better or worse, and most current state tests tend to ignore this effect or just hope for the best. While not all test items can emulate high-quality learning experiences, a system that includes both traditional sit-down assessments and classroom-embedded assessments can more positively influence teaching and learning.

Furthermore, research finds that when teachers become experienced in developing and evaluating high-quality performance assessments, they are more able to design and deliver high-quality learning experiences because they have a stronger understanding of what kinds of tasks elicit thoughtful work, how students think as they complete such tasks, and what a quality standard looks like (Darling-Hammond & Rustique-Forrester, 2005). In many U.S. states that have used performance assessments in mathematics and English language arts, studies find that teachers spent more time on problem solving, mathematical communication, writing, and assignments requiring complex thinking (see Stecher, Barron, Kaganoff, & Goodwin, 1998, as well as Darling-Hammond & Rustique-Forrester, 2005).

In states that are working to produce more useful and informative assessments, there is an effort to expand the range of performance assessments and integrate them into teaching and learning. As open-ended tasks offer more information about how students think and perform, they are also more useful for formative purposes, although they can and should offer information for summative judgments as well. We need to move from an overemphasis on summative testing that offers little information for instruction to a proper emphasis on formative assessments that improve learning, with summative testing serving an appropriately modest role (figure 9.1).

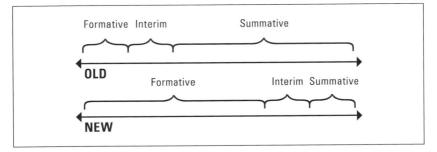

Source: P. Leather, personal communication, September 3, 2013. Used with permission.
Figure 9.1: Relative emphasis on assessment purposes.

Rich performance assessments provide a vehicle for teachers to examine student work so they and their students may gain insights into how students learn in the specific content area and how teachers can facilitate improvements in this learning. Because they model worthwhile tasks and expectations, embed assessment in the curriculum, and develop teachers' understanding of how to interpret and respond to student learning, the use of performance assessments typically improves instruction (Darling-Hammond & Rustique-Forrester, 2005).

Postsecondary Readiness

Right now, U.S. state tests are unable to perform these functions. Because they are typically limited to multiple-choice and short-answer formats, they provide little useful information to teachers about how students think and what they understand. Neither do they provide much insight to postsecondary institutions about how ready students are for college-level work or to prospective employers about work readiness or specific technical skills required for careers.

College and career readiness is a complex construct. The model developed by David Conley (2014) contains fifteen aspects and a total of forty-two components organized into four keys (figure 9.2): key cognitive strategies, key content knowledge, key learning skills and techniques, and key transition knowledge and skills.

Key Cognitive Strategies	Key Content Knowledge	Key Learning Skills and Techniques	Key Transition Knowledge and Skills
Think	**Know**	**Act**	**Go**
Problem Formulation Hypothesize Strategize	**Structure of Knowledge** Key Terms and Terminology Factual Information Linking Ideas Organizing Concepts	**Ownership of Learning** Goal Setting Persistence Self-Awareness Motivation Progress Monitoring Self-Efficacy	**Contextual** Aspirations Norms/Culture
Research Identify Collect			**Procedural** Institution Choice Admission Process
Interpretation Analyze Evaluate	**Attitudes Toward Learning** Content Challenge Level Value Attribution Effort	**Learning Techniques** Time Management Test-Taking Skills Note-Taking Skills Memorization/ Recall Strategic Reading Collaborative-Learning Technology	**Financial** Tuition Financial Aid
Communication Organize Construct			**Cultural** Postsecondary Norms
Precision and Accuracy Monitor Confirm	**Technical Knowledge and Skills** Specific College- and Career-Readiness Standards		**Personal** Self-Advocacy in an Institutional Context

Source: Conley, 2014.

Figure 9.2: Four keys to college and career readiness.

No one test, however innovative it is in terms of item types, can hope to address all of these variables. More importantly, many of them need to be measured in low-stakes contexts, with feedback provided to students on where they stand relative to the goal of becoming college and career ready—not with the intent of classifying them or withholding a benefit, such as access to a program, curriculum, or diploma.

For example, here are a number of important Common Core standards that, due to their very nature, the consortia assessments cannot measure directly.

- Conducting extended research using multiple forms of evidence

- Communicating ideas—discussing or presenting orally or in multimedia formats

- Collaborating with others to define or solve a problem

- Planning, evaluating, and refining solution strategies

- Using mathematical tools and models in science, technology, and engineering contexts

It is easy to see from these examples that many of these standards are very important to becoming well prepared for completing a bachelor's degree or a career certificate. It is also readily apparent that these standards require a wider range of assessment techniques, many of which will work best in a classroom environment. For example, assessing student ability to conduct research and synthesize information would best be done via a research paper. The standard for planning, evaluating, and refining solution strategies suggests a multistep process through which evidence is generated at multiple points. Designing and using mathematical models is a task that occurs most naturally in other subject areas, such as the natural and social sciences and engineering, via complex problems set in real-world contexts.

The consortia assessments plan to be more directly aligned with postsecondary readiness expectations in English and mathematics. However, because the Common Core State Standards represent only this subset of the full range of college- and career-readiness expectations, states that rely solely on college admissions tests and the new CCSS assessments will have two overlapping measures of the same domain. Even together, they will not capture all the important aspects of readiness; nor will they be sufficiently actionable to guide instruction.

However, a system of assessments could offer greater insight into college and career readiness and flexibility by allowing states to assemble the set of measures they feel best gauge a wider and more complex range of knowledge and skills in ways that begin to approximate how they will be applied in postsecondary settings.

Such a system might begin with an on-demand assessment of the new Common Core State Standards developed by PARCC or Smarter Balanced. (Figure 9.3 shows the relationships among college- and career-readiness competencies, the Common Core State Standards, and Smarter Balanced or PARCC assessment.) It would then strategically design a variety of ways to develop, value, and look at the full range of Common Core State Standards and, beyond those, many of the additional college- and career-readiness skills, including content knowledge beyond ELA and mathematics, key cognitive strategies, key learning skills and techniques, and key transition knowledge and skills.

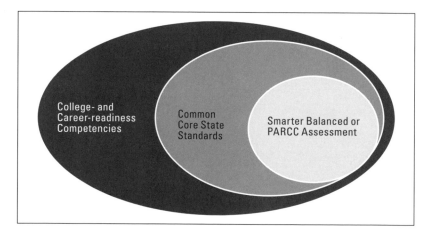

Source: Standford Center for Opportunity Policy in Education. Used with permission.

Figure 9.3: Relationship between college and career readiness, Common Core, and consortia assessments.

State Development of Systems of Assessment

As they seek to develop new systems of assessment, states should:

- Define *college and career readiness*

- Evaluate the gap between the system as it now exists and the desired system

- Identify policy purposes for state and local assessments
- Consider a continuum of assessments that address different purposes
- Identify the information assessments need to generate for different users, such as—
    + Policymakers (state/local)
    + Students and parents
    + Teachers
    + Higher education and employers
- Develop assessments that can provide a profile of student abilities and accomplishments
- Connect these assessments to curriculum, instruction, and professional development in a productive teaching and learning system
- Create an accountability system that encourages the kinds of learning and practice needed to reach the goals of college and career readiness

During the 1990s, a number of states developed thoughtful systems of assessment, and many countries have robust examples of such systems that have been in operation for long periods of time. As we shall see, many U.S. states developed standards-based systems of curriculum and assessment that included large-scale, on-demand tests in a number of subject areas—usually once in each grade span (3–5, 6–8, 9–12), plus classroom-based assessments that involved students completing performance tasks, such as science investigations and research, writing, or art projects, including portfolios of student work assembled over time to illustrate specific competencies.

These systems were designed to offer different kinds of information to different stakeholders. The on-demand tests usually included a combination of multiple-choice and short constructed-response items, with longer essays to evaluate writing. These scores informed state and local policymakers about how students were doing overall in key areas.

Going beyond these components, Connecticut, Maine, Maryland, New York, and Vermont involved students in classroom performance tasks of longer duration—from one class period to several—designed at the state level and administered and scored locally, with a moderated scoring process to ensure consistency. Maryland was able to mount an ambitious set of tasks across subject areas by using matrix sampling, which meant that different groups of students completed different tasks, and the results could be aggregated across an entire district or state to report on more aspects of learning culled from all the tasks.

Additionally, Minnesota, Oregon, Wisconsin, and Wyoming introduced more individualized student learning profiles that allowed students to demonstrate specified competencies through locally developed performance assessments. Minnesota's Profile of Learning set out expectations for graduation readiness in ten domains not tested in the state's basic skills tests. For example, in social studies, the inquiry standard could be met with an issue analysis that requires the student to research an issue and evaluate proposed positions or solutions by gathering information and assessing points of view, looking for areas of difference and agreement, analyzing the feasibility and practicality of proposed solutions, and comparing alternatives and their projected consequences. Oregon's Certificate of Initial and Certificate of Advanced Mastery included similar tasks that students could complete to demonstrate their competencies in various areas. These could then be recorded on the diploma. Students could use these competency demonstrations to meet proficiency-based entrance requirements at Oregon's public universities.

Graduation portfolios in states like Rhode Island and New York have taken this idea a step further. For example, the New York Performance Standards Consortium, a group of more than forty secondary schools (now expanding to other states), has received a state-approved waiver allowing its students to complete a graduation portfolio in lieu of some of the state Regents Examinations. This portfolio includes a set of ambitious performance tasks—a scientific investigation, a mathematical model, a literary analysis, and a social science research paper, sometimes augmented with other tasks like an arts demonstration or analyses of a community service or internship experience. These tasks meet common standards and are evaluated on common scoring rubrics.

New Hampshire's System of Assessments

To ensure its students' preparation for college and careers, New Hampshire has begun to create a system of assessments that is tightly connected to curriculum, instruction, and professional learning. In addition to the Smarter Balanced assessments for ELA and mathematics, this system will include a set of common performance tasks that have high-technical quality in the core academic subjects, locally designed assessments with guidelines for ensuring quality, regional scoring sessions and local district peer review audits to ensure sound accountability systems and inter-rater reliability, a web-based bank of local and common performance tasks, and a network of practitioner assessment experts to support schools.

The state's view is that a well-developed system of performance assessments augmenting the traditional tests will drive improvements in teaching and learning, as they "promote the use of authentic, inquiry-based instruction, complex thinking, and application of learning . . . [and] incentivize the type of instruction and assessment that support student learning of rich knowledge and skills" (New Hampshire Department of Education, 2013). The system will also offer a strategic approach for building the expertise of educators across the state by organizing professional development around the design, implementation, and scoring of these assessments, which model good instruction and provide insights about teaching and learning.

Assessment information gathered from the local assessment system, including common and locally developed performance tasks, is expected to provide the bulk of the information used for school, educator, and student accountability systems. Meanwhile, the large-scale assessment system will provide information to support school accountability determinations and, perhaps, to supplement educator accountability determinations. To accomplish this, over three years (from 2013 to 2015), the state will do the following:

- Develop college- and career-ready competencies reflecting higher-order thinking and performance skills for the core disciplines of ELA, mathematics, science, social studies, and the arts.

- Use these competencies to guide the development of common statewide performance tasks in each of these content areas at each grade span (K–5, 6–8, 9–12) with accompanying guidelines, tools, rubrics, student-work anchors, and data reports. Each task will be constructed as a complex, multistep, curriculum-embedded assignment that measures the depth and application of student learning.

- Develop a process, tools, and protocols for supporting districts and schools in developing and validating high-quality local performance tasks, along with guidance for teachers in how to use these to enhance curriculum and instruction.

- Assemble both the common and locally developed tasks into a web-based bank of validated performance tasks to be used for formative as well as summative assessments.

- Organize professional development institutes for cohorts of schools focused on the design, validation, and reliable scoring of tasks, as well as data analysis to track student progress and inform instruction.

- Create regional support networks led by practitioner assessment experts to help build capacity in schools and to support regional task validation and calibration scoring sessions, with a goal of 80 percent or greater inter-rater reliability on locally scored tasks.

- Maintain technical quality and consistency through district peer review audits, in which districts will submit evidence of their performance assessment systems to peer review teams of external practitioners, who will review the evidence based on common criteria, including whether the district has developed. A key part of the accountability system, these audits will examine how districts administer common and local tasks, manage a quality-assurance process, develop educators' skills, and design policies and practices that support the state performance assessment system (for example, performance-based graduation requirements) (New Hampshire Department of Education, 2013).

In its description of its new assessment framework, the New Hampshire Department of Education (2013) notes:

> Comprehensive assessment systems are generally defined as multiple levels of assessment designed to provide information for different users to fulfill different purposes. Most importantly, information gathered from classroom and school assessments should provide information to supplement accountability information generated at the state level, and state level assessments should provide information useful for evaluating local education programs and informing instructional practice. Further, the large-scale assessment should signal the kinds of learning expectations coherent with the intent of the standards and the kinds of learning demonstrations we would like to see in classrooms.

Testing regimes in most states typically lack this kind of coherence and synergy, and they fail to measure deeper learning skills. New Hampshire has also introduced a technology portfolio for graduation, which allows students to collect evidence to show how they have met standards in this field.

Kentucky Instructional Results Information System

The Kentucky Education Reform Act of 1990, passed in response to a school-funding lawsuit, brought about sweeping changes to Kentucky's public school system, including changes to school and district accountability for student performance. The Kentucky Instructional Results Information System (KIRIS) was a performance-based assessment system implemented for the first time in the spring of 1992. KIRIS tested students in grades 4, 8, and 11 in a three-part assessment that included:

- Multiple-choice and short-essay questions

- Performance "events" requiring students to solve applied problems

- Portfolios in writing and mathematics in which students presented the best examples of classroom work collected throughout the school year

Students were assessed in seven areas: (1) reading, (2) writing, (3) social science, (4) science, (5) mathematics, (6) arts and humanities, and (7) practical living and vocational studies. Schools were evaluated based on attendance, graduation rates, and school-climate surveys, as well as achievement scores.

Eventually, as the system evolved, the mathematics portfolio was replaced by performance tasks. The writing portfolio continued until 2012 in grades 4, 7, and 12, while an on-demand writing assessment was used in grades 5, 8, and 12. A four-piece portfolio was required in grade 12, and a three-piece portfolio was required in grades 4 and 7. The required content, prepared to meet state specifications, included examples of reflective writing, personal expressive or literary writing, and transactive writing (two of these in grade 12, at least one of them analytical and at least one outside of English class). The on-demand writing assessment provides students in grades 5 and 8 with the choice of two writing tasks that include a narrative writing prompt and a persuasive writing prompt. In addition, students in grade 12 are given one common writing task and the choice of one of two additional writing tasks (Kentucky Department of Education, 2009).

Teachers were trained to score the portfolios at the school level using analytical rubrics. Two readers, using double-blind scoring, scored each piece. If scores did not match in any domain, a third reader would also score. By 2008, the agreement rate for independent readers who audited school-level scores was over 90 percent (Kentucky Department of Education, 2009).

More important, in many schools, the portfolio became a tool for transforming teachers' practice and students' learning opportunities. As one high school English teacher noted of her school's approach, which engaged all the school's teachers in assigning and scoring writing for the portfolio,

> Whole-school assessment . . . is the one tool that brought all of us, administrators and teachers, together in a common effort. As we addressed the needs of the writing portfolio, we were discussing learning needs of all kinds: the need to critically engage students with the content as well as present it; the need to communicate for a variety of purposes and audiences as well as for the teacher-as-examiner. A dialogue about learning started that almost certainly would never have occurred without whole-school portfolio assessment. Our discussions gave us a very practical sense that all of us are responsible for the kind of learning that goes on in our school. (Moore & Russell, n.d.)

International Systems of Assessments

Other countries with highly effective educational systems rely on a mix of measures that usually include classroom-based assessments of more complex academic tasks and exams that have open-ended essays with other item types that get at constellations of student knowledge and skill applied in a more holistic fashion.

Examination systems in England, Singapore, and Australia, for example, have common features that can also be found in the International Baccalaureate (IB) system, used in more than one hundred countries around the world. Students typically choose the subjects or courses of study they will take examinations in to demonstrate their competence or qualifications, based on their interests and strengths. These qualification exams are offered in vocational subjects as well as traditional academic subjects. Part of the exam grade is based on externally developed "sit-down" tests that feature open-ended essays and problems; the remainder—which can range from 25 to 60 percent of the total score—is based on specific tasks undertaken in the classroom to meet syllabus requirements. (For a more in-depth treatment, see Darling-Hammond & Wentworth, 2010.)

These classroom-based assessments are generally created by the examinations board and are scored by local teachers according to common rubrics in a moderation process that ensures scoring consistency. They may range from a portfolio-like collection of assignments, like the tasks shown in table 9.1 that are required for Britain's GCSE exam in English, to single, large projects that complement the sit-down test, like the science investigation required as part of Singapore's high school science examinations, in which students must demonstrate their ability to:

- Follow instructions and use techniques, apparatus, and materials safely and effectively

- Make and record observations, measurements, methods, and techniques with precision and accuracy

- Interpret and evaluate observations and experimental data

- Identify problems, design and plan investigations, and evaluate methods and techniques (Singapore Examinations and Assessment Board, 2009)

Table 9.1: British GSCE English Language Examination Components

Unit and Assessment	Tasks
Reading literacy texts Controlled assessment (coursework)	Responses to three texts from choice of tasks and texts. Candidates must show an understanding of texts in their social, cultural, and historical context.
Imaginative writing Controlled assessment (coursework)	Two linked continuous writing responses from a choice of text development or media.
Speaking and listening Controlled assessment (coursework)	Three activities: (1) a drama-focused activity, (2) a group activity, and (3) an individual extended contribution. One activity must be a real-life context in and beyond the classroom.
Information and ideas Written exam with two sections	Nonfiction and media: Responses to previously unseen authentic passages. Writing information and ideas: One continuous writing response—choice from two options.

In Queensland, Australia, national testing occurs at grades 3, 5, 7, and 9, and the state offers a reference exam at grade 12. Most assessment is conducted through common statewide performance tasks that are administered locally, plus a very rich system of local performance assessments that are developed at the school level but subject to quality control and moderation of scoring by a state panel. The Queensland Curriculum, Assessment and Reporting Framework (QCAR; table 9.2) helps provide consistency from school to school based on the state's content standards, called *Essential Learnings*, which include unit templates and guidance for assessments in each subject. These include extended research projects, analyses, and problem solutions across fields.

Table 9.2: Queensland Curriculum, Assessment, and Reporting Framework

	Pre-Secondary Level	Senior Level (Grades 11–12)
Curriculum guidance	Essential Learnings: Scope and sequence guides, unit templates, plus assessable elements and quality descriptors (rubrics)	Syllabi for each subject outlining content and assessments
External tests	National tests of literacy and numeracy at grades 3, 5, 7, 9—centrally scored	Queensland Core Skills Test, grade 12
Locally administered performance tasks	Queensland Comparable Assessment Tasks (QCAT): Common performance tasks at grades 4, 6, and 9—locally scored	Course assessments, outlined in syllabus—locally scored and externally moderated
Locally developed assessments	Local performance assessment systems—locally scored and externally moderated	Graduation portfolios—locally scored and externally moderated

The kinds of tasks used are intended to develop students' abilities to guide their own learning, which becomes deeper over time, as they have repeated opportunities to engage complex tasks, and their teachers learn to incorporate this kind of work into the curriculum. Clearly, as shown in the following examples of a Queensland common task used in grade 7 in science, as well as one expected of students at the senior level (Queensland Curriculum and Assessment Authority, n.d.), students are expected and supported to develop very sophisticated skills that indicate college readiness.

QCAT for 7th Grade Science: 90 minutes over 1–2 days. Given some contextual information, students must analyze and construct food webs in two environments. Through multiple prompts, students must show an understanding of food chains and the impact of environmental disruptions on populations.

Extended Experimental Investigation at the Senior Level (Grades 11–12): Over four or more weeks, students must develop and conduct an extended experimental investigation to investigate a hypothesis or to answer a practical research question. Experiments may be laboratory or field based. The outcome of the investigation is a written scientific report of 1500 to 2000 words.

The student must:
- Develop a planned course of action
- Clearly articulate the research question and provide a statement of purpose for the investigation
- Provide descriptions of the experiment
- Show evidence of student design
- Provide evidence of primary and secondary data collection and selection
- Execute the experiment(s)
- Analyze data
- Discuss the outcomes of the experiment
- Evaluate and justify conclusion(s)

Within schools, groups of teachers develop, administer, and score the assessments with reference to national curriculum guidelines and state syllabi (also developed by teachers). At the high-school level, a student's work is collected into a portfolio that is used as the primary measure of college readiness. Portfolio scoring is moderated by panels that include teachers from other schools and professors from the higher-education system. A statewide examination serves as an external validity check, but not as the accountability measure for individual students (Tung & Stazesky, 2010).

This type of assessment can be used as a reliable and valid measure because educators have, over time, acquired very similar ideas of what adequate performance on these papers and tasks looks like. In nations as varied as the Netherlands and Singapore, these shared mental models of student performance on robust tasks shape teacher judgments. They are developed from the earliest stages of teacher education and are reinforced by high-quality in-course assessments and grading practices based on scoring guides that are closely aligned with standards.

In this system, as in those described earlier in this section, the combination of training, moderated scoring, and auditing have allowed performance assessments to be scored at high levels of reliability, while they also offer a more valid method for evaluating higher-order thinking and performance skills (Darling-Hammond & Adamson, 2010). Where school systems have devoted resources to assessment at the classroom level and have invested in classroom-based performance assessors, teachers have developed deep expertise that translates into shared judgments and common mental models of what constitutes acceptable student performance on complex types of learning.

In these systems, instruction is guided and enriched by assessments that place value on deeper learning. Teachers' capacity to teach for deeper learning is strengthened through the process of planning for curriculum and assessments, scoring student work, and reflecting collectively on how to improve instruction. Students are able to work on these assessment tasks intensively, revise them to meet standards, and display their learning to parents, peers, teachers, and even future professors and employers. Policymakers are able to track general trends as scores from multiple measures are aggregated, reported, and analyzed.

A Continuum of Assessments
This section is adapted, in part, from Conley, 2014.

A key characteristic of a system of assessments is the continuum of options and methods for determining what students know and can do, as shown in figure 9.4 (page 258).

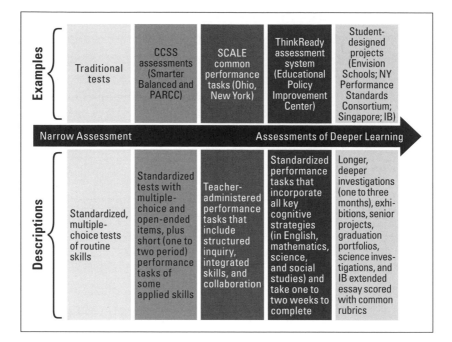

Figure 9.4: Assessment continuum.

A benefit of this approach is that different types of information can be used for different purposes, instead of trying to have one assessment address all needs. Performance assessments can be designed to gauge student growth on learning progressions, can be incorporated into proficiency determinations or end-of-course exams, or can be combined in a culminating fashion, as in the case of a graduation portfolio.

At one end are the multiple-choice and close-ended items found in traditional tests. These measure recall and recognition but do not measure deeper learning skills as defined by the Hewlett Foundation (Conley, 2011; Conley, 2014) or by such taxonomies as Webb's (2002) Depth of Knowledge framework. The tasks become more complex and extend over longer periods of time at each step along the continuum. They also measure larger and more integrated sets of knowledge and skill, which provide insight into more cognitively complex aspects of learning as well as the application of knowledge to new settings and situations. The more challenging tasks require greater student initiation of designs, ideas, and performances; these tasks encourage and tap the planning and work-management skills needed for college and careers.

The types of useful performance tasks or measures in a system of assessments can cover a wide span—from a single class period to a semester. They are generally graded by teachers (for their own students or, in a system moderated across schools, for other students) and can yield the kinds of information needed to help inform a range of decisions.

Performance tasks may also be subject to external quality control. This can be accomplished by specifying task content, including creating common tasks at the state or district level, designing the conditions for task administration, managing how tasks are scored, and deciding how results are reported. Figure 9.5 is an example of a state-developed common task used in classrooms and evaluated by teachers with training and moderation that produce reliable scores. The Ohio Performance Assessment Pilot Project, from which it is drawn, has developed and piloted tasks in English, mathematics, history and social studies, and science that are being used in high schools throughout the state.

Ohio "Heating Degrees" Task

Students are given the scenario of a homeowner, Mrs. Johnson (Kevin and Shana's mother), who has installed insulation to bring her heating bills down but finds in the following winter that the bills are not much lower. When she calls the contractor to complain, he points out that the prior month was much colder than usual and that the rates had gone up. To figure out whether Mrs. Johnson's insulation did indeed save her money, students must evaluate how heating costs may change as a simultaneous function of temperature, fuel costs, and savings due to insulation.

Continued →

Figure 9.5: State-developed performance task with out-of-class work.

On the basis of the situation painted here and some initial information to help them begin to research "heating degree days" on the Internet, students are given two tasks.

1. Assess the cost effectiveness of Kevin and Shana's mom's new insulation and window sealing. In their assessment, you must do the following:

   + Compare Mrs. Johnson's gas bills from January 2007 and January 2008.

   + Explain Mrs. Johnson's savings after the insulation and sealing.

   + Identify circumstances under which Mrs. Johnson's January 2008 gas bill would have been at least 10 percent less than her January 2007 bill.

   + Decide if the insulation and sealing work on Mrs. Johnson's house was cost effective, and provide evidence for this decision.

2. Create a short pamphlet for gas company customers to guide them in making decisions about increasing the energy efficiency of their homes. The pamphlet must do the following:

   + List the quantities that customers need to consider in assessing the cost effectiveness of energy efficiency measures.

   + Generalize the method of comparison used for Mrs. Johnson's gas bills with a set of formulas, and provide an explanation of the formulas.

   + Explain to gas customers how to weigh the cost of energy efficiency measures with savings on their gas bills.

Source: Adapted from Ohio Performance Assessment Pilot Project.

Another type of performance assessment can be classified as the culminating project. This demonstration is a means to cumulatively gauge student knowledge and skill. Taking the project one step further, students study one topic for a semester or even an entire year and apply what they are learning in their academic classes to their work on the project. The results are presented to a panel that includes teachers, experts from the community, and fellow students. The culminating project may be interdisciplinary and generally includes a terminal paper and accompanying documentation, reflecting overall cognitive development and a range of academic skills.

This method of juried exhibitions is used in examination systems abroad (for example, in the Project Work task required in Singapore, figure 9.6) and by U.S. schools (such as in the New York Performance Standards Consortium and a number of networks, including schools working with the Center for Collaborative Education in Boston, the Internationals High School Network, New Technology High Schools, Envision Schools, the MetSchools, and others). It allows students to communicate their ideas in writing, orally, and in other formats, such as with the use of multimedia technology or through products they have created, and to demonstrate the depth of their understanding as they respond to questions from others, rather like a dissertation defense. In Singapore, the project must also be collaborative, integrating another key skill.

Project Work is an interdisciplinary subject that is compulsory for all pre-university students. The tasks are designed by the Singapore Examinations and Assessment Board (SEAB) to be sufficiently broad in order to allow students to carry out a project they are interested in while meeting the task requirements.

- It must foster collaborative learning through group work. Together as a group that is randomly formed by the teacher, students brainstorm and evaluate each others' ideas, agree on the project that the group will undertake, and decide on how the work should be allocated among themselves.

Continued →

Figure 9.6: Project Work in Singapore.

- Every student must make an oral presentation in the presence of an audience, individually and together as a group.

- Both product and process are assessed; there are three components for assessment.

  + The written report, which shows evidence of the group's ability to generate, analyze, and evaluate ideas for the project

  + The oral presentation, in which each group member is assessed on his or her fluency and clarity of speech, awareness of audience, and response to questions; the group as a whole is also assessed in terms of the effectiveness of the overall presentation

  + The group project file, in which each individual group member submits three documents that serve as snapshots of the processes involved in carrying out the project; these documents show the individual student's ability to generate, analyze, and evaluate the following:

    • Preliminary ideas for a project

    • A piece of research material gathered for the chosen project

    • Insights into and reflections on the project

Classroom teachers assess all three components of the project, using a set of assessment criteria provided by the SEAB, which also provides training for assessors and internal moderators. Like all other assessments, the grading is both internally and externally moderated.

Source: Singapore Examinations and Assessment Board, 2009.

A slight variation on this model is for the culminating demonstration to be based on a portfolio of work rather than one project alone. In this model, students may present the results of several projects independently or they may integrate findings and observations from assignments into a final demonstration organized around a topic such as sustainability, public mental health services in the community, or a business plan for starting an enterprise chosen by the student.

Rich performance tasks can also generate insight into other aspects of student-learning skills and strategies. For example, teachers can report on student ability to sustain effort when confronted with difficult tasks; manage time to complete complex, multistep assignments; and work with others to improve both individual and group performance. This evidence of readiness for college and career pathways can be used in combination with test scores to provide a more balanced view of students' abilities, including those critical to success, such as evidence of effective study habits, good collaborative skills, and resourcefulness. Essentially, teachers can use scoring guides to rate these types of learning skills alongside content knowledge. Such performance-task scores can identify students with postsecondary potential who may not demonstrate their capacity fully on tests, but who respond well to performance tasks as a means to express their knowledge and skills, their ability to learn independently, and their capacity to find resources when needed.

New Systems of Accountability

As states develop new systems of assessment, it will be important to develop new systems of accountability as well. It is important to incorporate productive uses of new assessments while recognizing that assessments of student performance provide information for an accountability system, but *they are not the system itself.*

Genuine accountability can occur only when useful processes exist for using information to improve what schools and teachers do on behalf of students (Darling-Hammond, 1993). Assessments and outcome standards alone cannot guarantee that schools will know how to improve or make the changes that will help students learn more effectively. In fact, if such standards are improperly designed, they can actually undermine accountability.

Accountability for education is achieved when the policies and operating practices of a school, school system, and state work both to provide quality education and to correct problems as they occur. There must also be methods for changing school practices—even totally rethinking certain aspects of schooling—if they are not working well. Assessment data are helpful to the extent that they provide relevant, valid, and timely information about how individual students are doing and how schools are serving them, but these kinds of data are only a small part of the total process.

An accountability system is a set of commitments, policies, and practices that are designed to:

- Increase the probability that schools will use good practices on behalf of students

- Reduce the likelihood that schools will engage in harmful practices

- Encourage ongoing assessment on the part of schools and educators to identify, diagnose, and change courses of action that are harmful or ineffective

Thus, in addition to *outcome standards* that rely on many kinds of data, accountability must encompass *professional standards of practice*—how a school, school system, or state hires, supports, and evaluates its staff; how it makes decisions about curriculum and ensures that the best available knowledge will be acquired and used; how it organizes relationships between adults and students to allow the needs of learners to be known and addressed; how it creates incentives and safeguards to ensure that teachers and students are supported in their efforts and that problems are effectively addressed; how it establishes communication mechanisms between and among teachers, students, and parents; how it evaluates its own functioning as well as student progress; and how it provides incentives for continual improvement. These are the core building blocks of accountability. They reveal the capacity of educational institutions to serve their students well.

Accountability tools must address the barriers to good education that exist not only within schools and classrooms but also at the district, state, and national levels. Although schools may be appropriately viewed as the unit of change in education reform, the structuring of inequality in learning opportunities occurs outside the school in the governmental units where funding formulas, resource allocations, and other educational policies are forged. In sum, if students are to be well served, accountability must be *reciprocal*. That is, federal, state, and local education agencies must meet certain standards of delivery while school-based educators and students are expected to meet certain standards of practice and learning.

This tripartite conception of accountability should include at least the following. (For a fuller discussion of such a system, see Darling-Hammond, 1993.)

- Accountability for resources (based on standards of delivery), encompassing:

    + Adequate and equitable school *resources*, allocated based on student needs (dollars, instructional materials, and equipment, including technology)

    + Equitable access to *curriculum*, supported by policies that do not unnecessarily deny students access to programs of study from which they could benefit

    + Access for all students to well-prepared *teachers and other professional staff*, based on policies that create incentives for equitable distribution of educators

- Accountability for professional practice, ensuring:

    + *Educator capacity* that enables teachers to teach for deeper learning and administrators to understand and support this work at the school and district level, using such tools as the following—

        • High-quality preparation, induction, and professional development

        • Licensing based on evidence of teacher and administrator performance in supporting diverse learners to meet challenging standards

- • Evaluation based on multiple indicators of practice, contributions to student learning, and contributions to colleagues that support ongoing learning

  + Schools designed to support *personalization and deeper learning* for students

  + Processes that support *continuous improvement* for learners, teachers, and schools, including cycles of inquiry, goal setting, and shared learning

- • Accountability for learning, based on:

  + *Multiple measures* that are complementary and contribute to a comprehensive picture of the quality of learning in classrooms, schools, school systems, and states

  + *High-quality assessments* that encourage and reflect deeper learning and authentic evidence of student readiness to succeed in college and in work

  + *Profiles of information* about students, teachers, schools, and districts that move beyond a single cut score to a richer set of data that can provide indicators of accomplishment and grist for ongoing improvement

In the context of a comprehensive system of accountability, a system of assessments should strive to recognize and acknowledge that education is a complex process and that meeting goals for students, teachers, and schools requires indicators that draw from direct measures of the actual knowledge and skills associated with subsequent success. Most important, all of the elements of a system of assessments should be actionable and under the control of educators. The more directly educators can address the accountability measures and effect changes in student behavior associated with them, the more likely they are to do so.

Conclusions and Recommendations

States interested in pursuing a system of assessments within a productive approach to accountability should consider the following five steps.

1. **Define college and career readiness comprehensively**, and note what will be involved with measuring all the components of the definition and supporting students to meet these goals, which includes the following actions:

    + Realign other policy areas, program requirements, and funding to these goals so the state has a focused system of efforts that pulls in a common direction.

    + Identify the information needed to determine if students are college and career ready based on this definition. Be sure to identify sources that are actionable—in other words, what students and teachers can act on to improve readiness.

    + Determine the relationship between the definition of college and career readiness and school accountability needs. In other words, which aspects of the definition are most important for schools to be held accountable to address, and which are important but may not necessarily lend themselves well to inclusion in an accountability system?

2. **Determine the professional learning, curriculum, and resource supports** schools and educators need in order to provide a high-quality, personalized education for students that enables college and career readiness. This work includes the following measures:

    + Consider which opportunity to learn and educational process measures are needed to enable attainment of the outcome measures. Developing a plan to undertake the changes that may be needed in school funding systems, curriculum frameworks, and professional development supports—and launching work on these fronts— communicates that the state is serious about taking responsibility for its aspects of accountability.

    + Develop, disseminate, and implement comprehensive standards (in subject areas beyond the CCSS), curricular frameworks, learning progressions, instructional tools and modules, exemplars of student work, and other materials aligned to the college and career readiness goals that support classroom practices and advance deeper learning outcomes. Strengthen teacher education standards and the programs that enable educators to learn these practices.

+ Support schools in developing approaches that offer all students opportunities to learn the new content in ways that enable them to develop college and career readiness skills. Offer all teachers opportunities to learn to teach to new standards. Consider the ways in which changes in the use of time and technologies may factor into these new approaches.

3. **Establish a clear framework for a comprehensive system of assessments** aligned with CCSS and college and career ready outcomes as follows:

+ Assess the ways in which information and accountability needs could be met by a variety of measures, including performance assessments, and integrate measures appropriately into curriculum development and professional learning opportunities.

+ Ensure that these include opportunities for teachers to design, score, and discuss rich assessments of student learning.

+ Consider how measures could be triangulated—in other words, how more than one source of information could be combined to reach a more accurate or complete judgment about a particular aspect of performance. For example, many important metacognitive learning skills can best be measured both as processes and products.

+ Create a system of multiple measures for assessment uses that results in decisions about students, educators, or schools. Where cut scores are proposed or may have been used, identify supplemental data that will reduce the misclassification rate when combined with a benchmark score. Develop profiles of information for evaluating and conveying insights about students and schools.

4. **Work with postsecondary and workforce representatives** when developing new measures and implementing a system of accountability to ensure acceptance of the system and its measures of college and career readiness. Determine beforehand how data from the system will be used by postsecondary institutions and employers, and develop safeguards to avoid misuse of data, particularly cut scores. Define, with postsecondary stakeholders, how the results of rich measures of student learning can be best conveyed and used (for example, digital portfolios or summary data supplemented by a taxonomy of work samples) and what kinds of student information profiles will be most useful.

5. **Develop means for system learning** to support continuous improvement at all levels of the system. These will include involving educators in the development and scoring of assessments so that they deeply learn the standards and have opportunities to share practice; documenting best practices and disseminating knowledge through online platforms that share studies and highlight exemplars; scheduling school study visits; attending conferences focused on the sharing and development of practice; creating feedback loops to inform students, educators, and schools about their work (for example, through exhibitions, educator evaluation systems, and school quality reviews); and ensuring collaboration opportunities within and across schools and networks.

Research and experience make it clear that educational systems that accomplish the deeper learning goals now before us must also incorporate assessments that honor and reflect those goals. New systems of assessment, connected to appropriate resources, learning opportunities, and productive visions of accountability, are a critical foundation for enabling students to meet the challenges that face them in 21st century college and careers.

References and Resources

Conley, D. (2005). *College knowledge: What it really takes for students to succeed and what we can do to get them ready.* San Francisco: Jossey-Bass.

Conley, D. (2011). *Crosswalk analysis of deeper learning skills to Common Core State Standards.* Palo Alto, CA: Hewlett Foundation.

Conley, D. (2014). *Getting ready for college, careers, and the Common Core: What every educator needs to know.* San Francisco: Jossey-Bass.

Conley, D., Lombardi, A., Seburn, M., & McGaughy, C. (2009). *Formative assessment for college readiness: Measuring skill and growth in five key cognitive strategies associated with postsecondary success.* San Diego, CA: American Educational Research Association Annual Conference.

Darling-Hammond, L. (1993). Creating standards of practice and delivery for learner-centered schools. *Stanford Law and Policy Review, 4,* 37–52.

Darling-Hammond, L. (2013). *The assessment curriculum.* Stanford, CA: Stanford Center for Assessment, Learning, and Equity.

Darling-Hammond, L., & Adamson, F. (2010). *Beyond basic skills: The role of performance assessment in achieving 21st century standards of learning.* Stanford, CA: Stanford University, Stanford Center for Opportunity Policy in Education.

Darling-Hammond, L., Herman, J., Pellegrino, J., Abedi, J., Aber, J. L., Baker, E., et al. (2013). *Criteria for high-quality assessments.* Stanford, CA: Stanford Center for Opportunity Policy in Education.

Darling-Hammond, L., & Rustique-Forrester, E. (2005). The consequences of student testing for teaching and teacher quality. In J. Herman & E. Haertel (Eds.), *The uses and misuses of data in accountability testing: The 104th Yearbook of the National Society for the Study of Education, part II* (pp. 289–319). Malden, MA: Blackwell.

Darling-Hammond, L., & Wentworth, L. (2010). *Benchmarking learning systems: Student performance assessment in international context.* Stanford, CA: Stanford Center for Opportunity Policy in Education. Accessed at http://edpolicy.stanford.edu/publications/pubs/115 on April 4, 2014.

Gordon Commission on the Future of Assessment in Education. (2013). *A public policy statement.* Princeton, NJ: Educational Testing Service.

Kentucky Department of Education. (2009). *On-demand writing released prompts in grades 5, 8, and 12.* Accessed at www.education.ky.gov/kde/administrative+resources/testing+and+reporting+/district+support/link+to+released+items/on-demand+writing+released+prompts.htm on August 1, 2014.

Lundell, D. B., Higbee, J. L., & Hipp, S. (Eds.). (2005). *Building bridges for access and success from high school to college: Proceedings of the Metropolitan Higher Education Consortium's Developmental Education Initiative.* Paper presented at the Metropolitan Higher Education Consortium's Developmental Education Initiative, Minneapolis, MN.

Moore, L., & Russell, D. R. (n.d.). *Portfolios across the curriculum: Whole school assessment in Kentucky.* Accessed at www.public.iastate.edu/~drrussel/EJ99.html on April 4, 2014.

New Hampshire Department of Education. (2013). *Enriching New Hampshire's assessment and accountability systems through the quality performance assessment.* Concord, NH: Author. Accessed at www.education.nh.gov/assessment-systems/documents/executive -summary.pdf on August 1, 2014.

Queensland Curriculum and Assessment Authority. (n.d.). *Queensland comparable assessment tasks.* Accessed at www.qcaa.qld.edu.au/3163.html on August 1, 2014.

Stecher, B. M., Barron, S., Kaganoff, T., & Goodwin, J. (1998). *The effects of standards-based assessment on classroom practices: Results of the 1996–97 RAND Survey of Kentucky Teachers of Mathematics and Writing* (CSE Technical Report 482). Los Angeles: Center for Research on Evaluation, Standards, and Student Testing.

Tung, R., & Stazesky, P. (2010). *Including performance assessments in accountability systems: A review of scale up efforts.* Boston: Center for Collaborative Education.

Webb, N. L. (2002). *Depth-of-knowledge levels for four content areas.* Accessed at http://facstaff .wcer.wisc.edu/normw/All%20content%20areas%20%20DOK%20levels%2032802.doc on August 24, 2011.

Yuan, K., & Le, V-N. (2012). *Estimating the percentage of students who were tested on cognitively demanding items through the state achievement tests.* Santa Monica, CA: RAND.

PART III

What Lessons Will Work?

Michael Fullan

Recognized as a worldwide authority on educational reform, Michael Fullan advises policymakers and local leaders around the world on the moral purpose of all students learning. From 2004 to 2013, Michael served as special adviser in education to the premier of Ontario, Canada. He is a prolific, award-winning author whose books have been published in many languages. His book *Leading in a Culture of Change* was named the 2002 Book of the Year by Learning Forward. His book *Breakthrough* (with Peter Hill and Carmel Crévola) won the 2006 Book of the Year Award from the American Association of Colleges for Teacher Education. His latest books are *Motion Leadership in Action*, *Stratosphere, The Professional Capital of Teachers* (with Andy Hargreaves), and *The Principal*.

To learn more about Michael's work, visit www.michaelfullan.ca.

Chapter 10

Breakthrough Learning

Michael Fullan

The term *21st century learning skills* has been around for a decade and probably more; and the concept behind the term—deep learning—has existed at least since Socrates. The problem has been that 21st century learning skills have become a catchphrase with too little accompanying progress on the ground. In the meantime, traditional schooling is increasingly becoming outmoded. For reasons that I will spell out in this chapter, the situation is dramatically changing. Whatever solutions arise will have to work for the whole system. This is not the time for sporadic innovations.

The four major components of what I call *breakthrough learning*—deep learning on a whole-system basis—are emerging and converging at a rapid rate:

1. The dynamics of push-pull forces

2. New pedagogies linked to deep learning

3. New change leadership

4. An explosion of activity

The Dynamics of Push-Pull Forces

Students are increasingly bored, and teachers are alienated. The data are crystal clear on both fronts. Lee Jenkins asked teachers at different grade levels how enthusiastic their students were about school. The percentage of students enthused at kindergarten was 95 and steadily declined until it bottomed out at 37 percent in grade 9 (Jenkins, 2013). Students themselves echo this disaffection with schooling. When comparing U.S. sixth graders with eleventh graders in the large-scale 2012 My Voice National Student Report (Quaglia Institute for Student Aspirations, 2012), the percentage of students who say "I put in my best effort at school" declined from 87 percent to 69 percent; on a related statement, "Teachers make school an exciting place to learn," the percentages went from 60 to 33 percent. We are talking about up to two-thirds of the students being bored at best.

Teachers, for both micro and macro reasons, reflect this trend as well. The micro reasons pertain to facing bored students and experiencing working conditions that make it difficult for regular teachers to break the mold. One principal we filmed while in a school that was engaged in breakthrough learning (more about this later) observed smartly that "teachers were bored too, they just didn't realize it" until they experienced the alternative. (For our films see our YouTube channel on our website www.michaelfullan.ca.) At the macro level, policies designed to strengthen the teaching profession are actually backfiring and making matters worse, as I have argued in *Professional Capital*. Thus, in the MetLife surveys of teachers conducted every two years, we see an incredible decline in satisfaction and in the intention to stay in teaching from 68 percent in 2008 to 40 percent in 2012 (Hargreaves & Fullan, 2012).

Student boredom and teacher alienation are our "push factors." They are psychologically and literally pushing people out of traditional schooling. At the same time, powerful "pull factors" are rapidly emerging. I have captured some of these in *Stratosphere* (Fullan, 2013), which argues that three forces are beginning to converge: (1) seductive technology, (2) new pedagogies for learning, and (3) new change knowledge about how to foster and respond to change opportunities. These pull factors are not necessarily positive (in *Stratosphere*, an early chapter is devoted to the dark side of the Internet), but together they form a combination powerful enough to change the learning landscape. Thus, the allure of digital and new engaging pedagogies is drawing teachers and students into more exciting and productive learning.

In short, when relentless push and pull factors comingle, it becomes a dead certainty that the status quo will not prevail. I believe that the time has come, and we are seeing and will continue to see radical breakthroughs on a large scale from 2014 onward.

New Pedagogies Linked to Deep Learning

Any solution, as I said in *Stratosphere* (2013), must meet four criteria:

1. Irresistibly engaging for students and for teachers

2. Elegantly efficient and easy to use

3. Technologically ubiquitous

4. Steeped in real-life problem solving

The first step in creating a new pedagogy is to define the roles of students in this new partnership. We can start by ruling out the extremes—for instance, teachers dominating knowledge is obviously off the table, but I would also say that students learning on their own is not viable for the majority. We get a good glimpse of the problem in one of the comparisons that John Hattie derives from his meta-analysis of over one thousand research studies. He compared the roles of teacher as facilitator with teacher as activator. Note that he suggests that effect sizes of 0.40 and above are worth looking at, while those below 0.40 are insignificant. This is what he finds:

- **Teacher as facilitator** (effect size of 0.17)—Using problem-based learning, simulations and gaming, individualized instruction, and web-based, inductive teaching

- **Teacher as activator** (effect size of 0.72)—Providing feedback to students, helping students access their own thinking, and furnishing challenging goals (see Hattie, 2012)

These findings are instructive. They basically say that the teacher as "mere" facilitator will not, in most cases, generate much learning. The guide on the side, if you will, is a poor pedagogue. Note also that there are two Internet-based practices in the facilitator list that are associated with weak impact. We don't have the details, but I would say it is a good bet that the reason involves technology used superficially or poorly from a pedagogical standpoint.

On the other hand, teacher as activator, change agent, or proactive partner in learning does make a significant difference. What is needed, then, is a revamping of the roles and relative roles of teachers and students in a new pedagogy. We define these role changes as "a new learning partnership between and among students and teachers. Roles in which students are more proactive in their own learning, and teachers as designers and enablers of deep learning" (Fullan & Langworthy, 2014). We see it partially in the works of Will Richardson, Marc Prensky, Guy Claxton, and others, and I have worked with Maria Langworthy (2014) to map out a version in a new report titled *A Rich Seam*. In these new roles, students will be more in charge of their own learning but under the guidance and influence of teachers and, indeed, other students. Everyone will be a learner.

This new work must be characterized by precision, specificity, and clarity. With a knowledge-building framework and sharing of practices, this new developmental work can move very quickly. We have already seen some of this clarity in our filming of regular schools moving naturally in these directions (visit www.michael fullan.ca to see the motion leadership film series). I cannot stress enough that these new developments must be characterized by precision, not in order to prescribe them, but in order to be clear about what the practices entail. So, defining and operationalizing the new pedagogies is job one.

Close on the heels of this will be the definition and measurement of deep learning outcomes. Over the past fifteen years, some of these outcomes have been referred to as *21st learning skills*: critical thinking and problem solving, communication, collaboration, and creativity and imagination. The yield, however, has been virtually nothing, as little progress has been made in defining either the pedagogies or their associated outcomes. What is needed now is a more comprehensive job of defining and measuring the learning goals, as well as the pedagogical practices that will produce them.

I have formulated one version of a more comprehensive list of deep learning goals for Ontario that we have called the 6Cs (Fullan,

2013). Essentially what I did was take the original 4Cs and add two key missing ones: character education and citizenship. Here is a brief description of the set:

- **Character education**—Honesty, self-regulation and responsibility, perseverance, empathy for contributing to the safety and benefit of others, self-confidence, personal health and well-being, career and life skills

- **Citizenship**—Global knowledge, sensitivity to and respect for other cultures, active involvement in addressing issues of human and environmental sustainability

- **Communication**—Communicate effectively orally, in writing and with a variety of digital tools; listening skills

- **Critical thinking and problem solving**—Think critically to design and manage projects, solve problems, make effective decisions using a variety of digital tools and resources

- **Collaboration**—Work in teams, learn from and contribute to the learning of others, social networking skills, empathy in working with diverse others

- **Creativity and imagination**—Economic and social entrepreneurialism, considering and pursuing novel ideas, and leadership for action (Fullan, 2013, p. 9)

The latter four Cs concern what people usually refer to as the 21st century learning skills. It is critical to add character education and citizenship to this list because they pertain to the personal and well-being qualities that learners must also have to succeed in the world we live in.

There are enormous developmental requirements embedded in the new pedagogies for deep learning. First, current assessment measures and systems not only do not assess the 6Cs, they actually address more narrow goals in a way that distracts educators from moving in the new directions—that is, traditional assessment systems focus narrowly on rote knowledge and narrow forms of literacy and mathematics. While there is a strong move afoot (such as the

Common Core State Standards), new forms of assessment are not yet available to support the desired deeper learning goals. Second, the new pedagogies themselves (the learning partnership) are not well developed and will require radical changes in how teachers teach and how students (and teachers) learn. In other words, the shift from traditional teacher-led learning to students as partners has not yet occurred (Fullan & Langworthy, 2014).

In summary, while the first component is the powerful push-pull that creates the opportunity for fundamental change, the second element involves the new work necessary to develop and implement the substance of the pedagogy and the outcomes that will be required for deep progress. This leads to the third component: savvy change leadership that is suited to the new dynamics.

New Change Leadership

To move forward, we require a new kind of leadership that is suitable to fast-paced change. I would characterize the process of change in terms of repeated cycles of having a visional direction with a commitment to linking actions with learning outcomes; letting go to innovate, while sharing what you learn; and reining in to consolidate.

The vision does have direction—namely, new pedagogies for deep learning, as described in the last section. It is directional rather than blueprinted, because the details remain to be developed through learning-oriented actions and developments.

Letting go to innovate is related to classical change theory. If you want people to try new things, you have to take the fear out of change. Thus, leaders must create and foster a climate of non-judgmentalism in which people feel free to try out things and learn from them. A culture of risk-taking allows people to move things forward, and a key part of innovating is making sure there are norms and mechanisms by which people learn from each other. Recall also that actions are always tested in terms of their impact on learning outcomes.

Reining in consists of taking stock of the new developments in order to sort out what is working and should be retained and further developed, and to discard what is not working.

These phases are not as linear as I describe them, but they are approximate. We see this process very clearly in our film of Park Manor in Elmira, Ontario. Park Manor is a senior public school with about three hundred students. When they began the change process in 2008–2009, Park Manor was an average school with flatlined results. James Bond, the new principal, followed the process I have just described. He was committed to developing students who would be global critical thinkers collaborating to change the world—obviously a directional vision. He established a climate of trying things, began to make additional technology available, and like all key leaders, exemplified that effective leaders participate as learners with staff to improve the school. He made it clear that he was a learner along with the teachers, and indeed teachers describe their relationships with students as ones in which they are both learners. To be specific, the principal established with teachers a climate of trust (it is okay to make mistakes as long as you learn from them), participated with them in learning about most effective teaching, and linked these developments to data and action that was explicitly linked to student learning for all individuals. The evidence of impact was dramatic: the percentage of students who met the high provincial standard for writing increased from 42 percent to 83 percent in fewer than five years (see our film, www.michaelfullan.ca/category/videos).

Teachers began to identify what practices most engaged students. They developed a low-technology system—the use of sticky notes for each student with his or her picture that indicated how well he or she was doing in literacy, mathematics, and other subjects. The sticky notes for all students were permanently displayed in a locked staff room where all the teachers' meetings were held. There were various instructional strategies identified and used by all teachers: case sample profiles, use of technology that really connected, and so on. Park Manor is a clear example of explicitly pursuing new pedagogical practices linked to deep learning. The school developed an accelerated learning framework that specifically focused on all 6Cs, and all of this work paid off within three years. The school's grade 6 proficiency scores on the high-standard provincial assessment increased dramatically. This change process happens rapidly, accomplishing deep change in short order.

Leadership for such change requires those who immerse themselves with teachers, rapidly building the professional capital of teachers. Leaders "use the group to change the group" (Hargreaves & Fullan, 2012). In a 2014 publication, I elaborate on the role of the principal in terms of what maximizes impact (Fullan, 2014a). In our large-scale work, we use these strategies for whole-system reform, allowing schools and districts to learn from each other as the system moves forward.

An Explosion of Activity

The final component of breakthrough learning is the explosion of activity, which is occurring because of the constellation of converging forces that we have been discussing in this chapter. The new pedagogies, accelerated by technology and supported by leaders with strong change knowledge, provide an outlet for the frustrations of boredom and alienation; they feed on the intrinsic motivation of learners (they are irresistibly engaging); they fit well with another fundamental human motivation—working with others to accomplish something meaningful; and they draw on the prodigious power of technology to access and harness information and to create and make available new ideas and products. Because these conditions are becoming so widespread, we are witnessing the unleashing of forces that cannot be stopped, or to put it positively, can be readily leveraged for deep learning on a large scale. The world will be replete with such learning in short order—2015–2020 and beyond will witness incredible new developments on a scale never before witnessed.

For our part, we are involved in several activities and projects that exemplify the integration of new pedagogies, powerful technologies and better change leadership that supports innovation and collaborative learning. First, we have created an index based on the three dimensions from *Stratosphere:* technology, pedagogy, and change (Fullan & Donelly, 2013). The index allows users to assess given digital innovations according to their strengths on the dimensions: what is their quality as a technology, how specific or linked are they to quality pedagogy, and how amenable are they to supportive change conditions. We are currently building additional tools and strategies to enable the more effective use of technologies. At the outset we are finding that digital innovations are weakest with respect to the pedagogy and the change dimensions.

Second, we have mapped out some of the details of each of the domains of new pedagogy, deep learning, new leadership, and something we call "the new economies" (Fullan & Langworthy, 2014).

Third, we have moved these ideas into action. We have set up a large-scale action research project in which we have recruited ten clusters of one hundred schools, each in ten different countries—a total of over one thousand schools that have signed on for three years to pursue the ideas into practice while learning from their own and each other's experience (www.newpedagogies.org). Each cluster will have two or more cluster leaders whom we will support with tools and ideas for implementing and assessing these new learning examples.

Conclusion

When you put all of these components together, we have a potential breakthrough in terms of both learning conditions and the level of change, the likes of which we have not seen since the industrial factory model of public schooling was established in the 19th century. What is especially noteworthy about this breakthrough learning phenomenon is that the nature of the changes is becoming clear. Even more importantly, the pathways to get there are also more evident. The possibilities are real, and the journey will be exciting. This could very well be learning at its best.

References and Resources

Fullan, M. (2013). *Stratosphere: Integrating technology, pedagogy, and change knowledge*. Toronto: Pearson.

Fullan, M. (2014a). *The principal: Three keys for maximizing impact*. San Francisco: Jossey-Bass.

Fullan, M. (2014b). *Motion leadership film series*. Accessed at www.michaelfullan.ca/category /videos on May 23, 2014.

Fullan, M., & Donnelly, K. (2013). *Alive in the swamp: Assessing digital innovations*. London: New Schools Venture Funds.

Fullan, M., & Langworthy, M. (2014). *A rich seam: How new pedagogies find deep learning*. London: Pearson.

Hargreaves, A., & Fullan, M. (2012). *Professional capital: Transforming teaching in every school.* New York: Teachers College Press.

Hattie, J. A. C. (2012). *Visible learning for teachers: Maximizing impact on learning.* London: Routledge.

Jenkins, L. (2013). *Permission to forget: And nine other root causes of America's frustration with education.* Milwaukee, WI: American Society for Quality Press.

Metropolitan Life Insurance. (2013). *The MetLife survey of the American teacher.* New York: Author.

Quaglia Institute for Student Aspirations. (2012). *My voice national student report (grades 6–12) 2012.* Portland, ME: Author.

Steven Zipkes

Steven Zipkes is principal of Manor New Technology High School, in Manor, Texas, which has received numerous awards, including recognition as an Apple Distinguished School for the past four years, as a model school by the International Center for Leadership in Education, and as a showcase school by the Center for Secondary School Redesign. In 2012, Manor New Technology was chosen as a nationally recognized high school by *U.S. News & World Report* and was featured on Edutopia's "Schools That Work" webpage. Steven has led two high schools and one middle school to their first exemplary ratings and in 2011 was named an Apple Distinguished Educator, one of only approximately fifteen hundred worldwide.

Steven received his bachelor of science degree in radio-television-film from the University of Texas at Austin and his master's in education in school administration from Sul Ross State University in Alpine, Texas.

To learn more about Steven's work, visit www.manornewtech.com and www.thinkforwardpbl.org, or follow him on Twitter @newtechguy.

Chapter 11

All or Nothing: A Deeper Learning Experience

Steven Zipkes

After years of watching minor adjustments to the high school program fail, the Manor (Texas) School District's board of education elected to change its approach—dramatically. With collaboration from community, parents, teachers, and other organizations inside and outside the state, the district asked that I use my thirteen years of experience as a high school principal to take a different route. That was 2006. It was all or nothing.

The board decided to create an innovative high school open to all in-district students who wished to apply. The school would be an alternative to the district's traditional comprehensive high school but not a dumping ground. This is the story of how Manor New Technology High School (MNTHS) came to be a nationally recognized, top-performing school able to offer Manor students a deeper learning path to 21st century college and career success.

The success of MNTHS as a Texas Science, Technology, Engineering and Mathematics (T-STEM) initiative school was the result of an intentional effort to bring deeper learning to this semirural Texas school district, located almost at the end of Austin's airport runways. That success sprang from the school's 100 percent project-based learning (PBL) instruction in a collaborative school culture marked by 21st century learning outcomes and a transformative school structure.

This was not to be PBL by a few teachers, a department, or an elective or two. There were other innovative and unique transformations that were encased in our 100 percent model. And our teaching and learning attracted the attention of President Obama, Secretary of Education Arne Duncan, politicians from around the nation and the state of Texas, educators from around the globe, *U.S. News & World Report*, and the Public Broadcasting Service. Our change process caused MNTHS's scores on the four major subject areas of the Texas Assessment of Knowledge and Skills (TAKS) to soar from the mid 30s to the high 90s within six years (figure 11.1), its dropout and absenteeism rates to fall nearly to zero, and the number of graduates accepted into college to nearly double. We also became a state leader in the number of students—many the first in their family—who entered and stayed in college. So how did all of this happen in spite of the school's socioeconomic statistics, which predict that since the majority of the school comes from a minority population and is on free or reduced lunch programs, it should not have done well (Texas Education Agency, 2012a)?

Figure 11.1 shows TAKS test scores for our first three cohorts of students. The chart shows how each class's scores increased or decreased as students moved from ninth to eleventh grade.

The answer is complex, and it rests in part in the major whole-school restructuring that the school board adopted, ensuring that the results would be positive and long lasting. One of the outward signs of change was clearly visible from the earliest days, when students escorted visitors through the reconstructed middle school. The previous middle school featured architecture typical of its time—small classrooms, limited technology, and isolated learning environments. As they walked down the halls, they saw large, long glass windows opening onto each classroom, allowing them to easily watch students at work and teachers guiding from the side. With deeper observation, visitors saw the following:

- One hundred percent PBL in a collaborative classroom culture in which students teamed at their workstations

Class of 2010	Percent Who Met Standard ELA	Percent Who Met Standard Mathematics	Percent Who Met Standard Science	Percent Who Met Standard Social Studies
9th	86	64	NA	NA
10th	96 ⇧	78 ⇧	85	96
11th	95 ⇩	84 ⇧	95 ⇧	98 ⇧

Class of 2011	Percent Who Met Standard ELA	Percent Who Met Standard Mathematics	Percent Who Met Standard Science	Percent Who Met Standard Social Studies
8th	77	59	65	90
9th	87 ⇧	64 ⇧	NA	NA
10th	90 ⇧	67 ⇧	84 ⇧	98 ⇧
11th	90 ⇨	84 ⇧	94 ⇧	99 ⇧

Class of 2012	Percent Who Met Standard ELA	Percent Who Met Standard Mathematics	Percent Who Met Standard Science	Percent Who Met Standard Social Studies
8th	80	61	78	90
9th	93 ⇧	73 ⇧	NA	NA
10th	90 ⇩	77 ⇧	84 ⇧	98 ⇧
11th	99 ⇧	90 ⇧	97 ⇧	97 ⇩

Source: Texas Education Agency, 2012f.

Figure 11.1: Manor New Tech High School data chart.

- Projects, created by teachers and based on state standards, helping students integrate and assess the 21st century skills of critical thinking, collaboration, creative problem solving, innovation, communication, and research

- Students earning the opportunity to graduate with six years of mathematics credits, seven and a half years of science credits, and four years of engineering credits

- The use of technology as an invisible tool supporting students in solving problems and answering questions in a course's subject area

- Time being restructured to fit learning that includes the 21st century skills

Before examining in depth the system changes and successful practices that led to success at MNTHS, however, let's review why and how MNTHS came to be and how adaptive leadership led to its redesign for the sake of its clients—the students.

The Roots of Success

In education, theory and practice often split from each other, producing the opposite of the intended results. Too many school districts have responded to dropout rates in ways that only increase the numbers of students quitting school early. By embracing the emphasis on and amount of state and national testing as the dominant driver of instruction, school districts present struggling learners with the impossible task of passing even more tests for a curriculum they already have a hard time negotiating and learning. The result: unintended consequences.

When Manor New Technology High School opened in 2006, these same test pressures played a part in the new school's effort to close an ever-widening achievement gap. The board charged the development team with bringing up attendance, eliminating dropouts, creating a college-going culture, providing a safe learning environment, and improving teacher retention. All this was to be accomplished at a public school focused on STEM. A good number of MNTHS's potential students were trapped in a world of endless struggle. With so many students suspended, sent to disciplinary alternative educational settings, truant, or needing to work at night to help out their families, the number of those destined to drop out was high.

Given the depth of the problem, the district felt an urgent need to take a different, more innovative tack. This allowed for freer collaboration, focused leadership, and the adoption of a positive growth mindset—one that called for new strategies to replace all of the failed turnaround efforts that had been guided by a dictated institutional system driven by high-stakes tests.

Taking what Daniel Pink (2009) describes as "autonomy, mastery, and purpose" as the guiding lights for the MNTHS campus and staff, I and the other faculty on our team adopted a common sense approach. Following Pink's ideas, providing autonomy to the students would allow them to see a purpose to their work and develop mastery. It would be the MNTHS faculty's job to ensure that every student learned what was needed to graduate ready for college and career success. However, it would not be all about *what* we teach but rather *how* we teach.

The Growth Mindset: A Precondition to Deeper Learning

Almost every secondary teacher's professional preparation has been about *what* we teach, whether it's mathematics, science, or any other subject. Pre- and professional development have also revolved around the *what* of each separate discipline's content—the curriculum and its subjects—and not the individual's growth over time as a learner, thinker, or creator.

From the start, the MNTHS team challenged the content-centered curriculum's first-place rank. The team's thinking went like this: if teaching is first and foremost about what we teach, every school in the United States should be successful, because we have been spotlighting the *what* for over a century. Instead, our further thinking affirmed, focusing on a growth mindset allows teachers to consider what is most important for reaching all students, including the many on the negative side of the achievement gap. With the growth mindset, how we teach will impact how students learn, and how they learn must end in their growth. Thus, *how* is our mindset.

The MNTHS faculty, led by a growth-proactive principal freed by the district to adopt a full-growth mindset, arrived at the conclusion that more deeper learning opportunities were needed for all students—from the fast-charging, high-achieving digital natives to the most struggling not-yet performers—and that replacement of their obsolete, content-centered curriculum with a new focus on how they learned and how they were taught was a bottom-line necessity.

The switch was made immediately, and from the start, MNTHS faculty walked the talk of this new belief. In addition, the school abandoned traditional schedules and structures that revolved around where buses had to be when, a reliance on teaching silos in which content topics were isolated from each other, long hours of teacher talk, and a state-mandated curriculum with set minutes for students to "sit and git" each subject in readiness for high-stakes tests.

In the place of a school structure that isolated every action within little boxes, MNTHS faculty started with a shift in practices that reflected the paradigm shift to the growth mindset. First, there was a pedagogical shift in the delivery of instruction by adopting PBL as the complete core model of instruction. This led immediately to abandonment of curriculum departments, teaching in isolation, and other out-of-date remnants of the early factory-school days.

In order to provide authentic real-world projects that were multifaceted, like real-world problems, other changes followed. Teachers were free to incorporate 21st century skills—the new essential competencies for navigating today's society without worrying that they were soft skills that couldn't be checked by conventional short-answer tests. Now teachers were able to allot significant time for student goal setting and reflection, intensive inquiry, problem solving, and large doses of collaboration.

The STEM Challenge

Being a Texas designated STEM school raised the ante against MNTHS's growth mindset. Before the state minimum requirements were changed in 2006, Texas schools could be considered STEM schools by having only one additional mathematics and one additional science course than in a traditional school (Sadowski, 2006).

It was thought that by increasing the amount of student time on task in these rigorous disciplines, performance would soar. But how was it possible to get students who had traditionally struggled with mathematics and science to get excited about taking *more* mathematics and science? Knowing students struggled with the boredom of daily doses of severely menial tasks—of passively listening to teachers push information out to them, answering questions at the end of chapters, doing busywork, retaining as much of the information as they could, and using that information to answer bubble-sheet tests without any sense of real-world application—the faculty agreed that mere replication of the usual strategy would most likely continue the low results from this demoralizing model of instruction.

In order to develop deeper learning with STEM, the method of pedagogy had to be different. Without that difference, there would be no increases in student engagement and no closing of the achievement gap. Without adding the growth mindset to the mix, the faculty was convinced that little change would occur and "drop-outitis" would continue.

The faculty focused its *how* on four elements. First was *project-based learning.* From the start, PBL became the core model of instruction in all STEM course work all of the time. Teachers discovered quickly that PBL allowed for pedagogical shifts in the delivery of instruction, giving them autonomy to be as creative as they dared while developing standards-based projects that were authentic and had real-world application. This shift allowed teachers to fill students with a sense of purpose, which explained why these newly alive learners were gathering information through active research, creating a final product, and presenting their findings—a complete shift from sit and git.

Second was *collaboration in the classroom.* In PBL, students collaborate in groups of two to four to complete each project. They take charge of developing and running the project by drawing up a contract with each other, defining their roles and responsibilities. The students learn to rely on each other and hold each other accountable. If a student fails to follow the contract, the group may start a "firing" process to remove a nonproductive member from the group, even though the remaining students must complete the project without the fired worker.

At significant stages in a project, students help each other self-assess both content for mastery and 21st century skills for personal development. Each of these stages allows students opportunities to provide powerful input to refine and finalize shared work. This process provides a vehicle for deeper learning in a real-world application.

In a traditional high school schedule, the extensive thinking required by such assessment and reflection is hampered by short time limits for each class period. At MNTHS, moving away from traditional short-period time slots and subject matter isolated in silos was an outward sign of movement toward deeper learning. Both prompted faculty to seek out team teaching opportunities through which content could be integrated within authentic projects that did not focus on the recall of factual material. By having time to complete work that integrated content areas, students were able to synthesize the curriculum across the spectrum, tying tasks and ideas together and experiencing the learning of knowledge in an authentic scenario, a major component of deeper learning.

The third element in promoting deeper learning at MNTHS was *explicit teaching and assessing of 21st century skills.* The 4Cs became accepted as real learning outcomes that were as defined and valued as much as the mandated state or national content outcomes. In education, both quantitative and qualitative results have shown how relatively little the U.S. education system has changed in the last fifty years to improve student outcomes. From my personal experience as a principal sending teachers to professional development opportunities around the United States, and hosting guests from schools across the world, I've seen that most secondary schools continue to focus on the *what* and try not to speak about *how.* Our school provides training to teachers interested in moving past this older paradigm. Sticking with outdated techniques will not prepare our students for today's or tomorrow's world. MNTHS faculty began to implement, evaluate, and assess the essential 21st century skills of collaboration, communication, critical thinking, work ethic, and research, as well as content, in every project.

Finally, *technology* became a powerful and valuable vehicle. MNTHS began to support and enhance teaching and learning by providing tools for students and teachers to visualize their creativity in ways not previously available. With technology at their fingertips, students now had a chance for anytime, anywhere, and anyplace learning. They could communicate with their team members through visuals and forms of expression not available before 2010. This personalization of technology reinforced our belief that autonomy, mastery, and purpose are the essence of deeper learning.

Thanks to a district bond, each student was provided with an iPad to use as a personal learning device, so students could expand their horizons through creativity and digital authorship. It provided them with a fresher, more meaningful, and deeper approach than the traditional drill-and-kill, lecture, worksheet mode of menial learning and boring teaching. As digital natives, students now had the ability to design, create, write, and publish their work for the world to view.

The instructional practices built on these four fundamental elements included additional *how* methods. These make a long list, but the following are especially important:

- Moving to a trimester schedule allowed for greater flexibility in closing the achievement gap by offering more time for remediation and more opportunities for students to take additional classes in the traditional school calendar year.

- Students were given a major voice in making sure they benefitted from the school's routines. For example, students' interests, not teachers', initiated clubs and organizations. The students wrote up a formal proposal, found sponsors, and developed the bylaws of a club or program before it could be granted permission for implementation.

- Student ownership was enhanced during "circle time," when students and faculty came together as a family once a week for fifteen minutes. Announcements, celebrations, and opportunities for personal growth abounded. Circle time was designed and run by the students, creating a powerful relationship among peers and staff.

- While most educators cite the three Rs as rigor, relevance, and relationships, at MNTHS the three Rs are relationships first, relevance second, and then rigor. When MNTHS students experienced genuine care about their well-being, they worked hard. When they found relevance in projects, they became more engaged. When students are engaged, they find ownership, and attendance goes up, discipline issues go down, deeper learning takes place, and the achievement gap closes. Rigor is built into the entire process—but rigor is really more about *what* we teach, not *how*. Thus, deeper learning takes place at MNTHS not because of rigor but because of the value students see in both the learning process of PBL and in working with their team members in ways that are similar to the real world.

Teacher Quality

At MNTHS, teacher quality was marked by the willingness of each faculty person to take learning to deeper levels for each and every student in the school's very diverse population. The faculty collaborated to achieve a clear understanding of how to use student data to design and create projects that were standards driven and to close the achievement gap. Teachers disaggregated each student's data by using slot analysis to identify strengths and weaknesses on the state-mandated curriculum. This data revealed which specific state standards give students the most difficulty. Then, based on the data, teachers built projects around the standards that students were struggling with. This was smart teaching that provided students the challenge of learning this material in order to apply it.

One area where this school excels is in the hiring of qualified, energetic, and open-minded teachers. When vetting applicants for teaching positions, I look for people willing to step out of their professional comfort zones. Our teachers come from diverse backgrounds and include lifelong teachers, people transitioning from previous careers, and those coming straight from college. The biggest indicators of whether or not a potential hire will fit in with our school culture are the applicant's willingness to let go of preconceived notions about classroom functions and an insatiable curiosity about new pedagogical techniques.

A Final Word

Deep diving into project-based teaching and learning is not done in isolation. Several organizations, such as Think Forward PBL, New Tech Network, Buck Institute for Education, Partnership for 21st Century Skills, Edutopia, and even the U.S. Department of Education, are helping create a tipping point of deeper learning for all students.

At MNTHS, we are proud of our bold steps forward in leading the charge for education redesign. Our students are prepared through deeper learning to meet the challenges of future societal expectations and careers we haven't even thought of. The work of our faculty, supported by the district and the community, has created an exemplar school. Our transformation has shown us that we can make the substantive changes needed to ensure that all students, regardless of skin color, economic status, or any other distinguishing mark, can ace the most difficult of accountability tests when they are indeed freed to think and create their own learning. By taking an all-or-nothing approach in place of quick-fix bandages, students can excel, teachers can excel, and the whole school can excel—as the hard data from Manor New Tech High School illustrates so well. Twenty-first century skills and deeper learning are not pie-in-the-sky theories. They are proven. All trumps nothing.

References and Resources

Pink, D. (2009). *The puzzle of motivation* [Video file]. Accessed at www.ted.com/talks/dan _pink_on_motivation on August 19, 2014.

Sadowski, C. (2006, September 1). *Texas increases graduation requirements*. Accessed at http://news.heartland.org/newspaper-article/2006/09/01/texas-increases-graduation -requirements on August 19, 2014.

Texas Education Agency. (2012a). *2007-08 Academic Excellence Indicator System*. Accessed at http://ritter.tea.state.tx.us/perfreport/aeis/2008/campus.srch.html on August 19, 2014.

Texas Education Agency. (2012b). *2008-09 Academic Excellence Indicator System.* Accessed at http://ritter.tea.state.tx.us/perfreport/aeis/2009/index.html on August 19, 2014.

Texas Education Agency. (2012c). *2009-10 Academic Excellence Indicator System.* Accessed at http://ritter.tea.state.tx.us/perfreport/aeis/2010/index.html on August 19, 2014.

Texas Education Agency. (2012d). *2010-11 Academic Excellence Indicator System.* Accessed at http://ritter.tea.state.tx.us/perfreport/aeis/2011/index.html on August 19, 2014.

Texas Education Agency. (2012e). *2011-12 Academic Excellence Indicator System.* Accessed at http://ritter.tea.state.tx.us/perfreport/aeis/2012/index.html on August 19, 2014.

Texas Education Agency. (2012f). *Academic Excellence Indicator System archives.* Accessed at http://ritter.tea.state.tx.us/perfreport/aeis/index.html on August 19, 2014.

Deborah Rosalia Esparza

Deborah Rosalia Esparza, EdD, started her first career path as an Allstate Insurance systems analyst directing the installation of IBM office systems well before the advent of the 21st century. Transferring to the education world—first as a foreign language intern, then as a bilingual teacher and mentor, award-winning principal, area instructional officer, and chief area officer—she brought a systemic business mindset with her. When directing Allstate's office system installation, she learned the importance of careful planning that not only included management of equipment but also careful attention to human needs impacted by scaling and long-term maintenance. Throughout her education career, Deborah has transferred to the world of education her prior knowledge, skills, and commitment in developing professional adults for work in a technology-driven shifting environment. With several years of experience working in the private sector and over twenty years as a teacher and school administrator, Deborah has used a hybrid approach to the administration of teaching and learning and was an early adopter of the 21st century skills agenda.

Chapter 12

Ears to the Ground: School Leadership in the New Millennium

Deborah Rosalia Esparza

As a school leader in this new millennium, I have faced many new and unique challenges and seen many exciting discoveries. Our students and their families are living in a world dramatically different from past generations. Rapidly developing technology tools, shifting national demographics with blended cultures, and changing accountability standards in our schools have brought a renewed and immediate need for public schools to proactively re-examine curriculum and instruction, school leadership models, and diverse stakeholder expectations. With the implementation of the Common Core State Standards and the Partnership for Assessment of Readiness for College and Careers or Smarter Balanced Assessment Consortium assessments in the majority of districts throughout the United States, many school leaders have accepted the challenge and put their ears to the ground. In order to implement new school leadership insights, 21st century instructional approaches, exemplars of sound practice, and new and unique challenges on a daily basis, I found it essential to do the same—to listen to stakeholders and prepare students to live, learn, and work in a new millennium.

Over the past twenty years as a supervisor, coach, and mentor for thirty-four school leaders and their school-based leadership teams, I learned to facilitate my area schools in making progress toward the 21st century instructional 4Cs (critical thinking and problem solving, communication, collaboration, and creativity and innovation; Kay, 2010). Looking through the lens of a former site-based and area-wide school leader, I identified four critical elements that directly and actively impacted either one or a collective of the schools I was directly responsible for developing.

The Four Cs of 21st Century Leadership

These four organizational elements were inspired by the work of Jim Collins (2005), and through his lens I address them as the *4Cs* of 21st century school leadership—context, culture, conditions, and competencies.

Context

As 21st century school leaders and educators, we needed to develop and nurture a keen awareness of the dynamic and ever-changing environment in which we operated. The identified areas in this element of the diagram arose from leading and persevering within a multicultural and multi-ethnic diverse school community. The examination of context inspired dialogue among school leaders about various aspects of community profiles and characteristics. These characteristics included:

- Dynamic and evolving technology learning tools continuously being promoted and marketed to our schools by a variety of external sources

- The critical need to discern instructionally relevant and effective staff development for every educator

- And, more importantly, equal and appropriate student access, where resources were already inequitably unbalanced and capital scarce, to appropriately and rigorously serve our diverse school community needs, due to the multicultural, multigenerational, and multilingual nature of our students and their families

Culture

We agreed that a healthy school culture is largely determined by a shared vision and organizational beliefs that correspond with and synergize the beliefs of each of its individual members. In our collective-culture diagnostic examination, we found that many of the identified school-culture factors were either internally agreed on or externally imposed. As an area support team, and in an era of decreasing resources, we encouraged a high level of distributive leadership efforts in order to achieve efficient and effective communication, implementation, and evaluation of all educational investments. The external context that directly impacted each individual internal school culture, whether due to district or local school community stakeholder demands, manifested in a variety of ways that were unique and applicable to each school's internal goals, values, beliefs, and ultimately culture. Transparency of teaching and learning priorities, the proactive recruitment of progressive staff, and ongoing support and mentoring of effective instructional strategies and practices were an integral and active component of every school culture development.

Conditions

We agreed that effective school leaders have a higher degree of control of school community conditions when they proactively align resources to student growth and factors that directly impact that primary goal. In addition, we stressed that principals and their leadership teams have the option to formatively construct and create internal school stakeholder consensus on several blueprints of internal resource allocation and plans of action, alongside the explicit expectations of their district's goals and objectives, based on effective use of relevant data. When we examined this aspect of our transformative analysis activity, we saw that creative and innovative conditions that increase participation, morale, coherence, cohesion, and problem solving within a school community also increase and influence effective and proactive change. However, it was also clear that time, a valuable resource for critical communication around formative and summative goal attainment, would be all too scarce.

Competencies

After investigating this element, we noted that savvy school leaders always seek a value-added approach to human-resource recruitment, retention, and development. We agreed on the need for a positive and on-board faculty to bring about a successful and sustainable school transformation. A collaborative, informed, and empowered parental and external school community would also dramatically impact available, underutilized, or even worse, nonutilized resources.

Having served eight years as a principal, I can readily attest to the importance of nurturing, supporting, and promoting the growth of both teacher and external school leadership. True teacher leaders have grounded, invested, and connected their personal development and success with that of the organization. The potential they have to make creative contributions, offer innovations and ideas, and contribute to peer acceptance and respect can be a powerful tool for administrators who are forging through challenging school scenarios.

My aim was to form an agreement among our thirty-four Area 2, Chicago Public Schools, District 299 principals and their school stakeholders regarding each school community's vision and ultimately reach consensus on the core objectives of what they wanted their students to contribute as adults to the global society. There was much to support the contention that any such agreement must provide all students with the equitable opportunity to become deeper learners competent with the 4Cs of learning. These were the competencies my team and I envisioned as the means to deepen students' content knowledge and ability to learn skills. We wanted all of our students to go well beyond the expectations held for students in prior generations.

To accomplish this agenda, it was important for the thirty-four school leaders in our urban sub-district to sharpen communication throughout all layers of our organizations. We agreed that these principals had to be astute in identifying teachers and other key stakeholders who believed in themselves, had a genuine desire for social justice, acted with a high level of emotional intelligence, nurtured their own growth, shared an active voice in key decision-making roles that recognized a new context for learning, created a culture of 21st century readiness, set the conditions for transforming the school to include a deeper learning agenda, and strived to increase the competencies of all staff and students as both teachers and learners.

Our Discovery

As we summed up these attributes, it became clear that our most effective 21st century school leaders would be those willing and able to transform the 4Cs of learning through the prism of the 4Cs of school leadership. We spelled out this challenge by constructing a multilayered Venn diagram (figure 12.1, page 306) in which the 4Cs of leadership were interwoven with each school community's shared goal.

The four leadership elements provided the interrelated framework. The baseline analysis (areas of concern are in gray) provided the current state of each 4C leadership element, while the transformative analysis (figure 12.2, page 307) promoted an open and productive dialogue through a new shift in viewpoint (see gray areas of renewed perspective).

Examining our comparative work both within each Venn and between the two, we discovered the essence of what we needed to do with each of the 4C leadership elements.

Actions and Strategies for Success

Educational leadership in the 21st century is unique in that it operates within an ever more varied mix of value systems, with new pressures for working and living that may not have existed even a decade ago. In the context of increasing diversity, a superabundance of data, and rapid changes in technology, today's learning environment requires an appreciation of school and community cultural backgrounds and a knowledge base of constituents' motives for migration and their educational expectations. To that end, our area team worked to identify actions and strategies for success in this unique and exciting environment.

Unlike corporations and the military, which train already developed adults to a predetermined set of objectives, school leaders need to facilitate young students' construction of their own knowledge

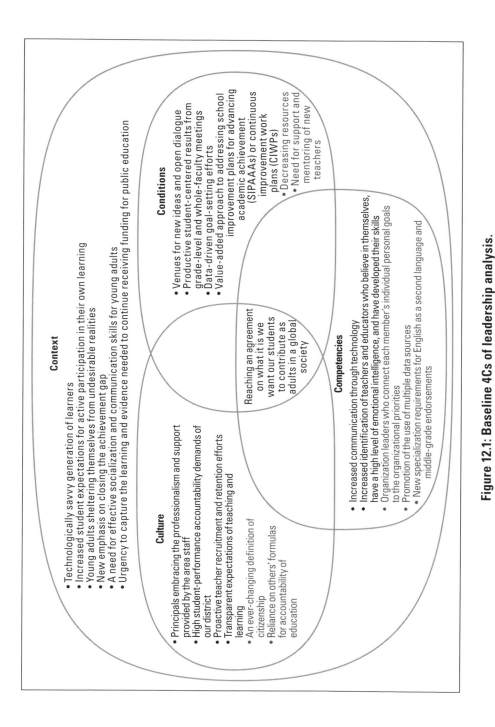

Figure 12.1: Baseline 4Cs of leadership analysis.

Context

- Technologically savvy generation of learners
- Increased student expectations for active participation in their own learning
- Young adults sheltering themselves from undesirable realities
- New emphasis on closing the achievement gap
- A need for effective socialization and communication skills for young adults
- Urgency to capture the learning and evidence needed to continue receiving funding for public education

Conditions

- Venues for new ideas and open dialogue
- Productive student-centered results from grade-level and whole-faculty meetings
- Data-driven goal-setting efforts
- Value-added approach to addressing school improvement plans for advancing academic achievement (SIPAAAs) or continuous improvement work plans (CIWPs)
- Decreasing resources
- Need for support and mentoring of new teachers

Reaching an agreement on what it is we want our students to contribute as adults in a global society

Culture

- Principals embracing the professionalism and support provided by the area staff
- High student-performance accountability demands of our district
- Proactive teacher recruitment and retention efforts
- Transparent expectations of teaching and learning
- An ever-changing definition of citizenship
- Reliance on others' formulas for accountability of education

Competencies

- Increased communication through technology
- Increased identification of teachers and educators who believe in themselves, have a high level of emotional intelligence, and have developed their skills
- Organization leaders who connect each member's individual personal goals to the organizational priorities
- Promotion of the use of multiple data sources
- New specialization requirements for English as a second language and middle-grade endorsements

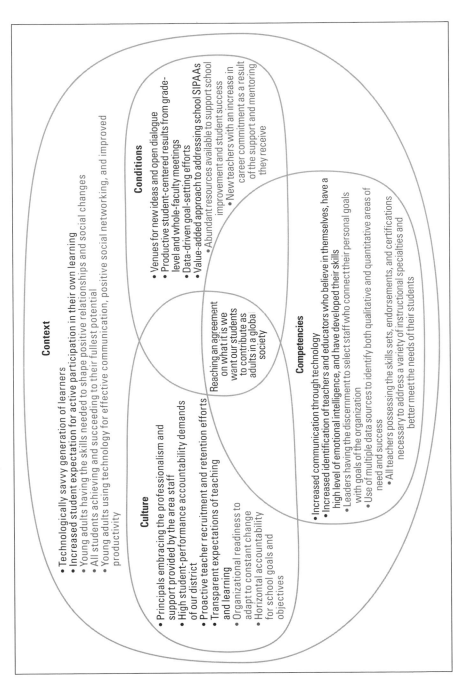

Figure 12.2: Transformative 4Cs of leadership analysis.

base and value systems. Since educational outcomes are complex, it is the school leaders' responsibility to introduce students to a new culture of 21st century, locally relevant expectations. Additionally, these leaders need to be conscious of the challenges and resiliency with which students lead their lives and channel these life skills into productive and lifelong successes.

Our school change effort depended on a partnership among our stakeholders, most notably the parents. This partnership continues to be constant. School leaders and faculty needed to acknowledge that beyond any differences in ideology, they were bonded with parents and the community by the goal of student success. This common goal was an invaluable asset toward building our dynamic learning community.

With these new challenges engulfing our area's schools, we could not leave our collaboration merely to talking about abstract principles. We felt compelled to move principles to practice and big ideas to concrete, achievable actions. To move from the leadership 4Cs to manageable goals, we facilitated our area stakeholder teams toward an action plan with relevant, data-driven, and specific strategies. The plan started with three focus strategies: (1) a focus on teacher capacity and efficacy to improve curriculum rigor, (2) a focus on improving student achievement and engagement, and (3) a focus on distributive leadership. In each focus strategy, we enumerated actions and resources that passed through the implementation continuum of preparing, envisioning, and enacting. In addition, we wanted to identify levers of change and impact within the components of data, accountability, and relationships, which were high-priority goals and objectives for our district.

Each identified strategy and pertinent actions for success was charted as passing through a continuum of implementation in order to gauge progress and continuously align appropriate resources. *Preparing, envisioning,* and *enacting* were terms used to define which stage of development each action was undergoing. Preparing was the stage of innovative thinking, brainstorming, goal setting, and implementation planning, usually in a collective discussion and consensus format. Envisioning required a broader perspective of the organizations' capacity, simultaneous initiative commitments, evaluation development, and a realistic alignment to limited, scarce, and competing resources. Enacting was the early stage of implementation, whether in full organizational scale or pilot group format. This continuum of change model provided us with a clear scenario of the multiple activities our school stakeholders were involved in and allowed us, as an area support system, the necessary perspective to advocate for and actively coach their progress and ultimate success.

The levers of change were identified in the areas of data, accountability, and relationships. These were selected as the most impactful areas that would drive school transformation and provide transparency to our investments in achieving the critical goal of continuous student achievement. The use of data in schools is not a new endeavor, since many schools have been collecting, analyzing, and using formative and summative data at varying degrees of effectiveness to measure and determine next steps and appropriate actions. We were looking for new data—data that would be more relevant and immediate to the needs of our students and that would also give them a voice and a venue for feedback. The accountability lever allowed us to directly identify which programs were contributing to the district goals and our local schools' site-based mission and vision statements. The relationship lever was of critical importance in our progressive multilingual and multicultural culture in order to gauge where we were stimulating, fostering, and promoting high levels of communication and collaboration among several school stakeholders. We held a firm belief that relationship building was a strong foundation for achieving whole-school community advocacy, awareness, and support for programs and actions designed to promote student growth.

Focusing on Teacher Capacity and Efficacy

Focusing on teacher capacity and efficacy to improve curriculum rigor (table 12.1, pages 310–311) was chosen as an area of high attention due to the direct and immediate effect teachers have on their students. CCSS and emerging diverse school models, along with new school populations and stakeholders, have fostered a renewed urgency to re-examine teacher readiness for 21st century educational expectations. Beyond traditional teacher preparation programs, including new online venues and alternative education degree options, it is imperative to structure ongoing data-driven professional development opportunities for teachers to stay abreast of local and global issues, develop competence and comfort with technology instructional tools, have expertise with data management, utilize a repertoire of student learning diagnostics and strategies, and consciously and deliberately seek opportunities to better meet the needs of their diverse populations.

Table 12.1: Strategies and Actions for Success

Sample Strategy: Focus on Teacher Capacity and Efficacy to Improve Curriculum Rigor						
Preparing	Envisioning	Enacting	Action	Data	Accountability	Relationships
✓			Participate in differentiated professional development, managed by a centralized database, to better target professional areas of need and track progress.		✓	
	✓		Promote and support the adoption of a district-wide common language for administrators, teachers, and support staff to describe best practices, increase self-reflection, and improve teaching practices. (Excellence in Teaching Program)		✓	✓
✓			Use World-Class Instructional Design and Assessment (WIDA) standards for lesson planning to provide high-quality instruction and close the achievement gap among English learners.	✓	✓	

Preparing	Envisioning	Enacting	Action	Data	Accountability	Relationships
		✓	Increase teacher expertise through university and museum partnerships and programs. (NLU cohorts: ESL, bilingual education, middle school; DePaul University High School Algebra Teacher Training, Shedd Aquarium navigators, Adler Planetarium partnership, Lincoln Park Zoo, National Geographic JASON Project promoting science, technology, engineering, and mathematics (STEM) exploratory learning, named after the mythological Greek explorer)		✓	✓
	✓		Refine language objectives and lesson planning to improve delivery of instruction for ELs. (Sheltered Instruction Observation Protocol [SIOP])	✓	✓	
		✓	Use high-quality curricula to improve instructional capacity and student learning in mathematics and science. (Chicago Math and Science Initiative)		✓	
	✓		Train teachers in planning and facilitating instructional strategies to address individual student needs, effectively closing the achievement gap among all students through differentiation of content, process, and/or product. (Applying Differentiated Strategies [ADS])	✓	✓	
		✓	Provide best practice informational sessions to promote fellowship and capacity of school staff, and increase student achievement, growth, and development. (Area Education Fair)		✓	✓
	✓		Improve literacy in all content areas through the use of primary sources. (Library of Congress primary sources tools)	✓	✓	

Focus on Improving Student Achievement and Engagement

This selected focus area facilitated necessary and pertinent dialogue, documentation, and prioritization around the investment of valuable and scarce school resources. This meant revisiting all direct and indirect student services and learning opportunities. This also meant engaging more student voice and analyzing authentic feedback data to create new curriculum-delivery-enhancement approaches and multicultural reach.

In an era of constant change and increased student expectations, any and all school programs, initiatives, or curriculum investments should enter through a careful filter of criteria in relation to their ultimate effects on student growth. The actions described within this sample strategy chart were highly vetted activities that directly contributed to our 21st century vision. Our students needed educational opportunities beyond the classroom doors. They wanted online portals, direct manipulation and examination of primary resources, external experiences, connections with the outside world of professionals, exposure to internships, and so on. If students are to develop the necessary skills to live and contribute in a global society, then we have the responsibility to afford them these opportunities throughout their educational learning encounters.

Successful 21st century school leaders need to possess high standards for all school community members and students, a relentless ability to motivate teachers and administrators with a 21st century vision, and the compassion to understand the realities of students' families' social conditions. The actions and strategies outlined in table 12.2 made the process of growth and goal setting more transparent and reflective. It has also provided for clarity in understanding the overlaps and synergy within the levers of change. Carefully crafted, multiple and measurable practices impacted the differentiated needs of schools and communities and provided necessary and relevant data for continued action or redesign. This method of formative reflection allowed for cost-effective investments, based on research supporting increased student achievement, high-implementation fidelity through schools, broad student reach, and emerging local sustainability.

Table 12.2: Focus on Improving Student Achievement and Engagement

Preparing	Envisioning	Enacting	Action	Data	Accountability	Relationships
			Sample Strategy: Focus on Improving Student Achievement and Engagement			
		✓	Improve student engagement, problem-solving ability, and higher-order thinking skills through use of a structured chess program. (First Move)	✓		✓
		✓	Increase instructional capacity for middle grade teachers to teach and improve student learning in earth science. (national Geographic JASON project)	✓	✓	
		✓	Provide real life, authentic experiences for students to supplement inquiry-based learning. (Shedd Aquarium navigators, Adler Planetarium Partnership, Lincoln Park Zoo)		✓	✓
	✓		Provide before-, during-, and after-school tutoring to support student mathematics learning. (Loyola University's Countdown Program)	✓		✓
		✓	Improve high school outcomes for success by offering high school preparation and content-level classes in the middle grades. (High school algebra for middle school students)	✓	✓	
✓			Support social studies teaching and learning. (Barat Foundation partnership)		✓	
		✓	Curriculum coherence with alignment to state standards and benchmark assessments, increasing student achievement through more effective and targeted instruction and assessment processes. (Supported Core Reading Materials Adoption [SCRMA], Lucy Calkins Writing Workshop, area curriculum maps, area standards-aligned reading charts)	✓	✓	
		✓	Increase student achievement in writing skills through use of a technology tool that provides immediate feedback. (MyAccess)		✓	✓

Develop Distributive Leadership

Progressive school leadership recognizes and values stakeholder input. The deliberate verb transition from *focus* to *develop* created a realization of how this particular strategy manifested at varying degrees, in different school sites, based on distinct school cultures. The actions and programs described within this school leadership approach (table 12.3) promoted the optimization of structures and the relationships operating within those structures to work and thrive in a highly driven 4C teaching and learning environment where all voices are heard, valued, and empowered. The strategic collection of student data being systemically examined through several lenses, the purposeful examination of organizational competencies to readily address student-achievement areas of need, the attention to social-emotional and student leadership development, the effective practice of professional learning communities, and proactive parental empowerment endeavors were actions that proved to be meaningful, useful, and sustaining.

Table 12.3: Develop Distributive Leadership

Sample Strategy: Develop Distributive Leadership						
Preparing	Envisioning	Enacting	**Action**	Data	Accountability	Relationships
	✓		School data teams collaborate to do a deeper analysis of student work and use multiple measures of summative and formative data to create an increased awareness of student needs. (Chicago Data Initiative [CDI])	✓	✓	✓
	✓		Employ technology to support the use of multiple measures of data for decision making and curriculum alignment to improve the use of differentiated instruction and increase student achievement. (Instructional Management Program and Academic Communications Tool [IMPACT] Curriculum and Instruction Management Tool [CIM])	✓	✓	

Preparing	Envisioning	Enacting	Action	Data	Accountability	Relationships
		✓	Develop an objective, data-based, and reliable method of focusing organizational energies on continuous improvement for leaders and members of their units in order to increase in the levels of organizational productivity and increase the leadership capacity of leaders and teams throughout the organization. (Organizational Health [OH])	✓	✓	✓
		✓	Establish professional learning communities (PLC) in which best practices for teaching and learning are reviewed, discussed, adapted, and adopted into practice. (Excellence in Teaching Program, book study groups, principal and assistant principal cohorts, teacher-specialty cohorts)		✓	✓
✓			Promote positive student leadership models to address the need for character education, anti-drug / anti-bullying education, and improved decision making to increase student involvement, improve attendance, and reduce discipline problems.		✓	✓
		✓	Facilitate communication between the home and school to empower parents as partners in education and increase parental knowledge of grade-level curricula and home-based interventions. (Parent conference/fair)		✓	✓

Takeaways

I have documented the change process my colleagues and I made to transform our schools to meet and exceed the challenges of a new century. In this plan, you have seen the specific results of our collaborative thinking and problem solving as we addressed the 4Cs of leadership.

From these four leadership elements—context, culture, conditions, and competencies—came specific strategies and actions that fit our schools. Each school's specific plan allowed us to track our progress individually and as a collective. Words became actions.

With this example—adjusted to each school's ideas, insights, and change efforts—it is possible for school leaders to adopt this framework for directing their own pathway through a 21st century transformation. The challenge is to outline how you would take what you have read here, adapt the processes from the 4Cs of leadership, work with colleagues, and develop your own analysis and actions.

We live in an increasingly complex sociopolitical and economic landscape that promotes division and obfuscates human connection. The most successful citizens will be those able to define and solve problems thoughtfully and thoroughly, taking into account the impact of their actions on others.

Our information age has linked us into a world of new responsibilities. As a global society, educators have the mandate to prepare future leaders for a more challenging and dynamic existence. As educational leaders, we are in a unique and privileged position of influence to guide students toward a deeper understanding of the past, present, and future. More importantly, as professionals, we need to forge our organizational models and frameworks from successful practicing environments to optimize student-learning outcomes. The successful school leader of the new millennium will exercise common sense approaches of analysis, be conscious of the value others possess, make decisions without deviation from objectives, develop a culture of dynamic growth, utilize every venue available to maximize opportunities for their organization, and have the skills required to reassess and redirect courses of action whenever and wherever necessary.

References and Resources

Boyatizis, R., & McKee, A. (2005). *Resonant leadership: Renewing yourself and connecting with others through mindfulness, hope, and compassion.* Boston: Harvard Business School Press.

Chalker, D. (1992, February). Refocusing and redirecting school leadership for the 21st century. *Thresholds in Education,* 26–30.

Collins, J. (2005). *Good to great and the social sectors: Why business thinking is not the answer—A monograph to accompany Good to Great.* New York: HarperCollins.

Denzin, N. K., & Lincoln, Y. S. (1994). *Handbook of qualitative research.* Thousand Oaks, CA: SAGE.

Goleman, D. (1995). *Emotional intelligence: Why it can matter more than IQ.* New York: Bantam.

Hodgkinson, C. (1991). *Educational leadership: The moral art.* New York: State University of New York Press.

Fiedler, F. E., & Chemers, M. M. (1984). *Improving leadership effectiveness: The leader match concept.* New York: Wiley.

Kay, K. (2010). Foreword. In J. A. Bellanca & R. Brandt (Eds.), *21st century skills: Rethinking how students learn* (pp. xiii–xxxi). Bloomington, IN: Solution Tree Press.

Krause, D. G. (1997). *The way of the leader.* New York: Pedigree.

Owens, R. G. (1995). *Organizational behavior in education.* Boston: Allyn & Bacon.

Peterson, K. D. (1982). Making sense of principals' work. *The Australian Administrator, 3*(3), 1–3.

Salovey, P., & Mayer, J. D. (1990). Emotional intelligence. *Imagination, Cognition, and Personality, 9*(3), 185 211.

Ken Kay

Ken Kay is the chief executive officer of EdLeader21, a professional learning community for education leaders committed to 21st century education. Ken cofounded the Partnership for 21st Century Skills in 2002 and served as its president for eight years.

Along with Valerie Greenhill, he authored *The Leader's Guide to 21st Century Education: 7 Steps for Schools and Districts*.

Ken is a graduate of Oberlin College and the University of Denver College of Law and currently serves on the board of the Buck Institute for Education (www.bie.org). He and his wife, Karen, have three adult children, a daughter-in-law, and a grandson, Ollie. They live in the desert outside Tucson, Arizona, with their golden retriever, Bisbee.

To learn more about Ken's work, visit www.edleader21.com, or follow him on Twitter @kenkay21.

Valerie Greenhill

Valerie Greenhill leads EdLeader21's capacity-building work. She is currently focused on supporting district leaders with efforts to integrate the 4Cs into teaching and learning systems. She leads member work in key national initiatives, such as STEP21 (Systemic Transformation Evaluation Protocol for 21st Century Education), the 4Cs Performance Assessment System, and Common Core/4Cs implementation. From 2004 to 2010, Valerie served as the director of strategic initiatives for the Partnership for 21st Century Skills, where she established and led the work of integrating college- and career-readiness skills into standards, assessments, curricula, instruction, and professional development. Along with Ken Kay, she authored *The Leader's Guide to 21st Century Education*.

Valerie earned her master's degree in educational media and computers from Arizona State University and a master's degree in English from the University of Arizona and is an honors graduate of Vassar College. She lives with her husband and two daughters in Tucson, Arizona.

To learn more about Val's work, visit www.edleader21.com, or follow her on Twitter @val_green.

Chapter 13

The Pivotal Role of the District

Ken Kay and Valerie Greenhill

In 2012, the San Jose Unified School District embarked on a bold mission: eliminate the opportunity gap and ensure that all students receive the finest 21st century education. To that end, the California district of 32,000 students adopted a five-year strategic plan that emphasizes critical thinking and problem solving, creative thinking, communication, collaboration, and global citizenship, along with digital literacy.

"The concept of 21st century skills is hugely supported by our leaders, teachers, parents, students, and community," says Superintendent Vincent Matthews.

> In fact, we developed our 5 Cs in partnership with these stakeholder groups. . . . Early in our strategic planning process, we held roundtables where some of the leading companies in Silicon Valley engaged on the skills they would like to see from their future employees. We consistently heard the message that our local businesses must hire globally because they *do not see 21st century skills locally*. This hammered home that we must focus in this area, not only for the good of our students, but also the local economy. (EdLeader21, 2013)

Across the United States, Fairfax County Public Schools in Virginia has been on a similar journey. Its fourth annual education summit, Portrait of a 21st Century Graduate and School System, held in 2013, drew parents, educators, students, and citizens from the suburban district of about 184,500 students. They discussed ways for families to foster critical thinking, creativity, communication, and collaboration at home. They heard about classrooms that are changing to reflect innovations in programs and curriculum delivery, the impact of technology, flexible and adaptable learning spaces, and environmental sustainability. They learned how postsecondary education and the world of work have changed drastically over the past twenty years—and how upcoming high school graduates can prepare to succeed in this new world (Fairfax County Public Schools, 2013).

In media coverage of the summit, Jocelene Aquino, who is the parent of three children in the district, said that the U.S. education system compares unfavorably with those of Hong Kong and Jerusalem, two other places she has lived. "We're so far behind," Aquino said, noting that tests such as Virginia's Standards of Learning "are an antiquated way to look at educating our children" (as cited in Shapiro, 2013).

"We need to find new ways we can measure learning and the ways our teachers are teaching without taking the joy out of both," echoed Superintendent Karen Garza (as cited in Shapiro, 2013). To that end, the Fairfax district will use the international assessment known as Programme for International Assessment (PISA) to benchmark student skills and creative application of knowledge with that of students around the world and across the district. The superintendent and the school board are working with an advisory group to develop a profile of a 21st century student, and they want the district to become a national model for assessment of 21st century competencies.

Our Theory of Action: Scaling Transformation in Districts

In our view, frank talk and innovative approaches to 21st century education at the *district* level—as in San Jose and Fairfax County—are exactly what is needed to scale deeper learning. Deeper learning requires:

- A deeper vision, deeper commitment, and deeper community consensus on priorities for student learning

- Deeper implementation to embed that vision and community priorities into standards, professional learning, instructional practices, curriculum, and assessment

- Deeper innovation to spur continuous improvement

Since 2004, many cutting-edge principals and teachers have made remarkable progress in fostering 21st century competencies and deeper learning in classrooms. Federal and state leadership and incentives make a difference, but the serious work must take place in districts. Communities must imagine and embrace the future they want for their children. Districts represent communities—and district leaders must take ultimate ownership and responsibility for making the community's vision a reality.

In addition, a model of systemic change that relies in large part on forward-thinking teachers and principals to transform educational practices is not sustainable. Make no mistake: these teachers and principals are doing wonderful work. But without more support from their districts, the impact they can make is limited. Even the most committed and passionate educators can do only so much before they bump up against barriers to innovation, from limited capacity and resources to lack of support and authority to disjointed standards, curricula, and assessments. In districts committed to rethinking education, however, educators who have been deepening their practices can become tremendous assets and role models for their peers.

Finally, in our work we've considered the numbers and the question of scale. There are almost 99,000 public elementary and secondary schools in the United States (U.S. Department of Education, National Center for Education Statistics, Common Core of Data, 2012). We are continually inspired by individual school models that are achieving amazing results for students. To scale these promising practices, however, we must look to the 13,600 regular U.S. school districts (Keaton, 2012), the biggest of which affect thousands of schools and millions of students. District leaders have the power to transform entire systems, create a seamless and coherent plan for educating students at every grade level and subject, and drive entire school communities toward a common purpose: preparing students to succeed in the 21st century.

What About the Common Core?

Many states have adopted the Common Core State Standards in English language arts and mathematics, and districts are therefore focused on Common Core implementation.

We support the Common Core, which raises the bar on student expectations. We applaud the emphasis in the Common Core on developing higher-order skills, such as analyzing, reasoning, constructing logical arguments based on evidence, and applying knowledge and skills to real-world issues and challenges in the context of core academic content. Critical thinking and communication are well aligned with the Common Core (for example, see Partnership for 21st Century Skills, 2011a).

We caution, however, that the Common Core is not a *de facto* vision or path for a 21st century education—and it should not be equated with career readiness. The Common Core is the floor, not the ceiling, for deeper learning. It is not comprehensive in covering all academic subjects, for example, and many important competencies (such as creativity, collaboration, and financial literacy) are not addressed.

We advocate a "Common Core and more" approach (Kay & Lenz, 2013). We see two paths emerging as educators work to implement the Common Core—a minimalist path and a visionary path. Educators on the first path go through a compliance exercise, mapping existing curricula and grade-level requirements to the Common Core and concluding that, for the most part, "we're already doing that." Educators on the second path view the Common Core as a unique opportunity to leverage the strengths of the standards to transform teaching and learning by aligning the Common Core with 21st century skills and deeper-learning outcomes, professional development, and assessment.

Our Model for Creating 21st Century Districts

Our model for 21st century education is centered on student outcomes. *All* students need to master the full range of core academic subjects, the 4Cs (critical thinking and problem solving, communication, collaboration, and creativity and innovation, plus life and career skills, such as self-direction), and 21st century themes, such as financial, economic, business, and entrepreneurial literacy (Partnership for 21st Century Skills, 2011b) (See figure 13.1.)

20th Century	Common Core	and More
Student A	**Student B**	**Student C**
Mathematics	Content Mastery	Content Mastery
Science	Critical Thinking	Critical Thinking
English	Problem Solving	Problem Solving
Social Studies	Communication	Communication
		Collaboration
		Creativity
		Global Competence
		Self-Direction

Source: EdLeader21.

Figure 13.1: Which student would you choose?

Similarly, deeper learning emphasizes mastering core academic content, thinking critically and solving problems, working collaboratively, communicating effectively, and learning how to learn (for example, through self-directed learning), according to a National Academy of Sciences report (Pellegrino & Hilton, 2012). Deeper learning is closely aligned to our vision of 21st century education. This alignment validates the strong consensus around the key elements for preparing world-ready students. Whether it's labeled deeper learning or 21st century education, the movement toward more rigor and relevance in education is broadly shared. We're working under the same big tent toward a unified set of student outcomes. All over the United States, there is a sense of urgency for a new model of education.

Through our experiences advocating at the national and state levels for 21st century education, we became convinced that many districts are eager to move education into the 21st century in practice—not just with disingenuous lip service or by virtue of having flipped the calendar into a new century. But a true 21st century education is a dramatic departure from business as usual—and districts want help. To that end, we launched EdLeader21, a national network of district and school leaders focused on integrating the 4Cs into education. More than 125 districts in thirty-four states are now working with us, with one another, and on their own to better prepare students for the realities they are likely to face.

EdLeader21 has become a bellwether for 21st century education and an incubator for innovation. Common themes and strategies are emerging as district leaders take on the fundamental and practical challenges of districtwide transformation. Superintendents, their cabinets, and education leaders need to be deeply invested in this process. Outsourcing this work amounts to devaluing it—not an auspicious beginning.

Where should district leaders start? Our book, *The Leader's Guide to 21st Century Education* (Kay & Greenhill, 2013), synthesizes the trajectory of the process we're seeing, turning it into a blueprint for action. (An *Edutopia* blog series [Kay, 2011a] provides a succinct summary of the steps.) The seven steps are:

1. Developing a vision

2. Creating community consensus

3. Aligning the system

4. Building professional capacity

5. Focusing curriculum and assessment

6. Supporting teachers and students

7. Improving and innovating

Developing a Vision

In step 1, developing a vision, we recommend that district leaders define a vision of 21st century education outcomes for students, with the 4Cs of critical thinking and problem solving, communication, collaboration, and creativity and innovation as the centerpiece of this vision. In our view, these competencies are not optional; there is overwhelming agreement that they are essential to student success—no matter how or where students pursue their dreams after high school.

The vision must reflect real commitment. A deep vision results from serious inquiry and reflection. A good way for leaders to go about this is to ask some fundamental questions, such as:

- What's different about 21st century life?

- How does a changed world impact education?

- What will today's kindergarteners need to learn and be able to do by the time they graduate?

- What knowledge and skills will empower students to succeed in college, careers, and life?

- Which indispensable skills do *I*, as a leader, rely on now—and which skills do I want to improve?

Impatience can be a virtue when it comes to school improvement. But district leaders shouldn't skip or speed through the process of reflection and envisioning. Developing a *personal* vision and a deep understanding of 21st century outcomes is time well spent. Many district leaders find it valuable to learn how their peers are reimagining and reinventing their systems. No one district has all the answers. EdLeader21 offers a professional learning community that fosters conversations and collaborative learning around every step of the journey. In 2015, we will release a STEP21 guide aligned to these seven steps, which will provide a rubric and peer review process that districts can use to conduct a systematic analysis of what it means to be a 21st century district or school.

Creating Community Consensus

Leadership conviction is critical for communicating and refining the vision with the leadership team and with the community—and for staying the course when challenges inevitably arise during implementation. That leads to step 2: creating community consensus. Moving from a personal conviction to a shared vision means more than issuing a dictum from on high that change is coming. It requires deeper, intentional engagement, led by superintendents and principals, with educators, parents, students, and the entire community. District and school leaders need to communicate, demonstrate, and showcase their commitment to their vision and the 4Cs in leadership team meetings, public appearances, and digital forums, such as blogs or online communities.

A decided benefit of this outreach could be partnerships with the business community, community organizations, and other stakeholders that can support the district vision. That's what happened in the East Syracuse-Minoa Central School District in New York, where the 21st century education initiative led to partnerships with the local federal credit union to support financial literacy and with regional, national, and international companies and organizations to support STEM skills for middle and high school students.

The Ballston Spa Central School District, also in New York, is partnering with the Hudson Valley Community College and Saratoga Technology + Energy Park (STEP) to prepare high school students with knowledge and skills related to careers in clean technologies and sustainable industries.

District and school leaders should also model the 4Cs in their interactions with stakeholders. In this way, the 4Cs become *attributes* of 21st century leadership and professionalism. We see districts using the 4Cs in three ways: (1) as expectations for student learning, (2) as qualities of great pedagogy, and (3) as characteristics of great leadership. To be 21st century leaders, district administrators must demonstrate these skills. Otherwise, leaders will lose all credibility in advocating for their vision of 21st century education. In fact, when we asked school leaders which skills they used most in their deeper learning work, they listed the 4Cs.

In this process of defining a vision and building community consensus, districts might consider adding additional skills and knowledge to the 4Cs as expected learning outcomes. In the Catalina Foothills School District in Tucson, Arizona, for example, teachers were teaching systems thinking to K–5 students. Superintendent Mary Kamerzell and other district leaders were so impressed with the robust examples of systems thinking from elementary students that they decided to use systems thinking tools to examine the school system and plan transformation practices. The district developed a common definition for systems thinking: Systems thinking is a vantage point from which one sees a whole, a web of relationships, rather than focusing only on the detail of any particular piece. Events are seen in the larger context of a pattern that is unfolding over time. Systems thinking provides students with a more effective way of interpreting the complexities of the world in which they live—a world that is increasingly dynamic, global, and complex (Catalina Foothills School District & Waters Foundation, 2007). This definition is now infused in all curricula, assessments, and professional development.

Communities need to be convinced and educated about the district vision. And leadership matters. District leaders must play a key role in instilling the vision of 21st century education deep into the culture of the community.

Aligning the System

With a deeper vision and community consensus, districts are ready to begin the most difficult work: taking action to ensure *all* students are benefiting from this vision. In step 3 toward 21st century education—aligning the system—districts integrate the 4Cs and any other student outcomes into curricula, instruction, and assessments in an aligned, coordinated way. Alignment, like the process of developing a vision and community consensus, is a strategic process that demands leadership engagement.

Alignment of standards, curricula, instruction, and assessments might be a familiar concept and exercise, especially in high-performing districts. But 4Cs alignment is a new and different challenge for most districts. In fact, we've discovered a surprising lack of attention in most alignment efforts to 21st century student outcomes—the most important goal of a 21st century education.

So what does 21st century alignment *really* mean? It entails systemic integration of the 4Cs into every major area of district activity:

- Curriculum
- Instruction
- Professional capacity
- Assessment

- Learning environments
- Leadership and administration
- Partnerships with the community
- Continuous improvement

Obviously, this list requires a deep dive into all the elements of a district that affect 21st century student outcomes—and connecting the dots so that they all work together to achieve these outcomes. While this work is difficult and sometimes daunting, district leaders and educators who do undertake systematic, 21st century alignment find it incredibly rewarding and dynamic work. There are excellent resources to help districts with the alignment process. Our Step21 work, for example, will take districts through a self-assessment of where they are on the path to 21st century education and help them set benchmarks and goals to make progress.

Alignment becomes a window through which districts can begin to see what they're really driving toward—and make adjustments along the way. That's what happened in Virginia Beach City Public Schools, where the effort involved:

- **Community alignment**—Defining 21st century student outcomes for the community and building support for them
- **Strategic plan alignment**—Setting five key objectives to empower students to achieve the outcomes: (1) engage every student, (2) create balanced assessment, (3) improve achievement, (4) create opportunities, and (5) build capacity
- **Implementation team alignment**—Pairing a cabinet-level leader and a school principal to collaborate as a team for accountability on each of the five objectives
- **School alignment**—Aligning school improvement plans to the district strategic plan

Virginia Beach has been relentless about alignment at every level—district, school, and classroom—and has created structures for that alignment to happen. For example, educators from every discipline are leaders within their PLC, which focuses on 21st century skills, such as communication and collaboration. They've developed concrete tools, such as rubrics and assessments, that are now changing classroom instruction.

Building Professional Capacity

With the strategic work of developing a vision of 21st century education, building community consensus, and system alignment completed, districts are truly ready to take on the tactical work of supporting deeper teaching and learning. The overarching goal of this tactical work should be to embed the 4Cs into teaching and learning practices. Traditionally, professional development, curriculum and assessment, and instructional practices have centered on core academic content, not on skills. Skills have been treated as a nice-to-have, not a must-have. That has to change. Only by putting the 4Cs at the center of a 21st century education, thoroughly and deliberately, can districts ensure that students will master both the knowledge and skills they need to succeed. More and more, in fact, educators understand that when they are intentional about the 4Cs in the context of core academic content teaching and learning, they see their students becoming more engaged. The 4Cs focus is a more effective way for students to truly learn, understand, and think critically about academic content, while also developing the competencies they need to succeed in college, career, and citizenship.

Districts need to change both the culture and the content of professional learning. As we write,

> We have all had the experience of attending a seminar where none of the 4Cs is present: No critical thinking is required, no collaboration is expected, and no creativity is encouraged. . . . When this is the kind of "professional development" being provided, how can we possibly engage educators in lifelong professional learning? (Kay & Greenhill, 2013, p. 58)

To counteract the irrelevance of most teacher training, districts should consider the 4Cs as the design principles of professional development. What if professional development challenged educators to think critically, communicate more effectively, and collaborate with colleagues around authentic work, and inspired them to be more creative and innovative? To state the obvious, just as math teachers need a deep understanding of math to teach this subject effectively, 4Cs teachers need to master and model the 4Cs to teach them. And make no mistake: if the 4Cs are truly integrated into curricula, instruction, and assessments, *every* teacher needs to be a 4Cs teacher.

PLCs are a powerful way to move away from static training sessions toward a culture of continual inquiry, teamwork and collaboration, creative problem solving, and fresh ideas—all toward the goal of improved student learning. Albemarle County Public Schools in Virginia have begun to focus on job-embedded professional development to support teachers in implementing new ideas and strategies. This model of staff development is collaborative, using both face-to-face and online interaction as opposed to simply having teachers attend professional development workshops that may be one-time events. The New Tech Network, as another example, requires every new teacher to participate in both a school-based team and an online collaborative team with teachers across the network.

Beyond infusing the 4Cs into the culture of professional development, districts need to make the 4Cs the *content focus* of professional development. What do we mean by that? A PLC can provide the structure within which to practice the 4Cs. Teachers' participation in a PLC will not, in and of itself, impact student learning of the 4Cs *unless this is their essential purpose.* Thus, professional development should be all about empowering teachers to embed the 4Cs into their practice.

Teachers in every subject and grade level must develop a deep understanding of and specific strategies for the 4Cs. Given that most teachers were never explicitly prepared to do this, sustained professional learning is critical. In the Upper Arlington Schools in Ohio, the superintendent and his leadership team focused for two years on critical thinking. Two years! Every teacher, in every school, department, and grade, worked within the PLC to share and develop examples of how to teach critical thinking.

A wonderful insight emerges from Upper Arlington's elevation of critical thinking as a priority: untapped expertise exists in our schools right now. Coaches in the district recruited thirty-eight district teachers who already had compelling examples of teaching critical thinking, but as in many districts, their expertise had never been broadly recognized or shared. These teachers led a kick-off event to launch the critical-thinking focus, modeling their practices for other teachers—a powerful professional development approach. Teachers all had their own individual breakout room where they explained their most effective critical thinking pedagogical practices. The event created incredible demand for ongoing support around critical-thinking practices.

Focusing Curriculum and Assessment

Many districts are familiar with writing or rewriting curricula to align with new standards and adjust to new assessments. Focusing the interlocking components of curricula and assessments on the 4Cs is a different challenge—and one that requires districts to go deeper into both curricula and assessment to support 21st century student outcomes.

Consider typical 20th century curricula, the *what* that is taught in the classroom. These curricula focus on content mastery, with the emphasis on discrete facts, and are aligned to standards that emphasize a breadth of academic content coverage. Student work is expected to demonstrate factual mastery. Textbooks selected by administrators serve as curricular stand-ins, with little or no customization by districts or schools. Curriculum revisions are based on the textbook adoption cycle.

Contrast this with 21st century curricula with a 4Cs focus (table 13.1, page 332). These curricula require deep understanding of content knowledge *and* skills, acquired through exploration of essential questions that probe for deeper meaning and set the stage for deeper learning and higher-order thinking skills. Curricula with a 4Cs focus are aligned to standards that emphasize Depth of Knowledge and skills and essential understandings. Student work requires complex performances that demonstrate deep content knowledge and competencies in the 4Cs. Teams of district educators, including classroom teachers, lead curricula selection, design, and development, making them highly customized, using a wide range of source materials drawn from research and best practice.

Table 13.1: Comparison of 20th and 21st Century Curricula

20th Century Curricula Versus 21st Century Curricula		
	20th Century Curricula	**21st Century Curricula**
Content Model	Content mastery with emphasis on discrete facts	Deep understanding of knowledge and skills with focus on essential questions
Adoption/ Authorship Model	Curricula selection by administrators with little input from teachers; writing by commercial publishers with little customization by school or districts	Curricula selection, design, and development are highly customized using a wide range of source materials
Standards Model	Aligned to standards that focus on breadth of academic content coverage	Aligned to standards that emphasize essential understandings (with a focus on Depth of Knowledge and skills)
Revision Model	Revisions based on textbook adoption cycle; student performance data rarely used	Continual revisions led by collaborative teacher teams using current student performance data
Student Work Model	Student work demonstrates factual mastery	Student work emphasizes complex performances that demonstrate deep content understanding along with competencies such as the 4Cs

Source: Kay, Ken; Greenhill, Valerie, Leader's Guide to 21st Century Education: The 7 Steps for School Districts, 1st edition © 2001, p. 76. Reprinted by permission of Pearson Education, Inc., Upper Saddle River, NJ.

See the difference? Any curriculum with a 4Cs focus should be rigorous, with student understanding as the goal and a balanced combination of core academic content, performance-based tasks, and assessments *for* learning (Stiggins, 2005). And it should be a living document, in the sense that educators help create it, use it to improve their professional capacity and daily practice, and continually refine it. That means educators attend to all three levels of curricula: (1) the intended, written curricula; (2) the taught curricula; and (3) the learned (and assessed) curricula.

In North Salem Central School District north of New York City in Westchester County, New York, district leaders, site leaders, and classroom teachers collaborated to map and unpack standards; identify essential questions for each discipline, course, and unit; and create common, course-level performance tasks in one of the district's focus areas—creative problem solving. These elements were intrinsic to the way in which curricula are designed and used throughout the system.

In addition to performance tasks, another way to embed the 4Cs into the curriculum is through project-based learning (PBL), which requires students to *practice* the 4Cs and other skills (see, for example, Boss, 2013). Among other benefits within 21st century curricula, projects require inquiry and the creation by the student of something new. PBL empowers students to explore open-ended, driving questions that give them some choice and a voice in their work.

Student work on performance tasks and projects also provides educators with evidence of how well the curricula are working. Examination and sharing of student work helps educators reflect on the curricula and their instructional practices. In a 21st century district, curriculum design is a professional learning activity and an iterative process—embedding the 4Cs into curricula, monitoring student performance, identifying areas for improvement, and then refining the curricula to improve results (Berger, 2003).

We take issue with critics who declare that the 4Cs cannot be well defined or measured or that there is no hope for changing an entrenched assessment system. In fact, a decade into the era of accountability, we see positive developments all around us in the assessment landscape. It might not be possible—yet—to measure the 4Cs on most state accountability tests, but assessments that measure content knowledge and key skills are out there, and more are in the works.

Take the Common Core assessments, AP exams, and PISA, all of which place more emphasis on higher-order thinking skills such as the 4Cs, integrated with subject-area knowledge. Likewise, the College and Work Readiness Assessment for high school students measures critical thinking and communication skills. This assessment enables schools to benchmark their students' performance against that of their peers around the United States and, for twelfth graders, against that of first-year college students, in order to track college readiness.

Now, districts and schools will have a new assessment tool—the OECD Test for Schools, based on PISA. EdLeader21 members have participated in this assessment since 2013. It provides school-level results that indicate how well students can *apply* content knowledge in reading, mathematics, and science. This assessment will help districts understand how well fifteen-year-olds in their high schools can think critically and solve problems in comparison to their peers around the world, in the United States, and even in schools within their districts.

Our member districts are excited about the OECD Test for Schools. They see many ways in which it can support 4Cs teaching and learning (Greenhill, 2013). Detailed, school-level data about student performance—and student attitudes about learning and the school environment—will help ground and guide school improvement. The results provide an evidence-based lever for change and a sense of urgency around the 4Cs, particularly in schools where the perception is that "we're doing everything right already." Teachers can review sample items, learn how competencies such as critical thinking and problem solving can be measured, and see how good is good enough. This is already proving to be a rich, powerful professional development experience. To support districts and schools in analyzing school results and considering changes in policies and practices that can lead to school improvement, EdLeader21 released an OECD Test for Schools Toolkit (Greenhill & Martin, 2014), with support from the Hewlett Foundation. The toolkit is free and available at www.edleader21.com.

A true 21st century education system also requires districts to create their own deeper assessments for learning. For each of the 4Cs, they can create rubrics for teachers and students that specify expectations for performance along a continuum toward mastery, and they can incorporate the 4Cs into grading and report cards. The Catalina Foothills School District in Arizona, for example, includes 21st century outcomes in the context of each subject area. In addition to content knowledge, students are graded on one or more of the following 21st century skills and personal and social responsibility areas: self-direction, teamwork, leadership, critical and creative thinking, cultural competence, systems thinking, communication, class participation, work completion and effort, and behavior. EdLeader21 has created a set of nationally vetted rubrics to support district and school efforts to integrate 4Cs assessment strategies into teaching and learning systems. The master set of rubrics covers grades 3–4, 7–8, and 11–12 in each of the 4Cs (www.edleader21.com).

Other meaningful assessments of the 4Cs that we see districts implementing are PBL assessment strategies, portfolio-based assessments, and capstone projects.

PBL Assessment Strategies

As we mentioned earlier, project-based learning is a terrific way to embed the 4Cs into the curriculum. Districts are finding innovative ways to assess skills that students demonstrate on their projects as well. For example, the New Tech Network brings students into the assessment loop. At the end of a project, students use a common, schoolwide rubric to evaluate other students. Teachers support this process by guiding students in providing constructive feedback in an online system. Teachers monitor the feedback, and each student receives a detailed report of these peer reviews. Teachers also use the electronic gradebook in the online system, which is set up to allow them to easily enter grades for skills competencies.

Portfolio-Based Assessments

Portfolios, long used by artists and designers, are a way for students to collect their best examples of core academic subject mastery along with 21st century outcomes for evaluation. For example, students at Envision Schools in California work with an advisor to assemble and curate their best work. Seniors present and defend their portfolios to teachers, advisors, students, and guests, such as parents and community members. The district requires students to pass this public "defense" to graduate—a notable policy that goes beyond state graduation requirements. Most students are well prepared to defend their portfolios, but those who don't pass on the first try have multiple opportunities, and extra support, to do so. The Envision team plans to offer its portfolio system, called the Deeper Learning Student Assessment Initiative, to any interested school or district. The system is aligned to the Common Core standards and assessments and will be supported by a web-based platform.

Capstone Projects

Capstone projects are longer-term projects, typically the culmination of learning at the end of elementary, middle, or high school, that require students to take a deep dive into content and demonstrate the 4Cs and other skills. In the Upper Arlington School District in Ohio, a capstone project is required of all high school seniors. Every student does a community project around an essential question and produces three pieces of work: (1) a research paper, (2) a product related to the community, and (3) a presentation. When the district adopted 21st century student outcomes, educators realized that these outcomes would be perfect for assessments of capstone projects. So the district created rubrics to evaluate these projects at midyear and at the end of the year. Students were directly involved in developing these rubrics—and they insisted that the rubrics be easy to understand and that teachers actually use them to assess the projects. These capstone projects and rubrics have helped deepen conversations, instruction, learning, and assessments.

Supporting Teachers and Students

Too often, districts adopt a new program or practice neglect to couple it with sustained, job-embedded professional development and support for teachers. That inattention to effective implementation absolutely undermines the culture of teacher collaboration and support necessary for deeper learning. Thus, step 6 of our model focuses on sustained support for teachers in the context of their daily work.

Here again, leadership is critical. To do this work, district and school leaders need to demonstrate, not just proclaim, that they understand the needs of educators in the system. Do teachers have sufficient time for the planning and collaboration involved in delivering 4Cs instruction? Do they have enough autonomy, mastery, and purpose around the 4Cs? Are they encouraged to take risks and innovate? Are they supported in PLCs and focused on the 4Cs? Do they receive timely, constructive support and feedback from principals, coaches, and other administrators? Answering these questions in ways that actually support teachers often requires changes in policies and practices that are impeding progress.

We don't believe, as some do, that teachers are the problem in education. They are a big part of the solution—but only if they are engaged, motivated, and supported in making a difference. We've seen teachers energized by the promise and practice of 21st century education. We've also, unfortunately, seen 21st century education initiatives falter when districts fail to build in enough time or structured approaches for teachers to learn and collaborate with one another. Some efforts devolve into checklist activities—check, we're aligned; check, it's in the curriculum; check, we're already doing that; check, we teach critical thinking; check, here's a laundry list of instructional strategies. Checklists are fine as part of a thoughtful process of inquiry and as a starting point or final review of substantive work. In and of themselves, however, checklists are unlikely to spur change.

On a related note, this point has bearing on the pipeline of future teachers. It's common knowledge that the best and brightest U.S. students don't often choose to become teachers. Just think about the work of a 4Cs teacher versus that of a teacher who works in a compliance-driven environment. What professional wants to work in a check-the-box culture? A 4Cs model of education, in which teachers know they will spend their careers reinventing and reinvigorating education, has the potential to attract more of our best and brightest students into the field.

Two key practices for engaging teachers, which have emerged from EdLeader21 members, are worth noting: engaging with student work and rethinking evaluations.

Engaging With Student Work

A deeper way to begin more meaningful work with today's teachers is to engage them in student work. Educators can look at real examples of student work and ask, "Does this work display any of the 4Cs?" If every teacher in a group brings a piece of student work that he or she believes exemplifies the 4Cs, the group can then compare and contrast the work samples. Examining student work forces leaders and teachers to focus concretely on what the 4Cs look like in terms of student performance—and it leads the conversation to instructional practices in the 4Cs (see, for example, Berger, 2003).

With a shared and clearer understanding of what the 4Cs do (or should) look like in student work, teachers are more open and ready to talk about the implications for instructional practice. In *The Leader's Guide to 21st Century Education*, we summarize a number of pedagogical models that are used in districts to support 4Cs instruction (Kay & Greenhill, 2013). All of them embed strategies that foster the 4Cs and other skills into instruction, such as active listening, collaborative dialogue, persistence, interpretation, inquiry, reflection, and learning how to learn.

As teachers learn about and practice different 4Cs-focused strategies, it's a good idea to monitor how deeply these strategies are infused into the learning environment. Learning walks, also known as instructional walks, are a way for teams of leaders and teachers to take the pulse of instruction and learning in classrooms and schools. Learning walks typically focus on gathering evidence that a particular practice, such as critical thinking, is being used. They are meant to be informative, not evaluative. They can help educators plan professional development and provide feedback to teachers, as well as help them monitor and adjust their school improvement strategies.

Instructional coaches can be another powerful way to deepen support for teacher engagement. Albemarle County Public Schools employs 21st century skills coaches to help teachers integrate these skills into their daily practices. Accomplished teachers compete for these positions and then rotate back to their classrooms after four or five years. There is no set agenda for the coaches other than to integrate into the culture of the school and support teacher-identified professional needs.

Rethinking Evaluations

Embedding the 4Cs into teaching and learning requires rethinking teacher and principal evaluations as well. Educators should be recognized and rewarded for aligning their practices with the district or school vision for 21st century education. Many states are implementing teacher and principal evaluations that require multiple measures of effectiveness. The 4Cs should be represented in those multiple measures. In Colorado, the State Model Evaluation System for Teachers bases 50 percent of a teacher's evaluation on quality standards for professional practice and the other 50 percent on student growth in performance or student learning over time—using multiple measures, not a single assessment (Colorado Department of Education, 2013). The system is not mandatory, but it provides an option for districts.

The Douglas County School District in Colorado collaborated with the teachers' union on its Continuous Improvement of Teacher Effectiveness initiative. This teacher evaluation system integrates the 4Cs and other student outcomes into teacher expectations in five teaching standards—(1) standards, (2) assessment, (3) instruction, (4) culture and climate, and (5) professionalism—with multiple indicators of effectiveness. Here are two examples of the standards.

1. "Teacher uses performance assessments/tasks that require students to demonstrate World Class Outcomes," including creativity, communication, collaboration, and critical thinking (4Cs).

2. "Teacher integrates 21st century skills (financial literacy, global awareness, problem solving, resiliency, systems

thinking, health and wellness, and civic responsibility) where authentic" (Douglas County School District, 2013).

The evaluation process starts with goal setting, moves to an observation cycle (preobservation conference, classroom observation, postobservation conference, and additional evidence), and concludes with a summative evaluation. Teachers are evaluated on a four-point matrix on their mastery of each standard and the frequency with which they demonstrate they are meeting each standard.

At the Odyssey School, an Expeditionary Learning school in Denver, Colorado, a school team and some colleagues in the Expeditionary Learning network spent several months designing a framework for teacher evaluation that reinforces the school's vision for 21st century education. Their framework incorporates core practices of Expeditionary Learning—curriculum, instruction, assessment, culture and character, and leadership—and an approach to teaching and learning that is active, challenging, meaningful, public, and collaborative. Notably, the evaluation system treats teachers like learners, with an online system for collecting and sharing evidence and artifacts of teacher practice, and for ongoing feedback and collaboration between teachers and the school director. This system came about because the school knew it wanted to use portfolios in similar ways with students. The school employed the smart strategy of building a portfolio system for *adults* first. This gave teachers two years of experience creating, managing, and revising their own portfolios—and the skills they would need to help students do the same.

Improving and Innovating

Implementing the meaningful changes that will lead to deeper learning requires a continual focus on the 4Cs, with improvement along the way. As we've stressed throughout this chapter, creating a true 21st century education system will be a big stretch for districts. Reaching the vision of 21st century learning requires substantive changes throughout every major part of the system—and very different practices for leaders, teachers, and students. While best practices and PLCs that focus on the 4Cs exist, there is no one size fits all. Every district will need to take its own path—and course corrections are a given. In fact, the journey should never be considered complete, because skill demands on students will continue to evolve.

For this reason, step 7 of our model focuses on improving and innovating, so that the seven steps of continuous cycle of improvement look like this:

1. Create a common vision.

2. Share outcomes.

3. Take action.

4. Measure progress.

5. Reflect on progress.

6. Revise action.

7. Repeat.

The 4Cs should be the centerpiece of continuous improvement, both as student learning outcomes and as indispensable skills for educators.

Our experiences at the national, state, and district levels over more than a decade leave us cautiously optimistic that we could be on the verge of a renaissance in K–12 public education. We are seeing a critical mass of district leaders who are willing to push the boundaries to achieve 21st century learning. We see educators, students, parents, and communities all over the United States eager for their schools to catch up with the world.

Our education system needs vivid imaginations, bold ideas, relentless drive, and a willingness to experiment, take risks, and craft new solutions. Innovation is key. To spur this innovation and take it to scale, two conditions are essential:

1. **Courageous leadership**—Leadership drives change. EdLeader21 superintendents and principals show what is possible when engaged leaders stand up before their cabinets, administrative teams, teachers, and communities to say: "We can and we must do a better job preparing students to take command of their futures."

District leaders must maintain that courageous stance as they develop their personal vision for 21st century education and take strategic and tactical actions to build community consensus and align standards, curriculum, assessment, professional learning, and instructional practices to the 4Cs and other competencies. They must assert their leadership to ensure that a culture of continuous improvement takes hold in their organizations. And when challenges present themselves, they must hold fast to their vision and exert calm but firm influence.

2. **A policy environment that empowers district leaders, teachers, and students to drive toward 21st century education**—Right now, districts and schools that are leading the way toward 21st century learning are doing courageous work in spite of state and national policies, not because of them. Visionary district leaders are operating under the assumption that state and national policies won't take their schools as far as they need to go.

In many states and districts, Common Core implementation is a major undertaking right now. We believe the Common Core will move schools to higher performance—but it's only one piece of the work that will truly transform education. We urge policymakers to give district leaders the space and flexibility both to implement the Common Core *and* to create a true 21st century education for all students. If policymakers choke off innovation with a host of top-down, inflexible requirements for change, we'll never accomplish deeper learning for all students.

In this vein, we encourage policymakers to look to states like New Hampshire, which is initiating a high-school redesign that replaces "seat time" (Carnegie units) with a competency-based system focused on personalized learning, strong teacher-student relationships, flexible supports, and the development of 21st century skills (New Hampshire Department of Education, 2007). In Kentucky, districts can apply for exemptions from certain administrative regulations and statutory provisions, as well as for waivers on local board policy to "rethink what a school might look like" and "redesign student learning in an effort to engage and motivate more students and increase the numbers of those who are college and career ready" (Kentucky Department of Education, 2013). This is the kind of outside-the-box policymaking that inspires innovation that can propel deeper learning.

Final Thoughts

Within the next decade or so, every district in the United States will recognize the need to move from 20th century education, in which rote learning and fill-in-the-bubble tests are the flawed but strong determinants of students' futures, to 21st century education, in which deeper learning and mastery of the 4Cs are the coins of the realm. Already, deeper learning and 21st century education are in evidence in many U.S. schools and classrooms. This progress is well worth noting. However, these incremental steps may not scale unless district leaders are championing transformation as well. District systems have the critical mass, influence, and connections to communities to instill the 4Cs systemically.

As they undertake this work, district and school leaders and teachers will be looking for models of 21st century learning and blueprints for how to achieve it. EdLeader21 districts are among those creating innovative models of teaching and learning on their journey to 21st century education. While every district is unique, and districts differ in the details of their pathways, we encourage all district leadership teams to focus on the seven steps highlighted in this chapter: (1) developing a vision, (2) creating community consensus, (3) aligning the system, (4) building professional capacity, (5) focusing curriculum and assessment, (6) supporting teachers and students, and (7) improving and innovating.

Finally, as leaders in the national dialogue on 21st century education, we believe we must remain aware of the limits of policies that are too top-down and too specific to promote true innovation, scale, and sustainability. We must give district leaders the freedom to redesign their systems to reflect their own visions of the content knowledge and 21st century competencies students need to succeed—and their own approaches to implementation and improvement. The more innovation we see, the more likely we are to scale up successful practices for deeper learning.

References and Resources

Berger, R. (2003). *An ethic of excellence: Building a culture of craftsmanship with students.* Portsmouth, NH: Heinemann.

Boss, S. (2013). *PBL for 21st century success: Teaching critical thinking, collaboration, communication, and creativity.* Novato, CA: Buck Institute for Education.

Catalina Foothills School District & Waters Foundation. (2007, August 24). *CFSD 21st century skill rubric: Systems thinking.* Accessed at http://cfsd16.org/public/_century/pdf/Rubrics/CFSDSystemsThinking_Rubric.pdf on July 28, 2014.

Colorado Department of Education. (2013). *Colorado State Model Evaluation System.* Accessed at www.cde.state.co.us/educatoreffectiveness/statemodelevaluationsystem on November 5, 2013.

Douglas County School District. (2013, August 15). *Continuous Improvement of Teacher Effectiveness (CITE) 2013.* Accessed at https://docs.google.com/viewer?a=v& pid=sites&srcid= ZGNzZGsxMi5vcmd8ay0xMi1lZ HVjYXRpb258Z3g6M2QwMGM1 NWMzNzAwNmJjZg on July 28. 2013.

EdLeader21. (2013, October 21). Superintendent Vincent Matthews on school redesign [Web log post]. Accessed at www.edleader21.com on August 1, 2014.

EdLeader21. (2014). *4Cs rubrics.* Accessed at http://edleader21.com/order.php on August 1, 2014.

Fairfax County Public Schools. (2013). *Fairfax Education Summit: Portrait of 21st century graduate and school system* [Agenda]. Accessed at www.fcps.edu/news/summit/2013/summit-agenda.pdf on September 29, 2013.

Greenhill, V. (2013, October 4). OECD test for schools and 4Cs school improvement [Web log post]. Accessed at http://p21.org/news-events/p21blog/1271-oecd-test-for-schools-and-4cs-school-improvement on November 1, 2013.

Greenhill, V., & Martin, J. (2014). *OECD Test for Schools: Implementation toolkit.* Accessed at http://edleader21.com/info/EdLeader21_OECD_TFS_Toolkit.pdf on July 28, 2014.

Kay, K. (2011a). The seven steps to becoming a 21st century school or district [Web log series]. Accessed at www.edutopia.org/blog/21st-century-leadership-overview-ken-kay on November 1, 2013.

Kay, K. (2011b, November 8). Unleashing locally driven innovation. *Education Week Commentary.* Accessed at www.edweek.org/ew/articles/2011/11/09/11kay_ep.h31.html on November 1, 2013.

Kay, K., & Greenhill, V. (2013). *The leader's guide to 21st century education: 7 steps for schools and districts.* Boston: Pearson Education.

Kay, K., & Lenz, B. (2013, March 22). Which path for the Common Core? *Education Week Commentary.* Accessed at www.edweek.org/ew/articles/2013/03/22/26kay.h32.html?qs=which+path+for+the+common+core on November 1, 2013.

Keaton, P. (2012). *Numbers and types of public elementary and secondary local education agencies from the Common Core of data: School Year 2010–11* (NCES 2012–326 rev). Accessed at http://nces.ed.gov/pubsearch on September 30, 2013.

Kentucky Department of Education. (2013, July 25). *Districts of innovation.* Accessed at http://education.ky.gov/school/innov/pages/districts-of-innovation.aspx on November 5, 2013.

New Hampshire Department of Education. (2007). *New Hampshire's vision for redesign: Moving from high schools to learning communities.* Accessed at www.education.nh.gov /innovations/hs_redesign/documents/vision.pdf on November 5, 2013.

Partnership for 21st Century Skills. (2011a). *P21 Common Core toolkit: A guide to aligning the Common Core State Standards with the framework for 21st century skills.* Accessed at http://p21.org/storage/documents/P21CommonCoreToolkit.pdf on March 27, 2014.

Partnership for 21st Century Skills. (2011b). *Framework for 21st century learning.* Accessed at www.p21.org/storage/documents/1.__p21_framework_2-pager.pdf on November 1, 2013.

Pellegrino, J. W., & Hilton, M. L. (Eds.). (2012). *Education for life and work: Developing transferable knowledge and skills in the 21st century.* Washington, DC: National Academies Press.

Shapiro, T. R. (2013, September 28). *New Fairfax Schools chief outlines challenges at education summit.* Accessed at www.washingtonpost.com/local/education/fairfax-schools -challenges-include-overcrwding/2013/09/28/753d953e-285d-11e3–9256–41f018d21b 49_story.html on September 29 2013.

Stiggins, R. K. (2005). From formative assessment to assessment FOR learning: A path to success in standards-based schools. *Phi Delta Kappan, 87*(4), 324–328.

U.S. Department of Education, National Center for Education Statistics, Common Core of Data. (2012, October). *Public elementary/secondary school universe survey, 1990–91 through 2010–11.* Accessed at http://nces.ed.gov/programs/digest/d12/tables/dt12_108.asp on September 30, 2013.

Wagner, T. (2008). *The global achievement gap: Why even our best schools don't teach the new survival skills our children need—and what we can do about it.* New York: Basic Books.

Helen A. Soulé

Helen A. Soulé, the executive director for Partnership for 21st Century Skills, previously led the organization's state recruitment and support effort, working with P21's nineteen state partners and directing outreach to connect with new partner states. In her new role, she identifies exemplar schools to be included in the online national network. Helen's experience as an educator spans from teacher to district administrator, chief of staff at the U.S. Department of Education to the assistant secretary for Office of Postsecondary Education, and former executive director of Cable in the Classroom. She is a catalyst for change in education policy and helping others apply policy to pedagogy.

To learn more about Helen's work, visit www.p21.org, or follow her on Twitter @helenasoule.

Steven Paine

Steven Paine, EdD, served as West Virginia's twenty-fifth state school superintendent from 2005 through 2011. He oversaw West Virginia's 21st Century Learning and Teaching program, renowned for including the development of internationally rigorous and relevant curriculum standards, research-based instructional practices, a parallel accountability system, aligned teacher preparation programs, and integration of technology tools and skills in state classrooms. Steven was a founder of the Smarter Balanced Assessment Consortium and has been a member of the National Assessment Governing Board and a member of the board's Committee on Standards, Design and Methodology. He has also served as president of the Council of Chief State School Officers, a member of the National Commission on Teaching and America's Future board of directors, and a member of the National Assessment Governing Board and High School Readiness Commission. Throughout his career in education, Steven has held numerous positions, including teacher, assistant principal, principal, curriculum director, school district superintendent, and deputy state superintendent of schools. He is also a past recipient of the prestigious Milken Family Foundation National Educator Award.

Chapter 14

Levers for Change: The Role of the States

Helen A. Soulé and Steven Paine

When you close your eyes and imagine "school," what do you see? Do you see desks in rows, teachers at a board (white, black, or green), and students engaged (or not) in individual activities intent on mastery of specific content knowledge with their tools of textbook, paper, and pencil? If you do, you stand with the majority of us who were educated in this manner. Yet, the question of what are (and how can we create) 21st century learning environments evokes a very different image of learning, for the expectations of learning have changed dramatically. Moreover, how each state's education system reacts to change leads to different results.

Because the expected outcomes of learning have changed dramatically, no longer do we envision mastery of discrete content as the primary or preferred outcome of twelve years of schooling. As this century dawned and business began to demand a different kind of worker for a global, competitive economy, a coalition of business, education, and policy experts became the Partnership for 21st Century Skills (P21) and collaborated to define a framework for learning that reflected the need for more comprehensive student outcomes. In addition to deep content knowledge mastery, P21 posits that all students must possess a collection of skills that would enable them to navigate any situation, profession, or educational setting throughout college, career, and life. These skills include the 4Cs—(1) critical thinking and problem solving, (2) communication, (3) collaboration, and (4) creativity and innovation—as well as life and career skills and media information and technology skills.

As of this writing, nineteen states have joined P21 and have provided leadership and insight into the states' role in this transformation process. Guided by P21's (2011) *Framework for 21st Century Learning* and other documents created though P21's collaborations, these states provide a bank of experiences that can serve as good examples of what works from their perspective and responsibility.

The *Framework* presents a holistic view of 21st century teaching and learning that combines a discrete focus on 21st century student outcomes (a blending of specific skills, content knowledge, expertise, and literacies) with innovative support systems to help students master the multidimensional abilities required of them in the 21st century and beyond. To help practitioners integrate these 21st century skills into the teaching of core academic subjects, P21 developed a unified, collective vision for learning, exemplified by the *Framework for 21st Century Learning* (figure 14.1).

Defining the Framework was only the first step. In order for every student to get the education he or she needs and deserves for this century and beyond, P21's members knew that for systemic transformation to occur, the real work had to start at the state level, where responsibility for statewide policies and programs begins.

Because education is primarily a shared state and local responsibility, reinventing school requires states, districts, and schools to effect comprehensive changes throughout all components of their educational systems. It is not enough to define the outcomes—states, districts, and schools must build a foundation for systemic change, fusing the Framework with all the necessary support systems—including standards, assessments, curriculum and instruction, professional development, and learning environments—in order to make 21st century learning a reality.

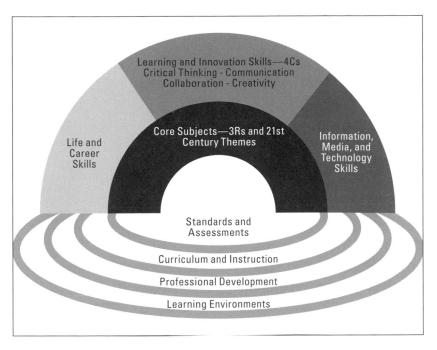

Source: Partnership for 21st Century Skills. Used with permission.

Figure 14.1: 21st century student outcomes and support systems.

State Roles in Enabling School Transformation

P21 and its nineteen state partners have been building and documenting what it takes for states to transform education since 2002. Although the amount of state influence varies according to state law, six primary levers of educational change, distilled from a decade of experiences among the nineteen state partners, provide guidance for how other states can influence 21st century change and produce significant transformation.

1. Developing a shared statewide 21st century vision and broad consensus through leadership and communication

2. Building the policy framework for 21st century learning

3. Aligning the operational and programmatic environments with the 21st century learning vision

4. Aligning standards, curriculum, assessment, and accountability to support 21st century learning

5. Ensuring technology access and integration to accelerate and support 21st century learning

6. Building capacity through ongoing professional learning and strategic partnerships

Developing a Shared Statewide 21st Century Vision and Broad Consensus

Building a shared statewide vision and developing broad consensus is essential for success and requires that state leaders from the highest levels, as well as stakeholders at all levels, are committed to 21st century learning. The role of education leaders encompasses not only effectively articulating the vision on a regular basis to the education community and public at large but also engaging the broader community in the actual development of the vision to increase understanding and buy-in. Education leaders must promote, facilitate, model, and support the comprehensive integration of 21st century skills into curricula, professional development, instructional practices, accountability and performance evaluation systems, resources, management, and operations.

Because state-level leaders have a cache of tools and resources available for communicating to multiple stakeholders that local districts or schools may not have access to, they are in a unique position to achieve consensus around a shared vision. A professionally trained communication staff and access to numerous information dissemination vehicles, such as statewide digital and print news outlets, provide valuable expertise and distribution capability for building understanding and commitment to 21st century learning. Key questions to consider when building a state's shared vision are:

- What should students know and be able to do to be successful in college, career, and life?

- Which state stakeholders should be engaged in developing and promoting the vision?

- How can momentum be developed and sustained across the state?

- What (existing and new) statewide vehicles are needed to effectively communicate?

State examples provide models for how to answer these questions. The West Virginia Department of Education (WVDE), with support from the governor, collaborated to build a vision for 21st century learning with its stakeholders. Using P21's resources, such as *Learning for the 21st Century* and *A State Leader's Action Guide to 21st Century Skills*, WVDE created a comprehensive framework of strategies, resources, and policies for implementing 21st century learning called the Global21 Initiative. Educators, business leaders, and community groups engaged in developing the shared vision: "To graduate all students with 21st century knowledge and skills, ready to succeed in appropriate postsecondary education programs, able to live responsibly, and able to live, learn, and thrive in a global society" (WVDE, 2011, p. 6).

A comprehensive statewide communication strategy sustained the active coalition of stakeholders. Numerous communications vehicles were employed, and a 21st century advisory council was formed and met regularly to provide advice. Regional Voices From the Field events were held, seeking educator input. In one series, teachers were asked to provide insight on questions such as, What knowledge and skills does a West Virginia graduate need to succeed in the 21st century, and what does a teacher need to educate a 21st century learner? Student focus groups, superintendents' forums, and school system leadership team conferences brought students' and administrators' voices into the conversation. Next came the development of a series of guiding documents that framed the initiative and outlined thirty-nine critical implementation elements necessary for success that addressed target areas of the education system (WVDE, n.d.). A unified vision and communication strategy allowed West Virginia to successfully capture the voices of numerous stakeholders and build consensus for the state's Global21 Initiative.

The North Carolina State Board of Education and Department of Public Instruction (NCDPI) (www.learnnc.org) also set forth a robust vision for public schools, grounded in the belief that a strong public education system lays the foundation for democracy and a healthy economy. The fusion of 21st century knowledge and skills form an important part of the vision. An excerpt from the two-page summary vision statement (and longer ten-page paper submitted by Edward B. Fiske and Helen F. Ladd), which was formally adopted by the NC State Board of Education in October 2012, follows:

> A great public education system is one that prepares all students for postsecondary education, careers, citizenship and lifelong learning. It sets high standards and fosters the critical thinking and other skills needed in today's global economy. A great state education system must evolve over time in response to changes in the state's economic, technological, and social contexts as well as in response to developments in other states and the world. (North Carolina State Board of Education, 2012, p. 3)

Building the Policy Framework for 21st Century Learning

As would be expected, such change carries significant policy implications that must be addressed to align with the goal of preparing all students for the 21st century. This is one of the most important levers at the state level. The combination of legislation, executive orders, and state board policies form the legal framework for a state's educational system, acting as critical agents of change in determining success or failure. Attempting to build 21st century learning systems with outdated, rigid policies or requirements such as those involving seat time, credits, instruction, or Carnegie units can doom an initiative. Teams must undertake research and careful analysis of both current and desired state education policies to ensure that the policy framework facilitates rather than hinders implementation of the vision.

Key questions to consider when aligning existing and proposed policies at the state level are:

- Do policies consistently support student mastery of knowledge and 21st century skills?

- Are there tangible incentives for educators in their local districts to lead, teach, and assess 21st century skills? If not, what incentives can be created?

- Are state policies aligned with districts and schools to ensure 21st century learning?

- Do state policies around standards, assessments, professional learning, and curricula support 21st century learning?

- Do the criteria for licensure of educators and accreditation of teacher education institutions include the comprehensive integration of 21st century skills?

- Are there existing state policies that inhibit (or impede) the implementation of 21st century learning for *all* students?

Two examples may provide insight into how states have approached developing comprehensive policy frameworks. When Iowa embraced 21st century learning, the Iowa Department of Education asked, "How do we prepare the next generation for a world we cannot even imagine?" As a result, the state board of education, the governor, and the legislature collectively began to focus on competency-based education as a priority: the governor included competency-based pathways in his blueprint for education; the legislature eliminated the century-old dependency on the Carnegie unit as a basis for credit in Iowa high schools; and two school districts developed competency-based opportunities. In 2013, the legislatively created Competency-Based Education Task Force, led by the Iowa Department of Education, set out to study "competency-based instruction, standards, and options and the integration of competency-based instruction with the Iowa core curriculum, and to develop related assessment models and professional development focused on competency-based instruction" (Iowa Department of Education, 2013, p. 3). The resulting report outlines the outcome of the yearlong study and recommends broad policy changes to incorporate world-class competency-based opportunities for Iowa's students (Iowa Department of Education, 2013).

The West Virginia policy framework development began with a Senate bill that required the state board of education to establish a plan with specific goals and policy-oriented and performance-oriented objectives for public education, consistent with the 21st century. Over the next several years, a combination of new or adjusted legislation, executive orders, and state board policies further aligned policies with the Global21 vision and goals on a wide range of important topics, such as exceptional students, virtual learning, early childhood education, accreditation, assessment, professional development, and licensure. (A full list can be found at WVDE, 2009a.)

Aligning the Operational and Programmatic Environments With the 21st Century Learning Vision

Large-scale change requires a full review, alignment, and revamp of operations, processes, and programs, as well as a fresh analysis of the organizational structure and resources. Often this lever is overlooked, especially in bureaucracies, in which organizational change can be difficult. However, examining existing structures and programs through the lens of the 21st century framework and making necessary changes can accelerate efficiency, effectiveness, and organizational focus on the vision and desired outcomes.

Operational Environment

The operational environment directly impacts the overall success of the implementation, affecting organizational culture, efficiency, and effectiveness. A review of the organization should include a comprehensive analysis and alignment of the departmental structure, organizational norms, and staffing patterns. In addition, a periodic reevaluation and redesign (if needed) of processes should be performed by the state department of education or other appropriate external agency, such as educator or administrator certification, state assessment procedures, state or district strategic plan review and evaluation, and professional development. Key questions to consider when aligning the operational environment are:

- How should the organization be structured and operate to *effectively* and *efficiently* fulfill the vision?

- What current processes assist or hinder implementation of the vision?

- How can the organizational structure and processes be streamlined to advance implementation?

- What data are needed to make sound decisions?

The example that follows describes one model for approaching alignment of the operational environment.

The WVDE reviewed the internal structure and breadth of programs as well as the allocation of resources, making adjustments as needed. All documents were revised and aligned with the Global21 Initiative to provide cohesive guidance for operationalizing the vision. The five strategic goals were translated into strategic plans, which included objectives for achieving the goals; timelines, activities, and responsibilities to implement the plan; and evidence to measure progress toward achieving each goal. The WVDE also developed a process for evaluation of the plans, and the thirty-nine associated critical implementation elements. A similar process was utilized by the districts and schools when re-envisioning their strategic plans, using the WVDE's online strategic-planning tool.

West Virginia utilized several important research reports that provided recommendations for the Global21 Initiative. *Closing the Achievement Gap for 21st Century Learners in West Virginia* (WVDE, 2009b) was designed to establish a structure of comprehensive data analysis, report on the status and improvement of student achievement in West Virginia, and provide recommendations for consideration as a result of the identified findings. The West Virginia Professional Development Stakeholder Group report (Paine, 2006) provided further recommendations to guide a comprehensive professional development program that would further the goals of the Global21 Initiative. Other reports included the *Report on the Recommendations of the Education Performance by the Audit Study Committee* (West Virginia Office of Education Performance Audits, 2006), *Improving Results for Students in High Need Populations* (WVDE, 2006), *West Virginia State Educational Technology Plan 2007–2010* (WVDE, 2007), and *A Vision for Student Success: High School for West Virginia's Future* (WVBE, 2005). This planning process includes regular assessment and revision. States should engage in comprehensive, ongoing analyses of data in order to effectively implement a regular cycle of planning, implementation, assessment, and revision.

Programmatic Environment

State departments of education are responsible for countless programs funded through federal, state, public, and private channels that are ultimately implemented in local schools. It is imperative to conduct a careful analysis of existing programs to ensure that they align with the vision and strategic direction of the state or district and that they can be effective in producing desired outcomes with students.

Key questions to consider when addressing the programmatic environment are:

- What existing programs are aligned with the vision and strategic plan? What programs should be discontinued?

- What new programs (if any) are needed?

- What appropriate funding mechanisms support and monitor progress on the comprehensive integration of 21st century skills across the education system?

These are difficult questions to answer, as long-standing programs or processes are often popular and difficult to dismantle. However, a comprehensive, thoughtful, yet practical analysis can result in important insights and effective changes.

The WVDE developed a comprehensive set of initiatives that included new and redesigned existing programs to support the 21st century learning needs of the state's students, ensuring that a comprehensive array of programs would be available to support all aspects of curriculum, instruction, assessment, professional development, and needs of diverse learners. The initiatives span all grades, universal preK, response to intervention, online standards-based individualized education program, financial literacy, foreign language, the LINKS (Learning Individualized Needs, Knowledge, and Skills) Program, Arts Alive!, and an online learning pilot for secondary mathematics. More information on these programs can be found in *Closing the Achievement Gap Report for 21st Century Learners in West Virginia* (WVDE, 2009b).

Aligning Standards, Curriculum, Assessment, and Accountability

The alignment of standards, curriculum, assessment, and accountability in support of 21st century learning is essential for a successful statewide implementation. At the state level, authority and responsibility for standards, curriculum, and assessment varies widely, from states that have almost full responsibility to those with little or no authority over standards or curriculum. States have considerably more authority over assessment and accountability programs, which are required by federal law. Changes made to the standards, curriculum, assessment, and accountability systems have far-reaching influence all the way to the classroom.

Standards and Curriculum

In spite of the uneven levels of state responsibility regarding standards and curriculum, most state departments of education do have some authority to develop or adopt curricular standards, and over half the states have a role in adoption of educational textbooks and supplementary materials. This authority may be granted through legislation, board policy, or department of education process. A key lever for change when approaching 21st century learning is aligning state standards (and curriculum, where state authority exists) with the *Framework for 21st Century Learning*. To accomplish this alignment requires careful planning and execution with substantive educator involvement.

For example, with grassroots support from organizations such as the California Center for 21st Century Education (http://our -future-now.org), California's governor, Jerry Brown, signed a bill requiring the state to incorporate the 4Cs into state curriculum frameworks. Similarly, the West Virginia Department of Education surveyed and revised the state's curriculum standards to incorporate 21st century skills. The standards were also evaluated for appropriate levels of rigor and relevance and were aligned with rigorous new graduation requirements as well as national and international standards and assessments, like PISA.

It is important to ensure that the standards and curriculum development, alignment, and revision process is comprehensive, encompassing all subjects and grades—not only the core subjects of English, reading or language arts, mathematics, social studies, and science but also geography, history, government and civics, music, world languages, arts, economics, and others. Adopting a widely respected, generally aligned set of standards, such as the Common Core State Standards for ELA or mathematics or the Next Generation Science Standards, is a good starting place but should not be considered a substitute for a deep dive into what the 21st century standards should be.

In standards development, the incorporation of cross-disciplinary themes identified within the *Framework for 21st Century Learning*, including global awareness; financial, economic, business, and entrepreneurial literacy; and civic, health, and environmental literacy, should also be considered for inclusion. States and districts may choose to focus on one or more of these themes within the standards and curriculum as they relate to their priorities.

P21 has long advocated that the full range of knowledge and skills articulated in P21's *Framework for 21st Century Learning* be integrated explicitly into standards, assessments, curriculum, instruction, professional development, and learning environments. When approaching alignment of standards and curriculum with the Framework, it is important that the 4Cs be given considerable priority, as they are generally considered to form the backbone of the Framework.

Today's life and work environments require far more than critical thinking and content knowledge. The ability to navigate the complex life and work environments in the globally competitive information age requires students to pay rigorous attention to developing adequate life and career skills, such as flexibility and adaptability, initiative and self-direction, social and cross-cultural skills, productivity and accountability, and leadership and responsibility. When aligning standards and curricula, it is important to consider how, when, and where these critical life and career skills are being addressed.

From the *Framework for 21st Century Learning* perspective, the renewed focus on rigorous and relevant standards—whether from states such as Texas, Massachusetts, and Virginia or the multistate Common Core State Standards adopted by more than forty-five states—is a promising development in the standards movement. These standards explicitly call for and integrate critical-thinking skills as a means to achieve career and college readiness for all students. The CCSS in particular have established widespread consensus around a U.S. baseline for college and career readiness and a focus on rigorous core academic content mastery along with competencies like critical thinking, reasoning, communication, and collaboration. The CCSS also established media, information, and technology literacy in ELA and mathematics as key performance outcomes around which curricula and assessments should be focused. While the CCSS do not explicitly address every skill in the P21 framework, several areas (such as critical thinking, communication, and collaboration) are strongly represented throughout. These areas of the CCSS are good places for educators interested in 21st century skills to begin— but not end—the work of preparing students for success in college, career, and life. P21's Common Core Toolkit (P21, n.d.), available for free download, provides a valuable resource when beginning to delve into the alignment of standards with the *Framework for 21st Century Learning*. The toolkit also provides classroom-focused examples that help clarify what alignment between standards-based lessons and the 4Cs looks like.

Conducting a comprehensive standards and curriculum development, alignment, and revision process is a key step in building among educators awareness, buy-in, and ultimately understanding of the standards as well as of the curriculum and materials needed to make standards implementation possible. The more teacher and administrator leaders are involved in this process, the more successful the implementation will be.

Key questions to consider when aligning standards and curriculum are:

- How can the process be structured so that as many leaders and key stakeholders as possible and appropriate are involved?

- When performing a crosswalk between the new and previous standards, what standards must be added, revised, or deleted?

- What curricula and materials are needed to make the standards implementation possible?

- What implementation challenges arise, and how can they be addressed?

- What is the strategy for building stakeholder support for the new standards and curricula?

In West Virginia, teachers began with professional development designed to give them the tools to successfully accomplish this task. They participated in workshops on the *Framework for 21st Century Learning* and used the Depth of Knowledge assessment scale to examine U.S. and international assessments before they rewrote their standards and performance descriptors. Upon completion of the content standards and objectives (CSO), the WVDE sought state and national reviews and comments based on 21st century content and rigor. After a number of comment and revision rounds, the CSOs were approved by West Virginia's board of education. This comprehensive process is necessary not only to ensure that the standards and curricula are of the highest quality, rigor, and relevance but also that all stakeholders have an opportunity to participate in the process, build knowledge, and create support for the important changes that need to be made.

Attention must also be given to other important state standards, such as student-technology standards, graduation- or college-readiness standards, professional teaching standards, and online learning standards to ensure they appropriately incorporate 21st century learning. Once the full set of standards is in place, curricular, programmatic, and resource alignments to support rigorous content and student-achievement needs can be more easily accomplished.

Assessments and Accountability

Since 2002, with the implementation of No Child Left Behind, federal, state, and even local policymakers have defined educational accountability in very narrow terms—often only by student performance on selected subject-matter standardized tests (English, language arts, and mathematics primarily), end-of-course tests, or a few other aggregated data points, such as dropout or graduation rates. This is a general statement that did not come from a citation. As the body of knowledge and skills necessary for student success continues to grow, and the tools for information, communication, and learning expand, what outcomes will be most important to our students' success? Increasingly, studies are showing that expertise—skill mastery through the application of deep content understanding to real and relevant problems, questions, issues, and perspectives—translates into future success. As the system shifts to value students' 21st century expertise, it is imperative that assessments also be developed to measure both applied content understanding and mastery of 21st century skills and that accountability systems incorporate multiple measures for determining student success.

Assessments to inform instruction have unfortunately also changed little over the last decade, as teachers have been incentivized to prepare students for state standardized assessments on which everyone is judged (students, teachers, principals, schools, districts, and states), rather than to prepare students for a future for which there is no single multiple-choice answer. Educators need multiple tools and resources to effectively engage and evaluate students in authentic ways. Assessments should therefore come in all shapes and sizes, including formative tests, rubrics, projects, portfolios, presentations, and so on.

Most teachers who seek to immerse students in learning activities that focus on deeper understanding and 21st century skills are often on their own. They have little knowledge or exposure to the research, tools, and resources available to help them create 21st century learning environments. They might instead create their own classroom assessments and rely heavily on their own capabilities.

When educator support systems are missing, there is little educator collaboration between classrooms, schools, districts, or states.

Building a balanced system that includes multiple measures for summative, formative, and benchmark assessments; mastery of knowledge and skills; data for accountability measures; and accurate assessment of student learning to inform instruction continues to remain an elusive target. This new model must incorporate multiple measures that enable students to demonstrate proficiency not only to K–12 educational institutions but also to potential employers and postsecondary institutions.

Currently, there is no assessment of 21st century skills or even the 4Cs in widespread use in U.S. schools. There are, however, some promising practices.

- Two state testing consortia, the Smarter Balanced Assessment Consortium (in twenty-four states) and the Partnership for the Assessment Readiness for College and Careers (in eighteen states), are charged with creating new tests to measure progress on the Common Core State Standards (ELA and mathematics). The new assessments have the potential to broaden the capability of our assessment systems by measuring applied skills such as critical thinking and including open-ended items and short performance tasks, rather than solely relying on multiple choice. These new assessment systems are scheduled for implementation during the 2015–2016 school year.

- The 2012 international PISA measured fifteen-year-old students' reading, mathematics, and science literacy as well as problem-solving and financial literacy. PISA plans to measure collaboration and creativity in the future. One significant difference between PISA and other widely used tests is that PISA is not administered to every student but produces results from a representative sample. In addition, it includes open-ended items as well as multiple-choice items. For the time being, however, states continue to struggle with assessing students in ways beyond multiple-choice tests.

- The College and Work Readiness Assessment is for middle and high school students and measures student performance on the 21st century skills of critical thinking, analytic reasoning, problem solving, and written communication through realistic performance tasks.

- Ohio has incorporated teacher-developed performance tasks into that state's assessments. The Ohio Performance Assessment Pilot Project (OPAPP) (http://education.ohio .gov/Topics/Testing/Next-Generation-Assessments/Ohio-Performance-Assessment-Pilot-Project-OPAPP) calls for the development and pilot of a system of learning and assessment tasks (known as a "dyad" system) for elementary and high school students, as well as complementary professional development services. The performance tasks align with the CCSS for ELA and mathematics, as well as Ohio's Revised State Standards in science, social studies, and career technical pathways. They are delivered online using web-based software that supports e-portfolios and similar tools. These tasks "include structured inquiry, collaboration, and integrated skills" (excerpt from *Creating Systems of Assessment for Deeper Learning: Development of Assessment That Can Measure Deeper Learning Skills* [Conley & Darling-Hammond, 2013]).

- For further information, the RAND Education's 2013 report, *Measuring 21st Century Competencies*, conduct an analysis of existing instruments, which provides an in-depth look at the cognitive and noncognitive assessment landscape (Soland, Hamilton, & Stecher, 2013).

Assessments must be carefully and completely aligned to the content, context, and learning tools of the 21st century. Some states and districts are spending considerable time focusing on preparing teachers to administer multiple measures of student assessment, including traditional methods such as formative and summative assessments, as well as nontraditional methods such as rubrics, performance-based assessments, portfolios, and so on.

A comprehensive assessment program should be designed to measure a full range of knowledge and skills in all content areas, including formative and summative assessments, explore multiple approaches to student accountability, improve record keeping on crucial learning outcomes, and develop an accreditation and accountability process focused on 21st century learning.

Key questions to consider when aligning assessments and accountability are:

- How does the accountability system support evidence-based assessment that strengthens student mastery of 21st century skills?

- Do the standards and curriculum incorporate the 4Cs and facilitate 21st century learning outcomes for students?

- What multiple measures of assessment should be a part of the state system?

- How can multiple measures of assessment be incorporated into the state assessment system?

Ensuring Technology Access and Integration

State departments of education and other state agencies play multiple roles related to education technology integration. Some state agencies provide the state technology backbone and serve as the Internet provider for educational institutions in preK–12 (and beyond) with assistance from E-Rate funding. State departments of education manage large-scale student-level database systems, collecting data from schools and districts for state and federal accountability purposes.

Additionally, technology represents an important tool for educators and students to use in achieving 21st century outcomes. Students must understand not only how to manipulate the multiple screens with which they interact, but they must also build a strong set of digital literacy skills that enable them to be smart consumers of the wealth of information available—to analyze, critique, verify, and synthesize the information they encounter.

Building an environment with appropriate privacy and safety policies in place—in which *all* students have access to needed technologies as well as the skills they need to take full advantage of these tools—is a shared responsibility among the state, district, and school. It begins with a comprehensive technology plan, developed with input from a wide range of stakeholders, rigorous student and educator standards and curriculum, adequate staffing, and comprehensive professional development. A variety of high-quality digital resources are available at little or no cost to schools to build media and information literacy skills for teachers and students. Examples of such resources can be found through Cable in the Classrooms "InCtrl" (www.ciconline.org/InCtrl) and Common Sense Media (www.commonsensemedia.org).

Technology is not only a ubiquitous and increasingly critical part of the 21st century learning environment, it has also become an important systemwide component in professional development, instruction, assessment, and instructional resources. State educational technology plans form the foundation for implementing technology and outlining goals, policies, standards, and actions. The National Education Technology Standards for students and educators, created by the International Society for Technology in Education (www.iste.org) and adopted by many states, are highly correlated to 21st century skills and provide a solid foundation on which to build systemwide technology standards and plans.

Key questions to consider when ensuring technology access and integration are:

- Who is responsible (state, district, school) for educator and student access to technology? Often this is a shared responsibility; however, the various roles and responsibilities should be made very clear.

- What student and educator skills are needed to take full advantage of the digital access and resources available, while ensuring safety and security?

- Which digital access and resources should be available to fully sustain a 21st century learning environment?

- What strategies can be employed to ensure that *all* students have the access and skills necessary to be prepared for life, college, and career?

Specialized programs and resources to build capacity for technology integration exist in many states. For instance, the Kentucky Continuous Instructional Improvement Technology System, or CIITS, is a multiphase, multiyear project designed to provide Kentucky public school educators with the 21st century resources they need to carry out highly effective teaching and learning in every classroom in Kentucky. In CIITS, teachers access tools for building lesson plans, formative assessments, and instructional resources directly linked to the Kentucky academic standards.

Similarly, the North Carolina Department of Public Instruction, in partnership with the North Carolina Virtual Public School (NCVPS), created an Occupational Course of Study (OCS) Blended Learning Program. The program partners a NCVPS content teacher with an OCS classroom teacher to provide blended instruction to OCS students across the state. The OCS is rigorous, aligns to the core content standards, and prepares students with disabilities for a career or postsecondary education. The NCVPS developed the OCS Blended Learning Program courses with talented, highly qualified content teachers.

The NCVPS focuses on the learning needs of students with disabilities in three ways: through course design, course expectations, and teacher expectations. The unique partnership between the virtual teacher and the face-to-face teacher has produced solid results for students. Teachers support each other as they work together to individualize their students' learning, adapting instruction to students' learning styles, strengths, and weaknesses.

Building Capacity Through Ongoing Professional Learning and Strategic Partnerships

Achieving desired systemic changes in state educational institutions requires Herculean capacity and community-building efforts with internal and external stakeholders. These efforts must be ongoing, holistic, engaging, relevant to the role each participant plays, and laser-focused on the vision and goals with clearly articulated outcomes.

Ongoing Professional Learning

Ongoing professional learning opportunities are essential to build capacity and create supportive environments for teachers and administrators alike. Particular attention must be given to developing 21st century skills in leaders at all levels so they use these skills each and every day, serving as models for staff, students, parents, and the community. Learning Forward, the professional association devoted exclusively to advancing professional learning for student success, developed new professional learning standards (Learning Forward, 2014) that provide an excellent starting place when designing professional learning opportunities. Digital resources and tools can be invaluable, enabling just-in-time learning to occur.

Key questions to be considered when addressing ongoing professional learning are:

- What knowledge, skills, and dispositions do educators need in order to transform the educational environment?

- How might the gaps in capacity be filled?

- How can digital resources and tools contribute to ongoing professional learning?

- What resources and offerings are available, and what new resources must be created?

The WVDE developed a comprehensive professional development initiative focused on building the capacity of all involved in education, including staff at the state department of education, superintendents, district-level leadership teams, principals, and teacher leaders. These events focused on the urgent need for change, as well as what must happen and how it can be accomplished. Throughout the WVDE's menu of professional development offerings, from career technical education (CTE), social science, English as a second language, and foreign language institutes, to mathematics, health, and physical and special education leadership academies, to the more traditional conferences for gifted education, reading, universal preK, and so on, the focus remained on 21st century learning. Additionally, state-supported ongoing professional development promoted the inclusion of 21st century skills in teacher education programs and included competency in 21st century skills in the accreditation criteria of teacher education programs and the requirements for new-teacher licensure.

Developing professional learning resources and offerings that are multimodal can address individual learning styles and strengthen capacity-building efforts. West Virginia used a combination of face-to-face and digital vehicles for learning, including modules on 21st century learning that incorporated the curriculum content, technology tools, balanced assessment, and instructional design guidance. Utilizing a combination of free, open-education resources (OER) and state-created digital resources, they built a valuable library for professional learning.

Strategic Partnerships

P21 (2009) strongly believes that building 21st century schools is a communitywide endeavor in the broadest sense and urges states to create active coalitions of business, governmental, education, for-profit, nonprofit, and community organizations. Forging authentic partnerships with diverse organizations for mutual benefit requires all parties to practice the 4Cs, as well as patience. The rewards can be great, with each organization ultimately benefiting from the partnership. Care should be taken that organizational partnerships are significant, not superficial, and connect directly to the vision. Partnerships can take many forms and should include all types of stakeholders, including other government agencies, as well as business and industry.

Key questions to consider when developing strategic partnerships are:

- What asset or capability does each organization have that would be beneficial?

- What are common goals and needs among the organizations?

- What is the ROI (return on investment) for each organization?

- How will the partnership positively contribute to your organization's vision, goals, and outcomes?

- What obstacles may inhibit the formation of the partnership? How could they be overcome?

State partnerships take many different forms and address needs that are as individual as the states themselves. For example, a coalition of business and education partners in South Carolina, the South Carolina Council on Competitiveness, unveiled TransformSC, an initiative to transform public education in South Carolina. The initiative is a collaboration among leading South Carolina business leaders, such as AT&T and BT&T, school superintendents, school administrators, school board members, and others interested in rethinking public schools in South Carolina. TransformSC will provide tools and technical support to pilot districts interested in transforming their schools into 21st century learning systems. Such a strong and diverse partnership can greatly enhance its chances of success.

Similarly, in California, a group of education and business leaders launched a series of meetings to talk about the future of education. They called for the state to build a vision for California that prepares students for life in a globally connected world and ensures that they have the 21st century skills and knowledge needed for success. With the help of this coalition, significant educational legislation supporting the integration of the 4Cs into standards and curriculum has become law; local high school students petitioned the Anaheim, California, mayor and city council for support for 21st century learning; the mayor and city council declared Anaheim a "P21 City"; and in June 2013, the California Center for 21st Century Education, a nonprofit educational policy center, was formed through the North Orange County Community College District Foundation.

Conclusion

Since 2002, the Partnership for 21st Century Skills has advocated for 21st century readiness for every student. In working with nineteen state partners and numerous stakeholders, P21 has seen that what happens at the state level matters! The six levers described in this chapter can act as substantial change agents when implemented with focus, commitment, and strategic vision. These levers can significantly influence the transformation of a state's educational system from every level down to the classroom.

The state's role in effecting classroom change became particularly apparent as P21 began selecting exemplar schools and districts for the organization's 21st Century Learning Exemplar Program. Through this program, with funding from the Pearson Foundation, P21 is working to identify, document, promote, and celebrate examples of successful school and classroom 21st century learning through case studies, videos, podcasts, conferences, and other communication methods. Many of the schools and districts selected for recognition were directly and positively influenced by the state's vision, policies, partnerships, professional learning focus, standards, curriculum, and technology and assessment programs, to name a few. (Go to www.p21.org/exemplar-program-case-studies to view a full list.). Examples include the following:

- Embracing technology as a gateway to 21st century learning, students who attend Walker Elementary (http://walker .wawm.k12.wi.us) in Wisconsin experience next-generation, personalized learning environments with multiage classrooms, one-to-one tablet computing, and competency-based progressions.

- The teachers and leadership of Benjamin Franklin Elementary School (www.d41.org/schools/franklin) in Illinois have built a collaborative and innovative learning community through project-based and nontraditional instructional strategies.

- Spirit Lake High School (www.spirit-lake.k12.ia.us) in Iowa has instituted a creative, competency-based approach to learning that is helping Spirit Lake students develop critical thinking, collaboration, and problem-solving skills in an interdisciplinary environment.

- In Kentucky, educators at Bate Middle School (www.bms .danvilleschools.net) are using project-based learning, flexible scheduling, and a redesigned curriculum to intentionally incorporate critical-thinking, problem-solving, and communication skills.

- The students at North Carolina's Carolina Forest International Elementary School (http://carolinaforest.nc.oce.schoolinsites.com) are getting a global education right from the start, because the school is developing students' global awareness, collaboration, and critical-thinking skills.

- At Dana Elementary School (www.hendersoncountypublic schoolsnc.org/dan) in North Carolina, a collaborative mindset, a goal-oriented approach to learning, and a focus on ongoing professional learning for teachers enable students to develop problem-solving skills and become self-directed learners.

States cannot accomplish systemic transformation to 21st century learning alone. It requires full commitment and participation from educators and stakeholders at every level. The journey toward transformation is sure to be complex, with its share of successes and failures. Individual schools and districts can make progress on their own, but in order to reach the goal of *all* students having the knowledge and skills to be successful in college, career, and life, states must take a significant leadership role.

Visit **go.solution-tree.com/21stcenturyskills** for links to additional P21 resources.

References and Resources

Bloom, B. S., Engelhart, M. D., Furst, E. J., Hill, W. H., & Krathwohl, D. R. (1956). *Taxonomy of educational objectives: The classification of educational goals. Handbook I: Cognitive domain.* New York: McKay.

California Center for 21st Century Education. (n.d.). *California P21.* Accessed at www.cal21. org/california-p21.html on April 4, 2014.

Conley, D. T., & Darling-Hammond, L. (2013). *Creating systems of assessment for deeper learning: Development of assessment that can measure deeper learning skills.* Stanford, CA: Stanford Center for Opportunity Policy in Education.

Council for Aid to Education. (n.d.). *College work readiness assessment.* Accessed at http:// cae.org/participating-institutions/category/cwra-overview/ on August 1, 2014.

Iowa Department of Education. (2013, December 9). *Final report of the competency-based education task force.* Accessed at www.educateiowa.gov/documents/boards-committees -councils-and-task-forces/2013/12/final-report-competency-based-education on April 4, 2014.

Learning Forward. (2014). *Standards for professional learning.* Accessed at http://learning- forward.org/standards-for-professional-learning#.U4ZO1HJdW4R on May 28, 2014.

National Staff Development Council. (2005, September). *A study of professional development for public school educators in West Virginia.* Accessed at https://wvde.state.wv.us/boe /documents/NSDC%202005%20Study%20WV%20Professional%20Development.pdf on July 31, 2014.

North Carolina State Board of Education. (2012, October). *Vision of public education in North Carolina: A great public education system for a great state.* Accessed at http://stateboard .ncpublicschools.gov/resources/north-carolina-ambassador-resources/vision-report.pdf, 3 on August 1, 2014.

Paine, S. L. (2006). *RESA task force report.* Accessed at www.aesa.us/cms_files/resources/ finalresareport.pdf on October 6, 2014.

Partnership for 21st Century Skills. (2009). *The MILE guide: Milestones for improving learning and education.* Accessed at www.p21.org/storage/documents/MILE_Guide_091101.pdf on May 28, 2014.

Partnership for 21st Century Skills. (2011). *Framework for 21st century learning.* Accessed at www.p21.org/storage/documents/1.__p21_framework_2-pager.pdf on November 1, 2013.

Partnership for 21st Century Skills. (n.d.a). *Exemplar schools program: Case studies.* Accessed at www.p21.org/exemplar-program-case-studies on August 1, 2014.

Partnership for 21st Century Skills. (n.d.b). *P21 Common Core toolkit: A guide to aligning the Common Core State Standards with the Framework for 21st Century Skills.* Accessed at www.p21.org/storage/documents/P21CommonCoreToolkit.pdf on May 28, 2014.

Public Schools of North Carolina. (n.d.). *State board of education adopts vision of public education in North Carolina.* Accessed at www.ncpublicschools.org/newsroom/news/2012-13 /20121004-01 on August 1, 2014.

Soland, J., Hamilton, L., & Stecher, B. (2013). *Measuring 21st century competencies: Guidance for educators.* Accessed at http://asiasociety.org/files/gcen-measuring21cskills.pdf on July 31, 2014.

South Carolina's Council on Competitiveness. (2013). *Transform South Carolina.* Accessed at www.newcarolina.org/initiatives/educationworkforcedevelopment/transformsc.aspx on April 7, 2014.

Tait, T. (2014, January 28). *Anaheim California Mayor Tom Tait State of the City address.* Accessed at www.anaheim.net/articlenew2222.asp?id=5230 on April 7, 2014.

West Virginia Board of Education. (2005). *A vision for student success: High schools for West Virginia's future..* Accessed at https://wvde.state.wv.us/hstw/vision.pdf on July 31, 2014

West Virginia Department of Education. (2006, August). *Improving results for students in high need populations.* Accessed at http://wvde.state.wv.us/osp/highneedstrategic plan8-14-06.pdf on July 31, 2014.

West Virginia Department of Education. (2007). *West Virginia State educational technology plan 2007-2010.* Accessed at http://wvde.state.wv.us/technology/techplan /documents/StatePlan6.10.11.doc on July 31, 2014.

West Virginia Department of Education. (2009a, June). *A chronicle of West Virginia's Global21 Initiative.* Accessed at http://wvde.state.wv.us/oaa/pdf/WV%2021st%20 Century%20Learning%20Chronicle_FINAL.pdf on July 17, 2014.

West Virginia Department of Education. (2009b). *Closing the achievement gap for 21st century learners in West Virginia.* Accessed at http://files.eric.ed.gov/fulltext/ED508066.pdf on August 1, 2014.

West Virginia Office of Education Performance Audits. (2006, October). *Report on the Recommendations of The Education Performance Audit Study Committee.* Accessed at http://oepa.state.wv.us/PDFs/resources/OEPA%20Study%20Final%20Document%20 -%20Oct.%202006.doc on July 31, 2014.

Glossary

balanced assessment. The evaluation of standards-based student performance that gives equal weight to the stated process skill (verb or verb form such as *analyze* or *solve*) and the content (direct object) in the standard.

clarifying questions. The follow-up questions that students and teachers ask in order to get to the facts or details about a more abstract or unclear idea. Clarifying questions may include asking for details (Can you provide a description? A detailed example?) or checking for understanding (Do you mean . . . ? Are you telling me . . . ?). When asking about important points in a discussion or explanation, clarifying questions are considered essential.

cognitive engagement. The result of using instructional strategies that actively engage and develop the thinking functions and operations.

cognitive function. A term coined by cognitive psychologist Reuven Feuerstein that includes twenty-six prerequisites of thinking used for problem solving across the curriculum.

cognitive strategy. An instructional tool that brings about change in how learners understand a concept by helping them think in a specific pattern (for example, a graphic organizer).

collaboration. Two or more persons working together with a common goal, often using a common approach or technology tool (for example, a blog or wiki).

Common Core State Standards. Performance benchmarks the Council of Chief State School Officers and National Governors Association Center for Best Practices developed and most states adopted as a framework to guide balanced, rigorous instruction designed to advance academic and cognitive achievement and develop thinking skills and problem solving.

communication. A P21 skill marked by interaction between two or more persons to share ideas, feelings, goals, and values relating to their mutual interests and work.

competency. The ability to perform a task with a measureable amount of skill. (See also *proficiency*.)

constructivism theory of Reuven Feuerstein. The theory that equates learning with the cognitive act of understanding information via three mental phases: (1) gathering information, (2) making sense of information, and (3) communicating new ideas.

content. The facts, ideas, values, specific learning processes, and opinions that are the subject matter of any discipline. Reading, writing, and arithmetic made up the standard school content through the early 19th century. History, art, and other subjects blossomed after World War II and laid the stage for 21st century content, which includes financial, technological, and other literacies.

creative problem solving. A series of cognitive subskills, such as ideation and evaluation, which are learned, refined, and applied to crucial issues in all disciplines. Attributes are fluency, flexibility, and divergence, which, when applied to the solution of a problem, are said to be creative.

cross-curricular problem solving. A term used in the 2012 PISA to describe problem solving that is not mathematical but addresses ill-defined problems across several disciplines.

critical thinking. A category of thinking operations and functions crucial in 21st century learning experiences that highlights convergent-thinking processes such as analysis, comparison, and evaluation.

deeper learning. The type of learning that results from students' self-directed application of critical and creative thinking, problem solving, communication, and collaboration to deepen their understanding of key concepts in the curriculum. Deeper learning is also the outcome of those processes. (See also *shallow learning*.)

direct instruction. A 19th century model of teaching that received special attention in early school research as an effective model for helping students recall facts, procedures, and ideas for application with mathematics operations and basic reading skills.

disposition. A tendency to think or act in a certain way. (See also *mindset*.)

driving question. The essential question that starts every project-based inquiry unit. The best driving questions are authentic, driven by passion, thought inducing, and standards aligned. This is the most important question in a PBL unit, because it not only drives the inquiry and problem solving, but it also leads to the final answer created by the students. (See also *essential question*.)

engagement. The result of teachers using specific strategies and programs to keep students' attention on the material or content under study.

enriched instruction. Specific approaches to instruction that are carried out with on- and offline high-effects strategies identified by research to have the strongest effect on student achievement and complex cognitive skills.

entrepreneurship. An individual's ability to turn ideas into action and, therefore, a key competence.

essential questions. A generic term (sometimes wrongly substituted for *driving question*) that includes all those questions asked by teachers and students that are necessary for deepening student understanding within a unit. Three types of questions fall into the essential category: (1) driving, (2) guiding, and (3) clarifying.

explicit instruction. Purposefully direct inquiry models of instruction that help students learn the definition, criteria, use, and assessment of a 21st century skill prior to its application in a lesson or project. Explicit instruction leads to facilitated application and mediation of thinking and problem-solving skills.

focus. The essential cognitive function that allows learners or workers to concentrate intensely on one task at a time.

formative assessment. Determination of development in a lesson or project to identify progress and provide constructive feedback. (See *guiding assessment*.)

4Cs. The four 21st century competencies identified by P21: (1) critical thinking and problem solving, (2) communication, (3) collaboration, and (4) creativity and innovation

gathering information. The first phase of thinking in Feuerstein's constructivist learning framework. It requires the skills and attitudes necessary for collecting and evaluating data in order to answer an essential question or define a problem. The phase consists of searches for multiple sources of data, including prior knowledge, written text, visuals, enactments, lectures, surveys, interviews, and the like.

guiding questions. Questions found in PBL units that assist students in building foundational knowledge as they gather initial information to answer their driving questions. Students learn to ask guiding questions, which begin at the lowest rungs of Bloom's taxonomy "ladder" with *what, when, where,* and *who* and climb to *why* and *how.* These questions are considered essential when they provide the baseline background information students need to know to answer the driving question.

guiding rubric. A teacher-made assessment tool used to provide students with feedback that indicates their progress toward high performance of a Common Core or other standard. (See also *formative assessment*.)

high effect. The statistical description of instructional strategies that indicates which strategies have the greatest chance to raise student achievement.

intentional. The purposeful teaching or use of a specific instructional strategy, tool, or tactic to deepen content knowledge or complex-skill acquisition.

inquiry. The process of investigating a fact, topic, process, procedure, concept, or value in order to understand the investigation's focus more deeply. (See also *project-based inquiry*.)

innovative thinking. The cognitive process that enables the creation of novel products that are substantively different from existing products or ways of thinking. (See also *creative thinking*.)

making sense. The second phase in the Feuerstein's constructivist framework. In this phase, students are guided to draw conclusions about gathered data and make plans for communicating their understandings and conclusions to third parties.

Mediated Learning Experience. A term advanced by cognitive psychologist Reuven Feuerstein that describes how teachers can focus student learning on the prerequisite thinking and problem-solving skills sometimes referred to as dispositions or habits of mind.

mindset. An established way of thinking by an individual. (See also *disposition*.)

MOOC. A Massive Open Online Course that delivers content to an unlimited audience at any time via the web. MOOCs also include user forums to build community, in addition to traditional course materials such as videos and texts.

No Child Left Behind. An act of Congress that replaced the Elementary and Secondary Education Act as the federal funding mechanism. It requires states to develop assessments in basic skills at select grade levels in order to receive funding.

paradigm. A complete and unique way of thinking, with its own internal design and basic assumptions. A paradigm shift occurs when the basic assumptions change the design.

practical strategy. A learning activity used to intentionally advance student learning. *Practical* implies that the activity is highly transferable into various lessons or units as a means to facilitate student learning.

phase. A major segment of the constructivist learning process that includes a variety of cognitive strategies, tools, and tactics used to produce desired end results. There are three phases: gathering information, making sense, and communicating new ideas.

problem-based learning. A project-based learning model of instruction that starts with a loosely defined problem and ends with a novel solution or result.

problem definition. The cognitive function that is the first process in problem-solving tasks and units.

problem solving. The set of interactive critical- and creative-thinking strategies aligned to provide a solution to a problem that may range from being loosely to tightly structured. Loosely structured problems are those that require investigation and refinement into a specific problem statement, because the situation is considered messy (for example, water pollution). A tightly structured problem provides the specific definition of the problem (for example, in mathematics).

product-based learning. A project-based learning model of instruction that begins with an idea for a new or innovative product that fulfills a specific, defined need.

proficiency. A skill that reflects a high degree of expertise or competence. (See *competency*.)

Programme for International Student Assessment. A triennial, international, computer-based survey taken by fifteen-year-old students that evaluates education systems. In 2012, assessment of mathematical problem solving, reading literacy, and science literacy was joined by a review of financial literacy and cross-curricular problem solving.

project-based inquiry. A project-based learning model of instruction that starts with a driving question and ends with a student-created solution.

project-based learning. The overarching category that includes the problem-based, product-based, and inquiry-based learning models of instruction.

reflection. The teacher-facilitated process that enables students to learn from doing a project. Reflection may occur during any phase and can focus on process, product, and knowledge generation. It is often completed via rubrics that guide students' self-assessment of progress toward their self-identified goals. It is also the final step in PBL units.

self-directed learning. The process described by Malcolm Knowles, often called the father of self-directed learning. He saw it as a flow of thinking habits in which the learner takes the initiative, with or without the assistance of others, in diagnosing their learning needs, formulating learning goals, identify human and material resources for learning, choosing and implementing appropriate learning strategies, and evaluating learning outcomes.

shallow learning. Learning efforts that start and end with memorization of facts or demonstration of basic skills in a curriculum. The noticeable processes relied on to achieve these shallow or superficial, easily measured outcomes include reliance on worksheets and teacher-directed lessons and lectures. (See *deeper learning*.)

systematic. Thinking, working, or learning done according to a fixed plan or system.

systematic search. An essential cognitive function that directs examination of data in an orderly way.

systemic change. The result of any effort to modify an individual or organization through development of a fixed plan that begins with basic beliefs and assumptions and ends with new ways of thinking or acting.

21st century school. A school that intentionally creates a curriculum that investigates 21st century issues, explicitly teaches 21st century skills, and employs one or more versions of project-based learning to examine standards-based content 100 percent of the time for all students.

theory of action. A systematic plan, based on a hypothesis of what might happen, for bringing about specific changes in an individual or organization as the result of specific interventions.

theory of change. A systematic suppositing that contains all the building blocks required to bring about a given long-term goal in an organization or community. This sct of connected building blocks—interchangeably referred to as outcomes, results, accomplishments, or preconditions—establishes a framework for action.

transformation. The result of an act of deep change that brings about a new shape, form, or way of functioning for an individual or social institution. In its new form, the person or organization operates from a new set of assumptions, beliefs and practices, or behaviors.

understanding. The result of examining rigorous and relevant content through development of 21st century skills applied to an authentic content. Understanding is not a plateau; rather, it exists on a spectrum that proceeds from shallow to deep, dependent upon the length and seriousness of the investigation.

Web 2.0. Internet tools and sites that enable teachers to better manage and develop students' learning in a 21st century classroom.

Index

A

Academically Adrift (Arum and Roksa), 162
academic content, mastery of core, 4
academic mindsets, 6, 181–182
accountability
    need for educators to be involved
        with, 171–173
    new systems of, 263–266
    side effects of, 92–93
    states and alignment of, 360–364
accuracy and precision, striving for, 63
Achieve, 25
ACT, 27–28
    WorkKeys Assessments, 187
adult learning, supporting, 45–47
advisory programs, 182
Albemarle County Public Schools,
        Virginia, 330, 339
Alliance for Excellent Education, 36
allocentrism, 62
American Canyon High School, 197
American Institute of Research
        (AIR), Study of Deeper Learning
        Opportunities and Outcomes, 187
Ancess, J., 153
Aquino, J., 320
argumentation and reasoning, xx–xxi
Arum, R., 162
Asia Society, 178
Aspen Institute, 89–90
assessments
    authentic, 35–37
    changes needed in, xxii
    classroom-based, 187–188

consortia, what they do not measure,
        245, 246
districts and alignment of, 327–329
formative, 36–37, 44–45
performance, 9–10
portfolio-based, 336
school-based, 186–187
states and alignment of, 360–364
See also name of
assessment systems, high-quality
    accountability, new systems of,
        263–266
    college and career readiness, 243–246
    continuum of options, 257–263
    international, 253–257
    Kentucky Instructional Results
        Information System, 251–253
    New Hampshire's, 249–251
    objectives of, 239–243
    recommendations, 266–269
    role of, 237–239
    state development of, 246–249
Association of American Colleges and
        Universities, 172
Auerswald, P., 88–89, 90
Australia, 253, 254–256
authentic assessment, 35–37
autonomy, 99–100

B

Ballston Spa Central School District,
        New York, 326
Barber, M., 92

Bates Middle School, Kentucky, 370
Bellanca, J. A., 1–16
Beyond Current Horizons program, 208
Big Picture Learning, 178
Biscardi, W., Jr., 111
black-collar workers, 89
Blazevski, J., 131
blended and online learning, 125–128
Bloom's taxonomy, 7, 24, 55
Bock, L., 162, 167
Brandt, R., 1
Branson, R., 89
Breakpoint and Beyond (Land and
    Jarman), 91
breakthrough learning
    explosion of activity, 282–283
    leadership changes, 280–282
    new pedagogies, 277–280, 282–283
    push-pull forces, 275–277
Brown, J., 357
Brynjolfsson, E., 160
Buck Institute for Education (BIE), 114,
    201, 297
Buffum, A., 43
Business Education Partnership,
    198–199, 198
Busteed, B., 167

C

Cable in the Classrooms, 365
California Center for 21st Century
    Education, 357, 369
capstone projects, 336
Carnegie Foundation, 25
Carolina Forest International
    Elementary School, North Carolina,
    370–371
Catalina Foothills School District,
    Arizona, 326–327, 335
Center for Collaborative Education, 261
Center for Curriculum Redesign (CCR),
    212, 215, 223, 225, 226, 229
Center for Design and Technology
    (CDAT), 111, 124
Center for K–12 Assessment and
    Performance Management at ETS,
    36
Center for Public Education, 22
Center on Education and the Workforce, 22

Cervone, B., 178
character, 169–171, 225
character education, 279
checklists, 75
Chow, B., 2, 3
Christensen, C., 163
ChronoZoom, 117
Churchill, W., 178
citizenship, 279
Claxton, G., 278
Coalition of Essential Schools, 141
cognitive domain, xvi, xx–xxi
cognitive strategies, 57
collaboration, 4–5, 58, 279, 293–294
college and career readiness, 243–246
College and Work Readiness
    Assessment, 172, 186–187, 334, 362
Collegiate Learning Assessment, 162
Collins, J., 302
Coming Prosperity, The (Auerswald), 88
Committee on Defining Deeper
    Learning, 34, 36
Common Core State Standards (CCSS),
    xii, xx–xxi, 2, 4, 164, 166, 167, 178,
    235, 237, 322, 359
Common Sense Media, 365
communication, 5, 58, 279
Community High School, Vermont, 77
community partnerships, 182
competencies, 304–305
Compton, R., 165
conditions, 303
Conley, D., 57, 244
ConnectEd, 178
context, 302
continuous learning, 67
Council of Chief State School Officers,
    25, 235
Covey, S., 32
Coyle, D., 99–100
Creating Innovators (Wagner), 162, 167
creative thinking, 58, 65, 279
creativity
    age and, 91, 92
    decline in, 95–97
    digital, 112
critical thinking, 4, 58, 279
culture, 303
curriculum
    changes needed in, xxi–xxii, 207–230

changes, obstacles to, 228–229
comparison of 20th and 21st century, 332
deeper learning and, 25–27, 31–33
districts and alignment of, 327–329
key aspects of a 21st century, 213–214
resources, 208
states and alignment of, 357–360
what should students learn, 215–222
Cushman, K., 178

D

Dana Elementary School, North Carolina, 371
Darling-Hammond, L., 33–34
Davies, A., 208
Davis, V., 123
deBono, E., 62
deeper learning
    authentic assessment, 35–37
    common set of practices (ecosystem), 179–181
    creating the curriculum for, 25–27, 31–33
    defined, xii, xvi, 3–10, 24–25
    keys for teaching, 33–35
    prism model, 184–188
    schools, 178–184
    standards and, xix–xxi
    teacher education, changes needed in, xxii–xxiii, 30–31
    transforming to, 188–196
Deeper Learning (Martinez and McGrath), 178
"Deeper Learning for Every Student Every Day" (Schneider and VanderArk), 178
Deeper Learning Initiative, 168, 169
Deeper Learning Network, 131
Deeper Learning Student Assessment Initiative, 336
Deeper Learning Student Assessment System (DLSAS), 187
Defense Advanced Research Projects Agency, 128
Depth of Knowledge (DOK), 24–25, 26, 258, 360
Dewey, J., 97–98, 113
Dichter, A., 146–147

digital creativity, 112
dispositions
    as actions, 71
    applying, to many situations, 70–71
    behavioral questions transformed into thinking, 72
    checklists, 75
    as deeper learning, 67–69
    defined, 59
    explicit, 69–70
    modeling, 73–74
    portfolios, 76
    reasons for, 56–59
    rubrics, 75–76
    self-reflection, 72–73
    strategies for internalizing, 69–74
    vocabulary, building, 71–72
    vocabulary, using consistent, 70
dispositions, types of. See habits of mind
distributive leadership, 314–315
districts
    alignment of standards, curriculum, instruction and assessments, 327–329
    capstone projects, 336
    Common Core, 322
    community consensus, creating, 325–327
    curriculum and assessment, interlocking, 331–336
    improving and innovating, focusing on, 340–343
    model for creating 21st century, 322–329
    PBL assessment strategies, 335
    portfolio-based assessments, 336
    professional capacity, building, 329–343
    scaling transformation, 320–321
    teachers and students, supporting, 337–338–340
    vision, developing a, 324–325
Dobyns, L., 125, 126
Douglas County School District, Colorado, 339–340
Duckworth, A. L., 170
DuFour, R., 32, 35
Duncan, A., 2, 288

E

East Syracuse Minoa Central School District, New York, 326
Edison, T., 89
EdLeader21, 168, 169, 188, 189, 201, 323–324, 325, 334, 335, 338
Edmodo, 123
Edmonds, R., 16
education
  changes being made, 2–3
  changes needed in, xxi–xxii, 22–23, 207–230
  demands on, 211–213
  disparities in, xviii, 1–2, 28–29
  employee-oriented paradigm of, 84–89
  end of, 103–104
  entrepreneur-oriented paradigm of, 97–98
  four dimensions of, 222–227
  role of, xvii–xviii
  world-class, 98–103
Education and Experience (Dewey), 97–98
Education for Life and Work: Developing Transferable Knowledge and Skills in the 21st Century (Pellegrino and Hilton), xv, xix
education reforms
  problems with, 163–167
  those that are working, 168–169
Edutopia, 115–116, 297, 324
EdVisions Schools, 178
egocentrism, 62, 169
Eidman-Aadahl, E., 128–129
eight I's of innovation and education reinvention, 198–202
Einstein, A., 29, 86
Eisner, E. W., 1
Embedded Formative Assessment (Wiliam), 37
employee-oriented paradigm of education, 84–89
employment disparities, 159–163
End of Education, The (Postman), 103
England, 253, 254
entrepreneur-oriented paradigm of education, 97–98

entrepreneurial mindset, 89–92
entrepreneurship
  creativity, decline in, 95–97
  monitoring, 93–96
  need for, 87
  redefinition of, 87–89
environmental stress, 218–219
Envision Schools, 178, 261, 336
"Evolutionary Development, Accelerating Change, Our Digital Future, and Values of Progress" (Smart), 210
Expeditionary Learning, 115, 167, 168, 178, 340
explicit teaching, 294

F

Facer, K., 208
Fairfax County Public Schools, Virginia, 319–320
Feuerstein, R., 6
Feynman, R., 86
Fidler, D., 208
Finland Phenomenon, The, 165
Finnish Lessons: What Can the World Learn From Educational Change in Finland, The (Sahlberg), 83
Fiske, E. B., 352
Flat Classroom project, 122–123
flexible thinking, 62
Ford, H., 89
Forecast 3.0, 208
formative assessments, 36–37, 44–45
four Cs (essential skills), xviii, 5, 8, 9, 58, 168, 224, 279, 294, 322–343, 348
4Cs (leadership), 302–305, 306–307
Framework for 21st Century Learning, 348–349, 358–359
Franklin Elementary School, Illinois, 370
Franklin Institute, 121
Friedman, T., 123
Fry, A., 88
Fullan, M., 44, 188, 189–190, 202
Future Work Skills 2020 (Davies, Fidler, and Gorbis), 208

G

Gandhi, M., 74
Gardner, H., 91
Garza, K., 320
Gates, B., 86
Gates Foundation, 197
GEM (Global Entrepreneurship
    Monitor), 93–94
GERM (Global Education Reform
    Movement), 83–84, 92
Gerstner, L., 171
Global Achievement Gap, The
    (Wagner), 159, 161–162, 168, 169
Global Education Initiative, 87
globalization
    competency, 102–103
    disparities, 159–163
    influence of, 86–87, 217–218
    networks, 102
    perspective, 102
Global21 Initiative, 351, 354, 355
Google, 162–163, 166
Google Apps for Education, 122
Google Hangouts, 131
Gorbis, M., 208
Gordon Commission on the Future of
    Assessment in Education, 239–240
Greenhill, V., 324
growth mindset, 291–292
Gwaltney, M., 126–127

H

habits of mind
    accuracy and precision, striving for,
        63
    checklists, 75
    continuous learning, 67
    examples of, 76–78
    flexible thinking, 62
    humor, use of, 66
    impulsivity, managing, 60–61
    independent thinking, 66–67
    innovation/creativity, 65
    inquirers/questioners, 63–64
    listening with empathy and
        understanding, 61
    metacognition, 62–63

passionate and commitment, 65
past knowledge/experiences, use of, 64
persistence, 60
portfolios, 76
precise language, use of, 64
risk taking, 65–66
rubrics, 75–76
sensory data collecting, 65
Habits of Mind International, 77
Hattie, J., 44–45, 277
Hewlett Foundation, xii, 3, 7, 25, 168,
    178, 181, 185, 187, 258, 334
High Tech High, 115, 168, 178
High Tech High, teacher development at
    background information, 137–140
    daily schedule, 142–143
    design principles, 140–142
    formal structures for teacher
        development, 144–145
    guidelines for, 151–153
    hiring process, 143–144
    leadership development, 145–146
    peer collegial coaching, 148–151
    protocols, 146–148
    structures for, 142–146
    tools for, 146–151
Hilton, M. L., xv–xxiii, 117
Horizon Report, 121, 125
How Children Succeed (Tough), 170
Hudson Valley Community College, 326
humor, use of, 66
Hutchison, H., 118–119

I

impulsivity, managing, 60–61
independent thinking, 66–67
inner self-coaching, 68
innovation/creativity, 65
    eight I's of innovation and education
        reinvention, 198–202
    scaling, 171–173
inquirers/questioners, 63–64
inquiry-based learning, 34–35
*Inspired by Technology, Driven by
    Pedagogy* (OECD), 214
Institute of Education Sciences, 39
Internationals High School Network, 261

Internationals Network for Public
    Schools, 178
International Society for Technology in
    Education, 365
interpersonal domain, xvii, xxi
intrapersonal domain, xvi, xxi
intrapreneurs, 88
Invent to Learn (Martinez and Stager), 129
Iowa Department of Education, 353

J

Jarman, B., 91
Jenkins, L., 275
Jobs, S., 86, 89
Johnson, S. M., 153
Joseph, R., 116

K

Kamerzell, M., 326
Kay, K., 168, 324
Kennedy, J. F., 83
Kentucky Department of Education,
    342–343, 365–366, 370
Kentucky Instructional Results
    Information System (KIRIS),
    251–253
Khan, S., 163
Khan Academy, 125, 163
Kim, K. H., 95–97
knowledge/experiences
    Depth of Knowledge, 24–25, 26, 258, 360
    as a dimension of education, 223–224
    use of past, 64
KnowledgeWorks, 197, 208
Knowles, M., 5–6

L

Ladd, H. F., 352
Lady Gaga, 86
Land, G., 91
Langworthy, M., 278
Lanier High School, Georgia, 111
lateral thinking, 62
Latham, N., 153
*Leader's Guide to 21st Century
    Education, The* (Kay and
    Greenhill), 324, 338

Leaders of Learning (DuFour and
    Marzano), 32
leadership
    changes, 280–282
    developing distributive, 314–315
    4Cs, 302–305, 306–307
    strategies for success, 305, 308–309,
        310–311
    student achievement and engagement,
        improving, 312–313
    teacher capacity and efficacy, focusing
        on, 309–311
learning by doing, 113–114
Learning for the 21st Century (P21), 351
Learning Forward, 367
"Learning From Leaders" (Cervone and
    Cushman), 178
Lehmann, C., 119
Levy, F., 139
lifespan, affects of increased, 216–217
Lindsay, J., 123
listening with empathy and
    understanding, 61
Little, J. W., 46

M

maker spaces, 128–130
#Malala Project, 118–119
Manor New Technology High School
    (MNTHS), Texas
    background information, 287–290
    growth mindset, 291–292
    roots of, 290–291
    STEM challenge, 292–296
    teacher quality, 296–297
Manpower Group, 90
Martinez, M., 70, 178
Martinez, S., 129
Marzano, R., 32, 35
massively open online courses (MOOCs),
    163
mathematics with understanding, xx
Matthews, V., 319
Mattos, M., 43
McAfee, A., 160
McDonald, E., 146–147
McDonald, J., 146–147
McGrath, D., 178
McIntosh, P., 144

Mergendollar, J., 113
metacognition, 62–63, 225–226
MetLife surveys, 276
Met Schools, 261
Microsoft Office 365, 122
Microsoft Partners in Learning Global
    Forum, 116
mindset
    academic, 6, 181–182
    entrepreneurial, 89–92
    growth, 291–292
    student, 181
modeling, 73–74
Mohr, N., 146–147
Murnane, R., 139

N

NapaLearns, 200, 201
Napa New Tech High School, 197
Napa Valley Education Foundation, 200
Napa Valley Unified School District
    (NVUSD), 197, 199
    eight I's of innovation and education
        reinvention, 198–202
National Academy of Science, 323
National Assessment of Educational
    Progress (NAEP), 21, 25–26, 39–40
National Career Readiness Certificate
    Plus, 187
National Center for Education Statistics, 39
National Education Technology
    Standards, 365
National Governors Association, 25
National Research Council (NRC), xv–
    xvi, xxi, 24
Nation at Risk, A, 171
NETS, 4
New Hampshire, system of assessments,
    249–251, 342
Newsweek, 95
New Tech Foundation, 197
New Tech High Schools, 261
New Tech Network, 115, 123, 125, 178,
    297, 330, 335
New Visions for Public Schools, 178
New York Performance Standards
    Consortium, 248, 261
Next Generation Science Standards, xxi, 4, 9

Next 25 Years? Future Scenarios and
    Future Directions for Education
    and Technology, The (Facer and
    Sandford), 208
No Child Left Behind (NCLB), 9, 10, 26,
    96–97, 236, 360
North Carolina State Board of Education
    and Department of Public
    Instruction (NCDPI), 351–352, 366,
    370–371
North Salem Central School District,
    New York, 333

O

Obama, B., 235, 288
Odyssey School, Colorado, 340
Ohio Performance Assessment Pilot
    Project, 259–260, 363
online learning, 125–128, 163
Online School for Girls, 126
Organisation for Economic Co-operation
    and Development (OECD), xi, xiii,
    2, 26, 87, 208, 214, 225
    Test for Schools, 186, 334
outcome definition, 9–10, 278

P

paradigm of education
    employee-oriented, 84–89
    entrepreneur-oriented, 97–98
Park Manor, Ontario, 281
Partnership for Assessment of Readiness
    for College and Careers (PARCC),
    xxii, 2, 10, 26, 37–38, 41, 237, 246,
    362
Partnership for 21st Century Skills (P21),
    xviii–xix, 4, 47, 58, 168, 297, 347,
    351
    Common Core Toolkit, 359
    Framework for 21st Century
        Learning, 348–349, 358–359
    Learning Exemplar Program, 370
passionate and commitment, 65
pedagogies, new, 277–280, 282–283
Pellegrino, J. W., xv–xxiii, 7, 117
Penniman, L., 129–130
performance assessments, 9–10
Performance Standards Consortium, 2

persistence, 60
Petroski, H., 90
Pfeffer, J., 23
Piaget, J., 169
Pink, D. H., 57, 291
Popham, W. J., 37
portfolio-based assessments, 336
portfolios, 76
Postman, N., 103
practices, 227–228
precise language, use of, 64
Prensky, M., 278
prism model, 184–188
problem solving, xxi, 4, 279
process definition, 8
product-oriented learning, 100–101
Professional Capital (Fullan), 276
professional development
    changes needed in, xxii–xxiii
    ongoing, 366–368
    See also High Tech High, teacher
        development at
professional learning communities (PLCs)
    addressing the challenges of helping
        all students and, 27–30
    adult learning, supporting, 45–47
    defined, 23–24
    failure of current education, 28–29
    formative assessments and, 44–45
    implications for unsuccessful
        students, 29–30, 42–43
    student preparation beyond high
        school, 27–28
Programme for International Student
    Assessment (PISA), xi, 2, 10, 25, 26,
    40–41, 94, 95, 172, 186, 229, 362
project-based learning (PBL), 5, 182, 293,
    333, 335
project-based learning plus technology
    (PBLT)
    applications, 115–117
    blended and online learning, 125–128
    cloud computing, 121–122
    digital tools, 117–118
    essential elements in, 114–115
    implications for practice, 131–132
    learning by doing, 113–114
    maker spaces, 128–130
    mobile devices, use of, 122

personalization of, 123–125
role of, 112–113
support for teachers, 130–131
technology, role of, 117–121
trends in, 121–130
Project Foundry, 123
push-pull forces, 275–277

Q

Quadblogging, 117–118
questioners, 63–64

R

Race Against the Machine (Brynjolfsson
    and McAfee), 160
Race to the Top, 164, 166
Raikes Foundation, 181
RAND Corp., 236, 363
Ravitch, D., 40
Ravitz, J., 131
Reich, J., 123–124
Reilly, M., 111–112, 124–125
Richardson, W., 278
Rich Seam, A (Fullan and Langworthy), 278
risk taking, 65–66
Ritchhart, R., 58–59
Roberts, P., 116
Roksa, J., 162
Rowling, J. K., 89
rubrics, 75–76

S

Sahlberg, P., 83–84
Salomon, G., 59
Sandford, R., 208
San Jose Unified School District,
    California, 319
Saratoga Technology + Energy Park
    (STEP), 326
Schneider, C., 118, 178
school networks
    academic mindsets, 6, 181–182
    common set of practices (ecosystem),
        179–181
    description of, 178–179
    student agency, 182–184
    transforming to, 188–196

School Reform Initiative, 147
school-to-career movement, 141
Science Leadership Academy (SLA), 119, 121
Secretary's Commission on Achieving
    Necessary Skills (SCANS), 139
self-directed learning, 5–6
self-reflection, 72–73
sensory data collecting, 65
Silver, S., 88
Simplifying Response to Intervention
    (Buffum, Mattos, and Weber), 43
Singapore, 253, 257, 261–262
6Cs, 278–280
SketchUp, 117
skills
    as a dimension of education, 224
    See also 21st century skills
Skills, Understandings, and Mindsets
    (SUM), 184–185
Smart, J., 209–210
Smarter Balanced Assessment
    Consortium (Smarter Balanced),
    xxii, 2, 26, 38–39, 237, 246, 362
South Carolina Council on
    Competitiveness, 369
Spirit Lake High School, Iowa, 370
Stager, G., 129
standards
    deeper learning and 21st century
        competencies, xix–xxi
    defense of, 92–93
    districts and alignment of, 327–329
    problems with, 236
    states and alignment of, 357–360
    student-friendly language of, need for,
        41–42
Standards for Mathematical Practice,
    xx–xxi
Stanford Center for Assessment,
    Learning and Equity (SCALE), 187
*State Leader's Action Guide to 21st
    Century Skills, A* (P21), 351
State Model Evaluation System for
    Teachers, 339
states, role of
    alignment of standards, curriculum,
        assessments, and accountability,
        357–364

assessment development and,
    246–249
enabling school transformation and,
    349–350
exemplar schools and districts,
    370–371
operational environment, 354–355
policy framework for 21st century
    learning, creating, 352–354
professional learning and, 366–368
programmatic environment, 356
strategic partnerships and, 368–369
technology access and integration,
    ensuring, 364–366
vision and consensus development
    and, 350–352
STEM challenge, 292–296
Stratosphere (Fullan), 276, 277, 282
Strauss, S., 90
student achievement and engagement,
    improving, 312–313
student agency, 182–184
student mindsets, 181
students, implications for unsuccessful,
    29–30, 42–43
student work, engaging teachers with,
    338–339
Sutton, R., 23

T

Talent Code, The (Coyle), 99–100
teacher capacity and efficacy, focusing
    on, 309–311
teacher education
    changes needed in, xxii–xxiii, 30–31
    See also High Tech High, teacher
        development at
teacher evaluations, rethinking, 339–340
teachers, facilitators versus activators,
    277–278
teaching deeper learning, keys for, 33–35
Teaching the New Basic Skills
    (Murnane and Levy), 139
technology
    access and integration, state education
        departments and ensuring, 364–366
    influence of, 209–211, 219–222, 295

See also project-based learning plus technology

Tech Valley High School, New York, 129–130

Texas Assessment of Knowledge and Skills (TAKS), 288, 289

Think Forward PBL, 297

Think Scenarios (OCED), 208

Third Wave (Toffler), 86

Time for Deeper Learning (Traphagan and Zorich), 178

TIME International, 2

TodaysMeet, 120

Toffler, A., 86

Torrance test, 95

Tough, P., 57, 60, 170

transfer element, 7

transforming to deeper learning, 188
    assessment of results, 196–196
    chart, 202, 203
    district model steps for, 190–195
    eight I's of innovation and education reinvention, 198–202
    role of states, 349–350
    steps for, 189–190

Traphagan, K., 178

Trends in International Mathematics and Science Study (TIMSS), 94, 95

Trends Shaping Education (OCED), 208

Tuva Labs, 117

21st century skills, 235–236
    defined, xvi
    domains/competencies, xvi–xvii
    essential, 57–58
    initiatives for, xviii–xix
    6Cs, 278–280
    standards and, xix–xxi

21st Century Skills: Rethinking How Students Learn (Bellanca and Brandt), 1

21st century world challenges
    demands on education, 211–213
    key aspects on curriculum, 213–214
    living in, 208–209
    technology, influence of, 209–211

Twitter, 120, 131

U

UNESCO, 225

Upper Arlington Schools, Ohio, 330–331, 336

U.S. Department of Education, xxii, 39, 164, 297
    Office of Educational Technology, 57

V

Vander Ark, T., 118, 178

Virginia Beach City Public Schools, Virginia, 328–329

Vodafone Forecast 2020 program, 209, 211

Vogt, W. P., 153

VUCA, 209, 210

Vygotsky, L., 6

W

Wagner, T., 57, 91, 15973

Waikiki Elementary, Hawaii, 77–78

Walker Elementary, Wisconsin, 370

Webb, N., 24, 26, 258

Weber, C., 43

West Virginia Department of Education (WVDE), 351, 353–354, 355, 356, 357, 360, 367–368

WIDA, 4

Wiliam, D., 33, 37

Winfrey, O., 89

Wordle, 179

World-class education, 98–103

World Class Learners (Zhao), 101

World Economic Forum, 87–88

World Future Society, 210

World Is Flat, The (Friedman), 123

World Youth Report, The, 87

Z

Zorich, T., 178

Zuckerberg, M., 89

21st Century Skills
James A. Bellanca and Ron Brandt
Examine the Framework for 21st Century Learning from the Partnership for 21st Century Skills as a way to re-envision learning in a rapidly evolving global and technological world. Learn why these skills are necessary, which are most important, and how to best help schools include them.
BKF389

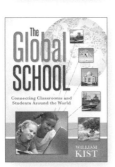

Bringing Innovation to School
Suzie Boss
Activate your students' creativity and problem-solving potential with breakthrough learning projects. Across all grades and content areas, student-driven, collaborative projects will teach students how to generate innovative ideas and then put them into action.
BKF546

The Global School
William Kist
Prepare students for an increasingly flat world where diverse people from divergent cultures learn and work together rather than in isolation. Learn specific steps to globalize your classroom and encourage higher-order thinking, all wrapped in a 21st century skills framework.
BKF570

Contemporary Perspectives on Literacy series
Heidi Hayes Jacobs
Today's students must be prepared to compete in a global society in which cultures, economies, and people are constantly connected. The authors explain three "new literacies"—digital, media, and global—and provide practical tips for incorporating these literacies into the traditional curriculum.
KTF130

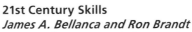

Solution Tree | Press   *a division of*

Visit solution-tree.com or call 800.733.6786 to order.

Wait! Your professional development journey doesn't have to end with the last pages of this book.

We realize improving student learning doesn't happen overnight. And your school or district shouldn't be left to puzzle out all the details of this process alone.

No matter where you are on the journey, we're committed to helping you get to the next stage.

Take advantage of everything from **custom workshops** to **keynote presentations** and **interactive web and video conferencing**. We can even help you develop an action plan tailored to fit your specific needs.

Let's get the conversation started.

Call 888.763.9045 today.

solution-tree.com